BALTIMORE CATECHISM #3

PRAYER TO THE HOLY SPIRIT

Come, Holy Spirit, fill the hearts of Thy faithful and enkindle in them the fire of Thy love.

V. Send forth Thy Spirit and they shall be created.

R. And Thou shalt renew the face of the earth.

LET US PRAY

O God, who didst instruct the hearts of the faithful by the light of the Holy Spirit, grant us in the same Spirit to be truly wise, and ever to rejoice in His consolation. Through Christ Our Lord. Amen.

(Indulgence of five years. Plenary indulgence, under the usual conditions, provided the prayer is recited daily for a month.)

INDULGENCES

Granted to those who devote themselves to teaching or learning Christian Doctrine.

I. A PLENARY INDULGENCE to all the Faithful who shall for approximately one-half hour or for not less than twenty minutes devote themselves at least twice a month to teaching or learning Christian Doctrine. The Indulgence can be gained twice during this same month on days which they may choose, provided they, being truly penitent, have gone to Confession and Holy Communion and have visited some church or public oratory and there prayed for the intention of the Roman Pontiff.

II. A PARTIAL INDULGENCE of 3 years to these same members of the Faithful as often as they devote themselves for the above mentioned space of time to teaching or learning Christian Doctrine. (S.P.Ap., May 26, 1949.)

FOREWORD BY FATHER CONNELL, C.SS.R.

In the spring of 1949 the Official Baltimore Catechism, No. 3, was issued under the auspices of the Confraternity of Christian Doctrine. It contains the same questions and answers as Catechism No. 2, issued in 1941, but with considerable additional matter in the form of Scriptural quotations and more extensive doctrinal explanations. This Catechism No. 3 is the product of several years of study and compilation by a committee of competent theologians and catechists.

The present Catechism, entitled THE NEW CONFRATERNITY EDITION OF THE REVISED BALTIMORE CATECHISM NO. 3, presents the entire text of the Official Baltimore Catechism No. 3, with additions to each lesson; these additions comprise a section summarizing the most important truths pertinent to the subject of the lesson and two sets of study helps. I take this occasion to express my deep gratitude to Father Thomas Chapman, C.SS.R, who composed most of the "Problems and Exercises" which are found in the second set of study helps.

It is my earnest hope and prayer that all who study this Catechism will be enlightened by the Holy Spirit to perceive the truth, the beauty, and the inspiration of the doctrines taught by the Holy Catholic Church.

Francis J. Connell, C.SS.R.

Washington, D.C., Feast of St. Alphonsus, August 2, 1949

THE NEW

CONFRATERNITY EDITION

REVISED

BALTIMORE CATECHISM

AND MASS

NO. 3

THE TEXT OF THE
OFFICAL REVISED EDITION 1949
WITH SUMMARIZATIONS OF DOCTRINE
AND STUDY HELPS
BY
REV. FRANCIS J. CONNELL, C.SS.R., S.T.D.
The Catholic University of America, Washington, D.C.
MASS SECTION
By
REV. DAVID SHARROCK, C.SS.R.
in collaboration with Father Connell

Reprinted by

The Seraphim Company, Inc.
P.O. BOX 26600
COLORADO SPRINGS, CO
80936-6600

IMPRIMATUR BY CARDINAL SPELLMAN — SEE PAGE 352

© 1949, 1952
by Benziger Brothers, Inc.

Reprinted by
The Seraphim Company, Inc.
1987, 1991, 1995, 2001

(Fourth Edition)

ISBN: 0-9656024-0-0

PRAYER INDEX

ILLUSTRATION INDEX

PRAYERS

Sign of the Cross

✠ In the name of the Father, and of the Son, and of the Holy Ghost. Amen. *(An indulgence of 3 years; with holy water, 7 years)*

Our Father

Our Father who art in heaven, hallowed be Thy name; Thy kingdom come; Thy will be done on earth as it is in heaven. Give us this day our daily bread; and forgive us our trespasses as we forgive those who trespass against us; and lead us not into temptation, but deliver us from evil. Amen.

Hail Mary

Hail Mary, full of grace! the Lord is with thee; blessed art thou among women, and blessed is the fruit of thy womb, Jesus. Holy Mary, Mother of God, pray for us sinners, now and at the hour of our death. Amen.

Glory Be

Glory be to the Father, and to the Son, and to the Holy Ghost. As it was in the beginning, is now, and ever shall be, world without end. Amen.

Apostles' Creed

I believe in God, the Father Almighty, Creator of heaven and earth; and in Jesus Christ, His only Son, Our Lord; who was conceived by the Holy Ghost, born of the Virgin Mary, suffered under Pontius Pilate, was crucified, died, and was buried. He descended into hell; the third day He arose again from the dead; He ascended into heaven, sitteth at the right hand of God, the Father Almighty; from thence He shall come to judge the living and the dead. I believe in the Holy Ghost, the Holy Catholic Church, the communion of saints, the forgiveness of sin, the resurrection of the body, and life everlasting. Amen.

Confiteor

I confess to Almighty God, to blessed Mary ever Virgin, to blessed Michael the Archangel, to blessed John the Baptist, to the holy Apostles Peter and Paul, and to all the saints, that I have sinned exceedingly in thought, word, and deed, through my fault, through my fault, through my most grievous fault. Therefore, I beseech blessed Mary ever Virgin, blessed Michael the Archangel, blessed John the Baptist, the holy Apostles Peter and Paul, and all the saints, to pray to the Lord our God for me.

May Almighty God have mercy on me, forgive me my sins, and bring me to everlasting life. Amen.

May the Almighty and merciful Lord grant me pardon, ✠ absolution, and remission of all my sins. Amen.

Act of Faith

O my God, I firmly believe that Thou art one God in three Divine Persons, Father, Son, and Holy Ghost; I believe that Thy Divine Son became man, and died for our sins, and that He will come to judge the living and the dead. I believe these and all the truths which the Holy Catholic Church teaches, because Thou hast revealed them, who canst neither deceive nor be deceived. *(3 years)*

Act of Hope

O my God, relying on Thy almighty power and infinite mercy and promises, I hope to obtain the pardon of my sins, the help of Thy grace, and life everlasting, through the merits of Jesus Christ, my Lord and Redeemer. *(3 years)*

Act of Charity

O my God, I love Thee above all things, with my whole heart and soul, because Thou art all good and worthy of all love. I love my neighbor as myself for the love of Thee. I forgive all who have injured me, and ask pardon of all whom I have injured. *(3 years)*

3

Act of Contrition

O my God, I am heartily sorry for having offended Thee, and I detest all my sins, because I dread the loss of heaven and the pains of hell, but most of all because they offend Thee, my God, who art all good and deserving of all my love. I firmly resolve, with the help of Thy grace, to confess my sins, to do penance, and to amend my life. Amen. *(3 years)*

Morning Offering

O my God, I offer Thee all my prayers, works, and sufferings in union with the Sacred Heart of Jesus, for the intentions for which He pleads and offers Himself in the Holy Sacrifice of the Mass, in thanksgiving for Thy favors, in reparation for my offenses, and in humble supplication for my temporal and eternal welfare, for the wants of our holy Mother the Church, for the conversion of sinners, and for the relief of the poor souls in purgatory. I wish to gain all the indulgences attached to the prayers I shall say and to the good works I shall perform this day.

Angelus

V. The angel of the Lord declared unto Mary.
R. And she conceived of the Holy Ghost.
 Hail Mary, etc.
V. Behold the handmaid of the Lord.
R. Be it done to me according to thy word.
 Hail Mary, etc.
V. And the Word was made flesh.
R. And dwelt among us.
 Hail Mary, etc.
V. Pray for us, O holy Mother of God.
R. That we may be made worthy of the promises of Christ.
 Let us pray.
Pour forth, we beseech Thee, O Lord, Thy grace into our hearts, that we to whom the Incarnation of Christ, Thy Son, was made known by the message of an angel, may by His passion and cross be brought to the glory of His resurrection, through the same Christ Our Lord. Amen.
(10 years each time, if recited at dawn, at noon and in the evening, or as soon thereafter as possible)

Regina Cæli

(Said during Eastertide, instead of the Angelus)
Queen of heaven, rejoice, Alleluia.
For He whom thou didst merit to bear, Alleluia.
Hath risen as He said, Alleluia.
Pray for us to God, Alleluia.
V. Rejoice and be glad, O Virgin Mary! Alleluia.
R. For the Lord is truly risen, Alleluia.
 Let us pray.
O God, Who, by the resurrection of Thy Son, Our Lord Jesus Christ, hast vouchsafed to make glad the whole world; grant, we beseech Thee, that through the intercession of the Virgin Mary, His Mother, we may attain the joys of eternal life. Through the same Christ Our Lord. Amen.
(At Eastertide, same indulgence as for the Angelus)

Hail Holy Queen

Hail Holy Queen, Mother of mercy, hail, our life, our sweetness, and our hope! To thee do we cry, poor banished children of Eve! To thee do we send up our sighs, mourning and weeping in this valley of tears! Turn then, most gracious advocate, thine eyes of mercy towards us; and after this, our exile, show unto us the blessed fruit of thy womb, Jesus! O clement, O loving, O sweet Virgin Mary!
(5 years)

Prayer to St. Michael

Holy Michael, the Archangel, defend us in battle; be our protection against the malice and snares of the devil. May God rebuke him, we humbly pray; and do thou, O Prince of the heavenly host, by the power of God, thrust into hell Satan and the evil spirits who roam through the world seeking the ruin of souls. Amen. *(3 years)*

4

Prayer to St. Joseph

To thee, O blessed Joseph, we have recourse in our affliction, and having implored the help of thy thrice holy Spouse, we now with hearts filled with confidence, earnestly beg thee also to take us under thy protection. By that charity wherewith thou wert united to the Immaculate Virgin Mother of God, and by that fatherly love with which thou didst cherish the Child Jesus, we beseech thee and we humbly pray that thou wilt look down with gracious eye upon that inheritance which Jesus Christ purchased by His blood, and wilt succor us in our need by they power and strength.

Defend, O most watchful guardian of the holy Family, the chosen offspring of Jesus Christ. Keep from us, O most loving Father, all blight of error and corruption. Aid us from on high, most valiant defender, in this conflict with the powers of darkness. And even as of old thou didst rescue the Child Jesus from the peril of His life, so now defend God's Holy Church from the snares of the enemy and from all adversity. Shield us ever under thy patronage, that, following thine example and strengthened by thy help, we may live a holy life, die a happy death, and attain to everlasting bliss in heaven. Amen.

Anima Christi

Soul of Christ, sanctify me.
Body of Christ, save me.
Blood of Christ, inebriate me.
Water from the side of Christ, wash me.
Passion of Christ, strengthen me.
O good Jesus, hear me.
Within Thy wounds, hide me.
Suffer me not to be separated from Thee.
From the malicious enemy, defend me.
At the hour of my death, call me.
And bid me come to Thee;
That with Thy saints I may praise Thee,
    Forever and ever. Amen.
(300 days, 7 years if said after Holy Communion)

Prayer Before a Crucifix

Look down upon me, good and gentle Jesus, while before Thy face I humbly kneel, and with burning soul I pray and beseech Thee to fix deep in my heart lively sentiments of faith, hope, and charity, true contrition for my sins, and a firm purpose of amendment; while with deep affection and grief of soul I ponder within myself and mentally contemplate Thy five most precious wounds, having before my eyes the words which David the prophet put on Thy lips concerning Thee, O good Jesus: "They have pierced My hands and My feet, they have numbered all my bones."
(10 years if said before an image of Christ crucified)

Prayer for Souls in Purgatory

Eternal rest grant unto them, O Lord, and let perpetual light shine upon them. May their souls and the souls of all the faithful departed, through the mercy of God, rest in peace. Amen.   *(300 days)*

Prayer to My Guardian Angel

Angel of God, my guardian dear,
To whom His love commits me here,
Ever this day be at my side,
To light and guard, to rule and guide.
Amen.

Prayer of St. Ignatius

Take, O Lord, and receive my entire liberty, my memory, my understanding, and my whole will. All that I am and all that I possess Thou hast given me; I surrender it all to Thee to be disposed of according to Thy holy will. Give me only Thy love and Thy grace; with these I will be rich enough and desire nothing more. *(3 years)*

Memorare

Remember, O most gracious Virgin Mary, that never was it known that anyone who fled to thy protection, implored thy help, or sought thy intercession was left unaided. Inspired with this confidence, I fly unto thee, O Virgin of virgins, my Mother. To thee I come, before thee I stand, sinful and sorrowful. O Mother of the Word Incarnate, despise not my petitions, but in thy mercy hear and answer me. Amen. *(3 years)*

Blessing Before Meals

Bless us, O Lord, and these Thy gifts, which we are about to receive from Thy bounty, through Christ Our Lord. Amen.

Grace After Meals

We give Thee thanks for all Thy benefits, O almighty God, who livest and reignest forever; and may the souls of the faithful departed, through the mercy of God, rest in peace. Amen. *(300 days)*

Ejaculations

Most Sacred Heart of Jesus, have mercy on us. *(500 days)*
My Jesus, mercy.
Mother of mercy, pray for us.
Jesus, Mary, and Joseph, bless us now and at the hour of our death.
(300 days each)

Mysteries of the Rosary

Five Joyful Mysteries

1. Annunciation
2. Visitation
3. Nativity of Our Lord
4. Presentation of Our Lord in the Temple
5. Finding of Our Lord in the Temple

Five Sorrowful Mysteries

1. Agony of Our Lord in the Garden
2. Scourging at the Pillar
3. Crowning with Thorns
4. Carrying of the Cross
5. Crucifixion and Death of Our Lord

Five Glorious Mysteries

1. Resurrection of Our Lord
2. Ascension of Our Lord into Heaven
3. Descent of the Holy Ghost upon the Apostles
4. Assumption of Our Blessed Mother into Heaven
5. Coronation of Our Blessed Mother in Heaven

(for Five Mysteries, 5 years once a day; 10 years once a day if recited with others; in the presence of the Blessed Sacrament, a plenary indulgence on condition of confession and Communion)

The Manner in Which a Lay Person Is to Baptize in Case of Necessity

Pour ordinary water on the forehead of the person to be baptized, and say while pouring it:

"I baptize thee in the name of the Father, and of the Son, and of the Holy Ghost."

N.B. Any person of either sex who has reached the use of reason can baptize in case of necessity, but the same person must say the words while pouring the water.

PART ONE — THE CREED

LESSON 1

The Purpose of Man's Existence

1. Who made us?

God made us.

(a) Reason unaided by revelation can prove that God exists. It knows that this vast universe could not have come into being by its own powers. The movement of creatures and their dependence upon one another, the various degrees of perfection found in them, the fact that they come into being and cease to be, and, finally, the marvelous order in the universe, demand the existence of an almighty power and the wisdom of an eternal intelligent cause that we call God.[1]

> SCRIPTURE:
> "In the beginning God created heaven and earth. . . . And God created man to his own image" (*Genesis 1:1, 27*).
> "God, who made the world and all that is in it . . . from one man he has created the whole human race" (*Acts 17:24-26*).

2. Who is God?

God is the Supreme Being, infinitely perfect, who made all things and keeps them in existence.

(a) This universe did not always exist; it came into existence at the beginning of time.

(b) All things depend on God; they begin and continue to exist by the power of God.

> SCRIPTURE:
> "Great is the Lord and greatly to be praised, and his greatness is unsearchable" (*Psalm 144:3*).
> "It is he who gives to all men life and breath and all things" (*Acts 17:25*).
> "In him we live and move and have our being" (*Acts 17:28*).

3. Why did God make us?

God made us to show forth His goodness and to share with us His everlasting happiness in heaven.

(a) By creating the world God did not increase His own happiness, since He was infinitely happy from all eternity, but He did manifest His glory externally by sharing His goodness. All creatures by their very existence show forth the glory of God, for all depend on God for their existence.

(b) God created man to manifest His glory in a special way. He gave man an intellect and a will that he might know, praise, and love his Creator. In the service of God man finds his true, though imperfect,

---

1. Atheists, who deny the existence of God, can offer no valid or convincing argument in proof of their denial.

5

happiness in this life. Perfect happiness has been promised in the next life as a reward for the merits man acquires here on earth. Thus the happiness of man is also a purpose of creation.

(c) The happiness of heaven consists in the direct vision, love, and enjoyment of God. This reward so far exceeds man's nature that without the supernatural help of God it could not possibly be attained. In heaven God gives us the light of glory, which enables us to see Him face to face. During our life on earth God gives us His grace, which enables us to live a supernatural life and to perform the actions that can earn this reward.

(d) The happiness of the blessed in heaven varies according to the merits of their lives on earth. All in heaven are perfectly happy, but one person may have a greater degree of happiness than another because he has more capacity for happiness, by reason of a more virtuous life on earth.

SCRIPTURE:

"The heavens declare the glory of God, and the firmament proclaims the work of his hands" (*Psalm 18:2*).

"He set his eye upon their hearts to show them the greatness of his works: That they might praise the name which he hath sanctified, and glory in his wondrous acts: that they might declare the glorious things of his works" (*Ecclesiasticus 17:7-8*).

"And every one that calleth upon my name, I have created him for my glory: I have formed him and made him" (*Isaias 43:7*).

"For the Son of Man is to come with his angels in the glory of his Father, and then he will render to everyone according to his conduct" (*Matthew 16:27*).

"What does it profit a man, if he gain the whole world, but suffer the loss of his own soul?" (*Mark 8:36*).

"In my Father's house there are many mansions" (*John 14:2*).

"Eye has not seen nor ear heard,
Nor has it entered into the heart of man,
What things God has prepared for those who love him" (*I Corinthians 2:9*).

"Now he who plants and he who waters are one, yet each will receive his own reward according to his labor" (*I Corinthians 3:8*).

"We see now through a mirror in an obscure manner, but then face to face" (*I Corinthians 13:12*).

4. What must we do to gain the happiness of heaven?

To gain the happiness of heaven we must know, love, and serve God in this world.

(a) Man must know, love, and serve God in a supernatural manner in order to gain the happiness of heaven. Man is raised to the supernatural order only by grace, a free gift of God.

(b) Man cannot be perfectly happy in this world, for nothing created can satisfy his desire for complete happiness. History and experience show that neither riches, nor honors, nor glory, nor reputation, nor power, nor pleasure, nor knowledge, nor any other worldly goods can fully satisfy man's longing for happiness.

(c) Man's earthly, imperfect happiness is in proportion to his approach to God—the final goal of his life. The more closely man approaches God by the practice of virtue under the influence of God's grace, the greater

6

will be his happiness. Worldly goods and pleasures may satisfy man for a time, but of themselves they cannot make him fully happy. Man may enjoy the innocent pleasures and reasonable comforts of life as long as they do not lead him away from God.

SCRIPTURE:

"Not everyone who says to me, 'Lord, Lord,' shall enter the kingdom of heaven; but he who does the will of my Father in heaven shall enter the kingdom of heaven" (*Matthew 7:21*).

"And thou shalt love the Lord thy God with thy whole heart, and with thy whole soul, and with thy whole mind, and with thy whole strength" (*Mark 12:30*).

"If you love me, keep my commandments" (*John 14:15*).

"Now this is everlasting life, that they may know thee, the only true God, and him whom thou hast sent, Jesus Christ" (*John 17:3*).

5. **From whom do we learn to know, love, and serve God?**

We learn to know, love, and serve God from Jesus Christ, the Son of God, who teaches us through the Catholic Church.

(a) In order to be saved, all persons who have attained the use of reason must believe explicitly that God exists and that He rewards the good and punishes the wicked; in practice they must also believe explicitly in the mysteries of the Blessed Trinity and the Incarnation.

(b) The supernatural happiness of heaven and such mysteries as the Holy Trinity, the Incarnation, and the Redemption are beyond anything man can know by his unaided powers of reason; they can be learned only through God's revelation.

SCRIPTURE:

"All power in heaven and on earth has been given to me. Go, therefore, and make disciples of all nations, baptizing them in the name of the Father, and of the Son, and of the Holy Spirit, teaching them to observe all that I have commanded you; and behold, I am with you all days, even unto the consummation of the world" (*Matthew 28:18-20*).

"He who hears you, hears me" (*Luke 10:16*).

"And without faith it is impossible to please God. For he who comes to God must believe that God exists and is a rewarder to those who seek him" (*Hebrews 11:6*).

6. **Where do we find the chief truths taught by Jesus Christ through the Catholic Church?**

We find the chief truths taught by Jesus Christ through the Catholic Church in the Apostles' Creed.

(a) A creed is a summary of the principal articles of faith. Since the Church received Christ's mandate to teach His way of salvation to all men in all ages, it was necessary to formulate at least the most important doctrines. To preserve unity of faith, it was first necessary to have the belief itself quite clearly stated. Thus there are records from the earliest times of a set profession of faith required of converts before their Baptism.

(b) With the spread of Christianity various erroneous teachings regarding the doctrines of faith were proclaimed. It thus became necessary to define the truths of revelation more explicitly. The Apostles' Creed underwent modification, not by the introduction of new doctrines but by an expression of the traditional belief in terms that left no room for error or misunderstanding. The principal creeds of the Church are the Apostles' Creed, the Athanasian Creed, and the Nicene Creed.

7. Say the Apostles' Creed.

I believe in God, the Father Almighty, Creator of heaven and earth; and in Jesus Christ, His only Son, Our Lord; who was conceived by the Holy Ghost, born of the Virgin Mary, suffered under Pontius Pilate, was crucified, died, and was buried. He descended into hell; the third day He arose again from the dead; He ascended into heaven, sitteth at the right hand of God, the Father Almighty; from thence He shall come to judge the living and the dead. I believe in the Holy Ghost, the Holy Catholic Church, the communion of saints, the forgiveness of sins, the resurrection of the body, and life everlasting. Amen.

(a) This collection of revealed truths is called the "Apostles' Creed" because it contains a summary of the principal truths handed down by the apostles and was in use from the earliest ages as the mark of a Christian.

(b) The twelve articles of the Creed contain the mystery of one God in three distinct Persons, Father, Son, and Holy Ghost, and the operations that are, for a particular reason, attributed to each Person.

(c) In the three main parts of the Apostles' Creed the doctrine of the mystery of the Trinity is so set forth that the first part tells of the first Person and the work of creation; the next, of the second Person and the work of redemption; and the third, of the third Person and the work of our sanctification, begun on earth by grace and completed in heaven by glory.

IMPORTANT TRUTHS ABOUT THE PURPOSE OF MAN'S EXISTENCE

No human being can live properly unless he knows the purpose of life. The present lesson tells us this purpose. We have been created by God in order to glorify Him and to merit eternal happiness with Him in heaven. Our own reason tells us that we have a spiritual soul; and a spirit is immortal — that is, it will never die. Reason also assures us that we can find perfect happiness only in God, for the desire for happiness in every human heart is unlimited, and hence no created good can fully satisfy it. As St. Augustine said: "The heart of man is made for Thee, O God, and it is restless till it rests in Thee."

God has revealed to us that the happiness to which He invites us in the next life is a share of His own happiness. It consists in seeing God directly in all His goodness and beauty, in loving Him, and in enjoying His presence for all eternity. This happiness, which is called the beatific vision, is a privilege to which human beings naturally have no strict right. It is true that, because of the spiritual and immortal nature of our soul, we have a right to everlasting happiness in the life to come if we serve God faithfully in this world. We have no claim, however, to the supernatural possession of God such as is given in the beatific vision. In order to merit this supernatural happiness God gives us while we are on earth sufficient grace to live a supernatural life and to perform the actions necessary to earn this reward.

8

The Sacred Scriptures, God's own word, frequently refer to the happiness prepared for us in heaven, and urge us to strive to attain it. God has called all men to this happiness, but some do not attain it because they commit mortal sin and die without repenting of it. These souls are cast into hell, and will never possess God. Hence, it is the most important duty of our lives to fulfill the conditions necessary to merit eternal happiness. These conditions are to know, to love, and to serve God in a supernatural manner.

The first condition is to know God in a supernatural manner — that is, by faith. To do this we must learn the truths He has revealed to us and become familiar with the duties we owe Him. Without such a knowledge it is impossible to love and to serve God as we should. The most important of the truths He has revealed are four — that God exists, that He rewards the good and punishes the wicked, that there are three Persons in the one God, and that the Son of God became man and died for our salvation. However, we should not be content with knowing these four truths, but should study the doctrines of revelation.

Catholics have no difficulty in knowing God in a supernatural manner, for the Catholic Church was established by Jesus Christ, the Son of God, to act as His representative in teaching men about God. The chief truths taught by Jesus Christ through the Catholic Church are found in the Apostles' Creed. There are also some important truths revealed by God which are not found in the Apostles' Creed, such as the Real Presence of Our Lord in the Holy Eucharist and the Immaculate Conception of the Blessed Virgin Mary. Moreover, other Creeds besides the Apostles' Creed are used in the Church, particularly the Nicene Creed which is recited in the Mass; it was composed at the Council of Nicaea, in 325 A.D. There is also the Athanasian Creed, named after St. Athanasius, a bishop of the fourth century.

Nowadays when it is so easy to procure books and pamphlets explaining the teachings of the Catholic Church, every Catholic able to read can acquire a thorough knowledge of the Catholic faith. Catholic programs on the radio are also a means of increasing our knowledge of the Church's teachings.

Catholic boys and girls should strive to learn their lessons in Catechism faithfully and thoroughly. They should always remember that in studying their religion they are preparing themselves to gain the happiness of heaven, for they are fulfilling the first condition of meriting that happiness — to know God. They must remember, however, that the knowledge of God does not consist in merely reciting the answers of the Catechism by memory. They must try to grasp the meaning of these answers, and apply to their own lives the truths they contain.

RESOLUTION: Resolve that during your entire life you will continue to study the truths of your Catholic religion, and thus by ever knowing God better and better, constantly prepare yourself for the happiness of heaven, which is the great goal of your life.

STUDY HELPS

A. TRUE OR FALSE. (*Check each of the following statements as either true or false. The correct answers can be found in the previous portions of this lesson.*)

	TRUE	FALSE
(1) We can prove by reason without the help of revelation that there is a God.	.....	.....
(2) We can learn by our own reason the doctrine of the Holy Trinity.	.....	.....
(3) Because we have a spiritual soul we are destined to live forever.	.....	.....

9

	TRUE	FALSE

(4) Because we have a spiritual soul we have a right to supernatural happiness, or the beatific vision. . . . .

(5) All the souls in heaven enjoy equal happiness. . . . .

(6) All the souls in heaven are perfectly happy. . . . .

(7) God became happier when He created the universe. . . . .

(8) The Athanasian Creed is recited in the Mass. . . . .

(9) The Apostles' Creed contains twelve articles. . . . .

(10) A Catholic knows God sufficiently if he can recite the answers in the Catechism from memory. . . . .

B. PROBLEMS AND EXERCISES. (*Answer the questions orally or write them as your teacher may direct*):

(1) Fabian, a Catholic Boy Scout, has a keen interest in wild flowers. Why did God create wild flowers?

(2) Name two other creeds besides the Apostles' Creed that are recited in the Catholic Church. From which century do these creeds date?

(3) Atlee, a Communist, wants his heaven here upon earth. He claims there is no future life. Is it possible for Atlee to be perfectly happy here on earth? Explain your answer in a paragraph of less than 100 words.

(4) Edna is asked the following question: "Why are we placed here on this planet?" She is confused by the wording of the question, and does not answer because she cannot remember a question in the Catechism being worded that way. What is your answer to this question?

(5) Timothy's religious training has been neglected by his careless Catholic parents. Explain briefly to him what is meant by the expression that occurs so frequently in this lesson: "the happiness of heaven."

(6) Ruth would like to know what price must be paid for this happiness. Tell her.

(7) We live in an age of highly organized efforts. Even journeys are sponsored by travel agencies, tour organizations, etc. Is there any agency or organization here on earth that will guide us through life to the happiness of heaven? Name it and its organizer.

(8) In the Apostles' Creed there are 109 words. Increase the number of words about 50% to 75% and express the same doctrines.

(9) Within 40 to 50 words show how some one or more of God's creatures promoted your happiness yesterday.

(10) Arthur, the youngest pupil in the seventh grade of St. Mary's school, has a perfect knowledge of this lesson in the Catechism. Why is it true that the young lad is really wiser than a world-famed, proud university professor who denies the existence of God?

(11) Orville made a beautiful crib for Christmas, and it gave him great happiness to realize that his skill had produced so fine a work. He remarks to his mother: "God must have been much happier after He made the world than He was before " Is Orville correct in his statement?

(12) Count the number of Catholic programs that you can get on your radio every week. To how many of these programs do you listen?

(13) Lorraine, who is poorly instructed in religion, wonders how God who is so good can send souls to the everlasting pains of hell. Explain to her that this is not opposed to God's goodness or justice.

10

God and His Perfections

"I BELIEVE IN GOD THE FATHER ALMIGHTY, CREATOR OF HEAVEN AND EARTH . . ."

8. What do we mean when we say that God is the Supreme Being?
When we say that God is the Supreme Being we mean that He is above all creatures, the self-existing and infinitely perfect Spirit.

(a) God is above all created things—the mineral, vegetable, and animal kingdoms, men, and angels. Some likeness of God is in every creature, from the highest to the lowest. The highest angel, however, is but a weak reflection of the infinite perfection of God, who is the infinite Creator and Governor of the universe.

    SCRIPTURE: "I am who am" (*Exodus 3:14*).

    "I am the First, and I am the Last, and besides me there is no God" (*Isaias 44:6*).

9. What is a spirit?
A spirit is a being that has understanding and free will, but no body, and will never die.

(a) The soul of man is a spirit which does not die because it is simple, having no integral parts, and because it is spiritual, that is, entirely independent of matter in its being and in its own proper acts; it does not depend on creatures for existence and cannot be destroyed by them.

10. What do we mean when we say that God is self-existing?
When we say that God is self-existing we mean that He does not owe His existence to any other being.

(a) God is the first and completely independent source of all being. Every other being is *given* existence, God *is* His own existence; God *is* His own life, or He who is.

(b) It is a manifest contradiction to hold that God, who is self-existent, could have been brought into being by anyone else.

    SCRIPTURE: *See Scripture, question 8, Exodus 3:14.*

11. What do we mean when we say that God is infinitely perfect?
When we say that God is infinitely perfect we mean that He has all perfections without limit.

(a) God has in Himself, in an eminent degree, the perfections of all things that ever existed or will or can exist. He is the cause of all perfection in creatures. The perfections of created things are in God in an infinitely superior manner.

(b) Every creature, even the highest angel, is finite for it has the limitation of dependence on the Creator for its existence.

SCRIPTURE:
"Great is the Lord ... and his greatness is unsearchable" (*Psalm 144:3*).

12. What are some of the perfections of God?

Some of the perfections of God are: God is eternal, all-good, all-knowing, all-present, and almighty.

13. What do we mean when we say that God is eternal?

When we say that God is eternal we mean that He always was and always will be, and that He always remains the same.

(a) If God had a beginning or if He could cease to be, He would be limited and would not be infinitely perfect or self-existing. If God changed, the change would be either for the better or for the worse. In either case God would not be infinitely perfect.

(b) Spirits such as angels and the souls of men are eternal in the sense that they will live forever, but both angels and the souls of men, unlike God, had a beginning and are subject to change.

SCRIPTURE:
"Before the mountains were brought forth and the earth and the world were born, and from everlasting to everlasting thou art, O God" (*Psalm 89:2*).

"Every good gift and every perfect gift is from above, coming down from the Father of Lights, with whom there is no change, nor shadow of alteration" (*James 1:17*).

" 'I am the Alpha and the Omega, the beginning and the end,' says the Lord God, 'who is and who was and who is coming, the Almighty' " (*Apocalypse 1:8*).

14. What do we mean when we say that God is all-good?

When we say that God is all-good we mean that He is infinitely lovable in Himself, and that from His fatherly love every good comes to us.

(a) Things are good and lovable in the degree that they are perfect. Since God is infinitely perfect, He is all-good and infinitely lovable in Himself, and all goodness of creatures must come from Him.

SCRIPTURE:
"With whose beauty, if they being delighted, took them to be gods: let them know how much the Lord of them is more beautiful than they. For the first author of beauty made all those things" (*Wisdom 13:3*).

15. What do we mean when we say that God is all-knowing?

When we say that God is all-knowing we mean that He knows all things, past, present, and future, even our most secret thoughts, words, and actions.

(a) God's knowledge is not gained like ours, by proceeding step by step from things known to those unknown. By knowing Himself perfectly, God knows from eternity all things past, present, and future, and even all things possible. Every creature, in its actions, depends entirely on God, and any goodness in creatures is but an imperfect reflection of God's perfection. Through His infinitely perfect knowledge God knows the extent to which creatures share His perfections.

(b) God's knowledge of the future does not take away our freedom, but leaves our wills free to act or not to act.

(c) We are responsible for our free actions, which will be rewarded by God if they are good and punished by Him if they are evil.

SCRIPTURE:

"Before man is life and death, good and evil: that which he shall choose shall be given him" (*Ecclesiasticus 15:18*).

"Who hath been tried thereby, and made perfect, he shall have glory everlasting. He that could have transgressed, and hath not transgressed: and could do evil things and hath not done them" (*Ecclesiasticus 31:10*).

"The Lord knoweth all knowledge and hath beheld the signs of the world. He declareth the things that are past and the things that are to come, and revealeth the traces of hidden things" (*Ecclesiasticus 42:19*).

"For I am God, and there is no god beside: neither is there the like to me" (*Isaias 46:9*).

"And there is no creature hidden from his sight; but all things are naked and open to the eyes of him to whom we have to give account" (*Hebrews 4:13*).

16. What do we mean when we say that God is all-present?

When we say that God is all-present we mean that He is everywhere.

(a) God is everywhere:

first, by His power, inasmuch as all things are under His dominion;

second, by His Presence. inasmuch as nothing is hidden from Him;

third, by His essence, inasmuch as He is in all things as the cause of their being.

SCRIPTURE:

"Whither may I go from thy spirit, or whither may I flee from thy face? If I ascend into heaven, thou art there; if I lie down with the dead, thou art present. If I lay hold of the wings of the dawn, if I dwell in the farthest part of the sea: Even there shall thy hand lead me, and thy right hand shall hold me" (*Psalm 138:7-10*).

17. If God is everywhere, why do we not see Him?

Although God is everywhere, we do not see Him because He is a spirit and cannot be seen with our eyes.

(a) Although we cannot see God, the splendid order and beauty of creation should constantly remind us of His wisdom, His power, His goodness, and His nearness to us.

SCRIPTURE:

"God is spirit, and they who worship him must worship in spirit and in truth" (*John 4:24*).

13

18. Does God see us?

God sees us and watches over us with loving care.

SCRIPTURE:

"The eyes of the Lord in every place behold the good and the evil" (*Proverbs 15:3*).

"And as for clothing, why are you anxious? Consider how the lilies of the field grow; they neither toil nor spin, yet I say to you that not even Solomon in all his glory was arrayed like one of these. But if God so clothes the grass of the field, which flourishes today but tomorrow is thrown into the oven, how much more you, O you of little faith! Therefore do not be anxious, saying, 'What shall we eat?' or, 'What shall we drink?' or, 'What are we to put on?' (for after all these things the Gentiles seek); for your Father knows that you need all these things" (*Matthew 6:28-32*).

19. What is God's loving care for us called?

God's loving care for us is called Divine Providence.

(a) Divine Providence is God's plan for guiding every creature to its proper end.

SCRIPTURE:

"All expect of thee, that thou give them food in season. What thou givest to them they gather up; when thou openest thy hand, they are filled with good. If thou hidest thy face, they are troubled; if thou takest away their breath, they die and return to their dust. If thou sendest forth thy spirit, they are created, and thou renewest the face of the earth" (*Psalm 103:27-30*).

"For God will not except any man's person, neither will he stand in awe of any man's greatness: for he made the little and the great, and he hath equally care of all" (*Wisdom 6:8*).

"Cast all your anxiety upon him, because he cares for you" (*I Peter 5:7*).

20. What do we mean when we say that God is almighty?

When we say that God is almighty we mean that He can do all things.

(a) God can do anything that is not opposed to His perfection, or that is not self-contradictory. The impossibility of God's doing anything wrong or acting falsely does not limit His divine power, since wrongdoing and falsity in themselves are evil and are manifest defects; they cannot be associated with an infinitely perfect Being.

(b) Although God, the first cause of all things, actually does all things, He does not thereby deprive the creature of its power of causality nor of its freedom of action. A creature is never more than a secondary cause, that is, always dependent on God, always a finite being. When this secondary cause is intellectual, it is constituted by Almighty God as a free agent.

SCRIPTURE:

"Whatsoever the Lord pleases, he does in heaven and on earth, in the sea, and in all the deeps" (*Psalm 134:6*).

"How often would I have gathered thy children together, as a hen gathers her young under her wings, but thou wouldst not!" (*Matthew 23:37*).

"For nothing shall be impossible with God" (*Luke 1:37*).

14

21. Is God all-wise, all-holy, all-merciful, and all-just?

Yes, God is all-wise, all-holy, all-merciful, and all-just.

(a) God, the first cause of all things, in His wisdom knows these things perfectly and disposes them to their ends according to appropriate means.

(b) If we do not understand why or how God does certain things or permits them to happen, it is because our limited minds cannot understand His secrets nor see the universal plan of creation.

(c) Because God is all-holy, He is entirely free from all sin and imperfection and is infinitely good and lovable.

(d) Because God is all-merciful, He gives to each creature even more than is its due. He rewards the good more fully and punishes the wicked less severely than they deserve. He is always ready to help His creatures and to forgive repentant sinners.

(e) Because God is all-just, He gives to each creature what is due to it. God rewards the good and punishes the wicked partially in this life and more fully in eternity.

SCRIPTURE:

"Be ye holy, because I the Lord your God am holy" (*Leviticus 19:2*).

"Thou art just, O Lord, and all thy judgments are just; and all thy ways mercy, and truth, and judgment" (*Tobias 3:2*).

"The Lord is merciful and kind, slow to anger and plenteous in mercy" (*Psalm 102:8*).

"The Lord is just in all his ways, and holy in all his works" (*Psalm 144:17*).

"Of his wisdom there is no measure" (*Psalm 146:5*).

"And they cried one to another, and said: Holy, Holy, Holy, the Lord God of hosts, all the earth is full of his glory" (*Isaias 6:3*).

"Oh, the depth of the riches of the wisdom and of the knowledge of God! How incomprehensible are his judgments and how unsearchable his ways!" (*Romans 11:33*).

22. Can we know by our natural reason that there is a God?

We can know by our natural reason that there is a God, for natural reason tells us that the world we see about us could have been made only by a self-existing Being, all-wise and almighty.[2]

SCRIPTURE: *See Scripture, question 3, Psalm 18:2.*

23. Can we know God in any other way than by our natural reason?

Besides knowing God by our natural reason, we can also know Him from supernatural revelation, that is, from the truths found in Sacred Scripture and in Tradition, which God Himself has revealed to us.

(a) Supernatural revelation is the communication of some truth by God to a creature through means that are beyond the ordinary course of nature. Some revealed truths, for example, the mystery of the Blessed Trinity, are strictly beyond the power of the human mind. We could

---

2. See question 1 (a); also Appendix I, question II.

never know such truths unless God revealed them. Other truths, for example, the immortality of the soul, while not beyond the power of the human mind, are objects of revelation because God has revealed them in a supernatural way. Although these latter truths could be known without revelation, they are grasped with greater ease and certainty once God has revealed them.

(b) God's public revelation of truths to men began with Adam and Eve and ended at the death of Saint John the Apostle.

(c) Divine revelation contained in the Old Testament is called pre-Christian. It can be divided into:

first, Primitive revelation, made to Adam and Eve;

second, Patriarchal revelation, made to the patriarchs, for example, to Abraham and Lot;

third, Mosaic revelation, made to Moses and the prophets.

(d) Christian revelation contains the truths revealed to us by Jesus Christ, either directly or through His apostles.

(e) The Church does not oblige the faithful to believe private revelations given, at certain times, to individuals. For our edification, however, the Church permits the publication of some private revelations. Those to whom private revelations are given are obliged to believe them when they are certain that the revelations are from God.

(f) Sacred Scripture, or the Bible, is the word of God written by men under the inspiration of the Holy Ghost and contained in the books of the Old and the New Testament.

(g) Inspiration is the act by which God moves and directs the sacred writers faithfully to commit to writing all those things and only those things that He wishes them to write. The sacred writers act as free instruments of God, who is the principal author of Sacred Scripture.

(h) Tradition is the unwritten word of God—that body of truths revealed by God to the apostles, and not committed by them to writing but handed down by word of mouth. These truths, which were later committed to writing, particularly by the Fathers of the Church, have been preserved and handed down to the present day.

SCRIPTURE:

"But I have called you friends, because all things that I have heard from my Father I have made known to you" (*John 15:15*).

"There are, however, many other things that Jesus did; but if every one of these should be written, not even the world itself, I think, could hold the books that would have to be written" (*John 21:25*).

"So then, brethren, stand firm, and hold the teachings that you have learned, whether by word or by letter of ours" (*II Thessalonians 2:15*).

"All Scripture is inspired by God" (*II Timothy 3:16*).

"God, who at sundry times and in divers manners spoke in times past to the fathers by the prophets, last of all in these days has spoken to us by his Son" (*Hebrews 1:1*).

IMPORTANT TRUTHS ABOUT GOD AND HIS PERFECTIONS

The most excellent knowledge that man can have is the knowledge of God. Our own natural reason tells us that there must be a Supreme Being who created

16

the entire universe. He alone *is* existence; all other things are *given* existence by Him. With our natural reason we can know also that the Creator possesses all possible perfections or all good qualities. He is the cause of all perfection in creatures; hence, the perfections of all created things must be in Him in an infinitely superior manner to what they are in creatures.

In order that men may know Him and His perfections more surely and more profoundly, God has given us divine revelations, which furnish us with clearer knowledge about His nature than reason could provide, and also manifest some truths about Him which natural reason could never learn by its own efforts. The first of God's revelations for the human race were given to Adam and Eve, and God continued to make such revelations until the death of the last apostle, St. John. Since that time there have been no new revelations for all mankind, although there have been private revelations for certain individuals. Moreover, there has been a growth of public revelation in the sense that, as time went on, men have gradually come to a deeper and clearer knowledge of the truths which God revealed of old. Thus it was only after hundreds of years that Catholics clearly perceived that the doctrine of Mary's Immaculate Conception is contained in revelation. The revelations given by God for the human race are contained in Sacred Scripture, or the Bible which is the written word of God, and in divine Tradition, which is the unwritten word of God, since it was handed down, without being written, by those who received it from God, namely the apostles.

The various perfections of God are mentioned in many passages of Scripture, as is evident from the many quotations from the Bible given in the preceding part of this lesson. Catholics should try to familiarize themselves with some of the principal texts which speak of God and of His infinite perfections. Moreover, the prayers employed or recommended by the Church abound with references to God and to His perfections. The liturgy of the Mass frequently speaks of the wonderful qualities of the Most High.

Some of God's perfections have a special relation to ourselves. For example, when we think of God's goodness we are inspired to love Him, not only because He is good to us but also because He is all-good in Himself. Thus we make an act of divine charity, the most excellent of the virtues. Again, the truth that God is all-present and hence always near us, should help us to avoid sin. The realization that God is all-knowing should remind us that He is aware of even our most secret thoughts and desires. The thought of His providence, of His loving care over us to help us to attain everlasting happiness, should inspire us to have unbounded confidence in Him. In trials and temptations we should remember that we are not alone; our loving Father is always near us.

RESOLUTION: Acquire the habit of remembering frequently that God is at your side and of concentrating briefly on one of His infinite perfections. Then in your heart make an act of adoration or of love.

STUDY HELPS

A. WORD SELECTION. (*Select the word or phrase in the parentheses which most exactly and most completely fills out the sentence*).

(1) When we say that God is self-existing we mean that (He is the cause of His own existence . . . He does not owe His existence to any other being . . . He loves Himself more than He loves any other being).

(2) Spirits are eternal (in the sense that they will live forever . . . in the same sense that God is eternal . . . in the sense that they never change).

(3) When we say that God is in all things as the cause of their being, we are referring to His presence by (presence . . . power . . . essence).

(4) God (wills . . . cannot prevent . . . permits) sin.

(5) The first public revelation was given to (Adam and Eve . . . Christ . . . Moses).

(6) Public revelation ended with (Christ . . . St. Peter . . . St. John).

(7) God rewards the good (as much as they deserve . . . more than they deserve . . . less than they deserve).

(8) Public revelation (is still going on . . . is all contained in the Bible, . . . is contained in the Bible and in Tradition).

(9) Private revelations (must be believed only by those for whom they are made . . . must be believed by everyone . . . must be believed by no one).

(10) The principal author of a book in the Bible is (the man who wrote it . . . the Church . . . God).

B. PROBLEMS AND EXERCISES. (*Answer the questions orally or write them as your teacher may direct*):

(1) What should we be inspired to do when we consider the goodness of God?

(2) Julius, an irreligious High School boy, claims we are forced to do all the things we do; he says that we are not free. Is this true? What is the reason for your answer?

(3) At this very moment, God knows what we shall do tomorrow. Does this mean we shall be forced to do those things tomorrow? Explain.

(4) Sometimes in religious art, the eye of God is represented within an equilateral triangle. What perfection of God is thus illustrated?

(5) In three or four sentences tell why the remembrance of the Presence of God is a great aid in practising virtue and in avoiding sin.

(6) Remembering that God's eye ever rests upon us, should we be frightened or encouraged? Tell us the reason for your answer.

(7) Occasionally atheists and scoffers at religion put such silly questions as these: "Can God make a square circle?—or a stick with only one end?" How do you answer such nonsense?

(8) Passing the announcement board of a Catholic church, Chester, a Protestant lad, notices the advertisement of a sermon: "The Mercy of God." He asks his Catholic friend, Alfred, what it means. Help Alfred to give the right answer.

(9) The timepieces of earth are regulated from the movements of the heavenly bodies. These timepieces—our watches and clocks—are made by intelligent beings outside of the timepieces themselves. Who then, made the Master Timepiece,—the heavenly bodies?

(10) Define: Supernatural Revelation; Divine Providence.

(11) Brigid is fond of spiritual books, especially the life of her patroness, recounting the wonderful revelations made to her. Other saintly men and women of God also have been favored with such revelations. How are these revelations classified? Are they the same as the supernatural revelations spoken of in this lesson?

(12) Explain in what sense there has been, for many centuries, (a) no growth of public revelation, and (b) such a growth.

(13) Leander wonders how it was possible for the prophets to describe the details of Our Lord's passion and death many centuries before they took place. Can you explain this to Leander?

18

The Unity and Trinity of God

24. Is there only one God?

Yes, there is only one God.

(a) Reason can prove that there is only one God. The assumption that there could be two infinitely perfect gods or two infinitely supreme beings independent of each other, is an absurdity.

(b) Revelation confirms our reasoning that there is only one God.

SCRIPTURE:

"That thou mightest know that the Lord he is God: and there is no other besides him" (*Deuteronomy 4:35*).

"Thus saith the Lord, the king of Israel and his redeemer the Lord of hosts: I am the First, and I am the Last: and besides me there is no God" (*Isaias 44:6*).

"I am the Lord, and there is none else: there is no God besides me" (*Isaias 45:5*).

"The first commandment of all is, 'Hear, O Israel! The Lord our God is one God'" (*Mark 12:29*).

25. How many Persons are there in God?

In God there are three divine Persons—the Father, the Son, and the Holy Ghost.

(a) Unaided by divine revelation, the human mind could not know the existence of the Blessed Trinity because it is a supernatural mystery.[3] Even after God has revealed the existence of the Blessed Trinity, we cannot understand it fully. When we believe, on the word of God, that there are three Persons in one God, we do not believe that three Persons are one Person, or that three gods are one God; this would be a contradiction.

SCRIPTURE:

"Go, therefore, and make disciples of all nations, baptizing them in the name of the Father, and of the Son, and of the Holy Spirit" (*Matthew 28:19*).

"And I will ask the Father and he will give you another Advocate to dwell with you forever, the Spirit of truth whom the world cannot receive, because it neither sees him nor knows him" (*John 14:16-17*).

"But the Advocate, the Holy Spirit, whom the Father will send in my name, he will teach you all things, and bring to your mind whatever I have said to you" (*John 14:26*).

26. Is the Father God?

The Father is God and the first Person of the Blessed Trinity.

(a) The first Person of the Blessed Trinity is called the Father because from all eternity He begets the second Person, His only-begotten Son.

---

[3] See question 34.

19

(b) God the Father is called the first Person not because He is greater or older than the other two Persons, but because He is unbegotten.

SCRIPTURE:
"This, then, is why the Jews were the more anxious to put him to death; because he not only broke the Sabbath, but also called God his own Father, making himself equal to God" (John 5:18).

"Blessed be the God and Father of our Lord Jesus Christ, the Father of mercies and the God of all comfort" (II Corinthians 1:3).

27. Is the Son God?

The Son is God and the second Person of the Blessed Trinity.

(a) The second Person of the Blessed Trinity is called the Son because, from all eternity, He is the only begotten of the Father. Proceeding from the Father, the Son is called the Divine Word or the Wisdom of the Father.

SCRIPTURE:
"All things have been delivered to me by my Father; and no one knows the Son except the Father; nor does anyone know the Father except the Son, and him to whom the Son chooses to reveal him" (Matthew 11:27).

"In the beginning was the Word,
and the Word was with God;
and the Word was God" (John 1:1).

"And we know that the Son of God has come and has given us understanding, that we may know the true God and may be in his true Son. He is the true God and eternal life" (I John 5:20).

"I and the Father are one" (John 10:30).

28. Is the Holy Ghost God?

The Holy Ghost is God and the third Person of the Blessed Trinity.

(a) The third Person of the Blessed Trinity is called the Holy Ghost because from all eternity He is breathed forth, as it were, by the Father and the Son. Proceeding from the Father and the Son, He is called the Gift or Love of the Father and the Son.

(b) The word "Ghost" applied to the third Person means "Spirit."

SCRIPTURE:
"But Peter said, 'Ananias, why has Satan tempted thy heart, that thou shouldst lie to the Holy Spirit and by fraud keep back part of the price of the land? While it yet remained, did it not remain thine; and after it was sold, was not the money at thy disposal? Why hast thou conceived this thing in thy heart? Thou hast not lied to men, but to God' " (Acts 5:3-4).

"Do you not know that you are the temple of God and that the Spirit of God dwells in you?" (I Corinthians 3:16).

29. What do we mean by the Blessed Trinity?

By the Blessed Trinity we mean one and the same God in three divine Persons.

SCRIPTURE: See Scripture, question 25, Matthew 28:19; John 14:26.

30. Are the three divine Persons really distinct from one another?
The three divine Persons are really distinct from one another.

(a) Although the Father, the Son, and the Holy Ghost are distinct Persons, they are not distinct in nature. The nature of the Father is entirely the nature of the Son; and the nature of the Father and the Son is entirely the nature of the Holy Ghost.

31. Are the three divine Persons perfectly equal to one another?
The three divine Persons are perfectly equal to one another, because all are one and the same God.

(a) No one of the three Persons precedes the others in time or in power, but all are equally eternal and all-powerful because they have the same divine nature.

32. How are the three divine Persons, though really distinct from one another, one and the same God?
The three divine Persons, though really distinct from one another, are one and the same God because all have one and the same divine nature.

(a) Because the three divine Persons have one and the same divine nature, they have the same perfections and the same external works are produced by them. But in order that we may better know the three divine Persons, certain perfections and works are attributed to each Person; for example, omnipotence and the works of omnipotence, such as creation, to the Father; wisdom and the works of wisdom, such as enlightenment, to the Son; love and the works of love, such as sanctification, to the Holy Ghost.

33. Can we fully understand how the three divine Persons, though really distinct from one another, are one and the same God?
We cannot fully understand how the three divine Persons, though really distinct from one another, are one and the same God because this is a supernatural mystery.

34. What is a supernatural mystery?
A supernatural mystery is a truth which we cannot fully understand, but which we firmly believe because we have God's word for it.

(a) In addition to those truths which can be attained by man's natural reason, there are certain mysteries hidden in God which we cannot know without divine revelation, but which we must believe because God has revealed them. Divine mysteries by their very nature are far above the power of human understanding and even when revealed and accepted on faith they remain obscure during our life on earth. To understand these things fully, a finite mind would have to comprehend the infinite.

(b) In heaven there will be a fuller understanding of these mysteries, but never an infinite comprehension of them.

21

21a

The Holy Trinity

This picture shows Jesus Christ seated in Heaven at the right hand of His Father on a throne of Glory. The angels and saints surround Him, and His throne is borne up by a multitude of celestial spirits. The Father holds a scepter and the Son His Cross, and both support the world, which was created by the Father, bought back by the Son, and sanctified by the Holy Spirit.

(c) It is reasonable to believe supernatural mysteries revealed by God because He can neither deceive nor be deceived. In our everyday life we believe many things on the word of human beings even though at times they deceive or are deceived.

IMPORTANT TRUTHS ABOUT THE UNITY AND TRINITY OF GOD

Both reason and revelation assure us that there is, and can be, only one God, for the very idea of the Supreme Being makes it impossible for God to have an equal; but from revelation we learn that the one God is three distinct Persons, known as the Father, the Son, and the Holy Ghost. Before the coming of the Son of God this truth was not manifested even to the Jews, although there are some texts in the Old Testament which seem to imply that there is more that one Person possessing the divine nature — for example: "Let *us* make man to our image and likeness" (*Genesis 1:26*).

In His discourse at the Last Supper our Blessed Lord mentioned the three Persons by name, and He clearly spoke of the doctrine of the Holy Trinity to the apostles just before He ascended into heaven. The texts of Sacred Scripture containing these words of Christ have been given in this lesson. There was also an external manifestation of the Holy Trinity at the time of Our Lord's baptism by St. John in the river Jordan. On that occasion it was God the Son in His human nature who was baptized, while God the Holy Ghost descended on Him in the form of a dove and God the Father announced from heaven: "This is my beloved Son, in whom I am well pleased" (*Matthew 3:17*).

Hence, according to Catholic belief, there are three divine Persons but only one divine nature. All three Persons are perfectly equal to each other, because all possess the same divine nature with all its infinite perfections. From all eternity the Son proceeds from the Father as the Word, the product of the intellectual act whereby the Father understands the divine nature; and the Holy Ghost proceeds from the Father and the Son as the product of the act of love of these two Persons for the divine goodness. All the actions of God outside of those whereby the second and third Persons proceed are acts of the three Persons operating together through the one divine nature. However, certain works performed by all three Persons are appropriated or attributed to particular Persons as if they individually performed them—for example, the work of creation to the Father, the work of producing the human nature of Christ to the Holy Ghost (*Luke 1:35*); but only the Second Person became incarnate.

Although the doctrine of the Blessed Trinity is a supernatural mystery— a truth which we cannot discover by reason nor understand in the present life— we believe it because it has been made known to us by God who can neither deceive nor be deceived. Even in natural things there are many mysteries which we accept on the testimony of our fellowmen. We believe what the astronomers tell us about the stars and the planets, although we cannot prove these truths ourselves. Not even the most learned scientist understands fully the nature of the force we call electricity; yet we all know that there is such a force and we unhesitatingly accept the information that scientists give us about it. How much more willing should we be to believe the marvelous truth which God Himself has made known to us—that He is one in nature and three in Persons— even though we cannot perceive this truth by our own reason nor understand how each divine Person can be identical with the divine nature, yet really distinct from the other two Persons!

On the first Sunday after Pentecost the Church celebrates a feast in honor of the Most Blessed Trinity. Moreover, on Sundays outside of the Christmas, Lenten and Easter seasons the Preface of the Holy Trinity is recited or chanted in the Mass. One of the favored devotions of the Catholic Church is the *Doxology*—the prayer: "Glory be to the Father and to the Son, and to the Holy

Ghost. As it was in the beginning, is now, and ever shall be, world without end. Amen." This Doxology is frequently repeated in the official prayers of the Church, particularly in the Divine Office which priests and the members of many religious orders recite every day. And whenever we make the Sign of the Cross we profess our faith in the mystery of the Most Blessed Trinity.

RESOLUTION: Whenever you recite the Doxology or make the Sign of the Cross, try to remember that you are expressing your faith in the most profound mystery of the Catholic religion, the mystery of the Most Blessed Trinity.

A. TRUE OR FALSE. (*Check each of the following statements as either true or false. The correct answers can be found in the preceding portions of the lesson*)

	TRUE	FALSE
(1) Although we say that God the Father is the creator of heaven and earth, all three divine Persons created the universe equally.	. . . . .	. . . . .
(2) The second Person of the Blessed Trinity is called the Word.	. . . . .	. . . . .
(3) The Father existed before the Son and the Holy Ghost.	. . . . .	. . . . .
(4) It is unreasonable to believe anything we cannot understand.	. . . . .	. . . . .
(5) The third Person is called the Gift or Love of the Father and the Son.	. . . . .	. . . . .
(6) The third Person proceeds from the Father alone.	. . . . .	. . . . .
(7) The names Father, Son and Holy Ghost are names for one divine Person considered under three different aspects.	. . . . .	. . . . .
(8) The producing of the human nature of Christ is appropriated to the third Person, though all three Persons actually produced this nature.	. . . . .	. . . . .
(9) All three divine Persons became incarnate, in Jesus Christ.	. . . . .	. . . .
(10) We shall understand the mystery of the Holy Trinity perfectly in heaven.	. . . . .	. . . . .

B. PROBLEMS AND EXERCISES. (*Answer the questions orally or write them as your teacher may direct*):

(1) Does Lazarus, your Jewish neighbor, believe in the doctrine of the Most Holy Trinity? Did his Jewish ancestors, before the coming of Christ, have this doctrine expressly revealed to them?

(2) When did Our Lord clearly reveal the sublime truth of the Most Blessed Trinity?

(3) In what words did Our Lord make this revelation?

(4) What saying of Our Lord, at the Last Supper, revealed the names of the two other Persons of the Blessed Trinity?

(5) At the beginning of Our Lord's public ministry, John the Baptist baptized Jesus in the waters of the river Jordan. Show how the three Persons of the Blessed Trinity externally manifested themselves then.

(6) Abner, a dealer in electrical supplies, and a Unitarian in religion, has great admiration for Jesus Christ, but he will not believe that Jesus

is God. He refuses to believe that there are three Persons in God. He says that his mind revolts at the idea of believing something he cannot understand. Try to persuade him that he is wrong in maintaining such an attitude.

(7) What induces you to believe in the Most Blessed Trinity?

(8) In what ways does the Church pay honor to the Most Blessed Trinity?

(9) Name three instances in which you have accepted on faith from human beings something you could not perceive yourself.

(10) In church, Bonaventure picks up a leaflet of devotion to the nine choirs of angels. On it is printed the invitation to "recite the Doxology nine times each day." Bonaventure doesn't know what is meant by that strange word—Doxology. Tell him its meaning.

(11) Rosamond fails to answer a test question: "By what common devotional practice do we render homage to the Blessed Trinity?" What is your answer?

(12) Is the Holy Spirit the same as the Holy Ghost?

(13) Is it correct to say that whatever is above reason is also against reason? Is the doctrine of the Holy Trinity either against reason or above reason?

(14) It is related in the life of St. Patrick, the apostle of Ireland, that when he was preaching on the doctrine of the Holy Trinity to the pagan people of that land he plucked a shamrock and held it up to their gaze to illustrate the mystery of one God in three distinct divine Persons. A shamrock has three leaves on one stem. How would you illustrate the mystery by a three-leaf clover? Can you think of any other object to illustrate this wonderful mystery of the Holy Trinity?

(15) In Catholic art when the three Persons of the Holy Trinity are portrayed, the Father is represented as a venerable man with a long beard, the Son is represented by the picture of Jesus Christ, and the Holy Ghost is represented as a dove. Does this mean that God the Father, as well as the Son, took human nature? Does the fact that the Father is represented as a very old man indicate that the Father existed before the Son and the Holy Ghost?

(16) In the pictures just mentioned why is the Holy Ghost portrayed as a dove? Describe the incident on which this method of portraying the third Person is based. Did the third Person on that occasion take to Himself the nature of a dove in the same way that the second Person took to Himself human nature at the Incarnation?

(17) In the present lesson you have learned that the second Person of the Holy Trinity is called the Word. Do you know which of the four Evangelists uses this term for the Son of God in his Gospel? Do you know at what part of the Mass we use this term in the expression "The Word was made flesh"?

(18) When Our Lord worked miracles, such as the healing of the sick, in the course of His mortal life, He used His divine power. Now, was this divine power exercised by the second Person only, or was it exercised by the three Divine Persons?

Creation and the Angels

35. What do we mean when we say that God is the Creator of heaven and earth?

When we say that God is the Creator of heaven and earth we mean that He made all things from nothing by His almighty power.

(a) Only God can create, that is, make something from nothing, because creation requires infinite power, which God alone possesses.

(b) All things except God depend on a cause for their existence and hence must have been created by God.[4]

(c) God did not have to create the world; He did so freely.

(d) God preserves all creatures; otherwise, they would at once return to nothingness. He also governs all things, and in the divine government of the world nothing does or can happen unless God wills or permits it.

(e) Evil is the lack of some perfection. God does not will physical evil in itself but only insofar as it is connected with some good.

(f) God wills or permits the physical evils of life in order to punish sin, to make sinners repent, to try the just and make them worthy of everlasting reward, or to be the occasion of some other greater good.

(g) God permits but does not will moral evils.

SCRIPTURE:
"Thus saith the Lord, thy redeemer, and thy maker from the womb: I am the Lord, that make all things, that alone stretch out the heavens, that establish the earth. And there is none with me" (*Isaias 44:24*).

"For in him were created all things in the heavens and on the earth, things visible and things invisible, whether Thrones, or Dominations, or Principalities, or Powers. All things have been created through and unto him, and he is before all creatures, and in him all things hold together" (*Colossians 1:16-17*).

36. Which are the chief creatures of God?

The chief creatures of God are angels and men.

(a) It is a matter of faith that God the Creator produced out of nothing creatures both spiritual and corporal, angelic and earthly.[5]

SCRIPTURE: *See Daniel 3:57ff.*

See also Scripture, question 35, Colossians 1:16-17.

37. What are angels?

Angels are created spirits, without bodies, having understanding and free will.

(a) Reason alone cannot prove that the angels exist. Reason indicates, however, that just as there are purely material creatures, and creatures

---

[4] Read the first book of the Bible, Genesis, which describes the creation of the universe.
[5] Fourth Lateran and Vatican Councils.

composed of both matter and spirit, so also it is fitting that there should be purely spiritual creatures.

(b) Angels are spiritual beings inferior to God and superior to man.

(c) Sacred Scripture frequently speaks of the angels and mentions three by name: the Archangels Michael, Gabriel, and Raphael.[6]

(d) The nine "choirs" of angels are the Seraphim, Cherubim, Thrones, Dominations, Virtues, Powers, Principalities, Archangels, and Angels.[7]

(e) The exact number of angels is unknown, but Sacred Scripture indicates that their number is very great.

SCRIPTURE:

"Thousands of thousands ministered to him, and ten thousand times a hundred thousand stood before him" (Daniel 7:10).

"Or dost thou suppose that I cannot entreat my Father, and he will even now furnish me with more than twelve legions of angels?" (Matthew 26:53).

"Are they not all ministering spirits, sent for service, for the sake of those who shall inherit salvation?" (Hebrews 1:14).

"Rash and self-willed, such men in their deriding do not regard majesty; whereas angels, though greater in strength and power, do not bring against themselves an abusive charge" (II Peter 2:11).

38. What gifts did God bestow on the angels when He created them?

When God created the angels He bestowed on them great wisdom, power, and holiness.

(a) God bestowed upon the angels supernatural grace by which they could gain eternal happiness.

(b) The angels were given the opportunity to merit the reward of heaven by remaining faithful to God.

39. Did all the angels remain faithful to God?

Not all the angels remained faithful to God; some of them sinned.

(a) We do not know the exact nature of the test to which God put the angels that they might prove themselves worthy of eternal happiness.

(b) The angels who were unfaithful committed a serious sin, for which they were punished.

SCRIPTURE:

"For God did not spare the angels when they sinned, but dragged them down by infernal ropes to Tartarus, and delivered them to be tortured and kept in custody for judgment" (II Peter 2:4).

"And the angels also who did not preserve their original state, but forsook their abode, he has kept in everlasting chains under darkness for the judgment of the great day" (Jude 6).

[6] Michael — Daniel 10:13-21; Jude 1:9; Apocalypse 12:7;
Gabriel — Daniel 8:16; 9:21; Luke 1:19-26;
Raphael — Tobias 3:25; 5:17; 6:16; 8:3; 9:6; 11:7; and 12:15.
[7] Seraphim — Isaias 6:2;
Cherubim — Genesis 3:24; Ezechiel 10:1-22; Ecclesiasticus 49:10;
Thrones, Dominations, Principalities, Powers — Colossians 1:16;
Virtues — Ephesians 1:21;
Archangel — I Thessalonians 4:16;
Angel — Matthew 18:10.

40. What happened to the angels who remained faithful to God?

The angels who remained faithful to God entered into the eternal happiness of heaven, and these are called good angels.

SCRIPTURE:
"See that you do not despise one of these little ones; for I tell you, their angels in heaven always behold the face of my Father in heaven" (*Matthew 18:10*).

41. What do the good angels do in heaven?

In heaven the good angels see, love, and adore God.

SCRIPTURE: *See Scripture, question 40.*

42. How do the good angels help us?

The good angels help us by praying for us, by acting as messengers from God to us, and by serving as our guardian angels.

(a) The Old and the New Testament refer frequently to the work of the good angels among men. A good angel was the guide of God's chosen people (*Exodus 23:20*); the protector of Tobias was a good angel (*Tobias 5 ff.*). The Archangel Gabriel announced the glad tidings of the Incarnation to Our Blessed Mother (*Luke 1:28*).

(b) Although angels are pure spirits, they can be seen by man when on special occasions God permits them to take on bodies or the appearance of bodies, which are visible to the human eye.

SCRIPTURE:
"For to his angels he has given thee in trust, to keep thee in all thy ways. In their hands they shall bear thee up, lest thou dash thy foot against a stone" (*Psalm 90:11-12*).

"Now in the sixth month the angel Gabriel was sent from God to a town of Galilee called Nazareth, to a virgin betrothed to a man named Joseph, of the house of David, and the virgin's name was Mary. And when the angel had come to her, he said, 'Hail, full of grace, the Lord is with thee. Blessed art thou among women" (*Luke 1:26-28*).

43. How do our guardian angels help us?

Our guardian angels help us by praying for us, by protecting us from harm, and by inspiring us to do good.

(a) It is a matter of faith that angels are deputed as the guardians of men.

(b) It is commonly held that each individual has a special guardian angel.

SCRIPTURE:
"When thou didst pray with tears, and didst bury the dead, and didst leave thy dinner, and hide the dead by day in thy house, and bury them by night, I offered thy prayer to the Lord. ... For I am the angel Raphael, one of the seven, who stand before the Lord" (*Tobias 12:12, 15*).

44. What happened to the angels who did not remain faithful to God?

The angels who did not remain faithful to God were cast into hell, and these are called bad angels, or devils.

27

(a) The devils, or the evil spirits, were created by God, not as bad beings but as good beings. By their own free acts, they chose evil and thereby became bad angels.

SCRIPTURE:
"Depart from me, accursed ones, into the everlasting fire which was prepared for the devil and his angels" (*Matthew 25:41*).

45. What is the chief way in which the bad angels try to harm us?

The chief way in which the bad angels try to harm us is by tempting us to sin.

(a) Devils are sometimes permitted to enter the body of a man and to exercise power over his faculties—a state known as diabolical possession; or they are permitted to torment a person from without—a state known as diabolical obsession.

(b) Diabolic possession and obsession are permitted by God to show forth His glory, to punish sin, to bring sinners to repentance, or to give occasion for the exercise of virtue.

(c) When the devil uses the body of a possessed person to say or do evil things, the person is not guilty of sin, provided he does not freely consent.

(d) Exorcism is the act of driving out or warding off evil spirits from persons, places, or things possessed or infested by them. The Church received from Christ the power of exorcism.

(e) An exorcist is one who has power, conferred by a bishop, to exorcise demons. The order of exorcist is the third of the four minor orders of the Western Church. Only with the permission of his bishop is a priest allowed to use his power of exorcising evil spirits.

SCRIPTURE:
"Then having summoned his twelve disciples, he gave them power over unclean spirits, to cast them out" (*Matthew 10:1*).

"Put on the armor of God, that you may be able to stand against the wiles of the devil" (*Ephesians 6:11*).

"Be sober, be watchful! For your adversary the devil, as a roaring lion, goes about seeking someone to devour. Resist him, steadfast in the faith, knowing that the same suffering befalls your brethren all over the world" (*I Peter 5:8-9*).

46. Do all temptations come from the bad angels?

Some temptations come from the bad angels; but other temptations come from ourselves and from the persons and things about us.

(a) The bad angels, the persons and things about us, and we ourselves can excite the senses and be an inducement to sin.

SCRIPTURE:
"For I am delighted with the law of God according to the inner man, but I see another law in my members, warring against the law of my mind and making me prisoner to the law of sin that is in my members" (*Romans 7:22-23*).

"Let no man say when he is tempted, that he is tempted by God; for God is no tempter to evil, and he himself tempts no one. But everyone is tempted by being drawn away and enticed by his own passion" (*James 1:13-14*).

"Do not love the world, or the things that are in the world" (*I John 2:15*).

47. Can we always resist temptations?

We can always resist temptations, because no temptation can force us into sin, and because God will always help us if we ask Him.

(a) God does not demand the impossible; however He warns us that in our efforts to overcome temptation we must not rely entirely on ourselves but must seek His help.

(b) God permits us to be tempted in order to make us realize our weakness, to test our faith, and to help us by His grace to strengthen virtue by practice and to obtain the reward of eternal life.

(c) The most effective means of overcoming temptation are prayer, mortification, frequent Confession and Holy Communion, and avoiding idleness and the near occasion of sin.

> SCRIPTURE:
> "Therefore let him who thinks he stands take heed lest he fall. May no temptation take hold of you but such as man is equal to. God is faithful and will not permit you to be tempted beyond your strength, but with the temptation will also give you a way out that you may be able to bear it" (*I Corinthians 10:12-13*).
>
> "And he has said to me, 'My grace is sufficient for thee' " (*II Corinthians 12:9*).

IMPORTANT TRUTHS ABOUT CREATION AND THE ANGELS

One of the usual names for God is "Creator." Both reason and revelation assure us that everything outside of God has been created, or brought into existence from nothingness by His almighty power. Moreover, after He has created something, God continues to keep in existence; this is called divine conservation.

In the first chapter of the Bible we read that in the beginning God created heaven and earth; and then the Sacred Scripture tells us that in the course of six days God made the various elements of the universe—the sun and moon and stars, the plants and the animals, and finally man. These six "days" need not be understood as days of twenty-four hours each—they may each have been periods of many thousands of years in duration.

Before He created men, God created another class of intellectual beings, known as angels—spirits without bodies, endowed with great perfections, particularly with profound intelligence. God wished the angels to share His supernatural happiness in heaven, but He wished them first to merit this privilege by their own free actions. Hence, while He raised the angels to the supernatural order by giving them sanctifying grace, God did not admit them at once to the beatific vision but imposed on them a test of their fidelity. Many of the angels were faithful to God; as a reward they were admitted immediately to the everlasting joys of heaven. Their leader was St. Michael. Others, led by Lucifer, who is now called Satan or Beelzebub, in their wilful pride rebelled against God. St. Thomas Aquinas, the great theologian, taught that the wicked angels committed sin either by rejecting the supernatural happiness to which God called them because they were satisfied with their own natural perfections, or by desiring to attain to supernatural happiness by their natural powers. Those sinful angels were cast into hell for all eternity and are now called devils.

The good angels, who praise and enjoy God in heaven, are employed by Him in the service of mankind. Many passages of Scripture record that God's designs for the human race were carried out through the ministry of angels. This was especially the case in connection with the Incarnation. The angel

Gabriel announced to our Lady that she was to be the Mother of the divine Redeemer; angels proclaimed His birth to the shepherds on the first Christmas night; an angel warned St. Joseph of Herod's murderous plan and bade him take the Child and His Mother into Egypt, and later informed him of Herod's death and commanded the Holy Family to return; angels ministered to Our Lord after His threefold temptation by the devil; an angel comforted Him during His agony in the garden; angels announced His Resurrection and His Ascension into heaven.

In His goodness, God protects us by the ministry of angels. It is commonly believed that each individual has a special guardian angel, athough it is not taught by the Church as an article of faith. Our angel guardian accompanies us from birth until death, praying for us in a special way, inspiring us with good thoughts, striving to protect us from dangers of body and of soul. On October 2nd the Church celebrates a feast in honor of the Guardian Angels. There are also three feasts in the course of the year to honor the three angels whose names we know from the Sacred Scripture— St. Michael (September 29th), St. Gabriel (March 24th), and St. Raphael (October 24th). There is also a feast on May 8th to honor an extraordinary apparition of St. Michael.

God allows the devils to tempt human beings by working on their imagination. Sometimes the devil is permitted by God to attack a human being more directly by obsession (from without) or by possession (from within the body). Sometimes very holy persons were tormented in this way. The devil can never force a person to commit sin; God will always give us sufficient grace to resist temptation.

RESOLUTION: Resolve to think of your guardian angel at least once a day, either in your morning or in your night prayers. Thank him for his protection, ask him to continue his loving care for you, so that one day you may be with him in heaven.

STUDY HELPS

A. COLUMN SELECTION. (*Join correctly the parts of the sentences in Columns I and II, by placing the right key letter in the proper parenthesis.*)

I	II
(1) The creation of the angels took place (. .).	(A) sanctifying grace.
(2) The leader of the good angels was (. .).	(B) diabolical obsession.
(3) The leader of the bad angels was (. .).	(C) the beatific vision.
(4) It is an article of faith that (. .).	(D) each individual has a special guardian angel.
(5) The angels are (. .).	
(6) The angels were endowed at their creation with (. .).	(E) diabolical possession.
(7) The angels were given the opportunity of meriting (. .).	(F) before the creation of man.
(8) It is commonly held, but it is not an article of faith that (. .).	(G) purely spiritual beings.
(9) When the devils enter the body of a person, it is called (. .).	(H) God created the angels out of nothing.
(10) When the devils torment a person from without, it is called (. .).	(I) Michael.
	(J) Lucifer.

B. PROBLEMS AND EXERCISES. (*Answer the questions orally or write them as your teacher may direct*):

(1) Dora's friends are praising her oil painting "The Good Shepherd." One of them calls it "a superb creation." Is it a "creation" in the sense of the word as it is used in this lesson? If not, why not?

(2) Winston, an historian and an unbeliever, is studying the most ancient historical documents. He is overlooking the Bible. May real scholars neglect a fair consideration of the Bible? Give the reason for your last answer.

(3) Heinrich wants to know how the shepherds watching their flocks on Christmas night on Bethlehem's hillside were able to see the angels, since angels are pure spirits without bodies. What reply is to be given to him?

(4) Mention two occasions in Our Lord's adult life when one, or several, of the angels appeared to Him.

(5) Did Lucifer ever enjoy the Beatific Vision? Add a reason to your answer.

(6) How did St. Michael win his present happiness in heaven?

(7) Geraldine, in the seventh grade of the school of St. Felicitas, was asked in religion class: "Have you any regular devotion to the Archangel, St. Michael?" She answered "No"; but she has,—and so have you, for at least once every week we pray to this great saint. When and where is this devotion practised?

(8) Of all the myriads of angels now with God, we know the names of how many? Who are they? Have we any knowledge of how the angels are classified or grouped? Explain your answer.

(9) Name the chief of the rebel angels. By what other scriptural names is he known? To what does St. Peter liken him?

(10) Godfrey, a lad inclined to be lazy, is bothered with many temptations to sin. May he justly blame all of them on the devil? Explain your answer. Advise him how to overcome his temptations.

(11) Learn the following prayer to your guardian angel, which is richly indulgenced by the Church:

> Angel of God, my guardian dear,
> To whom His love commits me here;
> Ever this day be at my side,
> To light and guard, to rule and guide. Amen.

(12) Do you think that your guardian angel knows what you are going to do tomorrow? Do you think the devil knows?

(13) St. John Baptist Vianney, a holy parish priest who lived in France about the middle of the nineteenth century, was frequently and violently assailed by the devil. Sometimes the evil spirit made loud noises in his room at night, thus depriving the good priest of his rest. What do we call this kind of activity by the devil? Do you think that God allowed it for some sins that St. John may have committed in his earlier days? What other reason can you suggest for this permission on the part of God? What would it be called if the devil had been allowed to take up his abode in the holy man's body and speak through his lips?

31

LESSON 5

The Creation and the Fall of Man

48. What is man?

Man is a creature composed of body and soul, and made to the image and likeness of God.

(a) The soul and the body are not loosely connected parts of man; they are united in a substantial union to form one complete human nature. The soul is not located in any particular member of the body but is whole and entire in each part.

SCRIPTURE:

"And the Lord God formed man of the slime of the earth, and breathed into his face the breath of life; and man became a living soul" (*Genesis 2:7*).

"And God created man to his own image; to the image of God he created him. Male and female he created them" (*Genesis 1:27*).

49. Is this likeness to God in the body or in the soul?

This likeness to God is chiefly in the soul.

(a) All creatures bear some resemblance to God inasmuch as they exist. Plants and animals resemble Him insofar as they have life, but none of these creatures is made to the image and likeness of God. Plants and animals do not have a rational soul, such as man has, by which they might know and love God.

50. How is the soul like God?

The soul is like God because it is a spirit having understanding and free will, and is destined to live forever.

(a) Men are especially like God when they know and love Him:

first, in a merely natural way without the aid of grace;

second, in a supernatural way here on earth, with the aid of grace;

third, in a perfect way in heaven, with the aid of the special light God gives to the souls of the blessed.

(b) Understanding is the power of the soul to apprehend, to judge, and to reason, and thus to know right and wrong.

(c) Conscience is that judgment by which we decide here and now what we should do as good or avoid as evil.

(d) Free will is that power of the soul to choose either to act or not to act.

(e) Human souls live forever because they are spirits.[8]

(f) The never-ending life of the soul is called immortality.

SCRIPTURE:

"And the dust return into its earth, from whence it was, and the spirit return to God, who gave it" (*Ecclesiastes 12:7*).

---

[8] See question 9.

32

"Do not be afraid of those who kill the body but cannot kill the soul" (*Matthew 10:28*).

"These will go into everlasting punishment, but the just into everlasting life" (*Matthew 25:46*).

51. Who were the first man and woman?

The first man and woman were Adam and Eve, the first parents of the whole human race.

(a) The theory of evolution which teaches that higher forms of life develop from lower forms has offered no convincing, scientific proof that the human body developed gradually from that of a lower animal.

(b) If scientific proof of such development of the body of man could be had, it would not be opposed to Catholic doctrine provided that some special action of God is admitted not only in the creation of the soul but also in the production of the body of Adam.

(c) The human soul, being spiritual, could not possibly have developed from a lower, material form of life.

(d) Sacred Scripture teaches that Adam's soul, like every human soul, was created directly by God.

SCRIPTURE: *See Scripture, question 48, Genesis 2:7.*

52. What was the chief gift bestowed on Adam and Eve by God?

The chief gift bestowed on Adam and Eve by God was sanctifying grace, which made them children of God and gave them the right to heaven.

(a) Sanctifying grace is a supernatural gift which is a sharing in the nature of God Himself and which raises men to the supernatural order, conferring on them powers entirely above those proper to human nature.

(b) Together with sanctifying grace God gave Adam and Eve the supernatural virtues and the gifts of the Holy Ghost.

SCRIPTURE:
"For just as by the disobedience of the one man the many were constituted sinners, so also by the obedience of the one the many will be constituted just" (*Romans 5:19*).

53. What other gifts were bestowed on Adam and Eve by God?

The other gifts bestowed on Adam and Eve by God were happiness in the Garden of Paradise, great knowledge, control of the passions by reason, and freedom from suffering and death.

(a) These gifts are not supernatural or above all created natures, but they are preternatural, that is, beyond the powers of human nature, though not above all created natures.

(b) If Adam had not sinned, these gifts would have been transmitted to all men as the possession of human nature.

SCRIPTURE:
"He created of him a helpmate like to himself: he gave them counsel, and a tongue, and eyes, and ears, and a heart to devise: and he filled them with

the knowledge of understanding. He created in them the science of the spirit: he filled their heart with wisdom, and shewed them both good and evil" (*Ecclesiasticus 17:5-6*).

"Therefore as through one man sin entered into the world and through sin death, and thus death has passed unto all men because all have sinned — for until the Law sin was in the world, but sin is not imputed when there is no law" (*Romans 5:12-13*).

54. What commandment did God give Adam and Eve?

God gave Adam and Eve the commandment not to eat of the fruit of a certain tree that grew in the Garden of Paradise.[9]

(a) God wished to test the obedience of our first parents in order that they might have the privilege of proving themselves faithful to Him and of meriting, in a special way, everlasting happiness in heaven.

SCRIPTURE:
"And he commanded him, saying: Of every tree of paradise thou shalt eat: But of the tree of knowledge of good and evil, thou shalt not eat. For in what day soever thou shalt eat of it, thou shalt die the death" (*Genesis 2:16-17*).

55. Did Adam and Eve obey the commandment of God?

Adam and Eve did not obey the commandment of God, but ate of the forbidden fruit.

(a) In eating the forbidden fruit Adam and Eve committed sins of pride and disobedience. Our first parents sinned grievously because they deliberately disobeyed a grave command of God.

SCRIPTURE:
"And the woman saw that the tree was good to eat, and fair to the eyes, and delightful to behold: and she took of the fruit thereof, and did eat, and gave to her husband who did eat" (*Genesis 3:6*).

56. What happened to Adam and Eve on account of their sin?

On account of their sin Adam and Eve lost sanctifying grace, the right to heaven, and their special gifts; they became subject to death, to suffering, and to a strong inclination to evil, and they were driven from the Garden of Paradise.

(a) The loss of sanctifying grace and the special gifts marked the beginning of that conflict between man's lower powers and his reason, of which Saint Paul says, "The flesh lusts against the spirit, and the spirit against the flesh . . ." (*Galatians 5:17*).

(b) Sacred Scripture teaches us that Adam, by the grace of God, later obtained the remission of his sin.

SCRIPTURE:
"In the sweat of thy face shalt thou eat bread till thou return to the earth, out of which thou wast taken: for dust thou art, and into dust thou shalt return" (*Genesis 3:19*).
"And the Lord God made for Adam and his wife garments of skins, and clothed them" (*Genesis 3:21*).
"And the Lord God sent him out of the paradise of pleasure, to till the earth from which he was taken" (*Genesis 3:23*).

[9] Read the third chapter of the Book of Genesis.

"She preserved him, that was first formed by God, the father of the world, when he was created alone, and she brought him out of his sin and gave him power to govern all things" (*Wisdom 10:1-2*).

57. What has happened to us on account of the sin of Adam?

On account of the sin of Adam, we, his descendants, come into the world deprived of sanctifying grace and inherit his punishment, as we would have inherited his gifts had he been obedient to God.

SCRIPTURE:
"But, by the envy of the devil, death came into the world" (*Wisdom 2:24*).

"For just as by the disobedience of the one man the many were constituted sinners, so also by the obedience of the one the many will be constituted just" (*Romans 5:19*).

58. What is this sin in us called?

This sin in us is called original sin.

59. Why is this sin called original?

This sin is called original because it comes down to us through our origin, or descent, from Adam.

SCRIPTURE: *See Scripture, question 53, Romans 5:12-13.*

60. What are the chief punishments of Adam which we inherit through original sin?

The chief punishments of Adam which we inherit through original sin are death, suffering, ignorance, and a strong inclination to sin.

(a) The fact of original sin explains why man is so often tempted to evil and why he so easily turns from God.

(b) Because of the ignorance resulting from original sin, the mind of man has difficulty in knowing many necessary truths, easily falls into error, and is more inclined to consider temporal than eternal things.

(c) The penalties of original sin—death, suffering, ignorance, and a strong inclination to sin—remain after Baptism, even though original sin is taken away.

(d) Although we have a strong inclination to evil as a result of original sin, our nature is not evil in itself; it can perform some good actions in the natural order without the aid of grace.

SCRIPTURE:
"For the imagination and thought of man's heart are prone to evil from his youth" (*Genesis 8:21*).

61. Is God unjust in punishing us on account of the sin of Adam?

God is not unjust in punishing us on account of the sin of Adam, because original sin does not take away from us anything to which we have a strict right as human beings, but only the free gifts which God in His goodness would have bestowed on us if Adam had not sinned.

35

35a

Original Sin

This picture shows the disobedience of Adam and Eve. God had forbidden them, under pain of death, to eat of the fruit of the tree of the knowledge of good and evil. Eve, deceived by the demon who hid himself under the form of a serpent, ate of the forbidden fruit and gave some to her husband who similarly ate of it.

Adam and Eve, having lost the grace of God by their sin, became subject to ignorance, uncontrolled passions, pain, and death, and they were banished from the earthly paradise.

At the bottom, the Angel of the Lord, armed with a flaming sword, is driving Adam and Eve from the earthly paradise. Subject to the miseries of life, they will fall under the blow of Death, who waits for them with a scythe in his hand.

The Cross of Jesus Christ, which is seen at the top left, signifies that Our Lord delivered us from original sin by His death. God had promised this deliverance to our first parents by announcing to them that one day a son of the woman would crush the head of the infernal serpent.

On the right, a priest is baptizing a little child, showing that baptism washes away the stain of original sin in us.

62. Was any human person ever preserved from original sin?

The Blessed Virgin Mary was preserved from original sin in view of the merits of her Divine Son; and this privilege is called her Immaculate Conception.

(a) In the first instant of her conception the Blessed Virgin Mary possessed the fullness of sanctifying grace, the infused virtues, and the gifts of the Holy Ghost. She was, however, subject to pain and suffering, as was her Divine Son.

(b) By a special privilege of Almighty God, Our Blessed Mother was free throughout her life from all actual sin, both mortal and venial.

SCRIPTURE:

"I will put enmities between you and the woman, between your seed and her seed: he shall crush your head, and you shall lie in wait for his heel" (*Genesis 3:15*).

"And when the angel had come to her, he said, 'Hail, full of grace, the Lord is with thee. Blessed art thou among women' " (*Luke 1:28*).

IMPORTANT TRUTHS ABOUT THE CREATION AND THE FALL OF MAN

There are many persons in the world who believe that human beings are merely animals of a higher type than the other animals on earth, and like them are destined to perish entirely with death. Against this materialistic view the Catholic Church holds the doctrine that every human being has a spiritual soul that is like to God Himself—a soul that will never die but will live for all eternity. Every human soul is directly created by God.

The Bible describes in great detail the beginning of the human race. God created a man, named Adam, forming his body from the dust of earth and creating his soul. Shortly afterward God made Eve from a rib of Adam, whose wife she was to be. Then the Almighty blessed the pair as husband and wife, bidding them: "Increase and multiply" (*Genesis 1, 28*). God bestowed on Adam and Eve wonderful privileges. They dwelt in a beautiful garden; they were free from inordinate inclinations to sin; they were preserved from suffering; they were destined never to die, but after a space of time on earth, to be taken, body and soul, into heaven. Above all, they were endowed with the precious gift of sanctifying grace, that made them the beloved children of God.

It was God's plan that these privileges should be transmitted from Adam to all his descendants. However, He made this dependent on the faithfulness of Adam in obeying His command not to eat the fruit of a particular tree. Adam disobeyed; and hence lost these precious gifts for himself and for all his descendants. Eve also sinned and lost the privileges for herself. There was no injustice on God's part in depriving Adam's descendants of these privileges because of his sin. The favors He gave our first parents were purely gratuitous; our first parents had no right to them. Hence, there was no injustice on the part of God in withholding them from Adam's descendants. It was as if a wealthy man told a poor man he could live in a splendid house on his property and pass it on to his descendants, if he would obey a certain command; if the poor man disobeyed, and accordingly lost the fine residence for himself and for his children, the rich man would be doing them no wrong by depriving them of the house.

The entire human race is descended from Adam and Eve; hence, we all enter the world deprived of the gifts we should have had if Adam had not sinned. The deprivation of sanctifying grace, called original sin, brings with it the necessity of submitting to suffering and to death. This is the significance of the words spoken by God to Adam after his sin, and repeated to each of the

36

faithful on Ash Wednesday when the priest places ashes on his brow: "Remember, man, that thou art dust, and into dust thou shalt return" (*Genesis 3: 19*). Yet, through the goodness of God we can recover sanctifying grace, and even though we are not restored entirely to the original state of our first parents, who were free from suffering and death and inordinate inclinations to sin, we can make these penalties of Adam's transgression the occasions of practicing virtue.

Nowadays many persons, claiming that man is descended from an animal, such as an ape, reject the account of creation given in the Bible. We admit that God could have brought the human race into existence in this way as regards the body of man; and if the evolutionary theory to this extent were ever proved, we should have no difficulty in admitting it. The soul of man, however, can come into being only by the direct act of the Creator.

Our Blessed Lord, since He is God, could have no original sin. Furthermore, original sin is transmitted to an infant by its father when he shares in giving it life, and Our Lord had no earthly father. Moreover, it is a doctrine of the Catholic faith that His Blessed Mother, Mary, on account of her great dignity as Mother of God, was preserved from original sin in the very first moment of her existence. This great privilege is known as her Immaculate Conception.

Catholics should have a clear idea of the meaning of the Immaculate Conception, since many persons confuse it with the virginal conception of Jesus Christ, which was an entirely different privilege of our Lady. God spoke of the Immaculate Conception immediately after the sin of our first parents, when He promised a Redeemer, and added that the Mother of the Redeemer would be at perpetual enmity with the devil, the author of sin: "I will put enmities between thee (the devil) and the woman, and thy seed and her seed: she shall crush thy head" (*Genesis 3:15*). This doctrine of Mary's Immaculate Conception is contained also in the Tradition of the Church, which has always attributed to Mary the fullest possible measure of holiness and freedom from sin. The feast of the Immaculate Conception is a holyday of obligation, celebrated on December 8th. Moreover, Mary Immaculate is the Patroness of the United States of America.

RESOLUTION: Resolve to call on our Blessed Mother in time of temptation with the prayer that honors her Immaculate Conception: "Mary, conceived without sin, pray for us who have recourse to thee"; (*Indulgence: 300 days; Plenary indulgence under usual conditions. S.P. Ap., April 15, 1932*).

A. TRUE OR FALSE. (*Check each of the following statements as either true or false. The correct answers can be found in the preceding portion of the lesson.*)

	TRUE	FALSE
(1) Every living creature has understanding and free will.	.....	.....
(2) There are some races of men who are not descended from Adam and Eve.	.....	.....
(3) If Adam had been obedient to God we should have come into the world in sanctifying grace.	.....	.....
(4) Baptism takes away all the effects of original sin.	.....	.....
(5) God does not deprive us, on account of original sin, of anything to which we have a strict right as human beings.	.....	.....
(6) The freedom from suffering and death granted to Adam and Eve was not a supernatural gift.	.....	.....

37

(7) A human being even in the state of original sin can perform some good deeds. . . . .

(8) Adam did not obtain the pardon of his sin. . . . .

(9) The sin of Adam and Eve was a mortal sin. . . . .

(10) The Immaculate Conception means that the Blessed Virgin Mary became the mother of Christ without losing her virginity. . . . .

B. PROBLEMS AND EXERCISES. (*Answer the questions orally or write them as your teacher may direct*):

(1) Alice and Zita are in an ice cream parlor and are about to order some refreshments. Show how they may exercise their free wills in the enjoyment of the treat.

(2) Bartholomew and his brother Yves are amused by the stunts of the trained animals at the circus. The animals can perform many wonderful tricks at the orders of their masters and mistresses. Are such animals intelligent? Have they understanding and free will? If not, how do you explain their actions?

(3) Amelia's pet kitten, Tabby, was run over and killed by an automobile. Amelia is greatly saddened over the mishap. Did Tabby have a soul? Will Tabby's soul ever come back to make Tabby live again? Explain your answers.

(4) Charlie says that conscience is a feeling that something is right or wrong. Bob says it is a judgment of the understanding. Which definition do you prefer? Why?

(5) Theresa tells Ursula there must necessarily be perfect and complete harmony between genuine scientific discoveries and the revelations of God in the Bible and in Tradition. Ursula asks why. Theresa's reply is: "God is the Author of the Bible and Tradition, and the same God is the Author of the Book of Nature. God cannot contradict Himself." Write two or three sentences containing your approval of Theresa's answer.

(6) Edith has a bad attack of the mumps. Do you think we should have had the mumps if Adam had not sinned?

(7) Caroline wonders if original sin has anything to do with her poor report card of last month. Has it? Explain your answer.

(8) If, up to the present day, the human race were sinless would there be any hospitals, funerals, cemeteries, prisons, insane asylums, or wars? What is the reason for your answer?

(9) With the preceding question and answer in mind, write a paragraph of four or five sentences telling what you think about the effects of original sin. Compare original sin with other evils.

(10) Annually how are we reminded by the Church of the penalty the human race must pay for original sin?

(11) Stanislaus is showing the parish church to his Protestant friend Schuyler. Schuyler wants to know about the statue representing a lady standing on the world, with a half moon beneath her feet; she is crushing the head of a serpent. Explain who the lady is and why she is thus represented.

Actual Sin

63. Is original sin the only kind of sin?

Original sin is not the only kind of sin; there is another kind, called actual sin, which we ourselves commit.

64. What is actual sin?

Actual sin is any willful thought, desire, word, action, or omission forbidden by the law of God.

65. How many kinds of actual sin are there?

There are two kinds of actual sin: mortal sin and venial sin.

66. What is mortal sin?

Mortal sin is a grievous offense against the law of God.

67. Why is this sin called mortal?

This sin is called mortal, or deadly, because it deprives the sinner of sanctifying grace, the supernatural life of the soul.

SCRIPTURE:
"Flee from sins as from the face of a serpent: for if thou comest near them, they will take hold of thee. The teeth thereof are the teeth of a lion, killing the souls of men" (*Ecclesiasticus 21:2-3*).

68. Besides depriving the sinner of sanctifying grace, what else does mortal sin do to the soul?

Besides depriving the sinner of sanctifying grace, mortal sin makes the soul an enemy of God, takes away the merit of all its good actions, deprives it of the right to everlasting happiness in heaven, and makes it deserving of everlasting punishment in hell.

SCRIPTURE:
"But, if the just man turn himself away from his justice and do iniquity according to all the abominations which the wicked man useth to work, shall he live? All his justices which he hath done shall not be remembered: in the prevarication by which he hath prevaricated and in his sin which he hath committed, in them he shall die" (*Ezechiel 18:24*).

"Then when passion has conceived, it brings forth sin; but when sin has matured, it begets death" (*James 1:15*).

69. What three things are necessary to make a sin mortal?

To make a sin mortal these three things are necessary:
first, the thought, desire, word, action, or omission must be seriously wrong or considered seriously wrong;
second, the sinner must be mindful of the serious wrong;
third, the sinner must fully consent to it.

(a) Things seriously evil are known to be such from Sacred Scripture, Tradition, the teachings of the Church, or from the nature of the acts themselves.

(b) The sinner is mindful of the serious wrong if at the time he commits the sin or places a cause from which he foresees the sin will follow, he either is clearly aware or at least thinks that the action is grievously sinful.

(c) A sinner fully consents to the wrong when he freely chooses to do evil, although he is entirely free not to do it. A person who deliberately consents to do something grievously sinful is guilty of mortal sin although he never actually does it, because his will has chosen evil in preference to good.

(d) When a sinner, mindful of evil, consents to it he is said to commit a *formal* sin.

(e) When a person does wrong but is in no way mindful of it, he is said to commit a *material* sin; for example, a person who misses Mass, unmindful that it is Sunday, commits a material sin. God does not hold us accountable for material sins and they do not deprive us of sanctifying grace.

SCRIPTURE:
"Before man is life and death, good and evil: that which he shall choose shall be given him" (*Ecclesiasticus 15:18*).

70. What is venial sin?

Venial sin is a less serious offense against the law of God, which does not deprive the soul of sanctifying grace, and which can be pardoned even without sacramental Confession.

(a) Venial sin, under certain conditions, can become mortal:
first, when an action which is not seriously wrong is performed by a person who thinks it is seriously wrong;
second, by reason of circumstances affecting the act; for example, if a person under oath to tell the truth were to lie about a light matter;
third, when the matter of several sins, in themselves not serious, adds up to a serious amount; for example, if someone were to steal small sums of money which would accumulate to a serious amount.

71. How can a sin be venial?

A sin can be venial in two ways:
first, when the evil done is not seriously wrong;
second, when the evil done is seriously wrong, but the sinner sincerely believes it is only slightly wrong, or does not give full consent to it.

(a) If a person being uncertain of the gravity of a sin nevertheless commits the sin, he is guilty of mortal sin because he shows himself willing to offend God seriously. One should not act in doubt but should form a certain conscience.

40

72. How does venial sin harm us?

Venial sin harms us by making us less fervent in the service of God, by weakening our power to resist mortal sin, and by making us deserving of God's punishments in this life or in purgatory.

SCRIPTURE:

"A workman that is a drunkard shall not be rich: and he that contemneth small things shall faii by little and little" (*Ecclesiasticus 19:1*).

"But I tell you, that of every idle word men speak, they shall give account on the day of judgment" (*Matthew 12:36*).

73. How can we keep from committing sin?

We can keep from committing sin by praying and by receiving the sacraments; by remembering that God is always with us; by recalling that our bodies are temples of the Holy Ghost; by keeping occupied with work or play; by promptly resisting the sources of sin within us; by avoiding the near occasions of sin.

74. What are the chief sources of actual sin?

The chief sources of actual sin are: pride, covetousness, lust, anger, gluttony, envy, and sloth, and these are commonly called capital sins.

(a) Pride is the inordinate seeking of one's own excellence. It is opposed to the virtue of humility.

(b) Covetousness is the inordinate seeking of temporal goods. Covetousness is two-fold:

first, the inordinate seeking of temporal goods by acquiring or possessing them unjustly. This form of covetousness is opposed to the virtue of justice and is often a mortal sin;

second, the inordinate seeking of temporal goods by loving or desiring them too much. This form of covetousness is opposed to liberality and is ordinarily a venial sin.

(c) Lust is the inordinate seeking of the pleasures of the flesh. It is opposed to the virtue of chastity.

(d) Anger is the inordinate seeking of revenge, or an unreasonable opposition to a person or thing. It is opposed to the virtue of meekness.

(e) Gluttony is the inordinate desire for food and drink. It is opposed to the virtue of temperance.

(f) Envy is sadness at another's good fortune because it is considered to be detracting from one's own excellence. It is opposed to the virtue of charity.

(g) Sloth is the distaste for spiritual things because their attainment requires much labor. It is opposed to the virtue of charity.

75. Why are these called capital sins?

They are called capital sins, not because they, in themselves, are the greatest sins, but because they are the chief reasons why men commit sin.

41

(a) Pride is the source of presumption, ambition, vainglory, and boasting.

(b) Covetousness is the source of hard-heartedness toward the poor, and of theft, fraud, and deceit.

(c) Lust is the source of blindness of mind, thoughtlessness, overhastiness, instability, love of oneself, hatred of God, worldliness, and despair.

(d) Anger is the source of contumely, blasphemy, quarrels, and murders.

(e) Gluttony is the source of dullness of mind, excessive talkativeness, and gross and vulgar speech.

(f) Envy is the source of hatred, calumny, detraction, joy in our neighbor's misfortunes, and distress at his prosperity.

(g) Sloth is the source of the neglect to perform good works that are of grave obligation.

76. What are the near occasions of sin?

The near occasions of sin are all persons, places, or things that may easily lead us into sin.

(a) There is a grave obligation to avoid the near occasion of mortal sin.

(b) If circumstances force us into the near occasion of sin, we are obliged to make use of the necessary safeguards, such as prayer and the frequent reception of the sacraments of Penance and Holy Eucharist.

IMPORTANT TRUTHS ABOUT ACTUAL SIN

By means of his free will, man can give God loyal and affectionate service; but by means of the same free will he can also offend God by committing actual sin. This sin can be committed in many ways. It can be entirely within man's mind and heart, as when he deliberately takes pleasure in something evil pictured in his imagination (sin of thought) or when he deliberately wishes something evil, even though he knows he can never do it (sin of desire). Or, a person can make use of his bodily faculties to offend God—by using his power of speech in bad language, such as blasphemy or cursing (sin of word), or by employing another bodily power, such as his hands to murder or to steal (sin of action). Finally a person can commit sin by neglecting to do something which he is obliged to do, as when he fails to go to Mass on Sunday or to help others in their need when he could and should do so (sin of omission).

When a person is in doubt as to whether or not a certain action is sinful, he is not allowed to do it until he has made reasonable efforts to solve his doubt. Usually the most practical way to solve such a doubt of conscience is to ask a priest, particularly in confession.

The most important division of actual sins, mortal and venial, is explained at length in the lesson. Some persons have the idea that it is sufficient to avoid mortal sins; they freely commit venial sins. This is a false notion. Venial sin is a great evil—next to mortal sin, it is the greatest evil in the world, worse than the most painful sickness or the most dreadful form of death. One who pays no heed to venial sins will soon fall into mortal sin. It is true, on account of the weakness of human nature brought on by original sin no one (unless he receives a special privilege from God, such as was given to the Blessed Virgin Mary), can abstain for a long time from semi-deliberate venial sins, committed without full consent of the will. But all should strive to avoid every deliberate sin, whether it be venial or mortal. No one can ever claim that God does not give him sufficient grace to avoid such sins, for St. Paul tells us: "God is faithful and will not permit you to be tempted beyond your strength" (*1 Cor. 10:13*).

However, venial sins, even though frequently committed, do not unite to form a mortal sin, though sometimes the *matter* involved in several sins, each of which in itself is venial, will accumulate to form a large amount, and thus eventually a mortal sin will be committed. Thus, if a clerk would steal fifty cents a day from the store in which he is employed, the total amount would soon become sufficient to render him guilty of mortal sin, even though the amount of each theft taken in itself would constitute only a venial sin.

We must all be on our guard against the capital sins, which are the sources of all the other sins. It is not sufficient to resolve not to give in to the capital sins—we must strive to practice the opposite virtues. Every one should honestly examine his own character and find out his predominant passion—that is, the type of sin to which he is most inclined—and try earnestly to overcome it. With God's grace, he shall eventually succeed.

We must particularly avoid the near occasions of sin. Nowadays there are many occasions of sin in the world, such as bad books, heretical or improper radio programs, indecent motion pictures, vile theatrical exhibitions, and persons who try to lead others into sin by their bad speech or wicked conduct. Those who frequent unnecessarily the occasions of sin are running a great risk. "He that loveth danger shall perish in it" (*Ecclus. 3:27*).

Above all, we have prayer and the sacraments to strengthen us against temptation to sin. Whenever an inclination to offend God besets our soul, our first thought should be to have recourse to prayer. It need not be a long prayer; even the devout calling on the names of Jesus and Mary will be of great help. And one who frequently receives Our Lord in Holy Communion obtains immeasurable spiritual strength against the weakness and evil inclinations of his nature that are the cause of so many sins.

RESOLUTION: Resolve frequently to suffer any evil, even death, rather than offend God by sin, especially mortal sin.

STUDY HELPS

A. WORD SELECTION. (*Select the word or phrase in the parentheses which most exactly and most completely fills out the sentence*):

(1) When a person eats meat on Friday without realizing that it is Friday he commits a (formal . . . material . . . venial) sin.

(2) When a person is in doubt whether or not a certain action is a sin he (is free to do it without further inquiry . . . may say a prayer and do it . . . may not do it until he has made a reasonable effort to find out whether or not it is sinful).

(3) Pride is called a capital sin because it is (one of the chief reasons why men commit sin . . . a sin that will not be forgiven . . . a mortal sin).

(4) A person's predominant passion is (pride . . . lust . . . the type of sin to which he is most inclined).

(5) If a man goes into a saloon, knowing that for him it is a near occasion of grave sins of intemperance, but on one particular occasion does not drink to excess, he commits (no sin . . . a mortal sin . . . a venial sin).

(6) A person who deliberately takes God's name in vain, erroneously thinking it is a mortal sin, commits (a mortal sin . . . a material sin . . . a venial sin).

(7) A person who eats too much commits a sin of (sloth . . . gluttony . . . covetousness).

(8) A person who inordinately seeks temporal goods by loving or desiring them too much commits a sin that is opposed to (justice . . . charity . . . liberality).

(9) When a person commits several venial sins of envy, they (remain distinct venial sins ... unite to form one greater venial sin ... unite to form one mortal sin).

(10) When a person in mortal sin goes to Mass he performs an action which (is a mortal sin ... is good but not meritorious of eternal life ... becomes meritorious when the person returns to the state of grace).

B. PROBLEMS AND EXERCISES. (*Answer the questions orally or write them as your teacher may direct*):

(1) Brian failed to go to Mass on Ascension Thursday because he entirely forgot that it is a holyday. Was his omission of Mass a formal sin or a material sin? Explain.

(2) Rosemary ate meat on a Thursday, thinking it was Friday, but deliberately willing to violate the law of the Church. Did she commit a sin? Was it material or formal? Explain.

(3) Six paydays in a row, Octavus, a Catholic laborer, got drunk. As he starts drinking on the seventh payday, his conscience warns him, reminding him how he missed Mass the last six Sundays from sickness following the drunkenness. The following Sunday afternoon he awakens from his drunken stupor. It is too late to go to Mass. Has he committed the mortal sin of missing Mass? Give the reason for your answer.

(4) What bad effects does venial sin work in our spiritual life?

(5) Percival wants to know how many venial sins it takes to make a mortal sin? How do you answer his question?

(6) On Quinquagesima Sunday, Tarcisius, a strong healthy fellow of twenty-two years, listens to the reading of the Lenten regulations. He wonders if he is exempted or excused from the strict fast. The doubt lingers with him all through Lent; then on Holy Saturday night, in confession, he says: "I didn't keep Lent because I didn't know whether or not I was bound to the strict fast." Do you approve of his manner of acting? Was he guilty of serious sins? Why? If he had asked you on Shrove Tuesday what he should do, what would you have suggested?

(7) Isabella asks if God ever allows anyone to be tempted beyond his strength to resist. Answer her, and in your answer tell her what St. Paul says about the matter.

(8) What are the virtues opposed to the capital sins, and which capital sins do they oppose?

(9) Evangeline is making her first school-retreat. The retreat master makes frequent reference to "our predominant passion." What does he mean? Write your explanation in three or four sentences.

(10) What does the Bible say about taking unnecessary moral risks?

(11) Wendelin is a vitamin enthusiast. He maintains that vitamins are great aids in building up bodily strength and general resistance to disease. Tell him how he can build up resistance to sinful temptations.

(12) Hortense goes to the movies frequently, but she never tries beforehand to find out whether the picture is good or bad, and consequently sometimes she goes to a picture that is a near occasion of sin for her. Does Hortense commit a sin? Explain.

The Incarnation

"I BELIEVE ... IN JESUS CHRIST, HIS ONLY SON, OUR LORD; WHO WAS CONCEIVED BY THE HOLY GHOST, BORN OF THE VIRGIN MARY ... "

77. Did God abandon man after Adam fell into sin?

God did not abandon man after Adam fell into sin, but promised to send into the world a Saviour to free man from his sins and to reopen to him the gates of heaven.

(a) God could have abandoned man and allowed the human race to suffer the just penalty of never seeing Him face to face in heaven. In His infinite love and mercy, God took pity on Adam and his descendants and gave them the chance of salvation through the promised Redeemer.

SCRIPTURE:

"But while he thought on these things, behold, an angel of the Lord appeared to him in a dream, saying, 'Do not be afraid, Joseph, son of David, to take to thee Mary thy wife, for that which is begotten in her is of the Holy Spirit. And she shall bring forth a son, and thou shalt call his name Jesus; for he shall save his people from their sins' " (*Matthew 1:20-21*).

"For God so loved the world that he gave his only-begotten Son, that those who believe in him may not perish, but may have life everlasting" (*John 3:16*).

"And we have seen, and do testify, that the Father has sent his Son to be Saviour of the world" (*I John 4:14*).

78. Who is the Saviour of all men?

The Saviour of all men is Jesus Christ.

(a) Not all men are saved, but all who attain salvation do so through the merits of Christ.

(b) That Jesus Christ is the promised Saviour can be proved from the prophecies of the Old Testament which are fulfilled in Him; from His own testimony, which is worthy of belief; and from the miracles He worked in proof of His divine mission, especially His Resurrection.

(c) The name "Jesus" means Saviour.

(d) "Christ," a Greek word meaning "anointed," signifies Jesus' three-fold office of King, Priest, and Prophet, because, of old, kings, priests, and prophets were anointed.

SCRIPTURE:

"For there is one God, and one Mediator between God and men, himself man, Christ Jesus, who gave himself a ransom for all, bearing witness in his own time" (*I Timothy 2:5-6*).

79. What is the chief teaching of the Catholic Church about Jesus Christ?

The chief teaching of the Catholic Church about Jesus Christ is that He is God made man.

45

SCRIPTURE:

"And the angel said to her, 'Do not be afraid, Mary, for thou hast found grace with God. Behold, thou shalt conceive in thy womb and shalt bring forth a son; and thou shalt call his name Jesus. He shall be great, and shall be called the Son of the Most High; and the Lord God will give him the throne of David his father, and he shall be king over the house of Jacob forever; and of his kingdom there shall be no end.' But Mary said to the angel, 'How shall this happen, since I do not know man?' And the angel answered and said to her, 'The Holy Spirit shall come upon thee and the power of the Most High shall overshadow thee; and therefore the Holy One to be born shall be called the Son of God' " (*Luke 1:30-35*).

"In the beginning was the Word, and the Word was with God; and the Word was God. ... And the Word was made flesh, and dwelt among us. And we saw his glory — glory as of the only-begotten of the Father — full of grace and of truth" (*John 1:1, 14*).

80. Why is Jesus Christ God?

Jesus Christ is God because He is the only Son of God, having the same divine nature as His Father.

(a) Jesus Christ is the second Person of the Blessed Trinity, who from eternity proceeds by true spiritual generation from the Father.

(b) We believe Jesus Christ is God because God Himself revealed this truth:

first, through the Prophets of the Old Testament who foretold that the promised Redeemer would be God;

second, through Christ Himself, who claimed to be God and confirmed His own testimony by the holiness of His life, by the fulfillment of His prophecies, and by the miracles He worked in His own name and by His own power, especially His Resurrection.

(c) A miracle is something that is not according to the usual course of created nature, surpasses the power of all creatures, and consequently can be produced only by the power of God.

(d) The senses must be able to observe a miracle if it is to have the value of a proof for us.

(e) Only God can be the principal cause of a miracle because a miracle surpasses the power of all creatures. God sometimes uses creatures as instruments in performing miracles.

(f) Since God, who is all-truthful, is the principal cause of a miracle, it cannot be worked in support of a lie.

(g) The following are some of Christ's miracles: He restored sight to the blind, cured lepers in an instant, walked on the waters of the sea, multiplied the loaves and fishes, raised the dead to life, and finally, rose from the dead Himself by His own divine power.

SCRIPTURE: The Divinity of Christ.

I. *Old Testament Prophecy*

"The Lord has said to me: 'Thou art my son, this day have I begotten thee. Ask of me and I will give thee the gentiles for thine inheritance, and the ends of the earth as thy possession' " (*Psalm 2:7-8*).

46

II. Christ Claimed to be God

"And the high priest said to him, 'I adjure thee by the living God that thou tell us whether thou art the Christ, the Son of God.' Jesus said to him, 'Thou hast said it. Nevertheless, I say to you, hereafter you shall see the Son of Man sitting at the right hand of the Power and coming upon the clouds of heaven' " *(Matthew 26:63-64)*.

"I and the Father are one" *(John 10:30)*.

III. Christ Confirmed His Testimony by Miracles

"But he answered and said to them, 'An evil and adulterous generation demands a sign, and no sign shall be given it but the sign of Jonas the prophet. For even as Jonas was in the belly of the fish three days and three nights, so will the Son of Man be three days and three nights in the heart of the earth' " *(Matthew 12:39-40)*.

"They let down the pallet on which the paralytic was lying. And Jesus, seeing their faith, said to the paralytic, 'Son, thy sins are forgiven thee.' Now some of the Scribes were sitting there and reasoning in their hearts, 'Why does this man speak thus? He blasphemes. Who can forgive sins, but only God?' And at once Jesus, knowing in his spirit that they so reasoned within themselves, said to them, 'Why are you arguing these things in your hearts? Which is easier, to say to the paralytic, "Thy sins are forgiven thee," or to say, "Arise, and take up thy pallet, and walk"? But that you may know that the Son of Man has power on earth to forgive sins' — he said to the paralytic — 'I say to thee, arise, take up thy pallet, and go to thy house.' And immediately he arose and, taking up his pallet, went forth in the sight of all, so that they were all amazed, and glorified God, saying, 'Never did we see the like' " *(Mark 2:4-12)*.

"Thomas answered and said to him, 'My Lord and my God!' Jesus said to him, 'Because thou hast seen me, thou hast believed. Blessed are they who have not seen, and yet have believed' " *(John 20:28-29)*.

81. Why is Jesus Christ man?

Jesus Christ is man because He is the Son of the Blessed Virgin Mary and has a body and soul like ours.

(a) Although Christ's conception and birth were miraculous, He, like other men, came into the world as an infant, having Mary for His Mother. Since His origin from the Blessed Virgin is true generation, Mary is the Mother of Jesus Christ, who is God, and she is therefore truly the Mother of God.

(b) Christ, like other men, ate, drank, became tired, slept, and walked through Judea, Galilee, and Samaria.

(c) Christ, as man, was the most perfect of all men. He was endowed with human intelligence and free will; but He was free from all ignorance and error, from all sin and imperfection.

(d) The human soul of Christ could suffer as well as His body. For example, Christ was sorrowful unto death. In the garden of Gethsemani He said to His disciples: "My soul is sad, even unto death. Wait here and watch with me" *(Matthew 26:38)*.

82. Is Jesus Christ more than one Person?

No, Jesus Christ is only one Person; and that Person is the second Person of the Blessed Trinity.

47

(a) It is heresy to say that there are two Persons in Christ.

SCRIPTURE:

"For a child is born to us, and a son is given to us, and the government is upon his shoulder: and his name shall be called, Wonderful, Counsellor, God the Mighty, the Father of the world to come, the Prince of Peace" (*Isaias 9:6*).

"For God so loved the world that he gave his only-begotten Son, that those who believe in him may not perish, but may have life everlasting" (*John 3:16*).

83. How many natures has Jesus Christ?

Jesus Christ has two natures: the nature of God and the nature of man.

(a) There is a difference between person and nature. Human nature is composed of body and soul; in a human person is found the added perfection which makes each one an individual, distinct from all others. A human person has only one human nature. Christ is a divine Person having the nature of God and the nature of man.

(b) Christ proved He had both the nature of God and the nature of man by doing some things that only God could do, and other things that men do.

(c) It is heresy to deny the divine nature of Jesus Christ by accepting Him as merely a perfect man; it is also heresy to deny His human nature.

(d) The following is the defined teaching of the Church: "I also believe in the Son of God, the Word, begotten of the Father in eternity, before all time . . . born in time of the Holy Ghost from Mary, ever virgin; born with a rational soul; having two nativities, one eternal of the Father, the other in time, of His Mother."[10]

SCRIPTURE:

"For I could wish to be anathema myself from Christ for the sake of my brethren, who are my kinsmen according to the flesh; who are Israelites, who have the adoption as sons, and the glory and the covenants and the legislation and the worship and the promises; who have the fathers, and from whom is the Christ according to the flesh, who is, over all things, God blessed forever, amen" (*Romans 9:3-5*).

"Have this mind in you which was also in Christ Jesus, who though he was by nature God, did not consider being equal to God a thing to be clung to, but emptied himself, taking the nature of a slave and being made like unto men. And appearing in the form of man, he humbled himself, becoming obedient to death, even to death on a cross" (*Philippians 2:5-8*).

84. Was the Son of God always man?

The son of God was not always man, but became man at the time of the Incarnation.

SCRIPTURE:

"But when the fullness of time came, God sent his Son, born of a woman, born under the Law, that he might redeem those who were under the Law, that we might receive the adoption of sons" (*Galatians 4:4-5*).

10. Leo IX, April, 1053.

48

85. What is meant by the Incarnation?

By the Incarnation is meant that the Son of God, retaining His divine nature, took to Himself a human nature, that is, a body and soul like ours.

(a) The union of the second Person of the Blessed Trinity with human nature is called the hypostatic union.

86. How was the Son of God made man?

The Son of God was conceived and made man by the power of the Holy Ghost in the womb of the Blessed Virgin Mary.

(a) The conception of the Son of God in the womb of the Blessed Virgin Mary is attributed to the power of the third Person of the Blessed Trinity because the Holy Ghost proceeds from the love of the Father and the Son, and the Incarnation is a work of God's great love for mankind.

(b) All three Persons of the Holy Trinity performed the act of divine power whereby the Incarnation took place. But Catholic faith teaches that only the second Person took to Himself a human nature.

SCRIPTURE:
"And the angel answered and said to her, 'The Holy Spirit shall come upon thee and the power of the Most High shall overshadow thee; and therefore the Holy One to be born shall be called the Son of God'" (*Luke 1:35*).

87. When was the Son of God conceived and made man?

The Son of God was conceived and made man on Annunciation Day, the day on which the Angel Gabriel announced to the Blessed Virgin Mary that she was to be the Mother of God.

(a) We commemorate this event when we say the Angelus.

(b) The miraculous privileges accorded the Blessed Virgin Mary by Almighty God testify to her position as the most exalted of God's creatures.

(c) Mary, the Mother of God, remained a virgin not only in the conception of Christ but also in His birth and during the rest of her life.

(d) Because of her consent to accept the office of Mother of the Redeemer, and also because of her merits in intimately sharing the sufferings of her Divine Son for the salvation of mankind, the Blessed Virgin is given the title of Co-Redemptrix of the human race.

(e) After her death, the body of the Blessed Virgin, reunited with her soul, was miraculously taken up into heaven. The Church observes this event in the Feast of the Assumption.

(f) Special veneration, called *hyperdulia*, is given to the Blessed Virgin, because of her excellence which far surpasses that of all the saints and angels.

88. Is Saint Joseph the father of Jesus Christ?

Jesus Christ had no human father, but Saint Joseph was the spouse of the Blessed Virgin Mary and the guardian, or foster father, of Christ.

49a

The Annunciation of the Blessed Virgin Mary

This picture shows the angel Gabriel greeting the Most Holy Virgin in prayer in her house at Nazareth. He announces to Her that God has chosen Her to be the Mother of the Savior. At the same instant, the Holy Spirit, through a great miracle, works in Her the mystery of the Incarnation.

According to St. Luke, we read:

"Now in the sixth month the angel Gabriel was sent from God to a town of Galilee called Nazareth, to a virgin betrothed to a man named Joseph, of the house of David, and the virgin's name was Mary. And when the angel had come to her, he said, 'Hail, full of grace, the Lord is with thee. Blessed art thou among women.' When she had heard him she was troubled at his word, and kept pondering what manner of greeting this might be.

"And the angel said to her, 'Do not be afraid, Mary, for thou hast found grace with God. Behold, thou shalt conceive in thy womb and shalt bring forth a son; and thou shalt call his Name Jesus. He shall be great, and shall be called the Son of the Most High, and the Lord God will give him the throne of David his father, and he shall be king over the house of Jacob forever, and of his kingdom there shall be no end.'

"But Mary said to the angel, 'How shall this happen, since I do not know man?'

"And the angel answered and said to her, 'The Holy Spirit shall come upon thee and the power of the Most High shall overshadow thee; and therefore the Holy One to be born shall be called the Son of God. And behold, Elizabeth thy kinswoman also has conceived a son in her old age, and she who was called barren is now in her sixth month; for nothing shall be impossible with God.'

"But Mary said, 'Behold the handmaid of the Lord; be it done to me according to thy word.' And the angel departed from her." (St. Luke 1)

49c

The Nativity of Our Lord

In the center, the Child Jesus is born in the stable of Bethlehem. He is surrounded with the loving care of the Blessed Virgin Mary, His Mother, and of St. Joseph, His foster-father. Near the manger where He lies, there are the ox and ass which, according to tradition, were present.

The shepherds come to adore Him and, from Heaven, the angels sing the joyful song, "Glory to God in the highest, and peace on earth to men of good will." (St. Luke 2:14)

(a) God the Father is the only true Father of Jesus Christ.

(b) Christ was the only child of Mary. The brothers and sisters of Christ mentioned in the Bible were cousins.

(c) Saint Joseph's high dignity, grace, holiness, and glory have their source in the fact that he was the husband of the Blessed Virgin Mary and the foster father of the Son of God. Saint Joseph is the patron of the Universal Church.

SCRIPTURE:

"But while he thought on these things, behold, an angel of the Lord appeared to him in a dream, saying, 'Do not be afraid, Joseph, son of David, to take to thee Mary thy wife, for that which is begotten in her is of the Holy Spirit. And she shall bring forth a son, and thou shalt call his name Jesus; for he shall save his people from their sins' " (*Matthew 1:20-21*).

"And Jesus himself, when he began his work, was about thirty years of age, being — as was supposed — the son of Joseph" (*Luke 3:23*).

89. When was Christ born?

Christ was born of the Blessed Virgin Mary on Christmas Day, in Bethlehem, more than nineteen hundred years ago.

IMPORTANT TRUTHS ABOUT THE INCARNATION

After the disobedience of Adam, God could in all justice have refused to restore the human race to His friendship or to give men another opportunity of gaining heaven. But in His goodness the Almighty determined to save men from their sins and to open to them again the gates of heaven. However, God willed that full satisfaction for sin should be made to Him, and since sin is an offense against the infinite dignity of God, only a person of infinite dignity— that is, a divine Person—could make full satisfaction for sin. But a divine Person in His divine nature cannot suffer and consequently cannot make satisfaction; hence, if God was to receive full satisfaction for sin, it was necessary that a divine Person should take our human nature and in that nature suffer in satisfaction for the sins of mankind. That is the reason why the Son of God became man in the Incarnation.

God promised this favor to Adam and Eve shortly after their fall, speaking of one that was to come into the world to crush the devil. The devil had led our first parents into sin, and God said to him: "I will put enmities between thee and the woman, and thy seed and her seed" (*Gen. 3, 15*). The woman is the Blessed Virgin Mary; the seed of the woman is our Saviour, Jesus Christ.

Many centuries passed. Sometimes it is said that four thousand years elapsed between the sin of our first parents and the coming of the Saviour. But this is a matter of much uncertainty; the Catholic Church has never made any statement on this matter, and so we can hold that many centuries or even hundreds of centuries passed from the beginning of the human race until the birth of Our Saviour. The world became very wicked; men forgot God and gave themselves freely to all manner of sins. Among the Jewish people, the chosen people of God, the hope of the Saviour-to-come was kept alive by prophets, men inspired by God to convey His message to their fellow men. These prophets foretold so accurately the circumstances of the birth, the life, the death and the resurrection of the future Saviour that no one could reasonably fail to recognize Him when He came.

The coming of the Redeemer was delayed so long in order that the world might learn from the many evils it suffered the great malice of sin and might know that God alone could raise up fallen man. Those who lived before the coming of the Redeemer could be saved if they had faith in God and kept His law. Thus they received sanctifying grace through the anticipated merits of the Saviour.

And when the time for the coming of the Saviour arrived, God announced it through an angel to a humble virgin of Nazareth named Mary, the daughter of Joachim and Ann. The angel told Mary that she was to be the mother of the world's Saviour, yet by a wonderful miracle she was to remain a virgin. We celebrate this great event on March 25, the Feast of the Annunciation. And nine months later in the stable of Bethlehem, where she and her spouse St. Joseph were obliged to pass the night because there was no room for them in the inn, the Blessed Virgin gave birth to the Child who was to save the world from sin. The name given Him was Jesus; and He was the Christ, the one destined to be the world's Redeemer.

When Christ began His preaching, He announced among other doctrines that He Himself was the true Son of God. By His wonderful miracles—which could be wrought only by divine power—he proved that God was vouching for the truth of His teaching. Hence, the Catholic Church has always held that Jesus Christ is true God. In other words, He is a divine Person—the second Person of the Blessed Trinity—possessing two distinct natures, the nature of God and the nature of man. His human nature is exactly like ours, consisting of body and soul with all its faculties. However, because of His divine personality certain imperfections to which we are subject could not be in His human nature. Thus, He could not have any sin, nor even any inclination to sin; neither could He be ignorant of any truth which it was fitting for Him to know. He was "full of grace and truth", as St. John says—enriched with the fullest measure of supernatural grace and virtue, and even in His human intellect endowed with a knowledge of all things that were or ever had been or ever were to be. Since the actions proceeding from a nature are truly the actions of the person possessing that nature, all the actions proceeding from the human nature of Jesus Christ are truly the actions of God, the second Person of the Holy Trinity. Thus we can correctly say: God walked on earth, God suffered, God died.

This is the great mystery of the Incarnation—which means "the being made flesh", because God took human nature, the most noticeable part of which is the body. Around this mystery Catholic faith and devotion are chiefly centered. The Gospel is the most important portion of the New Testament, relates the earthly life of Jesus Christ. Catholics are urged to read it and to ponder its lessons. Above all, the Incarnation is a manifestation of God's love for us, inasmuch as He could give us no more exalted Saviour than His only Son. "God so loved the world that he gave His only-begotten Son" (*John 3:16*).

RESOLUTION: Resolve that you will always pronounce the name of Jesus Christ with love and reverence and never speak that Holy Name irreverently.

STUDY HELPS

A. COLUMN SELECTION. (*Join correctly the parts of the sentences in Columns I and II, by placing the right key letter in the proper parenthesis*):

I	II
(1) Mary the Mother of God (. .).	(A) can have only a human nature.
(2) St. Joseph (. .).	(B) took to Himself a human nature.
(3) God the Father (. .).	(C) was the foster father of Jesus Christ.
(4) The Second Person of the Holy Trinity (. .).	(D) could not suffer and die.
(5) All three divine Persons (. .).	

51

(6) A human person (. .).

(7) It is heresy to say (. .).

(8) Jesus Christ in His human nature (. .).

(9) Jesus Christ in His divine nature (. .).

(10) The conception of Christ (. .).

(E) that there are two persons in Christ.

(F) performed the act of divine power whereby the Incarnation took place.

(G) could suffer and die.

(H) is attributed to the Holy Ghost.

(I) remained a virgin in the birth of Christ.

(J) is the only true father of Jesus Christ.

B. PROBLEMS AND EXERCISES. (*Answer the questions orally or write them as your teacher may direct*):

(1) In a short letter to a playmate, contrast God's treatment of Lucifer and His treatment of Adam after both had offended Him grievously.

(2) Amid the general corruption and decay of the human race in the centuries following the fall of our first parents, through what race, and by means of what class of men, did God keep alive the hope of a Saviour?

(3) Name three human imperfections to which we are subject that were excluded from Our Lord's human nature by His divine personality.

(4) Delia's boy friend, Horace, a Protestant student at a non-Catholic college, asks her little brother Robert, who is about to graduate from the eighth grade, whether or not Jesus Christ has a human personality. Delia is angry at the boy friend, claiming that his question is too difficult for Robert to answer. Is it? Explain your answer.

(5) Explain why it was necessary that a divine Person should take to Himself a human nature in the supposition that God required full satisfaction for the sins of men.

(6) In what section of the Bible is outlined the earthly life of Jesus? Are the gospels you hear read on Sundays at Mass taken from the Bible? From what part of the Bible?

(7) What dignitaries of ancient times were anointed with sacred oil?

(8) Rebecca, a little Jewess, lives near a Catholic church. She is curious to know why the bell in the church steeple rings every morning at 6:00 o'clock, every noontime, and every evening at 6:00 o'clock. Please explain to the little lady why the bell rings at those hours.

(9) Faith, a Baptist, says that she learned in her Bible class that Our Lord had some brothers and sisters. She claims that even our Catholic Bible mentions them. What comment have you to make in reply?

(10) Who was the first member of the human race to die in the state of grace? Explain how his soul was restored to the friendship of God, and how he managed to save his soul so many centuries before Our Lord was born. His name occurs in the Holy Sacrifice of the Mass shortly after the Consecration.

(11) Is it correct to say that God was born of the Blessed Virgin, God was hungry and thirsty, God suffered, God died? Explain your answer

LESSON 8

The Redemption

"I BELIEVE . . . IN JESUS CHRIST . . . WHO . . . SUFFERED UNDER PONTIUS PILATE, WAS CRUCIFIED, DIED, AND WAS BURIED. HE DESCENDED INTO HELL; THE THIRD DAY HE AROSE AGAIN FROM THE DEAD; HE ASCENDED INTO HEAVEN, SITTETH AT THE RIGHT HAND OF GOD, THE FATHER ALMIGHTY; FROM THENCE HE SHALL COME TO JUDGE THE LIVING AND THE DEAD . . . "

90. What is meant by the Redemption?

By the Redemption is meant that Jesus Christ, as the Redeemer of the whole human race, offered His sufferings and death to God as a fitting sacrifice in satisfaction for the sins of men, and regained for them the right to be children of God and heirs of heaven.[11]

(a) Satisfaction is compensation for an offense or injury against another.

(b) A redeemer is one who pays a price to regain something that has been lost or given up.

(c) No creature could, of himself, make adequate satisfaction for sin, which offends the infinite majesty of God. Every creature is finite and, as such, is unable to make infinite satisfaction.

(d) Although God wished all to be saved, and although Christ died for all, yet only those to whom the merits of His Passion are applied will benefit by His death.

(e) The death of Christ was a sacrifice of infinite merit and satisfaction, by which man was redeemed.

(f) Christ was both priest and victim in the sacrifice whereby He redeemed us. As priest He offered His Passion and death to God for us, and as victim He suffered and died.

SCRIPTURE:

"Walk in love, as Christ also loved us and delivered himself up for us an offering and a sacrifice to God to ascend in fragrant odor" (*Ephesians 5:2*).

"He has rescued us from the power of darkness and transferred us into the kingdom of his beloved Son, in whom we have our redemption, the remission of our sins" (*Colossians 1:13-14*).

" . . . looking for the blessed hope and glorious coming of our great God and Savior, Jesus Christ, who gave himself for us that he might redeem us from all iniquity and cleanse for himself an acceptable people, pursuing good works" (*Titus 2:13-14*).

91. What were the chief sufferings of Christ?

The chief sufferings of Christ were His bitter agony of soul, His bloody sweat, His cruel scourging, His crowning with thorns, His crucifixion, and His death on the cross.

11. See question 358.

53

(a) The Stations of the Cross and the Sorrowful Mysteries of the Rosary call to mind the chief sufferings of Christ.

(b) Christ suffered and died in His human nature; in His divine nature He could neither suffer nor die. All of His sufferings, even the least, were of infinite value because His human and divine natures were united in the divine Person of the Son of God.

92. When did Christ die?

Christ died on Good Friday.

93. Where did Christ die?

Christ died on Golgotha, a place outside the city of Jerusalem.

(a) The site of Christ's death is also called the Place of the Skull, and Mount Calvary.

SCRIPTURE:
"And they came to the place called Golgotha, that is, the Place of the Skull" (*Matthew 27:33*).

94. What do we learn from the sufferings and death of Christ?

From the sufferings and death of Christ we learn God's love for man and the evil of sin, for which God, who is all-just, demands such great satisfaction.

(a) We also learn that we should return God's great love and willingly take up our cross and follow Him.

95. What do we mean when we say in the Apostles' Creed that Christ descended into hell?

When we say that Christ descended into hell we mean that, after He died, the soul of Christ descended into a place or state of rest, called limbo, where the souls of the just were waiting for Him.

(a) Heaven had been closed by the sin of Adam. The just among the dead could not enter heaven until Christ satisfied for man's sin and repaired its injuries. They awaited their redemption in limbo.

SCRIPTURE:
"Put to death indeed in the flesh, he was brought to life in the spirit, in which also he went and preached to those spirits that were in prison" (*I Peter 3:18-19*).
"And Jesus said to him, 'Amen I say to thee, this day thou shalt be with me in paradise' " (*Luke 23:43*).

96. Why did Christ go to limbo?

Christ went to limbo to announce to the souls waiting there the joyful news that He had reopened heaven to mankind.

97. Where was Christ's body while His soul was in limbo?

While His soul was in limbo, Christ's body was in the holy sepulchre.

(a) Man dies when soul is separated from body. When Jesus died, His soul and His body were separated from each other but His divine Person remained united both to His body in the tomb and to His separated soul in limbo.

SCRIPTURE:

"And Joseph taking the body, wrapped it in a clean linen cloth, and laid it in his new tomb, which he had hewn out in the rock. Then he rolled a large stone to the entrance of the tomb, and departed" (*Matthew 27:59-60*).

98. When did Christ rise from the dead?

Christ rose from the dead, glorious and immortal, on Easter Sunday, the third day after His death.

(a) In the Resurrection the soul of Jesus was reunited to His body by His own divine power.

(b) The Resurrection is the most important of Christ's miracles. He Himself chose it as the most conclusive proof of His divine mission, and the apostles appealed to it to confirm the truth of their testimony.

(c) Christ's glorified body after its Resurrection was not subject to suffering or death; it possessed a certain radiance flowing from the supreme blessedness of His soul, it could move rapidly from place to place, it did not need food or sleep, and it could pass through other bodies.

SCRIPTURE:

"He said to them, 'Do not be terrified. You are looking for Jesus of Nazareth, who was crucified. He has risen, he is not here. Behold the place where they laid him'" (*Mark 16:6*).

"But he strictly charged them, and commanded them not to tell this to anyone, saying, 'The Son of Man must suffer many things, and be rejected by the elders and chief priests and Scribes, and be put to death, and on the third day rise again'" (*Luke 9:21-22*).

99. Why did Christ rise from the dead?

Christ rose from the dead to show that He is true God and to teach us that we, too, shall rise from the dead.

SCRIPTURE:

"Now if Christ is preached as risen from the dead, how do some among you say that there is no resurrection of the dead? But if there is no resurrection of the dead, neither has Christ risen; and if Christ has not risen, vain then is our preaching, vain too is your faith. Yes, and we are found false witnesses as to God, in that we have borne witness against God that he raised Christ — whom he did not raise, if the dead do not rise. For if the dead do not rise, neither has Christ risen; and if Christ has not risen, vain is your faith, for you are still in your sins" (*I Corinthians 15:12-17*).

100. Will all men rise from the dead?

All men will rise from the dead, but only those who have been faithful to Christ will share in His glory.

SCRIPTURE:

"Do not wonder at this, for the hour is coming in which all who are in the tombs shall hear the voice of the Son of God. And they who have done good shall come forth unto resurrection of life; but they who have done evil unto resurrection of judgment" (*John 5:28-29*).

"Now this is the will of him who sent me, the Father, that I should lose nothing

55a

Our Lord's Descent into Limbo

This picture shows the soul of Jesus Christ appearing to the captive souls in limbo. In the foreground are Adam and Eve on their knees. Immediately to the left, Abraham is raising a knife above Isaac, Jacob with a staff in his hand, David with his lyre, etc. On the right is Moses with rays of light coming from his head, Aaron with his rod, St. Joseph holding a lily, etc.

Our Lord stayed with them until His Resurrection.

At the bottom of the plate is the hell of the damned, where the demons and the condemned are punished. Jesus Christ did not descend to this place of eternal suffering nor to purgatory, but He did have an effect on the damned by making them recognize His divinity and on the souls of purgatory by giving them the hope of glory.

55c

The Resurrection of Our Lord

This picture shows the Resurrection of Our Lord Jesus Christ.

The holy women who are at left came, according to the Gospel, to embalm the body of Jesus, when suddenly there was a great earthquake. The angel of the Lord came from heaven, rolled back the stone, and sat upon it. The frightened soldiers fell to the ground as if dead. When the holy women entered the sepulcher, they were frightened by the sight of the angel. But he said to them, "Do not be terrified. You are looking for Jesus of Nazareth, who was crucified. He has risen, He is not here. Behold the place where they laid Him." (St. Mark 16:6)

55e

The Ascension of Our Lord

This picture shows the Ascension of Jesus Christ from the Mount of Olives. This mountain has three peaks, and it is from the middle one that Our Lord ascended to Heaven in the presence of His disciples and the holy women. While He was going up, as it is said, He left the imprint of His feet on the rock.

At the moment when Jesus Christ disappeared from the sight of His disciples in a luminous cloud, two angels appeared to them and said, "Men of Galilee, why do you stand looking up to heaven? This Jesus who has been taken up from you into heaven, shall come in the same way as you have seen Him going up to heaven."

of what he has given me, but that I should raise it up on the last day" (*John 6:39*).

"Behold, I tell you a mystery: we shall all indeed rise, but we shall not all be changed — in a moment, in the twinkling of an eye, at the last trumpet. For the trumpet shall sound, and the dead shall rise incorruptible and we shall be changed. For this corruptible body must put on incorruption, and this mortal body must put on immortality" (*I Corinthians 15:51-53*).

101. When did Christ ascend into heaven?

Christ ascended, body and soul, into heaven on Ascension Day, forty days after His Resurrection.

SCRIPTURE:
"Now he led them out towards Bethany, and he lifted up his hands and blessed them. And it came to pass as he blessed them, that he parted from them and was carried up into heaven" (*Luke 24:50-51*).

102. Why did Christ remain on earth forty days after His Resurrection?

Christ remained on earth forty days after His Resurrection to prove that He had truly risen from the dead and to complete the instruction of the apostles.

(a) Saint Paul tells us that Christ, after His Resurrection, appeared frequently to the apostles and to many others.

(b) Christ ascended into heaven from Mount Olivet, a hill outside Jerusalem.

SCRIPTURE:
"To them also he showed himself alive after his passion by many proofs, during forty days appearing to them and speaking of the kingdom of God" (*Acts 1:3*).

"Christ ... rose again the third day, ... he appeared to Cephas, and after that to the Eleven. Then he was seen by more than five hundred brethren at one time. ... After that he was seen by James, then by all the apostles. And last of all, ... he was seen also by me" (*I Corinthians 15:3-8*).

103. What do we mean when we say that Christ sits at the right hand of God, the Father Almighty?

When we say that Christ sits at the right hand of God, the Father Almighty, we mean that Our Lord as God is equal to the Father, and that as man He shares above all the saints in the glory of His Father and exercises for all eternity the supreme authority of a king over all creatures.

(a) Even as man, Christ of Himself has dominion over all creation. His Kingship rests on the fact that His human nature is immediately united to the divine Person of the Son of God, and on the fact that He redeemed all men with His precious blood.

(b) On earth Christ exercises His kingly authority in spiritual matters through His Church. His Kingship extends also over temporal and civil matters.

SCRIPTURE:
"All power in heaven and on earth has been given to me" (*Matthew 28:18*).

"For as the Father has life in himself, even so he has given to the Son also to have life in himself; and he has granted him power to render judgment, because he is Son of Man" (*John 5:26-27*).

"Pilate therefore said to him, 'Thou art then a king?' Jesus answered, 'Thou sayest it; I am a king. This is why I was born, and why I have come into the world, to bear witness to the truth' " (*John 18:37*).

"Therefore, if you have risen with Christ, seek the things that are above, where Christ is seated at the right hand of God" (*Colossians 3:1*).

"Jesus, who for the joy set before him, endured a cross, despising shame, and sits at the right hand of the throne of God" (*Hebrews 12:2*).

"And from his mouth goes forth a sharp sword with which to smite the nations. And he will rule them with a rod of iron, and he treads the wine press of the fierce wrath of God almighty. And he has on his garment and on his thigh a name written, 'King of kings and Lord of lords' " (*Apocalypse 19:15-16*).

104. What do we mean when we say that Christ will come from thence to judge the living and the dead?

When we say that Christ will come from thence to judge the living and the dead, we mean that on the last day Our Lord will come to pronounce a sentence of eternal reward or of eternal punishment on everyone who has ever lived in this world.

(a) Jesus Christ, both as God and as man, will judge all men because He is "King of kings and Lord of lords" (*Apocalypse 17:14; 19:16*), and it is His prerogative to pass judgment, to reward or punish according to merits.

SCRIPTURE:

"For the Son of Man is to come with his angels in the glory of his Father, and then he will render to everyone according to his conduct" (*Matthew 16:27*).

"For neither does the Father judge any man, but all judgment he has given to the Son" (*John 5:22*).

"And he charged us to preach to the people and to testify that he it is who has been appointed by God to be judge of the living and of the dead" (*Acts 10:42*).

IMPORTANT TRUTHS ABOUT THE REDEMPTION

Jesus Christ saved the world from the evil effects of both original sin and the actual sins of men by a life and death of suffering. His death on the cross was a sacrifice to His Father — a sacrifice in which He was both priest and victim. He was not obliged to suffer as much as He did in order to redeem us, for even the least suffering on His part would have sufficed to redeem all mankind because of the infinite dignity of His divine personality, which gave infinite satisfactory value to even the least of His sufferings. But He suffered so intensely and died the painful death of the cross in order to prove His great love for us.

Because His death means so much for the human race, the Catholic Church cherishes a great devotion to the representation of His death, the crucifix. The crucifix is the chief reminder of Jesus Christ. In every church and school the crucifix occupies a prominent place; and it should be found also in every Catholic home. Nothing is better calculated to teach us the greatness of God's love for men, and the malice of sin. It is because of the many lessons contained in Christ's Passion that the Church celebrates so solemnly Holy Week and recommends the devotion of the Way of the Cross.

Our Lord died on Good Friday. On the following Sunday He rose gloriously from the tomb in which His body had been placed. Thus He proved to the world the truth of His teachings, especially the doctrine that He is true God. There have always been men who denied the fact of Christ's Resurrection; but the proofs for it are so convincing that no reasonable person can doubt it. After His death on the cross He appeared on many occasions, eleven of which are mentioned in the Bible. Once He was seen by more than five hundred persons. He spoke with the disciples, ate with them, allowed them to touch the wounds in His hands and side. The very fact that the disciples willingly endured sufferings and death in testimony of the Resurrection, is a convincing proof that it took place, for men will not die for a cause unless they are sure of it.

To commemorate Christ's Resurrection, the Church celebrates Easter Sunday as one of the greatest and most joyous feasts of the year, and continues the Easter season for forty days in memory of the forty days Our Lord remained on earth. During this time the large paschal candle is kept in the sanctuary, as a symbol of the risen Christ; and to remind us of His Ascension into heaven, it is extinguished after the Gospel of the Mass on Ascension Thursday. His Ascension into heaven occurred on the fortieth day after His Resurrection.

In heaven Our Lord, even as man, is King of the entire universe. At the end of the world He will come to judge all mankind, as He Himself describes it in the twenty-fifth chapter of the Gospel of St. Matthew. There He says that at this last judgment He will place the just on His right and the wicked on His left. To the latter He will say: "Depart from me, accursed ones, into the everlasting fire which was prepared for the devil and his angels", while to the former He will give the consoling invitation: "Come, blessed of my Father, take possession of the kingdom prepared for you from the foundation of the world" (*Matthew, 25:34-41*).

The thought of Christ's sufferings and of His glorification should remind us that if we patiently accept the sufferings God allows to befall us, we shall merit one day to share in the glory and happiness of our divine Redeemer.

RESOLUTION: Resolve occasionally to perform the devotion of the Way of the Cross, particularly in Lent, and also to carry a crucifix on your person.

STUDY HELPS

A. TRUE OR FALSE. (*Check each of the following statements as either true or false. The correct answer can be found in the previous portions of this lesson.*)

	TRUE	FALSE
(1) The souls of those who had died in mortal sin before the time of Christ were in limbo.	.....	.....
(2) Even the least suffering of Christ would have sufficed to make satisfaction for all the sins of men.	.....	.....
(3) Our Lord proposed His Resurrection as the most conclusive proof of His divine mission.	.....	.....
(4) The divine Person was not united by hypostatic union to the dead body of Christ in the tomb.	.....	.....
(5) Sinners as well as saints will rise from the dead.	.....	.....
(6) The risen body of Christ needs food and sleep.	.....	.....
(7) Christ ascended into heaven from Mount Calvary.	.....	.....
(8) Christ died even for those who are now in hell.	.....	.....
(9) It is correct to say that God died on the cross.	.....	.....
(10) Christ suffered and died in His divine nature.	.....	.....

B. PROBLEMS AND EXERCISES. (*Answer the questions orally or write them as your teacher may direct*):

(1) From what evil did Our Lord rescue us?

(2) How did Our Lord prove after His Resurrection that His body could pass through other bodies?

(3) Give three names for the place where Christ was crucified?

(4) Griselda, reading an extract from St. Alphonsus' "The Passion and Death of Our Lord" is surprised to learn that a single tear shed by the Infant Jesus, or a baby cry from His lips, would have been sufficient to ransom a thousand worlds as sinful as ours. Can you tell her why? Then add to your explanation a reason why Our Lord suffered so much.

(5) On Good Friday afternoon, what remark did Our Saviour make to the Good Thief, Dismas? When did the Good Thief enter heaven? On his way thither did he pass through either purgatory or limbo, or did he go directly to heaven? State the reason for your answer.

(6) What is meant by limbo? Are any souls that were once in limbo now in the hell of the damned? Explain your answer.

(7) Is Christ a King only as God or only as man, or as both?

(8) In heaven, how is Our Lord exalted over the entire universe? What October feast commemorates this exaltation? What phrase of the Apostles' Creed expresses this exaltation?

(9) Pascal is curious to know if the "Easter season" mentioned in the third paragraph of this lesson's commentary is the same as the "Easter Duty season"? Explain matters to him.

(10) Hazel, an unbelieving college professor, flippantly denies an after-life, remarking: "No one ever came back to tell us about it!" Euphemia, the only Catholic girl in her class, remembers this lesson in Catechism, and makes an appropriate answer. What is her answer?

(11) Albert asks what Our Lord chiefly proved by His return from the dead? Give him your answer.

(12) About how many people, at the very least, saw Our Lord after He had returned from the dead? During the almost six weeks Our Lord remained on earth after Easter, on at least how many different occasions did He appear to His followers, and deal with them?

(13) Thelma is always deeply impressed by the services of Holy Week. Why does the Church celebrate them so solemnly?

(14) Marius always carries with him a small pocket crucifix. Do you approve this practice? Why?

(15) Our Lord's dead body was in the tomb from Good Friday until Easter Sunday. During that time was His body worthy of the highest form of adoration, the same type of adoration that is due to His living human nature today? Give the reason for your answer, remembering that the reason why Christ's human nature is given divine adoration is the fact that it is united to the Divine Person of the Word.

(16) Ethelreda has contracted marriage with a very wealthy non-Catholic, and has two children. Before her marriage she was a devout Catholic, but now she has given up many of her previous religious practices, though she still claims to be a good Catholic. She will not have a crucifix on the wall of any of the rooms in her house, because she asserts that the representation of the cruel sufferings inflicted on Our Lord will have a terrifying and depressing effect on the minds of her children. What do you think of her argument against the presence of a crucifix in her home?

LESSON 9

The Holy Ghost and Grace

"... I BELIEVE IN THE HOLY GHOST ..."

105. Who is the Holy Ghost?

The Holy Ghost is God and the third Person of the Blessed Trinity.

(a) The Holy Ghost is also called the Holy Spirit, the Paraclete, the Advocate, the Spirit of Truth, the Spirit of God, and the Spirit of Love.

> SCRIPTURE:
> "But Peter said, 'Ananias, why has Satan tempted thy heart, that thou shouldst lie to the Holy Spirit and by fraud keep back part of the price of the land? ... Thou hast not lied to men, but to God'" (*Acts 5:3-4*).
> *See Scripture, question 25, Matthew 28:19.*

106. From whom does the Holy Ghost proceed?

The Holy Ghost proceeds from the Father and the Son.

(a) The Holy Ghost does not proceed from the Father and the Son by spiritual generation. Only the Son proceeds from the Father by generation. This is one of the mysterious truths that we know only from revelation.

> SCRIPTURE:
> "But when the Advocate has come, whom I will send you from the Father, the Spirit of truth who proceeds from the Father, he will bear witness concerning me" (*John 15:26*).
> "But when he, the Spirit of truth, has come, he will teach you all the truth. For he will not speak on his own authority, but whatever he will hear he will speak, and the things that are to come he will declare to you. He will glorify me, because he will receive of what is mine and declare it to you. All things that the Father has are mine. That is why I have said that he will receive of what is mine, and will declare it to you" (*John 16:13-15*).

107. Is the Holy Ghost equal to the Father and the Son?

The Holy Ghost is equal to the Father and the Son, because He is God.

(a) Because of the oneness of nature in the Blessed Trinity, the Father is entirely in the Son and in the Holy Ghost; the Son is entirely in the Father and in the Holy Ghost; and the Holy Ghost is entirely in the Father and in the Son. No one of the three divine Persons is outside the other, for none precedes the other in eternity, nor surpasses the other in power, nor exceeds the other in any way. This indwelling of one divine Person in the others is called *circumincession*.

> SCRIPTURE:
> "Jesus answered, 'Amen, amen, I say to thee, unless a man be born again of water and the Spirit, he cannot enter into the kingdom of God'" (*John 3:5*).

108. What does the Holy Ghost do for the salvation of mankind?

The Holy Ghost dwells in the Church as the source of its life and sanctifies souls through the gift of grace.

(a) Although the sanctification of mankind, like all other outward works of God, is performed by all three Persons of the Blessed Trinity, it is attributed to the Holy Ghost, the third Person. The sanctification of mankind is attributed to the Holy Ghost because He is the love of the Father and the Son and because the sanctification of man by grace shows forth God's boundless love.

SCRIPTURE:

"And I will ask the Father and he will give you another Advocate to dwell with you forever, the Spirit of truth whom the world cannot receive, because it neither sees him nor knows him. But you shall know him, because he will dwell with you, and be in you" (*John 14:16-17*).

"Do you not know that you are the temple of God and that the Spirit of God dwells in you?" (*I Corinthians 3:16*).

"Guard the good trust through the Holy Spirit, who dwells in us" (*II Timothy 1:14*).

"But when the goodness and kindness of God our Savior appeared, then not by reason of good works that we did ourselves, but according to his mercy, he saved us through the bath of regeneration and renewal by the Holy Spirit; whom he has abundantly poured out upon us through Jesus Christ our Savior, in order that, justified by his grace, we may be heirs in the hope of life everlasting" (*Titus 3:4-7*).

109. What is grace?

Grace is a supernatural gift of God bestowed on us through the merits of Jesus Christ for our salvation.

(a) Grace is something real, just as the soul itself is real. It is not merely the absence of sin but rather a spiritual quality infused by God into the soul.

(b) The supernatural is that which surpasses the power of all created nature. It is of two kinds:

first, that manifested when the supernatural fact happens in a manner that is beyond the power of nature; for example, when a person is instantly cured of leprosy;

second, that manifested when the supernatural fact, in its essential character, completely surpasses the power of the whole natural order; for example, when, in some degree, God intimately shares His life with man through sanctifying grace.

(c) Because no man has a strict right to share in the life of God Himself, grace is a free gift, distributed by God according to His good pleasure.

(d) Jesus Christ, the Redeemer promised by God to Adam and Eve after their fall, merited all the graces since bestowed upon men. The graces bestowed by God on those who lived before the time of Christ were granted through anticipation of the merits of Our Lord.

(e) Man cannot attain eternal life by powers that are merely natural. He must be elevated to a supernatural plane through grace; and he constantly needs the impulse of God to merit eternal life.

61

61a

The Descent of the Holy Spirit on Pentecost

This picture shows the Cenacle where the apostles and disciples, waiting for the coming of the Holy Spirit, were praying with the Holy Virgin and several holy women. As St. Luke says in the Acts of the Apostles:

"And when the days of Pentecost were drawing to a close, they were all together in one place. And suddenly there came a sound from heaven, as of a violent wind blowing, and it filled the whole house where they were sitting. And there appeared to them parted tongues as of fire, which settled upon each of them. And they were all filled with the Holy Spirit and began to speak in foreign tongues, even as the Holy Spirit prompted them to speak." (Acts 2:1-4)

"And of his fullness we have all received, grace for grace. For the Law was given through Moses; grace and truth came through Jesus Christ" (*John 1:16-17*).

"And he said, 'This is why I have said to you, 'No one can come to me unless he is enabled to do so by my Father' " (*John 6:66*).

"But by the grace of God I am what I am, and his grace in me has not been fruitless — in fact I have labored more than any of them, yet not I, but the grace of God with me" (*I Corinthians 15:10*).

110. How many kinds of grace are there?

There are two kinds of grace: sanctifying grace and actual grace.

111. What is sanctifying grace?

Sanctifying grace is that grace which confers on our souls a new life, that is, a sharing in the life of God Himself.

(a) Sanctifying grace is also called habitual grace because we possess this divine gift as a habit of the soul, that is, as something permanent.

(b) Sanctifying grace is lost only through mortal sin.

"But to as many as received him he gave the power of becoming sons of God" (*John 1:12*).

"For in Christ Jesus neither circumcision nor uncircumcision but a new creation is of any account" (*Galatians 6:15*).

" ... through which he has granted us the very great and precious promises, so that through them you may become partakers of the divine nature, having escaped from the corruption of that lust which is in the world" (*II Peter 1:4*).

112. What are the chief effects of sanctifying grace?

The chief effects of sanctifying grace are:

first, it makes us holy and pleasing to God;

second, it makes us adopted children of God;

third, it makes us temples of the Holy Ghost;

fourth, it gives us the right to heaven.

"Jesus answered and said to him, 'If anyone love me, he will keep my word, and my Father will love him, and we will come to him and make our abode with him' " (*John 14:23*).

"For whoever are led by the Spirit of God, they are the sons of God. Now you have not received a spirit of bondage so as to be again in fear, but you have received a spirit of adoption as sons, by virtue of which we cry, 'Abba! Father!'"

"The Spirit himself gives testimony to our spirit that we are sons of God. But if we are sons, we are heirs also: heirs indeed of God and joint heirs with Christ, provided, however, we suffer with him that we may also be glorified with him" (*Romans 8:14-17*).

"Or do you not know that your members are the temple of the Holy Spirit, who is in you, whom you have from God, and that you are not your own? For you have been bought at a great price. Glorify God and bear him in your body' (*I Corinthians 6:19-20*).

"Therefore, since we receive a kingdom that cannot be shaken, we have grace, through which we may offer pleasing service to God with fear and reverence" (*Hebrews 12:28*).

"Behold what manner of love the Father has bestowed upon us, that we should be called children of God; and such we are" (*I John 3:1*).

113. What is actual grace?

Actual grace is a supernatural help of God which enlightens our mind and strengthens our will to do good and to avoid evil.

(a) Unlike sanctifying grace, actual grace is not a habit dwelling in the soul but a divine impulse moving a person to perform acts above his natural powers.

(b) A true Christian should view all his life in the light of grace. Under the general term of grace fall all the gifts that God freely bestows on man for his eternal salvation. For example, such external graces as a good mother and father, a Christian home, and even sickness and trials, must be accepted as ordained or permitted by Divine Providence for man's salvation.

(c) Persons in mortal sin cannot gain sanctifying grace without the help of actual grace.

(d) Christ, by His death, merited sufficient grace for all men to be saved.

SCRIPTURE:
"I am the vine, you are the branches. He who abides in me, and I in him, he bears much fruit; for without me you can do nothing" (*John 15:5*).

"... that the God of our Lord Jesus Christ, the Father of glory, may grant you the spirit of wisdom and revelation in deep knowledge of him: the eyes of your mind being enlightened, so that you may know what is the hope of his calling, what the riches of the glory of his inheritance in the saints" (*Ephesians 1:17-18*).

"For it is God who of his good pleasure works in you both the will and the performance" (*Philippians 2:13*).

114. Can we resist the grace of God?

We can resist the grace of God, for our will is free, and God does not force us to accept His grace.

(a) Although God wishes the salvation of all men, those who have attained the use of reason can be saved only by co-operating freely with the grace of God.

(b) Those who do not have the use of reason cannot choose to co-operate with God's grace. They can, however, be saved through Baptism.

SCRIPTURE:
"He that could have transgressed and hath not transgressed: and could do evil things and hath not done them" (*Ecclesiasticus 31:10*).

"Jerusalem, Jerusalem! thou who killest the prophets, and stonest those who are sent to thee! How often would I have gathered thy children together, as a hen gathers her young under her wings, but thou wouldst not!" (*Matthew 23:37*).

"Yes, working together with him we entreat you not to receive the grace of God in vain" (*II Corinthians 6:1*).

115. Why is sanctifying grace necessary for salvation?

Sanctifying grace is necessary for salvation because it is the supernatural life, which alone enables us to attain the supernatural happiness of heaven.

(a) Without sanctifying grace, the soul is unworthy to see God face to face. If the soul is in the state of mortal sin, it deserves eternal punishment.

116. Is actual grace necessary for all who have attained the use of reason?

Actual grace is necessary for all who have attained the use of reason, because without it we cannot long resist the power of temptation or perform other actions which merit a reward in heaven.

(a) The possession of sanctifying grace is also necessary in order to resist temptations for a long time.

SCRIPTURE:
"As the branch cannot bear fruit of itself unless it remain on the vine, so neither can you unless you abide in me. I am the vine, you are the branches. He who abides in me, and I in him, he bears much fruit; for without me you can do nothing" (*John 15:4-5*).

"God is faithful and will not permit you to be tempted beyond your strength, but with the temptation will also give you a way out that you may be able to bear it" (*I Corinthians 10:13*).

"Not that we are sufficient of ourselves to think anything, as from ourselves, but our sufficiency is from God" (*II Corinthians 3:5*).

117. What are the principal ways of obtaining grace?

The principal ways of obtaining grace are prayer and the sacraments, especially the Holy Eucharist.

(a) The sacraments of Baptism and Penance were instituted chiefly to give grace to those who do not possess it; the other sacraments, to increase it in those who are already in the state of grace.

SCRIPTURE:
"For we were buried with him by means of Baptism into death, in order that, just as Christ has arisen from the dead through the glory of the Father, so we also may walk in newness of life" (*Romans 6:4*).

118. How can we make our most ordinary actions merit a heavenly award?

We can make our most ordinary actions merit a heavenly reward by doing them for the love of God and by keeping ourselves in the state of grace.

(a) Supernatural merit is the right to a heavenly reward given to us by God for good actions in the supernatural order, provided we are in the state of grace.

(b) We can merit in this life only when we are in the state of sanctifying grace and perform good works freely.

(c) After death merit cannot be gained in heaven, in hell, or in purgatory.

(d) By mortal sin a person loses the merit of his good actions.

SCRIPTURE:
"Therefore, whether you eat or drink, or do anything else, do all for the glory of God" (*I Corinthians 10:31*).

IMPORTANT TRUTHS ABOUT THE HOLY GHOST AND GRACE

Although all three Persons of the Blessed Trinity perform the work of sanctifying human souls, this work is especially attributed to the third Person, the Holy Ghost, because He is the Person who proceeds from the Father and the Son as the breathing of their love; and sanctification is a work of love. God Himself indicated this when He attributed the Incarnation, the source of all man's sanctity, to the Holy Ghost, saying to the Blessed Virgin Mary, through the message of the Angel Gabriel: "The Holy Spirit shall come upon thee" (*Luke 1:35*).

God sanctifies the human soul by the supernatural gift of grace. The most exalted type of grace is sanctifying grace, which is a spiritual quality, dwelling in the soul, making it like God Himself. The New Testament is filled with allusions to this grace, which is referred to as a new life, a sharing in God's life. Our Lord spoke of the reception of this life as a spiritual birth, when He said: "Unless a man be born again of water and the Spirit, he cannot enter into the kingdom of God" (*John 3:5*). Once it has been received, sanctifying grace remains in the soul unless it is driven out by mortal sin. And when one has received sanctifying grace, he can grow in it constantly, for it increases with every worthy reception of a sacrament, and with every supernaturally meritorious work.

Actual grace, as the name indicates, is given for the performance of a good, supernatural action. It is a direct force from God Himself. It contains an enlightenment of the mind and an inspiration of the will. We should be very careful not to neglect it, for it is a precious gift of God, and if we neglect one such grace we may deprive ourselves of a whole chain of extraordinary graces that God had planned for us. Even sinners receive actual graces, impelling them to turn again to God. Indeed, without actual grace, we cannot perform any supernaturally good action; for our natural powers are unable to rise to the supernatural plane.

God does not distribute actual graces equally to all; some persons receive much more than others. There is no injustice in this on the part of God, for grace is a free gift from Him, and He can distribute it according to His good pleasure. But all receive sufficient grace to be saved.

The chief fruit of sanctifying grace is merit—a claim or right to receive an increase of sanctifying grace, together with a claim to a corresponding measure of glory and happiness in heaven. We can increase in heavenly merit indefinitely. Not only works which are by their nature good, such as prayer and the reception of the sacraments and attendance at Mass, but even the ordinary works of our day, such as the taking of our meals, study, our games and amusements, can become meritorious if we perform them under the proper conditions. These conditions are very easy—we must be in the state of grace, and offer our works to God out of love for Him. We do not have to make this offering with each work we perform. It is sufficient to make it from time to time, particularly every morning, intending to include in it all our thoughts, words and actions. Thus, it would suffice to say in our heart: "O my God, I offer Thee every deliberate action I shall perform, because I love Thee on account of Thy infinite goodness".

65

A person in mortal sin cannot merit any heavenly reward, even though he may perform very good deeds; but by performing good deeds from a supernatural motive he can prepare himself for repentance and for a return to the state of sanctifying grace.

RESOLUTION: Resolve out of love for God to offer Him frequently all the actions of the entire day, even the slightest.

STUDY HELPS

A. WORD SELECTION. (*Select the word or phrase in the parentheses which most exactly and most completely fills out the sentence*):

(1) A person in mortal sin cannot gain sanctifying grace without the help of (actual grace . . . the sacrament of Penance . . . the Church).

(2) Sanctifying grace is also called (the Holy Ghost . . . divine impulse . . . habitual grace).

(3) A good mother is (an external . . . an actual . . . a supernatural) grace.

(4) Grace is (freedom from sin . . . a spiritual quality . . . a source of peace).

(5) Circumincession is (a Jewish ceremony . . . the procession of one divine Person from another . . . the indwelling of each one divine Person in the others).

(6) The Holy Ghost proceeds from (the Father and the Son . . . the Father alone . . . the Son alone).

(7) The chief fruit of sanctifying grace is (charity . . . merit . . . happiness).

(8) Without actual grace we cannot perform (any action . . . any naturally good action . . . any supernatural action).

(9) The most exalted type of grace is (actual grace . . . sanctifying grace . . . external grace).

(10) The conferring of grace is attributed to (the Father . . . the Son . . . the Holy Ghost).

B. PROBLEMS AND EXERCISES. (*Answer the questions orally or write them as your teacher may direct*):

(1) What is the only thing that can expel sanctifying grace from the soul?

(2) How does an actual grace coming from God affect our mind? Our will?

(3) Laura is eating a bunch of grapes. An hour ago she completed her homework and her studies for tomorrow. Suddenly it occurs to her that there is something in this lesson's commentary about a vine and its branches. She cannot recall the saying of Our Lord nor the point it illustrates. Write out that text from memory, and explain how it illustrates this lesson.

(4) Albert is in mortal sin, but he went to Mass on Sunday, said his morning and night prayers and obeyed his mother when she told him to go to bed. Did Albert gain any merit for heaven by these good deeds? If not, what spiritual profit could he acquire from them?

(5) Camilla, 13 years old, and Rosabella 31, die as saints, with an equal amount of merit to their spiritual credit. In heaven, will one be

happier than the other? Will one have greater glory than the other? Explain both answers.

(6) Austin is having a glorious time at the altar boys' picnic. While he served Mass he said a short morning prayer, in which was the Morning Offering. The rest of the day is spent playing games, swimming, and eating. Tired out and happy, he tumbles into bed that night after saying an Our Father, a Hail Mary, a Glory be to the Father, and an Act of Contrition. The only other prayers he said all day were the meal prayers, and a couple of aspirations in the afternoon before the race that he won. He is in the state of grace. Have his games of the day, his meals, his swimming added to his merit with God? Explain your answer.

(7) From memory, write out the Morning Offering.

(8) Scholastica has the habit of repeating frequently during the day: "All for Thee, O Lord!" Once, Chloe, a non-Catholic playmate, overheard her whisper this aspiration before a game of tennis. Explain to Chloe what the prayer means, and why Scholastica says it frequently.

(9) Boniface, in the last religion test, explained that sanctifying grace stays in the soul as long as we enjoy God's friendship, doing good and avoiding serious sin. He further added that once sanctifying grace enters the soul it remains the same, neither decreasing nor increasing in degree. Are his answers correct? Explain your decisions.

(10) When the famous Dionne quintuplets, Yvonne, Annette, Cecile, Emilie and Marie received the sacrament of Baptism did all receive the same measure of sanctifying grace? What is the reason for your answer?

(11) Joachim, a pious lad of 8, observes that the pastor in his sermons to the children frequently refers to sanctifying grace, merit, and the good intention. He would like to know what is meant by "merit" and "the good intention." Can you tell him?

(12) Henrietta, Inez and Eloise, are exchanging confidences respecting their ambitions in life. Henrietta hopes to become a star movie actress in Hollywood, to make a fortune and win fame; Inez wants to become a stewardess on a transcontinental airliner, so that she may travel all around this country; Eloise says that she is praying for a vocation to the Poor Clares, so as to acquire an immense treasure of sanctifying grace. In a short composition of 150 to 175 words pass your judgment on the ambitions of all three girls.

(13) Helen, writing a religious test, states that an angel possesses sanctifying grace as something due to his nature, whereas grace is given to man as something entirely above his nature. She also writes that when a person is in mortal sin he cannot receive any actual graces. Finally, she asserts that the good works a person performs when he is in mortal sin will become meritorious when he returns to the state of sanctifying grace. What do you think of the correctness of Helen's answers?

(14) Justin wonders if many venial sins will add up to constitute a mortal sin—in other words, if a person will lose the state of grace by committing many venial sins, even though he does not commit any mortal sin. Can you answer Justin's question from the information given in the commentary on this lesson?

The Virtues and the Gifts of the Holy Ghost

119. What are the chief supernatural powers that are bestowed on our souls with sanctifying grace?

The chief supernatural powers that are bestowed on our souls with sanctifying grace are the three theological virtues and the seven gifts of the Holy Ghost.

(a) A virtue is a habit or permanent disposition which inclines a person to do good and to avoid evil.

(b) Virtues may be natural or supernatural. Natural virtues are acquired by frequent repetition of the same act; supernatural virtues are infused into the soul directly by God.

(c) Like sanctifying grace, the three theological virtues and the seven gifts of the Holy Ghost are supernatural habits. They are called "powers" because they enable us to perform supernatural acts that lead to God.

(d) Whoever is in the state of grace has the theological virtues and the gifts of the Holy Ghost, which are infused into the intellect and will by God.

SCRIPTURE:
"For this reason I bend my knees to the Father of our Lord Jesus Christ, from whom all fatherhood in heaven and on earth receives its name, that he may grant you from his glorious riches to be strengthened with power through his Spirit unto the progress of the inner man; and to have Christ dwelling through faith in your hearts: so that, being rooted and grounded in love, you may be able to comprehend with all the saints what is the breadth and length and height and depth, and to know Christ's love which surpasses knowledge, in order that you may be filled unto all the fullness of God" (*Ephesians 3:14-19*).
See Scripture, question 108, Titus 3:4-7).

120. Why are these virtues called theological virtues?

These virtues are called theological virtues because they have God for their proper object.

(a) All virtue has God for its last end, but not every virtue refers directly to Him. Some virtues deal directly with human things; for example, justice is concerned with human rights, such as the right to life and property. The virtues referring immediately to God are called theological, a term derived from the Greek word for God, *theos.*

121. What are the three theological virtues?

The three theological virtues are faith, hope, and charity.

SCRIPTURE:
"So there abide faith, hope and charity, these three; but the greatest of these is charity" (*I Corinthians 13:13*).

122. What is faith?

Faith is the virtue by which we firmly believe all the truths God has revealed, on the word of God revealing them, who can neither deceive nor be deceived.

(a) To believe is to assent to a truth on the word of another, even though it is not understood. A judge or jury believes the testimony of a witness. Such an obvious truth as two and two are four is not believed; it is understood. To understand is to assent to a truth because our intellect sees that it is true.

(b) To believe a mystery that can be known to us only because God has revealed it is to assent to it on divine faith. We believe men in human affairs; we should not find it difficult to believe God, even in matters we cannot understand, since God can neither deceive nor be deceived.

(c) To make a supernatural act of faith, one must have the help of grace. Grace enables one to have sufficient enlightenment and good will to accept God's word for what He has revealed.

(d) Our faith must have these qualities:

first, it must be firm; to be doubtful deliberately on matters of faith is equivalent to denying outright God's authority. Faith should not be confused with opinion, which considers an opposing statement as probably true. Saint Paul tells us, "Faith is the substance of things to be hoped for, the evidence of things that are not seen" (*Hebrews 11:1*). When he speaks of evidence he means that faith must be firm and certain. When he speaks of the things that are not seen, he means that faith is obscure;

second, it must be complete; our faith must include all the truths God has revealed. To accept one truth and deny another is equivalent to denying all the truths He has revealed.

(e) Without faith it is impossible to be saved. Adults must have the virtue and the act of faith; infants must have the virtue of faith, received in Baptism, although they are incapable of making an act of faith. When children are baptized in infancy they receive, along with sanctifying grace, the infused virtue of faith. This virtue supplies them with the supernatural power they will need to make an act of faith when they have reached the age of reason.

SCRIPTURE:

"He said to them, 'But who do you say that I am?' Simon Peter answered and said, 'Thou art the Christ the Son of the living God.' Then Jesus answered and said, 'Blessed art thou, Simon Bar-Jona, for flesh and blood has not revealed this to thee, but my Father in heaven' " (*Matthew 16:15-17*).

"He who comes from above is over all. He who is from the earth belongs to earth, and of the earth he speaks. He who comes from heaven is over all. And he bears witness to that which he has seen and heard, and his witness no one receives. He who receives his witness has set his seal on this, that God is true" (*John 3:31-33*).

"Blessed are they who have not seen, and yet have believed" (*John 20:29*).

"If we receive the testimony of men, the testimony of God is greater; for this is the testimony of God which is greater, that he has borne witness concerning his Son" (*I John 5:9*).

"Now faith is the substance of things to be hoped for, the evidence of things that are not seen; for by it the men of old had testimony borne to them" (*Hebrews 11:1-2*).

123. What is hope?

Hope is the virtue by which we firmly trust that God, who is all-powerful and faithful to His promises, will in His mercy give us eternal happiness and the means to obtain it.

(a) With the help of God man can gain heaven, a goal he could never attain of himself. In Sacred Scripture God promised to give man eternal life and the means to obtain it: ". . . he that putteth his trust in me shall inherit the land and shall possess my holy mount" (*Isaias 57:13*).

(b) Hope is absolutely necessary for salvation; adults must have the virtue and make the act of hope; infants must have the virtue. For the infused virtue of hope, like the infused virtue of faith, is given to the infant when he receives sanctifying grace.

(c) Our hope must be firm, since the motive for hope is God's almighty power, and since it is certain that God will give us sufficient means to obtain salvation. The firmness of hope founded in God does not exclude a reasonable fear of losing our souls because, ordinarily, we cannot be certain that we shall properly use the means of salvation.

SCRIPTURE:
"But hope that is seen is not hope. For how can a man hope for what he sees? But if we hope for what we do not see, we wait for it with patience" (*Romans 8:24-25*).

"Now may the God of hope fill you with all joy and peace in believing, that you may abound in hope and in the power of the Holy Spirit" (*Romans 15:13*).

"Christ is faithful as the Son over his own house. We are that house, if we hold fast our confidence and the hope in which we glory unto the end" (*Hebrews 3:6*).

"This hope we have, as a sure and firm anchor of the soul, reaching even behind the veil where our forerunner Jesus has entered for us, having become a high priest forever according to the order of Melchisedech" (*Hebrews 6:19-20*).

124. What is charity?

Charity is the virtue by which we love God above all things for His own sake, and our neighbor as ourselves for the love of God.

(a) Charity is called the queen of the virtues because it unites man to God most perfectly and most permanently in the bonds of love.

(b) Charity is the divine friendship uniting man to God and man to fellow-man in the bonds of mutual affection. As we love those who are truly our friends, for their own sake and not because of any advantage to us, so through charity, we love God for His own sake and our neighbor because of God.

(c) Our neighbor includes all living human beings, even our enemies, the souls in purgatory, the blessed in heaven, and the angels.

(d) The infused virtue of charity corresponds to the infused virtues of faith and hope. Like faith and hope it is given with sanctifying grace. When God gives us the infused virtue of charity, He gives us the means to make perfect acts of love, and the power to make these acts easily.

(e) We should frequently make acts of perfect love and open our hearts to God as friend to friend in intimate conversation.

(f) To love God above all things we must be willing to renounce all created things rather than offend God by mortal sin. It is not necessary that we have more feeling in our love of God than in our love of men, since love is essentially a matter of the will, not of the feelings.

(g) We return God's friendly love by making acts of perfect love, by promoting in ourselves and others an appreciation of His infinite goodness, and by striving to live constantly for Him.

(h) Faith and hope will cease once we have attained heaven, for we cannot believe what we see, and we cannot desire and hope for what we already have; but charity remains even in heaven, where we will love God whom we possess.

SCRIPTURE:

"If I should speak with the tongues of men and of angels, but do not have charity, I have become as sounding brass or a tinkling cymbal. And if I have prophecy and know all mysteries and all knowledge, and if I have all faith so as to remove mountains, yet do not have charity, I am nothing. And if I distribute all my goods to feed the poor, and if I deliver my body to be burned, yet do not have charity, it profits me nothing. Charity is patient, is kind; charity does not envy, is not pretentious, is not puffed up, is not ambitious, is not self-seeking, is not provoked; thinks no evil, does not rejoice over wickedness, but rejoices with the truth; bears with all things, believes all things, hopes all things, endures all things" (*I Corinthians 13:1-7*).

125. Which are the seven gifts of the Holy Ghost?

The seven gifts of the Holy Ghost are: wisdom, understanding, counsel, fortitude, knowledge, piety, and fear of the Lord.

(a) The gifts are infused with sanctifying grace. The Holy Ghost dwells in the souls of the just and He is never present without His gifts.

SCRIPTURE:

"And the spirit of the Lord shall rest upon him: the spirit of wisdom and of understanding, the spirit of counsel and of fortitude, the spirit of knowledge and of godliness. And he shall be filled with the spirit of the fear of the Lord" (*Isaias 11:2-3*).

126. How do the gifts of the Holy Ghost help us?

The gifts of the Holy Ghost help us by making us more alert to discern and more ready to do the will of God.

(a) The difference between the virtues and the gifts of the Holy Ghost consists in this, that the virtues help us to follow the guidance of our reason and faith, and the gifts help us to follow readily the inspirations of the Holy Spirit.

71

127. Which are some of the effects in us of the gifts of the Holy Ghost?

Some of the effects in us of the gifts of the Holy Ghost are the fruits of the Holy Ghost and the beatitudes.

(a) Beatitude, or happiness, consists in attaining what is desired. Man, notwithstanding human suffering, can gain a very real but supernatural happiness from the possession of God in this life through grace and charity. Man hopes for everlasting happiness in heaven, where suffering is excluded.

128. Which are the twelve fruits of the Holy Ghost?

The twelve fruits of the Holy Ghost are: charity, joy, peace, patience, benignity, goodness, long-suffering, mildness, faith, modesty, continency, and chastity.

(a) The fruits of the Holy Ghost are good works performed under the inspiration of the Holy Ghost and with a certain delight.

SCRIPTURE:
"But the fruit of the Spirit is: charity, joy, peace, patience, kindness, goodness, faith, modesty, continency" (*Galatians 5:22-23*).

129. Which are the eight beatitudes?

The eight beatitudes are:
1. Blessed are the poor in spirit, for theirs is the kingdom of heaven.
2. Blessed are the meek, for they shall possess the earth.
3. Blessed are they who mourn, for they shall be comforted.
4. Blessed are they who hunger and thirst for justice, for they shall be satisfied.
5. Blessed are the merciful, for they shall obtain mercy.
6. Blessed are the clean of heart, for they shall see God.
7. Blessed are the peacemakers, for they shall be called children of God.
8. Blessed are they who suffer persecution for justice' sake, for theirs is the kingdom of heaven.

(a) The eight beatitudes were announced by Our Saviour at the beginning of the Sermon on the Mount (*Matthew 5:3-10*).

(b) They are called beatitudes because the practicing of them will bring us happiness both on earth and in heaven.

130. Are there any other virtues besides the theological virtues of faith, hope, and charity?

Besides the theological virtues of faith, hope, and charity there are other virtues, called moral virtues.

131. Why are these virtues called moral virtues?

These virtues are called moral virtues because they dispose us to lead moral, or good, lives by aiding us to treat persons and things in the right way, that is, according to the will of God.

72

(a) The word moral generally signifies a way of acting, whether good or bad. It is sometimes used to mean good actions or things as opposed to immoral or evil actions and things.

132. Which are the chief moral virtues?

The chief moral virtues are prudence, justice, fortitude, and temperance; these are called cardinal virtues.

SCRIPTURE:
"And if a man love justice, her labours have great virtues. For she teacheth temperance and prudence and justice and fortitude, which are such things as men can have nothing more profitable in life" (*Wisdom 8:7*).

133. Why are these virtues called cardinal virtues?

These virtues are called cardinal virtues because they are like hinges on which hang all the other moral virtues and our whole moral life. The word "cardinal" is derived from the Latin word "cardo" meaning hinge.

(a) They are called cardinal or chief virtues not because they are the highest or even the most important virtues, but because all the other moral virtues depend upon them.

134. How do prudence, justice, fortitude, and temperance dispose us to lead good lives?

Prudence disposes us in all circumstances to form right judgments about what we must do or not do.

Justice disposes us to give everyone what belongs to him.

Fortitude disposes us to do what is good in spite of any difficulty.

Temperance disposes us to control our desires and to use rightly the things which please our senses.

(a) Prudence perfects the intelligence, which is the power of forming judgments. Knowledge and experience are important for prudence.

(b) Justice perfects the will and safeguards the chief rights of man: his right to life and freedom, to the sanctity of the home, to his good name and honor, and to his external possessions.

(c) Fortitude is especially important when one is in danger of death. Martyrs are the best examples of those who possess this virtue. Fortitude urges us forward in the face of trying difficulties.

(d) Temperance is especially necessary in moderating the use of food and drink, and in regulating the enjoyment of sex in the married state.

SCRIPTURE:
"Get wisdom, because it is better than gold: and purchase prudence, for it is more precious than silver" (*Proverbs 16:16*).

"He that followeth justice and mercy shall find life, justice, and glory" (*Proverbs 21:21*).

"Use as a frugal man the things that are set before thee: lest if thou eatest much, thou be hated" (*Ecclesiasticus 31:19*).

73

"Wine was created from the beginning to make men joyful, and not to make them drunk" (*Ecclesiasticus 31:35*).

"Or do you not know that the unjust will not possess the kingdom of God? Do not err; neither fornicators . . . nor thieves, nor the covetous, nor drunkards, nor the evil-tongued, nor the greedy will possess the kingdom of God" (*I Corinthians 6:9-10*).

135. Which are some of the other moral virtues?

Some of the other moral virtues are:

Filial piety and patriotism, which dispose us to honor, love, and respect our parents and our country.

Obedience, which disposes us to do the will of our superiors.

Veracity, which disposes us to tell the truth.

Liberality, which disposes us rightly to use worldly goods.

Patience, which disposes us to bear up under trials and difficulties.

Humility, which disposes us to acknowledge our limitations.

Chastity, or purity, which disposes us to be pure in soul and body.

Besides these, there are many other moral virtues.

(a) Religion is the highest moral virtue since it disposes us to offer to God the worship that is due Him. Religion, therefore, is rightly classed under the cardinal virtue of justice.

SCRIPTURE:

"An obedient man shall speak of victory" (*Proverbs 21:28*).

"Be patient in tribulation, persevering in prayer" (*Romans 12:12*).

"Let everyone be subject to the higher authorities, for there exists no authority except from God. . . . Render to all men whatever is their due; tribute to whom tribute is due; taxes to whom taxes are due; fear to whom fear is due; honor to whom honor is due" (*Romans 13:1, 7*).

"Rather are we to practise the truth in love, and so grow up in all things in him who is the head, Christ. . . . Wherefore, put away lying and speak truth each one with his neighbor, because we are members of one another" (*Ephesians 4:15, 25*).

"For this is the will of God, your sanctification; that you abstain from immorality; that every one of you learn how to possess his vessel in holiness and honor, not in the passion of lust like the Gentiles who do not know God. . . . For God has not called us unto uncleanness, but unto holiness" (*I Thessalonians 4:3-5, 7*).

"And all of you practise humility towards one another; for, 'God resists the proud, but gives grace to the humble.' Humble yourselves, therefore, under the mighty hand of God, that he may exalt you in the time of visitation" (*I Peter 5:5-6*).

IMPORTANT TRUTHS ABOUT THE VIRTUES AND GIFTS OF THE HOLY GHOST

When God sanctifies a soul, He gives it not only the sublime supernatural quality by which it is made like to Him and shares in His divine life—sanctifying grace—but also a number of other qualities or habits by which the soul can act supernaturally. These are called the supernatural virtues and the gifts of the

74

Holy Ghost. These supernatural habits are said to be *infused* by God—that is, *poured into* the soul. They are given in proportion to each one's measure of sanctifying grace, and they increase proportionately with the increase of that grace. The supernatural virtues do not destroy the natural virtues which one may have acquired by repeated good acts, but rather strengthen and perfect them. Neither do the supernatural virtues free one from the obligation of acquiring the natural virtues. The ideal Christian has both natural and supernatural virtues. However, it is possible to have one type without the other. Thus a baptized infant has the supernatural virtues, infused at Baptism, but he has no natural virtues. On the other hand, a sinner, who has not the supernatural moral virtues may have some natural virtues.

The noblest of the supernatural virtues are the three theological virtues, faith, hope and charity, by which the soul believes in God's revelations, hopes to possess Him for all eternity, and loves Him because of His infinite goodness. The infused moral virtues help one to use created things properly, employing them so as to gain eternal life from their use. These virtues, like the corresponding natural virtues, are grouped under the four chief or cardinal virtues of prudence, justice, fortitude and temperance. Finally, the gifts of the Holy Ghost make one docile to the movements of the Holy Spirit. Every good Christian knows that at times he chooses a certain course of action or performs a good deed so suddenly that it would seem that he is impelled by a power outside of himself; and afterwards he realizes that it was the proper thing to do. This is a manifestation of the activity of the Holy Ghost, working on the soul through His gifts. Often we find Catholics who believe that the gifts of the Holy Ghost are given only in Confirmation; but this is incorrect. They are always given with sanctifying grace, though the sacrament of Confirmation, since it makes us soldiers of Christ, urges us to use the gifts in a special degree.

The greatest of the theological virtues is charity, which is love for God because of His infinite goodness and love for our neighbor because he shares, or can share, in the goodness of God through the possession of sanctifying grace. Our Lord told us that we must love God with our whole heart and soul, which means that we must be willing to renounce every created good rather than offend God by mortal sin. We can have true love for God even though we are not sorry for our venial sins, though it is surely more perfect to repent of our venial as well as our mortal sins when we make an act of love for God. The goodness of God which is the motive of charity is His supernatural goodness, which is made known through revelation.

Similarly, love for our neighbor, to be charity, must be based on a supernatural motive—namely, the fact that every one of our fellow men either possesses sanctifying grace or is capable of possessing it. If we love a person merely because of his natural qualities, we are not making an act of charity. When Our Lord told us to love our neighbor as ourselves, He meant that we must love all our fellow men in the same *manner* as we love ourselves—that is, supernaturally—but not necessarily in the same *measure*. Moreover, we are not obliged to love all our fellow men in the same degree. We can and should have greater love for those who are united to us by the bonds of relationship, faith and nationality.

As long as we retain sanctifying grace, the infused virtues and the gifts remain in our soul. Mortal sin drives out all these supernatural habits, except faith and hope, which remain even in the soul of the sinner unless he commits a sin directly against hope—in which case only faith remains—or a sin directly opposed to faith, in which case all the supernatural qualities are driven out.

St. Paul in the Epistle to the Galatians (*5:22-23*) speaks of the fruits of the Holy Ghost—acts of virtue which bring sweetness and joy to the soul, like delicious fruit. Our Lord has given us the beatitudes (*Matthew 5:3-10*), eight

75

principles concerning the practice of virtue in an exalted manner, which will bring us happiness and peace, The Church is constantly urging her members to the practice of virtue. The first condition required in the process of canonization, or declaring one a saint, is to prove that this person practiced the theological and moral virtues in an heroic or extraordinary degree.

RESOLUTION: Resolve to make progress in virtue every day. It is best to center one's attention on a particular virtue, especially that which we find most difficult to practice, and perform acts of this virtue whenever the opportunity is offered.

STUDY HELPS

A. TRUE OR FALSE. (*Check each of the following statements as either true or false. The correct answers can be found in the previous portions of the lesson.*)

	TRUE	FALSE
(1) We shall retain faith and hope in heaven.	.....	.....
(2) It is not necessary that we have more feeling in our love for God than in our love for men.	.....	.....
(3) A baptized infant possesses the theological virtues.	.....	.....
(4) A baptized infant possesses the natural moral virtues.	.....	.....
(5) A baptized infant possesses the supernatural moral virtues.	.....	.....
(6) To make an act of charity toward God we must repent of all our venial sins.	.....	.....
(7) The gifts of the Holy Ghost are given only in Confirmation.	.....	.....
(8) The best examples of fortitude are the martyrs.	.....	.....
(9) Religion is classed under fortitude.	.....	.....
(10) We must love our neighbor as much as we love ourselves.	.....	.....

B. PROBLEMS AND EXERCISES. (*Answer the questions orally or write them as your teacher may direct*):

(1) Enumerate the chief supernatural powers that accompany sanctifying grace in our souls.

(2) Dolores has a well-merited reputation for being a virtuous girl. In a paragraph of three or four sentences explain what is meant by the expression 'virtuous girl.'

(3) Kent is an avowed atheist; but he is extremely honest in paying every penny he owes. What kind of virtue is he practicing, if any?

(4) Virginia's catechism paper would have come back marked 100% instead of 95% had she known St. Paul's text to the Corinthians, wherein charity is called the greatest of the virtues. What is that text?

(5) Kevin often quotes approvingly the expression: "Seeing is believing!" Is this true? Explain your answer.

(6) Susan, orphaned in childhood, is now a grown-up woman, without any form of religion. She believes in God, and reads the Bible regularly and reverently. Philomena, a Catholic girl of 12, runs errands for Susan. Yesterday Susan asked Philomena if God has any agency on earth doing His work and preserving His revealed truths. How would you answer Susan's question?

(7) Leo frequently makes acts of love for God, but he wonders if they are genuine acts of charity, because he does not feel any great fervor. Explain to him how these acts can be true acts of charity.

(8) Herman says that he would never do his neighbor any harm, but he would not put himself to any inconvenience to help anyone in need. Do you think he has the kind of love for his neighbor that Our Lord expects him to have?

(9) Yearly you hear read a parable that illustrates the love of our neighbor. What parable is it?

(10) Edith and Mabel, playmates, have a falling-out because Edith falsely accused Mabel of stealing a valuable wrist-watch from a classmate. Must Mabel continue to love Edith as her neighbor? Does that love imply an approval of Edith's injustice? Must Edith right the wrong she has done Mabel? With each answer, add a short explanation.

(11) Clement, Gerard and Alphonsus, 3 pals, are given ten apples by a friendly farmer. Clement keeps five for himself because he is the oldest and biggest of the three; three he gives to Gerard, and the remaining two he hands to Alphonsus, the smallest and the youngest of the trio. In his night prayers that night, Clement pauses when he reaches ". . . and I love my neighbor as myself for the love of Thee . . ." He wonders if he can truly say these words after what he did earlier in the day when sharing the apples. Tell him what to do, and why.

(12) Celine finds it hard to love her Protestant, Jewish and pagan neighbors in the same measure as she loves her own family and cousins. Her grandparents were all born in France. On that account she loves the French people more than those of any other nation except our own. Do any of her ideas on charity need correcting? State the reason for your solution.

(13) Lambert, the brightest boy in the sixth grade, claims he is not smarter than most of the boys in his class because he has any better brains but because perhaps he studies a little longer than most of them, and prays a bit more earnestly to the Holy Ghost and to Our Lady, Seat of Wisdom. In from 50 to 75 words let us know what you think of his theory.

(14) Regina wants to know if devotion to the Holy Ghost will help her become a saint? Answer her question, and add the reason why you think so.

(15) Enumerate any six of the moral virtues and give short definitions of them.

(16) What is an inspiration of the Holy Spirit?

(17) In this lesson you have learned that faith and hope will cease when the soul enters heaven, because it then sees and possesses God, and we cannot believe what we see nor hope for what we have. Do you think that the souls in purgatory have faith and hope? Do you think that faith and hope are present in the souls of any of those who are being punished in hell? Did the angels have faith and hope before they were submitted to the test whereby God tried their loyalty?

The Catholic Church

"I BELIEVE IN . . . THE HOLY CATHOLIC CHURCH . . ."

136. What is the Church?

The Church is the congregation of all baptized persons united in the same true faith, the same sacrifice, and the same sacraments, under the authority of the Sovereign Pontiff and the bishops in communion with him.

(a) Since Baptism, according to the ruling of Christ, is the gateway to the Church, a person becomes a member of the Church on receiving this sacrament. To remain a real member of the Church after Baptism a person must profess the one true faith and must not withdraw from the unity of the body of the Church in schism or heresy or be excommunicated by legitimate authority because of serious sins. Even schismatics, heretics, and those excommunicated are subjects of the Church and are obliged by its laws unless exempted by the Church.

(b) Sacred Scripture refers to the Church as the Body of Christ, as a sheepfold, as the kingdom of God, and as the kingdom of heaven.

SCRIPTURE:

"The kingdom of heaven is like a man who sowed good seed in his field . . . " (*Matthew 13:24*).

"But if I cast out devils by the finger of God, then the kingdom of God has come upon you" (*Luke 11:20*).

"I am the good shepherd, and I know mine and mine know me, even as the Father knows me and I know the Father; and I lay down my life for my sheep. And other sheep I have that are not of this fold. Them also I must bring, and they shall hear my voice, and there shall be one fold and one shepherd" (*John 10:14-16*).

"For as the body is one and has many members, and all the members of the body, many as they are, form one body, so also is it with Christ. . . . Now you are the body of Christ, member for member" (*I Corinthians 12:12, 27*).

" . . . one body and one Spirit, even as you were called in one hope of your calling; one Lord, one faith, one Baptism; one God and Father of all" (*Ephesians 4:4-6*).

137. Who founded the Church?

Jesus Christ founded the Church.

(a) Christ completed the founding of His Church just before His Ascension, when He commissioned the apostles to make disciples of all nations. Earlier in His public ministry He had instituted the sacraments, chosen the twelve apostles, instructed them by word and example, and conferred on them the power of teaching, ruling, and sanctifying.

(b) The Gospels show that Christ founded the Church in the form of a visible, hierarchical society, that is, one made up of subjects and superiors

78

who rightfully rule subjects. The Roman Pontiff and the bishops under him are the ruling hierarchy of the Church. The Church is also a monarchical society in which the Pope rules with full power, that is, with jurisdiction over the entire Church. Peter was the first head of the Church founded by Christ.

(c) After Pentecost Sunday the apostles began to carry out their mission, which through them and their successors continues and will continue until the end of time.

SCRIPTURE:

"And I say to thee, thou art Peter, and upon this rock I will build my Church, and the gates of hell shall not prevail against it" (*Matthew 16:18*).

"And Jesus drew near and spoke to them saying, 'All power in heaven and on earth has been given to me. Go, therefore, and make disciples of all nations, baptizing them in the name of the Father, and of the Son, and of the Holy Spirit, teaching them to observe all that I have commanded you; and behold, I am with you all days, even unto the consummation of the world' " (*Matthew 28:18-20*).

" . . . Christ also loved the Church, and delivered himself up for her, that he might sanctify her, cleansing her in the bath of water by means of the word; in order that he might present to himself the Church in all her glory, not having spot or wrinkle or any such thing, but that she might be holy and without blemish" (*Ephesians 5:25-27*).

138. Why did Jesus Christ found the Church?

Jesus Christ founded the Church to bring all men to eternal salvation.

(a) The Church instituted by Christ is the only way to eternal salvation. Christ gave the Church the means whereby man can be sanctified and saved.

SCRIPTURE:

"My sheep hear my voice, and I know them and they follow me. And I give them everlasting life; and they shall never perish, neither shall anyone snatch them out of my hand" (*John 10:27-28*).

"As the Father has sent me, I also send you" (*John 20:21*).

"For the grace of God our Savior has appeared to all men, instructing us, in order that, rejecting ungodliness and worldly lusts, we may live temperately and justly and piously in this world; looking for the blessed hope and glorious coming of our great God and Savior, Jesus Christ, who gave himself for us that he might redeem us from all iniquity and cleanse for himself an acceptable people, pursuing good works" (*Titus 2:11-14*).

139. How is the Church enabled to lead men to salvation?

The Church is enabled to lead men to salvation by the indwelling of the Holy Ghost, who gives it life.

(a) Although the work of salvation is the result of the operation of all three Persons of the Blessed Trinity, it is especially the result of the Redemption by Christ, and because this work is one of divine love it is attributed to the Holy Ghost, who is the soul of the Church, of which Christ is the Head.

"But you shall receive power when the Holy Spirit comes upon you, and you shall be witnesses for me in Jerusalem and in all Judea and Samaria and even to the very ends of the earth" (*Acts 1:8*).

140. When was the dwelling of the Holy Ghost in the Church first visibly manifested?

The dwelling of the Holy Ghost in the Church was first visibly manifested on Pentecost Sunday, when He came down upon the apostles in the form of tongues of fire.

(a) The word "Pentecost" means fiftieth and is applied to the fiftieth day after Our Lord's Resurrection.

(b) The apostles were sent by Christ to preach His doctrines to all men.

SCRIPTURE:

"And when the days of Pentecost were drawing to a close, they were all together in one place. And suddenly there came a sound from heaven, as of a violent wind blowing, and it filled the whole house where they were sitting. And there appeared to them parted tongues as of fire, which settled upon each of them. And they were all filled with the Holy Spirit and began to speak in foreign tongues, even as the Holy Spirit prompted them to speak" (*Acts 2:1-4*).

141. How long will the Holy Ghost dwell in the Church?

The Holy Ghost will dwell in the Church until the end of time.

(a) Christ foretold that the Holy Ghost would dwell in the Church until the end of time.

SCRIPTURE:

"And I will ask the Father and he will give you another Advocate to dwell with you forever, the Spirit of truth whom the world cannot receive, because it neither sees him nor knows him. But you shall know him, because he will dwell with you, and be in you" (*John 14:16-17*).

142. Who sent the Holy Ghost to dwell in the Church?

God the Father and God the Son sent the Holy Ghost to dwell in the Church.

(a) It is a matter of faith that the Holy Ghost proceeds from the Father and the Son and is sent by Both to dwell in the Church.

SCRIPTURE:

"But the Advocate, the Holy Spirit, whom the Father will send in my name, he will teach you all things, and bring to your mind whatever I have said to you" (*John 14:26*).

"But when the Advocate has come, whom I will send you from the Father, the Spirit of truth who proceeds from the Father, he will bear witness concerning me" (*John 15:26*).

"It is expedient for you that I depart. For if I do not go, the Advocate will not come to you; but if I go, I will send him to you" (*John 16:7*).

143. What does the indwelling of the Holy Ghost enable the Church to do?

The indwelling of the Holy Ghost enables the Church to teach, to sanctify, and to rule the faithful in the name of Christ.

80

(a) The Church must teach because otherwise men would not know the truths of divine revelation taught by Christ.

(b) The Church must sanctify, that is, bring grace to the world through the sacraments, because otherwise men could not be saved.

(c) The Church must rule because it was established by Our Saviour as a society, which is inconceivable without authority.

SCRIPTURE:

"But when he, the Spirit of truth, has come, he will teach you all the truth. For he will not speak on his own authority, but whatever he will hear he will speak, and the things that are to come he will declare to you. He will glorify me, because he will receive of what is mine and declare it to you" (*John 16:13-14*).

"Guard the good trust through the Holy Spirit, who dwells in us" (*II Timothy 1:14*).

144. What is meant by teaching, sanctifying, and ruling in the name of Christ?

By teaching, sanctifying, and ruling in the name of Christ is meant that the Church always does the will of its Divine Founder, who remains forever its invisible Head.

(a) The will of the Founder of the Church is expressed in the commission He gave to His apostles to teach all nations, to baptize them, and to have them observe all the things He had commanded. This commission, as well as the guarantee that Christ would be with His Church until the end of time, is related in the Gospel.[12]

145. To whom did Christ give the power to teach, to sanctify, and to rule the members of His Church?

Christ gave the power to teach, to sanctify, and to rule the members of His Church to the apostles, the first bishops of the Church.

(a) That Christ gave His apostles the power to teach, to rule, and to sanctify is evident from the Gospels, the inspired account of Our Lord's life written by Saints Matthew, Mark, Luke, and John. Christ gave the apostles the power to bind and loose, to baptize, to forgive sin, and to offer the sacrifice of the Mass.

(b) The power to teach and to rule is the power of jurisdiction; the power to sanctify is the power of orders. The power to sanctify sometimes requires jurisdiction, as in the sacrament of Penance.

SCRIPTURE:

"Go into the whole world and preach the gospel to every creature" (*Mark 16:15*).

"He who hears you, hears me; and he who rejects you, rejects me; and he who rejects me, rejects him who sent me" (*Luke 10:16*).

"He therefore said to them again, 'Peace be to you! As the Father has sent me, I also send you.' When he had said this, he breathed upon them, and said

---

12. See question 137.

81

to them, 'Receive the Holy Spirit; whose sins you shall forgive, they are forgiven them; and whose sins you shall retain, they are retained' " (*John 20:21-23*).

"You shall receive power when the Holy Spirit comes upon you, and you shall be witnesses for me in Jerusalem and in all Judea and Samaria and even to the very ends of the earth" (*Acts 1:8*).

146. Did Christ intend that this power should be exercised by the apostles alone?

No, Christ intended that this power should be exercised also by their successors, the bishops of the Church.

(a) Christ founded the Church to last until the end of time. The apostles lived for a short time only. Christ must, then, have intended that the apostles provide duly authorized successors to carry on the work of teaching, sanctifying, and ruling.

(b) The Acts of the Apostles and the Epistles of Saint Paul contain references to the work done by the successors of the apostles.

SCRIPTURE:
"And they prayed and said, 'Thou, Lord, who knowest the hearts of all, show which of these two thou hast chosen to take the place in this ministry and apostleship from which Judas fell away to go to his own place.' And they drew lots between them, and the lot fell upon Matthias; and he was numbered with the eleven apostles" (*Acts 1:24-26*).

"This saying is true: If anyone is eager for the office of bishop, he desires a good work" (*I Timothy 3:1*).

"For this reason I left thee in Crete, that thou shouldst set right anything that is defective and shouldst appoint presbyters in every city, as I myself directed thee to do" (*Titus 1:5*).

147. Did Christ give special power in His Church to any one of the apostles?

Christ gave special power in His Church to Saint Peter by making him the head of the apostles and the chief teacher and ruler of the entire Church.

(a) The power of the keys was promised to Saint Peter and was actually conferred on him.

(b) Saint Peter was recognized by the early Christians from the beginning as the head of the Church.

SCRIPTURE:
"Then Jesus answered and said, 'Blessed art thou, Simon Bar-Jona, for flesh and blood has not revealed this to thee, but my Father in heaven. And I say to thee, thou art Peter, and upon this rock I will build my Church, and the gates of hell shall not prevail against it. And I will give thee the keys of the kingdom of heaven; and whatever thou shalt bind on earth shall be bound in heaven, and whatever thou shalt loose on earth shall be loosed in heaven' " (*Matthew 16:17-19*).

"And the Lord said, 'Simon, Simon, behold, Satan has desired to have you, that he may sift you as wheat. But I have prayed for thee, that thy faith may not fail; and do thou, when once thou hast turned again, strengthen thy brethren' " (*Luke 22:31-32*).

"When, therefore, they had breakfasted, Jesus said to Simon Peter, 'Simon, son of John, dost thou love me more than these do?' He said to him, 'Yes, Lord, thou knowest that I love thee.' He said to him, 'Feed my lambs.' He said to him a second time, 'Simon, son of John, dost thou love me?' He said to him, 'Yes, Lord, thou knowest that I love thee.' He said to him, 'Feed my lambs.' A third time he said to him, 'Simon, son of John, dost thou love me?' Peter was grieved because he said to him for the third time, 'Dost thou love me?' And he said to him, 'Lord, thou knowest all things, thou knowest that I love thee.' He said to him, 'Feed my sheep' " (*John 21:15-17*).

"In those days Peter stood up in the midst of the brethren" (*Acts 1:15*).

"But Peter, standing up with the Eleven, lifted up his voice and spoke out to them" (*Acts 2:14*).

148. Did Christ intend that the special power of chief teacher and ruler of the entire Church should be exercised by Saint Peter alone?

Christ did not intend that the special power of chief teacher and ruler of the entire Church should be exercised by Saint Peter alone, but intended that this power should be passed down to his successor, the Pope, the Bishop of Rome, who is the Vicar of Christ on earth and the visible head of the Church.

(a) A successor to Saint Peter, the first Bishop of Rome, was required as chief teacher and ruler for the same reason that successors were required for the other apostles. From the very beginning it was acknowledged by the Church that the successor of Saint Peter as Bishop of Rome was at the same time the head of the entire Church. This successor of Saint Peter is called the Pope.

(b) The bishops of the Church are the successors of the apostles because they have received their power of orders by valid consecration through an unbroken line of successors of the apostles, and have received their power of jurisdiction through their union with the Pope, the successor of Saint Peter.

(c) The Pope is now elected by the College of Cardinals.

149. Who assist the bishops in the care of souls?

The priests, especially parish priests, assist the bishops in the care of souls.

(a) Although all priests assist the bishop of a diocese in the care of souls, parish priests especially are given the definite care of a section of a diocese, which is called a parish and is of ecclesiastical institution.

SCRIPTURE:
"And when they had appointed presbyters for them in each church, with prayer and fasting, they commended them to the Lord in whom they had believed" (*Acts 14:22*).

150. Who are the laity of the Church?

The laity of the Church are all its members who do not belong to the clerical or to the religious state.

(a) The clerical state includes all priests and all aspirants to the priest-hood who have received tonsure, which is the initiation into the ecclesias-

83a

The Confession of St. Peter

This picture shows Our Lord Jesus handing over the keys to St. Peter, as a sign of the power which He was giving him to forgive sins or to retain them, as shown in the account of St. Matthew:

"Now Jesus, having come into the district of Caesarea Philippi, began to ask His disciples, saying, 'Who do men say the Son of Man is?' But they said, 'Some say, John the Baptist; and others, Elias; and others, Jeremias, or one of the prophets.' He said to them, 'But who do you say that I am?' Simon Peter answered and said, 'Thou art the Christ, the Son of the living God.' Then Jesus answered and said, 'Blessed art thou, Simon Bar-Jona, for flesh and blood has not revealed this to thee, but My Father in heaven. And I say to thee, thou art Peter, and upon this rock I will build my Church, and the gates of hell shall not prevail against it. And I will give thee the keys of the kingdom of heaven; and whatever thou shalt bind on earth shall be bound in heaven, and whatever thou shalt loose on earth shall be loosed in heaven.' Then He strictly charged His disciples to tell no one that He was Jesus the Christ." (St. Matthew 16:13-20)

tical state. Students of minor and major seminaries are aspirants to the priesthood.

(b) The religious state includes men and women who embrace a community life and make the vows of poverty, chastity, and obedience. Those who are preparing to embrace the religious state are called aspirants, postulants, or novices.

(c) Religious and clerics enjoy special canonical privileges and have many more obligations than lay people have.

(d) Among the laity are secular persons who have embraced the state of celibacy or virginity, or the matrimonial state.

151. How can the laity help the Church in her care of souls?

The laity can help the Church in her care of souls by leading lives that will reflect credit on the Church, and by co-operating with their bishops and priests, especially through Catholic Action.

(a) The lay people can assist in a special way by prayer.

(b) Catholic Action is the participation of the laity in the apostolate of the hierarchy of the Church. There can be no Catholic Action without an episcopal commission.

SCRIPTURE:

"Even so let your light shine before men, in order that they may see your good works and give glory to your Father in heaven" (*Matthew 5:16*).

"I entreat Evodia and I exhort Syntyche to be of one mind in the Lord. And I beseech thee also, my loyal comrade, help them, for they have toiled with me in the gospel, as have Clement and the rest of my fellow-workers whose names are in the book of life" (*Philippians 4:2-3*).

"Behave yourselves honorably among the pagans; that, whereas they slander you as evildoers, they may, through observing you, by reason of your good works glorify God in the day of visitation" (*I Peter 2:12*).

IMPORTANT TRUTHS ABOUT THE CATHOLIC CHURCH

One of the most important articles of faith in the Catholic religion is the doctrine that Jesus Christ in the course of His lifetime on earth established a Church—that is, a visible organization which was to continue His work of bringing men to salvation until the end of time. This Church was to be an extension of Christ's own life and activities down through the ages. The account of Our Lord's life contained in the Gospel clearly indicates that He founded such an organization. He often spoke of it; He chose the apostles and disciples to be the first members of the Church; as time went on He made it clear that in the Church there were to be rulers who would teach, sanctify and govern the others; He made the apostles the first superiors of the Church, and gave them the power they needed for their office; He indicated that this power was to continue in their successors until the end of the world. As the chief of the apostles and the head of the Church, Christ chose Simon Peter. That Peter was to be the ruler of all the faithful, Christ frequently indicated, speaking of him as the foundation-stone of the Church (*Matthew 16:18*), giving him the commission to feed His lambs and His sheep—that is, the members of the Church (*John 21:17*)—saying to him: "I will give thee the keys of the kingdom of heaven" (*Matthew 16:19*). He gave Peter supervision over the other apostles, saying: "When once thou hast turned again, strengthen thy brethren" (*Luke 22:32*).

Such was the Church as Christ founded it; and such it continues to be today. The Catholic Church has remained the Church of Christ for more than nineteen centuries. It is ruled by the Pope, the successor of St. Peter and by the bishops, the successors of the other apostles. They exercise their authority in the name of Christ. To them He says, as He said to the apostles: "He who hears you hears me" (Luke 10:16). Whatever may be their personal abilities or disabilities, their perfections or imperfections, they teach and rule the faithful with power that comes to them from Our Lord Himself. And the members of the Church, clerical, religious and lay, are obliged to show them respect and obedience and to co-operate with their efforts toward the spread of the kingdom of Christ.

We call that portion of the Church that is governed by a bishop a diocese. The place from which the bishop teaches and rules is called a see—for example, the see of New York, the see of Boston. The see of the Pope in Rome, because of his special dignity and authority, is called the Holy See. Every diocese is divided into parishes, and the priest in charge is called the pastor or parish priest. The priests who aid him are called assistants or curates.

If the Church were a merely human organization, it could not have survived for nineteen hundred years. But the Church is a divine organization founded by the Son of God, receiving its life from the Holy Ghost, who on Pentecost came down upon the apostles, the first bishops, to give them light and strength, and to dwell in the Church, as its soul, until the end of time. As members of the Church we all share in this divine life.

These thoughts should urge us to be faithful to our obligations as Catholics. We should unhesitatingly accept the teachings of the Church, make use of the means of holiness the Church provides, and obey all the Church's laws, with the conviction that Christ Himself is teaching, sanctifying and ruling us through His representatives, the superiors of the Church. Above all, we should always be loyal to the Pope, the Vicar, or earthly representative, of Jesus Christ.

RESOLUTION: Resolve to say a special prayer at Sunday Mass and after Holy Communion for the Pope and for the freedom and exaltation of the Church.

STUDY HELPS

A. WORD SELECTION. (Select the word or phrase which most exactly and most completely fills out the sentence):

(1) The Holy Ghost began to dwell in the Church on (Good Friday . . . Easter Sunday . . . Pentecost).

(2) The Pope is elected by (the bishops . . . the cardinals . . . the people of Vatican City).

(3) The Pope uses his power of (teaching . . . sanctifying . . . ruling) when he appoints a priest to be a bishop.

(4) St. Peter was the first bishop of (Rome . . . Corinth . . . Jerusalem).

(5) Christ completed the founding of His Church (at His death . . . when He rose from the dead . . . just before His Ascension into heaven).

(6) A person becomes a Catholic (by professing the Catholic faith . . . by receiving Baptism . . . by acknowledging the supreme spiritual power of the Pope).

(7) The soul of the Church is (sanctifying grace . . . Jesus Christ . . . the Holy Ghost).

(8) Our Lord promised to give the power of the keys to (St. Peter . . . St. John . . . all the apostles).

(9) Novices are (candidates for the priesthood . . . those preparing to enter the religious state . . . those who have taken the vows of religion).

(10) Initiation into the clerical state takes place through (entrance into a seminary . . . ordination . . . reception of the tonsure).

B. PROBLEMS AND EXERCISES. (*Answer the questions orally or write them as your teacher may direct*):

(1) Blanche, the daughter of a Christian Scientist, is interested in our Church. In your own words, explain to her when Our Lord started the Catholic Church.

(2) Carl, a Lutheran Sunday-School boy, tells Patrick, a Catholic playmate, that he has read through his New Testament three times already, and he does not remember reading in it anything about the "Roman Catholic Church." Did Our Lord call His Church the "Roman Catholic Church?" By what names did He call it?

(3) Out in the lonely farming district where Miriam lives, each Summer a traveling minister erects a gospel tent which he calls the "Pentecost Tabernacle." Miriam is the only Catholic pupil in the seventh grade of the district school. When the teacher asked the class if anyone knew the meaning of 'Pentecost' not one child, including Miriam, knew the answer. Should Miriam have been able to answer correctly? Why?

(4) Lucius asks if any of the books of the Bible speak about bishops who were the successors of the apostles. Can you name any such books?

(5) Christopher is an ardent baseball fan. From memory, he can name the lineups of the sixteen clubs in the National and the American Leagues. The other day in a religion test he could give the names of only nine of the apostles. How many apostles did Our Lord choose, and what are their names? Do their names appear in the Mass? Where?

(6) What power did Our Lord give the apostles when He said to them: "Go ye into the whole world and preach the Gospel to every creature."?

(7) Does the Holy Ghost dwell in the Church today? Can you name any facts that indicate His indwelling in the Church?

(8) How many inspired accounts have we of Our Lord's life and works and sayings? Were all of them penned directly by apostles? Explain your answer.

(9) When did the apostles receive the command to say Holy Mass and to hear confessions? In carrying out these commands of Our Lord what power were the apostles exercising toward the first Christians?

(10) What is the difference between the power of orders and the power of jurisdiction? In which of the sacraments must both be employed? Which of these two powers does a bishop exercise when he ordains a man to the priesthood? When he sends a letter to be read to the people of the diocese? When he dispenses a person from the law of fasting?

(11) Name the present bishop of your diocese. When was he consecrated bishop? Do you know the name of the bishop who consecrated him? Does his power come to him from one of the apostles?

(12) Can you explain to a person who is not a Catholic the meaning of these terms: diocese; see; seminary; postulant; parish; Catholic Action?

The Marks and Attributes of the Church

152. Which is the one true Church established by Christ?

The one true Church established by Christ is the Catholic Church.

(a) Many churches which claim to be Christian have broken away from the one true Church established by Jesus Christ. These churches were founded by men who had no authority from God to found a church.

(b) Christ intended that there should be only one true Christian Church, for He always spoke of His Church as one.

SCRIPTURE:

"And other sheep I have that are not of this fold. Them also I must bring, and they shall hear my voice, and there shall be one fold and one shepherd" (*John 10:16*).

153. How do we know that the Catholic Church is the one true Church established by Christ?

We know that the Catholic Church is the one true Church established by Christ because it alone has the marks of the true Church.

SCRIPTURE:

"Holy Father, keep in thy name those whom thou hast given me, that they may be one even as we are" (*John 17:11*).

"Sanctify them in the truth. Thy word is truth. Even as thou hast sent me into the world, so I also have sent them into the world. And for them I sanctify myself, that they also may be sanctified in truth.

"Yet not for these only do I pray, but for those also who through their word are to believe in me, that all may be one, even as thou, Father, in me and I in thee; that they also may be one in us, that the world may believe that thou hast sent me" (*John 17:17-21*).

See Scripture, question 137, Matthew 16:18; 28:18-20.

154. What do we mean by the marks of the Church?

By the marks of the Church we mean certain clear signs by which all men can recognize it as the true Church founded by Jesus Christ.

(a) Jesus Christ willed that the true Church should have these marks, which would distinguish it from all false religions.

155. What are the chief marks of the Church?

The chief marks of the Church are four: It is one, holy, catholic or universal, and apostolic.

(a) Sacred Scripture teaches that the one true Church of Christ must have these marks.

(b) The marks of the Church are themselves an indication that God guides the Church.

156. Why is the Catholic Church one?

The Catholic Church is one because all its members, according to the will of Christ, profess the same faith, have the same sacrifice and sacraments, and are united under one and the same visible head, the Pope.

(a) Our Divine Saviour prayed explicitly that His Church might be one, and He made it one; thus men can recognize it as the true Church.

(b) Only the Catholic Church possesses this mark of unity. Various sects, having only fragments of Christianity, are divided in doctrine and practice and recognize no authority but their own judgment, which can easily lead them into error.

(c) There are many religious sects which claim to be Christian, but are separated from the unity of Christ by their rejection of the authority invested by Him in the Roman Pontiff, the successor to Saint Peter.

(d) Catholics accept all the doctrines of faith and morals which were taught by Our Lord and the apostles and are proposed by the Church for belief and practice. A person who deliberately denies even one of the doctrines of the Church cannot be a Catholic. The Church is one in faith.

(e) Catholics take part in the same sacrifice of the Mass and accept the same sacraments, although the same language and the same ceremonies are not used by all in the offering of Mass and in the administration of the sacraments. Everywhere the essential parts of the ceremonies are the same and substantially the same words are used in offering Mass. Hence the Church is one in worship. What Christ determined, the Church cannot change. Since Christ, however, did not determine many points of worship in non-essential matters, the Church has the authority to do so.

(f) Catholics are subject to their respective bishops who rule them. They must recognize the supreme authority of the Pope in matters of religion. A person who deliberately refuses to accept the legitimate and supreme authority of the Pope and the bishops in matters of religion cannot be a Catholic.

SCRIPTURE:
"For from the rising of the sun even to the going down, my name is great among the Gentiles: and in every place there is sacrifice and there is offered to my name a clean oblation" (*Malachias 1:11*).

"For just as in one body we have many members, yet all the members have not the same function, so we, the many, are one body in Christ, but severally members one of another" (*Romans 12:4-5*).

"Because the bread is one, we though many, are one body, all of us who partake of the one bread" (*I Corinthians 10:17*).

" ... one body and one Spirit, even as you were called in one hope of your calling; one Lord, one faith, one Baptism; one God and Father of all, who is above all, and throughout all, and in us all" (*Ephesians 4:4-6*).

See Scripture, question 152.

157. Why is the Catholic Church holy?

The Catholic Church is holy because it was founded by Jesus Christ, who is all-holy, and because it teaches, according to

88

the will of Christ, holy doctrines, and provides the means of leading a holy life, thereby giving holy members to every age.

(a) Holiness is a mark of the Church according to the will of Christ, as is evident from the prayer of Christ for His apostles.

(b) Even some of the enemies of the Church recognize the holiness of the doctrines which the Church teaches. The efforts of others to prove that the Church is not holy show that they acknowledge holiness as a mark of truth.

(c) The lives of the saints, of the martyrs, and of good Catholics prove how effective are the means of grace with which the Church is endowed. Moreover, God has always favored the Catholic Church with miracles.

(d) Bad Catholics do not disprove the holiness of the Church since they do not use the means of grace at their disposal. Christ foretold that there would be good and bad members of His Church as we read in the parables of the fishes in the net and the cockle among the wheat.

SCRIPTURE:
"Beware of false prophets, who come to you in sheep's clothing, but inwardly are ravenous wolves. By their fruits you will know them. Do men gather grapes from thorns, or figs from thistles? Even so, every good tree bears good fruit, but the bad tree bears bad fruit. A good tree cannot bear bad fruit, nor can a bad tree bear good fruit. Every tree that does not bear good fruit is cut down and thrown into the fire. Therefore, by their fruits you will know them" (*Matthew 7:15-20*).

". . . looking for the blessed hope and glorious coming of our great God and Savior, Jesus Christ, who gave himself for us that he might redeem us from all iniquity and cleanse for himself an acceptable people, pursuing good works" (*Titus 2:13-14*).

"And you know that he appeared to take our sins away, and sin is not in him" (*I John 3:5*).

See Scripture, question 153, John 17:17-21.

158. Why is the Catholic Church catholic or universal?

The Catholic Church is catholic or universal because, destined to last for all time, it never fails to fulfill the divine commandment to teach all nations all the truths revealed by God.

(a) Catholicity is a mark of the Church because Christ commissioned His apostles to go forth and make disciples of all nations, and to teach all that He had commanded. Christ further promised to be with them all days, even to the end of time.

(b) The Church today teaches the same doctrine it received from Christ. It has existed uninterruptedly since the day it was established down to the present time. The Church exists in a more flourishing condition in some nations than in others. It is always trying to preach the gospel to all races and in all places and sends its missioners to the most remote places on earth.

(c) Christian sects began later and for the most part exist in only some sections of the world. In trying to accommodate themselves to the changing conditions of the time, they have made changes in the doctrines of Christ without any divine authorization.

"And this gospel of the kingdom shall be preached in the whole world, for a witness to all nations; and then will come the end" (*Matthew 24:14*).

"And he said to them, 'Go into the whole world and preach the gospel to every creature. He who believes and is baptized shall be saved, but he who does not believe shall be condemned'" (*Mark 16:15-16*).

"But you shall receive power when the Holy Spirit comes upon you, and you shall be witnesses for me in Jerusalem and in all Judea and Samaria and even to the very ends of the earth" (*Acts 1:8*).

"Faith then depends on hearing, and hearing on the word of Christ. But I say: Have they not heard? Yes, indeed, 'Their voice has gone forth into all the earth, and their words unto the ends of the world'" (*Romans 10:17-18*).

See Scripture, question, 137, Matthew 28:19-20.

159. Why is the Catholic Church apostolic?

The Catholic Church is apostolic because it was founded by Christ on the apostles and, according to His divine will, has always been governed by their lawful successors.

(a) The true Church is apostolic because it is the Church Christ founded upon the apostles, and especially upon Peter whom He called the Rock on which the Church would be built. The supreme power of Saint Peter in the Church has been passed down through the unbroken line of his successors in the see of Rome.

SCRIPTURE:
"And I say to thee, thou art Peter, and upon this rock I will build my Church, and the gates of hell shall not prevail against it" (*Matthew 16:18*).

"Therefore, you are now no longer strangers and foreigners, but you are citizens with the saints and members of God's household: you are built upon the foundation of the apostles and prophets with Christ Jesus himself as the chief cornerstone" (*Ephesians 2:19-20*).

160. How do we know that no other church but the Catholic Church is the true Church of Christ?

We know that no other church but the Catholic Church is the true Church of Christ because no other church has these four marks.

(a) All other churches lack essential unity. They recognize no authority in religious matters vested in an individual who is the vicar of Christ. In the worship of God many Christian sects are guided more by sentiment and personal conviction than by the objective truths given to the world by Our Lord.

(b) The founders of Christian sects were not saints and generally were not holy or edifying men. The sects have not given saints to the world. Their truths are but fragments of the doctrines of the Catholic Church. The holiness of their members is due to the means that the sects have salvaged from Catholic worship. Moreover, these sects cannot point to miracles wrought in their favor.

(c) Not one of the Christian sects is universal or catholic; that is, not one has universality such as that of the Catholic Church.

(d) Not one of the Christian sects can trace its origin to the apostles.

(e) The Greek Orthodox or Schismatic Church began in the ninth century with its rejection of the authority of the Pope. From it have come various national churches, subject in some degree to civil authority. The Protestant churches began in the sixteenth century when their founders, rejecting certain doctrines of faith, broke away from Catholic unity. Many Protestant denominations are offshoots of the earliest sects. The Lutherans were founded by Martin Luther, the Presbyterians by John Knox, and the Methodists by John Wesley.

161. What are the chief attributes of the Catholic Church?

The chief attributes of the Catholic Church are authority, infallibility, and indefectibility. They are called attributes because they are qualities perfecting the nature of the Church.

162. What is meant by the authority of the Catholic Church?

By the authority of the Catholic Church is meant that the Pope and the bishops, as the lawful successors of the apostles, have power from Christ Himself to teach, to sanctify, and to govern the faithful in spiritual matters.

(a) Christ Himself gave this authority to Saint Peter and the other apostles when He bestowed the power of binding and loosing, of teaching and baptizing. He implicitly guaranteed the same power to the successors of the apostles when He promised to be with them all days, even to the consummation of the world.

(b) Outside the Church there generally is no real recognition of authority in spiritual matters and this disregard for spiritual authority has lessened the respect for civil and domestic authority.

(c) The Church has authority over temporal matters which are closely connected with spiritual matters, as the administration of Church property.

(d) The Pope, as the supreme head of the Church, cannot rightly be made a subject of any temporal power on earth. The present position of the Pope, as head of the Vatican City, shows to the world that he and his household are not the subjects of other temporal powers. When we speak of the temporal power of the Pope, we do not mean thereby merely to classify him with earthly rulers. The Pope's temporal power is a means to an end, guaranteeing that freedom of word and action which he must rightfully enjoy as the supreme spiritual ruler of the Church.

SCRIPTURE:

"And if he refuse to hear them, appeal to the Church, but if he refuse to hear even the Church, let him be to thee as the heathen and the publican" (*Matthew 18:17*).

"Take heed to yourselves and to the whole flock in which the Holy Spirit has placed you as bishops, to rule the Church of God, which he has purchased with his own blood" (*Acts 20:28*).

"On behalf of Christ, therefore, we are acting as ambassadors, God, as it were, appealing through us" (*II Corinthians 5:20*).

See Scripture, question 147, Matthew 16:17-19; question 158, Mark 16:15-16.

91

163. What is meant by the infallibility of the Catholic Church?

By the infallibility of the Catholic Church is meant that the Church, by the special assistance of the Holy Ghost, cannot err when it teaches or believes a doctrine of faith or morals.

(a) Infallibility, especially papal infallibility, is a doctrine often misunderstood and derided by those outside the Church. The term "infallibility" is often distorted to mean impeccability, that is, freedom from all sin. The Church has never held that the Pope cannot sin.

(b) It is unthinkable that an institution established by God for the salvation of souls could lead men into error and turn them away from God. If the Church could and did err in matters of faith or morals, it would not be a true teacher; it would fail in its ministry of sanctification and would not lead men to salvation but would be responsible for their condemnation.

(c) A doctrine of faith or morals is a truth revealed by God dealing with what we must believe or what we must do in order to be saved.

(d) The Church cannot change its defined teachings on faith and morals, though it may restate them more clearly and more completely.

(e) We know that the Church is infallible in matters of faith or morals because Christ promised that He would be with the apostles and their successors in their work of teaching until the end of time. It would be impossible for Christ to be with the official teachers of the Church and permit them to teach error.

SCRIPTURE:

"And I will ask the Father and he will give you another Advocate to dwell with you forever, the Spirit of truth" (*John 14:16*).

"But the Advocate, the Holy Spirit, whom the Father will send in my name, he will teach you all things, and bring to your mind whatever I have said to you" (*John 14:26*).

See Scripture, question 143, John 16:13-14; question 147, Luke 22:31-32.

164. When does the Church teach infallibly?

The Church teaches infallibly when it defines, through the Pope alone, as the teacher of all Christians, or through the Pope and the bishops, a doctrine of faith or morals to be held by all the faithful.

(a) The Holy Father must intend to use his supreme, apostolic authority when he teaches infallibly.

(b) The Pope can teach without speaking infallibly; for example, he does this in his encyclical letters. Catholics must accept such teachings, not on faith, but in obedience to the authority of the Pope and in respect for his wisdom.

165. What is meant by the indefectibility of the Catholic Church?

By the indefectibility of the Catholic Church is meant that the Church, as Christ founded it, will last until the end of time.

(a) This indefectibility of the Church is in conformity with the will of Christ, who promised to be with His Church until the end of time.

SCRIPTURE:

"For as often as you shall eat this bread and drink the cup, you proclaim the death of the Lord, until he comes" (*I Corinthians 11:26*).

166. Are all obliged to belong to the Catholic Church in order to be saved?

All are obliged to belong to the Catholic Church in order to be saved.

(a) The principle, "It makes no difference what religion a person practices so long as he leads a good life," is deceptive because it attaches the same importance to the teaching and practice of a false religion as it does to the teaching and practice of the one, true religion revealed by Christ and taught by His Church. No one can be saved without sanctifying grace, and the Catholic Church alone is the divinely established means by which grace is brought to the world and the full fruits of Our Lord's Redemption are applied to men.

SCRIPTURE:

"And as Moses lifted up the serpent in the desert, even so must the Son of Man be lifted up, that those who believe in him may not perish, but may have life everlasting" (*John 3:14-15*).

"Jesus said to him, 'I am the way, and the truth, and the life. No one comes to the Father but through me' " (*John 14:6*).

"In the name of Jesus Christ of Nazareth, whom you crucified, whom God has raised from the dead, even in this name does he stand here before you, sound. This is 'The stone that was rejected by you, the builders, which has become the corner stone.' Neither is there salvation in any other. For there is no other name under heaven given to men by which we must be saved" (*Acts 4:10-12*).

167. What do we mean when we say, "Outside the Church there is no salvation"?

When we say, "Outside the Church there is no salvation," we mean that those who through their own grave fault do not know that the Catholic Church is the true Church or, knowing it, refuse to join it, cannot be saved.

(a) "Outside the Church there is no salvation" does not mean that everyone who is not a Catholic will be condemned. It does mean that no one can be saved unless he belongs in some manner to the Catholic Church, either actually or in desire, for the means of grace are not given without some relation to the divine institution established by Christ.

168. Can they be saved who remain outside the Catholic Church because they do not know it is the true Church?

They who remain outside the Catholic Church through no grave fault of their own and do not know it is the true Church, can be saved by making use of the graces which God gives them.

(a) Those who are outside the Church through no fault of their own are not culpable in the sight of God because of their invincible ignorance.

(b) Persons who make use of the graces God gives them, even though they are not members of the true Church, actually have the desire to become

93

members inasmuch as they wish to use all the means ordained by God for their salvation.

(c) We should pray and try to persuade others to investigate the teachings of the Catholic Church because charity obliges us to do all we can to lead others to salvation. We should also pray for Catholic missioners and help them in their work of bringing the faith to those outside the Catholic Church.

169. Why is the Catholic Church called the Mystical Body of Christ?

The Catholic Church is called the Mystical Body of Christ because its members are united by supernatural bonds with one another and with Christ, their Head, thus resembling the members and head of the living human body.

SCRIPTURE:

"Abide in me, and I in you. As the branch cannot bear fruit of itself unless it remain on the vine, so neither can you unless you abide in me. I am the vine, you are the branches. He who abides in me, and I in him, he bears much fruit; for without me you can do nothing. If anyone does not abide in me, he shall be cast outside as the branch and wither; and they shall gather them up and cast them into the fire, and they shall burn. If you abide in me, and if my words abide in you, ask whatever you will and it shall be done to you" (*John 15:4-7*).

"Yet not for these only do I pray, but for those also who through their word are to believe in me, that all may be one, even as thou, Father, in me and I in thee; that they also may be one in us, that the world may believe that thou hast sent me. And the glory that thou hast given me, I have given to them, that they may be one, even as we are one: I in them, and thou in me; that they may be perfected in unity" (*John 17:20-23*).

"And all things he made subject under his feet, and him he gave as head over all the Church, which indeed is his body, the completion of him who fills all with all" (*Ephesians 1:22-23*).

"Again, he is the head of his body, the Church" (*Colossians 1:18*).

See Scripture, question 156, Romans 12:4-5; question 153, John 17:11.

IMPORTANT TRUTHS ABOUT THE MARKS AND ATTRIBUTES OF THE CHURCH

Since Christ founded only one Church and commanded that all men should join that Church in order to be saved, it is most important to discover which of the many churches that exist in the world is the one true Church. To discover this we have only to pick out the distinctive qualities of the Church as Christ founded it, and then find out which of the churches has these qualities. This process is quite similar to the modern methods of identifying a person by means of his fingerprints. No two persons have the same kind of fingerprints; and so, when we have a record of a person's fingerprints, we can find him in a group by having all make their fingerprints and then examining to see which one has the fingerprints of the person we are seeking. So too, we find in the Gospel a record of the fingerprints or marks of the true Church as Christ established it. The chief marks are unity, holiness, universality and apostolicity. And when we look for these marks or fingerprints among all the churches which claim to be established by Christ, we find that the marks are found in only one of these churches—the Catholic Church.

These marks are not the only proofs we have that the Catholic Church is the one true Church of Jesus Christ. We have another convincing argument in the many miracles that have always been wrought in the Catholic Church, in support of the Church's doctrines or at the intercession of a saint or a holy person. For example, in recent times many sick persons have been cured at the shrine of the Blessed Virgin Mary at Lourdes in France, in a manner that could not have been produced naturally. These must be wrought by God as a special favor to His Mother and to the Church which venerates her. Now, the God of truth would not work miracles for a false religion, and so the Catholic religion in whose favor these miracles take place must be true. Again, the fact that the Church has survived all kinds of obstacles and persecutions for almost twenty centuries is a proof that the Catholic Church is the Church of God; since any merely human organization would have perished long ago.

Besides the marks, the Church has certain important attributes or qualities— authority to command its members, indefectibility or permanence; and, above all, infallibility in its official teachings. The claim of the Catholic Church to possess infallibility meets with great opposition from the enemies of the Church; yet, any one who believes that Christ is truly God must admit that He can give the teachers of the Church a special protection whereby they are preserved from teaching error, and the Gospel clearly indicates that He willed to do so. This privilege of infallibility is possessed in the first place by the Pope, in whom the fulness of the teaching power resides; but it is present also in the bishops, not individually but as a group united with the Pope.

One of the attributes of the Catholic Church which is much misunderstood is the necessity of the Church for salvation. The doctrine of the necessity of the Church does not mean, as some non-Catholics claim, that everyone who dies without being an actual member of the Church will be lost for all eternity. It means that Our Lord Himself made His Church a necessary means for salvation for all men, in such wise that a person must be joined to the Church at least by desire in order to be saved. Those who through no fault of their own do not realize that the Catholic Church is the one true Church of Jesus Christ, but try to serve God faithfully and love Him with their whole heart, will be saved, even though they are not actual members of the Church, because they are joined to the Church by implicit desire. But such persons are deprived of many graces which they would receive as members of the true Church. Speaking of those outside the Catholic Church, Pope Pius, in his Encyclical on the Mystical Body, said: "From a heart overflowing with love we ask each and every one of them to be quick and ready to follow the interior movements of grace and to look to withdrawing from that state in which they cannot be sure of their salvation. For even though unsuspectingly they are related to the Mystical Body of the Redeemer in desire and resolution, they still remain deprived of so many precious gifts and helps from heaven, which one can enjoy only in the Catholic Church."

Oftentimes Catholics are accused of intolerance; and in the United States, where personal rights are valued so highly, it is regarded as very wrong to be intolerant. Now, the truth is this: Catholics are intolerant toward *doctrines* opposed to the teaching of the Catholic Church; but they are tolerant toward the *persons* who hold those doctrines. Any intelligent person who examines this attitude of Catholics will admit that it is quite fair and reasonable.

When we say that Catholics are intolerant toward doctrines opposed to the teaching of the Catholic Church we mean that Catholics regard those doctrines as false. We must do this if we are honest. Since we are convinced that the Catholic religion is true and that it is the one religion established by the Son of God for all mankind, we logically hold that all other religions are erroneous, and that their existence is not in accordance with the will of Christ, who prayed that "there should be one fold and one shepherd." For this reason we try to persuade those who hold those false doctrines to examine the claims of the Catholic Church to be the one true Church of Christ.

Catholics, however, are tolerant toward persons who hold false doctrines. In other words, we believe that we are obliged to show Christian charity to all such persons, to love them as our brothers and sisters, to aid them in their necessities. We should presume that they are honest and sincere in holding their religious beliefs, and we should pray that God may bless and enlighten them. Even if some of them are unkind to us and persecute us because we are Catholics, we should not manifest a like spirit of bigotry toward them.

It is indeed a great privilege to belong to the one true Church. Hence, it is one of the best works of Catholic Action for Catholics to try to persuade their non-Catholic friends to study the arguments for the truth of the Catholic religion. And Catholics themselves can never sufficiently thank God for the favor of being members of the true Church. They should remember the sublime teaching of St. Paul that the Church is a living body with Christ as its Head. "You are the body of Christ, member for member" (1 Cor. 12:27). Just as each member of the body receives vital power from the head, so we, if we are living members of the Church—that is, if we retain in our souls the life of grace—are constantly receiving supernatural power and vigor from Christ, our Head.

RESOLUTION: Thank God every day for giving you the grace of being a member of the one true Church, the Catholic Church.

STUDY HELPS

A. COLUMN SELECTION. (*Join correctly the parts of the sentences in Columns I and II, by placing the right key letter in the proper parenthesis*):

I

(1) The Pope teaches without ordinarily speaking infallibly (..).

(2) The Greek Orthodox Church (..).

(3) The Protestant churches (..).

(4) A person who deliberately denies one doctrine of the Catholic Church (..).

(5) The Pope has authority in temporal matters (..).

(6) The bishops can teach infallibly (..).

(7) The Catholic Church alone (..).

(8) To be saved a person must belong to the Catholic Church (..).

(9) The Head of the Mystical Body is (..).

(10) St. Peter (..).

II

(A) at least by desire.

(B) was called the Rock by Christ.

(C) is the divinely established means of grace.

(D) in his encyclical letters.

(E) only when they are united with the Pope.

(F) Our Lord Jesus Christ.

(G) began in the ninth century.

(H) when they are closely united to spiritual matters.

(I) began in the sixteenth century.

(J) cannot be a Catholic.

B. PROBLEMS AND EXERCISES. (*Answer the questions orally or write them as your teacher may direct*):

(1) Prove to Sydney, a non-Catholic boy interested in the subject, that our Blessed Saviour established only one Church.

(2) Wenceslaus, 10 years old, lives in a mining town. There are three Catholic churches close to one another on Main Street. He wonders how the Church is One when the Ukrainians and the Syrian Catholics are using different churches, different languages and different ceremonies in their services. Explain matters to him.

(3) Nelson, a very fine Protestant boy, tells Sylvester, his Catholic chum, that once his whole family were on the point of joining the Catholic Church, but changed their minds because some of their Catholic neighbors were disreputable characters. In the face of Nelson's testimony, how can Sylvester uphold the claim of the Church that she is holy?

(4) How many Popes have governed the Church during the present century? Name them.

(5) What is the name of the territory that now is under the temporal power of the Pope?

(6) Theresa, who is not a Catholic, admits that sometimes she wonders if the Catholic Church is the true Church, but she does not make further inquiries because some of the duties of Catholics are hard, and she does not wish to be convinced that she must join the Catholic Church. Will Theresa be saved if she dies in this state of mind? Explain your answer.

(7) Grace, a non-Catholic high school girl, wants to know if the Pope's infallibility prevents him from mistakes in arithmetic, spelling, geography and history? Enlighten her on the point.

(8) Samuel, a Jewish labor leader, listened to a Catholic priest speaking at a Labor Day celebration. The priest made several references to "Rerum Novarum" and "Quadragesimo Anno" well-known papal encyclicals. He asks Matthias a Catholic member of his local unit what is meant by the term "papal encyclicals." What should Matthias answer?

(9) Does infallibility make the Pope impeccable, that is, does it mean that the Holy Father cannot commit sin?

(10) Phoebe, a salesgirl in a department store, now and then remarks to her co-worker, Lillian, a member of the Blessed Virgin's Sodality, that "it doesn't make much difference what religion a person practises, as long as she leads a good life." May Lillian agree with that statement? State the reason for your answer.

(11) Alfred is asked by a non-Catholic friend if the Pope claims the authority to tell the Catholics of the United States how they should vote in the presidential elections. What should Alfred answer?

(12) Should we be anxious to have others become Catholics? Why?

(13) Besides the four marks of the Church, what other convincing proof have we that the Catholic Church is the one true Church of Jesus Christ?

(14) When do the bishops enjoy the privilege of infallibility?

The Communion of Saints and Forgiveness of Sins

"I BELIEVE IN ... THE COMMUNION OF SAINTS, THE FORGIVENESS OF SINS ... "

170. What is meant by "the communion of saints" in the Apostles' Creed?

By "the communion of saints" is meant the union of the faithful on earth, the blessed in heaven, and the souls in purgatory, with Christ as their Head.

(a) The blessed in heaven comprise the Church triumphant; the souls in purgatory, the Church suffering; and the faithful on earth, the Church militant.

SCRIPTURE:

"It is therefore a holy and wholesome thought to pray for the dead, that they may be loosed from sins" (*II Machabees 12:46*).

"In him (Christ Jesus) the whole structure is closely fitted together and grows into a temple holy in the Lord; in him you too are being built together into a dwelling place for God in the Spirit" (*Ephesians 2:21-22*).

" ... rendering thanks to the Father, who has made us worthy to share the lot of the saints in light" (*Colossians 1:12*).

"But you have come to Mount Sion, and to the city of the living God, the heavenly Jerusalem, and to the company of many thousands of angels, and to the Church of the firstborn who are enrolled in the heavens, and to God, the judge of all, and to the spirits of the just made perfect, and to Jesus, mediator of a new covenant" (*Hebrews 12:22-24*).

171. Through the communion of saints, what can the blessed in heaven do for the souls in purgatory and the faithful on earth?

Through the communion of saints, the blessed in heaven can help the souls in purgatory and the faithful on earth by praying for them.

(a) The prayers of the blessed in heaven are always efficacious because they are always in accord with God's will.

SCRIPTURE:

"When thou didst pray with tears, and didst bury the dead, and didst leave thy dinner, and hide the dead by day in thy house, and bury them by night, I offered thy prayer to the Lord" (*Tobias 12:12*).

"And there was given to him much incense, that he might offer it with the prayers of all the saints upon the golden altar which is before the throne" (*Apocalypse 8:3*).

172. Should the faithful on earth, through the communion of saints, honor the blessed in heaven and pray to them?

The faithful on earth, through the communion of saints, should honor the blessed in heaven and pray to them, because they

98

are worthy of honor and as friends of God will help the faithful on earth.

(a) Many saints have special feast days. All the saints are honored on the Feast of All Saints, November 1.

SCRIPTURE:
"Let us now praise men of renown, and our fathers in their generation" (*Ecclesiasticus 44:1*).

173. Can the faithful on earth, through the communion of saints, relieve the sufferings of the souls in purgatory?

The faithful on earth, through the communion of saints, can relieve the sufferings of the souls in purgatory by prayer, fasting, and other good works, by indulgences, and by having Masses offered for them.

(a) Mass can be frequently offered for the repose of a soul. There are special Requiem Masses for the day of the funeral, the thirtieth day after death or burial, and the anniversary of the death or burial. On All Souls' Day, November 2, Masses are offered for all the souls in purgatory.

(b) Most indulgences granted by the Church are applicable to the poor souls in purgatory.

(c) A plenary indulgence can be gained by the celebration of Mass at a privileged altar. This indulgence can be applied only to the soul in purgatory for whom the Mass is offered.

(d) Bishops and other prelates designated in the Code of Canon Law can determine and declare one altar, in churches specified by law, as privileged daily and perpetually, under the conditions prescribed by the Sacred Canons.

(e) All Masses celebrated at any altar on All Souls' Day, and during its octave, and during the Forty Hours' Devotion enjoy the same privilege as those offered on a privileged altar, but only in favor of the soul for whom the Mass is said.

SCRIPTURE:
"It is therefore a holy and wholesome thought to pray for the dead, that they may be loosed from sins" (*II Machabees 12:46*).

174. Can the faithful on earth help one another?

The faithful on earth, as members of the Mystical Body of Christ, can help one another by practicing supernatural charity and, especially, by performing the spiritual and corporal works of mercy.

(a) Prayer, one of the spiritual works of mercy, is of value not only for the living but also for the dead. The other spiritual works of mercy and most of the corporal works are concerned primarily with the living.

SCRIPTURE:
"Then the king will say to those on his right hand, 'Come, blessed of my Father, take possession of the kingdom prepared for you from the foundation of the world; for I was hungry and you gave me to eat; I was thirsty and you gave me to drink; I was a stranger and you took me in; naked and you covered

99a

The Mystical Body of Christ

This picture shows the Communion of Saints. The assembly of the Angels and Saints in Heaven, the faithful on earth, and the souls in Purgatory are all shown.

On top, the Angels and Saints adore the three Persons of the Holy Trinity and pray to them for the faithful who still live on earth.

In the middle, the faithful on earth assist at the Holy Sacrifice of the Mass, where they invoke the Saints in Heaven, pray for each other, and ask for the deliverance of the Poor Souls from Purgatory.

At the bottom are the souls in Purgatory. The refreshing waters which two Angels pour upon them symbolizes the relief which the Holy Sacrifice of the Mass obtains for them.

me; sick and you visited me; I was in prison and you came to me.' Then the just will answer him, saying, 'Lord, when did we see thee hungry, and feed thee; or thirsty, and give thee drink? And when did we see thee a stranger, and take thee in; or naked, and clothe thee? Or when did we see thee sick, or in prison, and come to thee?' And answering the king will say to them, 'Amen I say to you, as long as you did it for one of these, the least of my brethren, you did it for me' " (*Matthew 25:34-40*).

"By this will all men know that you are my disciples, if you have love for one another" (*John 13:35*).

"I urge therefore, first of all, that supplications, prayers, intercessions and thanksgivings be made for all men" (*I Timothy 2:1*).

"Pray for one another that you may be saved. For the unceasing prayer of a just man is of great avail" (*James 5:16*).

175. What is meant in the Apostles' Creed by "the forgiveness of sins"?

By "the forgiveness of sins" in the Apostles' Creed is meant that God has given to the Church, through Jesus Christ, the power to forgive sins, no matter how great or how many they are, if sinners truly repent.

(a) The Church exercises the power to forgive sin when sins committed before the reception of Baptism are forgiven by that sacrament; but especially does the Church exercise this power in the sacrament of Penance.

SCRIPTURE:
"He therefore said to them again, 'Peace be to you! As the Father has sent me, I also send you.' When he had said this, he breathed upon them, and said to them, "Receive the Holy Spirit; whose sins you shall forgive, they are forgiven them; and whose sins you shall retain, they are retained' " (*John 20:21-23*).

IMPORTANT TRUTHS ABOUT THE COMMUNION OF SAINTS AND FORGIVENESS OF SINS

We all desire, particularly in times of sorrow, to have loving friends. The Catholic doctrine of the communion of saints teaches us that we can have many good friends at all times. The word "communion," as we use it in this connection, has nothing to do with Holy Communion. It means "society" or "union." And the word "saints" does not mean merely those who are in heaven with God. It means all who are joined to Christ by sanctifying grace. In a word, the Catholic doctrine of the communion of saints means that we have millions of friends, bound to us by the supernatural ties of sanctifying grace and divine charity flowing from Jesus Christ, the Head of this society.

These friends are: *first*, those living on earth with sanctifying grace and charity in their souls; these make up the Church militant, so called because its members are still engaged in the spiritual warfare against the world, the flesh and the devil, hoping to be victorious and to win the crown of eternal life; *second*, the souls in purgatory—those who have left this world in the state of grace but must still make atonement to God for a debt of temporal punishment; these make up the Church suffering; *third*, the saints in heaven, called the Church triumphant, because they have won the victory and are now enjoying their triumph with God for all eternity.

These friends aid us in our needs, especially our spiritual necessities. There are many devout persons on earth who pray for us every day, even though we have never met them. The saints in heaven, particularly those to whom we pray, aid us also by their prayers. Above all, the Mother of God, the Queen of Saints, is praying for us before the throne of her Son, because she loves every soul for which He died, since she loves Him so much. The souls in purgatory probably pray for us also, although this is not entirely certain. The Church never prays publicly to the suffering souls, asking for their prayers, but she allows her members to do this privately, if they wish.

There are millions of saints in heaven, but only certain ones have been canonized, or officially declared by the Church to be in heaven. When the Church canonizes a saint, we have absolute certainty that this person is in heaven, for the Church is infallible in canonizations. We can also be sure that baptized children who die before they reach the age of reason—perhaps members of our own family—are in heaven, and we can invoke them in our private devotions. The saints in heaven help in a particular way those who were dear to them in life and those who ask their prayers.

But if the communion of saints brings us advantages, it also brings us obligations. We should pray to our friends, the saints in heaven; we should pray for our friends, the souls in purgatory. Toward those members of the communion of saints who are still in this world we must exercise charity, not only by praying for them but also by assisting them whenever they are in need either of body or of soul, especially through the corporal and spiritual works of mercy. We must not consider their natural traits, which may be unpleasant, but must rather view them as sharers in the divine life that flows from Christ, and as persons who are destined to be our companions for all eternity in His kingdom. If we put into practice in this manner the doctrine of the communion of saints, we shall never be lonely or sad, even though all our worldly friends turn against us.

RESOLUTION: Resolve to remember the suffering souls in purgatory after every Holy Communion, especially the souls of your deceased relatives and friends.

STUDY HELPS

A. TRUE OR FALSE. (*Check each of the following statements as either true or false. The correct answer can be found in the previous portions of this lesson*).

	TRUE	FALSE
(1) The blessed in heaven compose the Church militant.	.....	.....
(2) The indulgence of the privileged altar means that the Church grants a plenary indulgence to the soul in purgatory for whom the Mass is said.	.....	.....
(3) It is a truth of the Catholic faith that the souls in purgatory pray for those on earth.	.....	.....
(4) All Saints' Day is celebrated on November 1.	.....	.....
(5) All persons in sanctifying grace can be called saints.	.....	.....
(6) It is possible that some canonized saints are still in purgatory.	.....	.....
(7) We are allowed to pray privately to a baptized child who died before reaching the age of reason.	.....	.....
(8) The saints in heaven pray for the souls in purgatory.	.....	.....
(9) Some sins are so grievous that the Church cannot forgive them.	.....	.....
(10) All the spiritual works of mercy are concerned with the living.	.....	.....

101

3. PROBLEMS AND EXERCISES. (*Answer the questions orally or write them as your teacher may direct*):

(1) Abigail, an elderly Catholic lady, laments the fact that she is practically friendless in the world. Write a short note to the poor soul, wherein you remind her that no Catholic is really friendless who has a lively faith in the communion of saints. Explain that truth in your note.

(2) What spiritual bonds unite the three classes of saints that form the Church Triumphant, the Church Suffering, and the Church Militant?

(3) Why is our branch of this union, or communion, called Militant?

(4) Anastasia's wealthy parents are very generous to foreign missionaries. Their little girl is apt to be vain and boastful of the fact that her family is being prayed for by these grateful missionaries in all parts of the world. After studying this lesson, Theodora, a poor child, concludes that her family is being prayed for also in every part of the world. Is Theodora correct? Why?

(5) Silvia wonders is anyone in heaven praying for her and her family. Give her your answer.

(6) Placida, a child in the fifth grade, has difficulties with her lessons. She studies faithfully enough, but her memory of things is not very good. Sabina, her sister in the seventh grade, urges Placida to pray to the souls in purgatory whenever her memory fails her. What do you think of Sabina's advice?

(7) What obligations have we as members of the union, or communion of saints?

(8) Can you name five canonized saints? Can you name two saints canonized by Pope Pius XII? Can you name anyone who died in America and may one day be a canonized saint?

(9) Roberta hears her parish priest announce that on All Souls' Day he will celebrate three Masses. On what two days of the year may every priest offer the Holy Sacrifice three times?

(10) In the sense of the word "saint" as used in this lesson are only extraordinarily holy men and women and children meant? Explain.

(11) Explain to Cleopatra, a Protestant neighbor about your own age, what is meant by the title we Catholics confer on our Blessed Mother: "Mediatrix of All Graces." Though not a Catholic, the young girl has a tender regard for the "Virgin", as she calls her.

(12) For the benefit of Liborius, a Lutheran boy in your neighborhood, distinguish between All Saints' and All Souls' Day. Tell him what you know about them and what good Catholics must do, or are expected to do, on both days.

(13) Paula, a popular switchboard operator in a downtown office is drowned while on vacation. Her fellow workers collect $100 to buy flowers for the funeral. Then one of them suggests that instead of giving flowers they use the money as stipends for Masses for the repose of Paula's soul. Which plan is the better? Would you suggest a different plan?

LESSON 14

The Resurrection and Life Everlasting

"I BELIEVE IN . . . THE RESURRECTION OF THE BODY, AND LIFE EVERLASTING."

176. What is meant by "the resurrection of the body?"
By "the resurrection of the body" is meant that at the end of the world the bodies of all men will rise from the earth and be united again to their souls, nevermore to be separated.

(a) No man knows when the world will end. The signs preceding the destruction of the world, as given in Scripture, are: wars, famine, pestilence, the coming of Antichrist, the darkening of the sun and moon, and the appearance of the cross in heaven.

SCRIPTURE:
"But immediately after the tribulation of those days, the sun will be darkened, and the moon will not give her light, and the stars will fall from heaven, and the powers of heaven will be shaken. And then will appear the sign of the Son of Man in heaven; and then will all tribes of the earth mourn, and they will see the Son of Man coming upon the clouds of heaven with great power and majesty. And he will send forth his angels with a trumpet and a great sound, and they will gather his elect from the four winds, from one end of the heavens to the other" (*Matthew 24:29-31*). (*See also Romans 8:11*).

See Scripture, question 99; question 100, John 5:28-29; I Corinthians 15:51-53.

177. Why will the bodies of the just rise?
The bodies of the just will rise to share forever in the glory of their souls.

(a) During their earthly life the bodies of the just were the temples of the Holy Ghost; they were the instruments of the good acts by which the souls of the just merited eternal life. Respect should be shown for the bodies of the faithful departed; special burial places should be set aside for them, and their graves should be blessed.

(b) After the resurrection the bodies of the just will be in a glorified state. There will then be no need for food and drink to preserve the body, which will be endowed with qualities it did not possess in this life.

178. Has the body of any human person ever been glorified and taken into heaven?
By the special privilege of her Assumption, the body of the Blessed Virgin Mary, united to her immaculate soul, was glorified and taken into heaven.

(a) This question emphasizes *human person* because the Divine Person, Jesus Christ, in His human nature has risen from the dead, glorious and immortal, and ascended into heaven (question 98).

(b) Since she was free from all sin, both original and actual, it was most fitting that the Blessed Virgin Mary should be preserved from the consequences of sin; the corruption of death and the deferment of glory until the last day. Moreover, since the Son of God took His flesh and blood from the chaste body of Mary, it was most appropriate that her body shall be glorified as soon as her earthly life was ended. From the early centuries, the doctrine of Mary's bodily glorification and assumption

103

was accepted by the Church as contained in Christian Tradition. It was declared a doctrine of divine-catholic faith by Pope Pius XII on November 1, 1950. The Feast of the Assumption is celebrated on August 15.

(c) It is not certain whether the Blessed Virgin Mary first died and was shortly afterward taken into heaven, in body and soul, or was preserved from death and taken immediately to heavenly glory when her life on earth was ended. Pope Pius XII refrained from making a decision on this question when he issued his solemn definition of the Assumption of the Blessed Virgin.

179. Why will the bodies of the damned also rise?
The bodies of the damned will also rise to share in the eternal punishment of their souls.

(a) Since the body is the instrument of the soul in committing sin, it is just that the body also share in eternal punishment.

180. What is the judgment called which will be passed on all men immediately after the general resurrection?
The judgment which will be passed on all men immediately after the general resurrection is called the general judgment.

(a) The general judgment was described by Our Saviour Himself.

(b) Every deliberate thought, word, deed, and omission of every person's entire life will be manifested at the general judgment.

(c) The Lord Christ will be the judge.

SCRIPTURE:
"For the Son of Man is to come with his angels in the glory of his Father, and then he will render to everyone according to his conduct" (*Matthew 16:27*).
"Then the king will say to those on his right hand, 'Come, blessed of my Father, take possession of the kingdom prepared for you from the foundation of the world; for I was hungry and you gave me to eat; I was thirsty and you gave me to drink; I was a stranger and you took me in; naked and you covered me; sick and you visited me; I was in prison and you came to me.' Then the just will answer him, saying, 'Lord, when did we see thee hungry, and feed thee; or thirsty, and give thee drink? And when did we see thee a stranger, and take thee in; or naked, and clothe thee? Or when did we see thee sick, or in prison, and come to thee?' And answering the king will say to them, 'Amen I say to you, as long as you did it for one of these, the least of my brethren, you did it for me.'

"Then he will say to those on his left hand, 'Depart from me, accursed ones, into the everlasting fire which was prepared for the devil and his angels. For I was hungry, and you did not give me to eat; I was thirsty and you gave me no drink; I was a stranger and you did not take me in; naked, and you did not clothe me; sick, and in prison, and you did not visit me.' Then they also will answer and say, 'Lord, when did we see thee hungry, or thirsty, or a stranger, or naked, or sick, or in prison, and did not minister to thee?' Then he will answer them, saying, 'Amen I say to you, as long as you did not do it for one of these least ones, you did not do it for me.' And these will go into everlasting punishment, but the just into everlasting life" (*Matthew 25:34-46*).
"And he charged us to preach to the people and to testify that he it is who has been appointed by God to be judge of the living and of the dead" (*Acts 10:42*).

181. What is the judgment called which will be passed on each one of us immediately after death?
The judgment which will be passed on each one of us immediately after death is called the particular judgment.

104

(a) The existence of the particular judgment is apparent from the parable of Lazarus and Dives, which shows that one soul was rewarded and another punished immediately after death. Reward or punishment follows the sentence of judgment.

(b) The sentence of this judgment is final and will not be reversed.

(c) The particular judgment will be given immediately after the soul leaves the body. The soul will go at once either to its reward in heaven or to its punishment in purgatory or hell.

SCRIPTURE:
"For it is easy before God in the day of death to reward everyone according to his ways. The affliction of an hour maketh one forget great delights: and in the end of a man is the disclosing of his works" (*Ecclesiasticus 11:28-29*).

182. **If everyone is judged immediately after death, why will there be a general judgment?**

Although everyone is judged immediately after death, it is fitting that there be a general judgment in order that the justice, wisdom, and mercy of God may be glorified in the presence of all.

(a) Man is a social being as well as an individual. The general judgment will manifest God's Providence, the majesty of Christ, and the glory of the elect.

SCRIPTURE:
"Then shall the just stand with great constancy against those that have afflicted them and taken away their labors. These seeing it, shall be troubled with terrible fear, and shall be amazed at the suddenness of their unexpected salvation. Saying within themselves, repenting, and groaning for anguish of spirit: These are they whom we had some time in derision and for a parable of reproach. We fools esteemed their life madness and their end without honor. Behold how they are numbered among the children of God, and their lot is among the saints. Therefore we have erred from the way of truth, and the light of justice hath not shined unto us, and the sun of understanding hath not risen upon us. We wearied ourselves in the way of iniquity and destruction, and have walked through hard ways: but the way of the Lord we have not known. What hath pride profited us? Or what advantage hath the boasting of riches brought us? All those things are passed away like a shadow, and like a post that runneth on" (*Wisdom 5:1-9*).

See Scripture, question 180, Matthew 25:34-46.

183. **What are the rewards or punishments appointed for men after the particular judgment?**

The rewards or punishments appointed for men after the particular judgment are heaven, purgatory, or hell.

184. **Who are punished in purgatory?**

Those are punished for a time in purgatory who die in the state of grace but are guilty of venial sin, or have not fully satisfied for the temporal punishment due to their sins.

(a) There will be no purgatory after the general judgment.

(b) Since we do not know how long individual souls are detained in

105

purgatory, there is need for persevering prayer for the repose of the souls of all those who die after reaching the use of reason, except those who are canonized or beatified by the Church.

(c) The souls in purgatory are certain of entering heaven as soon as God's justice has been fully satisfied.

SCRIPTURE:
"The fire will assay the quality of everyone's work: if his work abides which he has built thereon, he will receive reward; if his work burns he will lose his reward, but himself will be saved, yet so as through fire" (*I Corinthians 3:13-15*).

See Scripture, question 173, II Machabees 12:46.

185. Who are punished in hell?

Those are punished in hell who die in mortal sin; they are deprived of the vision of God and suffer dreadful torments, especially that of fire, for all eternity.

(a) The souls in hell are beyond all help. They do not belong to the Mystical Body of Christ or to the Communion of Saints. They are not included among our neighbors and are not the objects of charity. They are doomed to the company of the devils for all eternity.

(b) The souls in hell do not have supernatural faith. They believe, however, in the truths revealed by Almighty God, not with divine faith, but because they cannot escape the evidence of God's authority.

(c) The privation of the beatific vision is called the pain of loss; the torment inflicted by created means on the soul, and on the body after its resurrection, is called the pain of sense.

(d) It is not against God's mercy to punish souls in hell for eternity. God's justice demands that He thus punish those who, sinning gravely and refusing to repent, deliberately turn themselves from God, their last end.

(e) The punishment of hell is eternal; Our Lord referred to it as "everlasting fire."

SCRIPTURE:
"Then he will say to those on his left hand, 'Depart from me, accursed ones, into the everlasting fire which was prepared for the devil and his angels'" (*Matthew 25:41*).
"Indeed it is just on the part of God to repay with affliction those who afflict you, and to give you who are afflicted rest with us at the revelation of the Lord Jesus, who will come from heaven with the angels of his power, in flaming fire, to inflict punishment on those who do not know God, and who do not obey the gospel of our Lord Jesus Christ. These will be punished with eternal ruin, away from the face of the Lord and the glory of his power, when on that day he shall come to be glorified in his saints, and to be marvelled at in all those who have believed (*II Thessalonians 1:6-10*).

186. Who are rewarded in heaven?

Those are rewarded in heaven who have died in the state o grace and have been purified in purgatory, if necessary, from all venial sin and all debt of temporal punishment; they see God face to face and share forever in His glory and happiness.

(a) The happiness of heaven consists in the beatific vision and the consequent joy of the blessed. This happiness is not postponed to the end of the world but begins as soon as all venial sin and the temporal punishment for sin have been remitted.

(b) The body participates in this happiness only after the resurrection at the end of the world.

(c) The blessed rejoice in the company of Our Saviour, the Blessed Virgin Mary, all the angels and saints, and the friends they knew on earth who have attained the reward of eternal life.

(d) There is no sorrow or pain in heaven; the joy is complete, though unequal, throughout all eternity.

SCRIPTURE:
"Then the king will say to those on his right hand, 'Come, blessed of my Father, take possession of the kingdom prepared for you from the foundation of the world' " (*Matthew 25:34*).

"Now this is everlasting life, that they may know thee, the only true God, and him whom thou hast sent, Jesus Christ" (*John 17:3*).

"But, as it is written, 'Eye has not seen nor ear heard, nor has it entered into the heart of man, what things God has prepared for those who love him' " (*I Corinthians 2:9*).

"We see now through a mirror in an obscure manner, but then face to face" (*I Corinthians 13:12*).

"We know that, when he appears, we shall be like to him, for we shall see him just as he is" (*I John 3:2*).

"And there shall not enter into it anything defiled, nor he who practices abomination and falsehood" (*Apocalypse 21:27*).

187. **What is meant by the word "Amen" with which we end the Apostles' Creed?**

By the word "Amen" with which we end the Apostles' Creed, is meant "So it is," or "So be it"; the word expresses our firm belief in all the doctrines that the Creed contains.

(a) Our Divine Saviour frequently used this term to emphasize His teaching.

SCRIPTURE:
"Amen I say to you, I have not found such great faith in Israel" (*Matthew 8:10*).

"Amen I say to you, unless you turn and become like little children, you will not enter into the kingdom of heaven" (*Matthew 18:3*).

IMPORTANT TRUTHS ABOUT THE RESURRECTION AND LIFE EVERLASTING

We know that we must all die. When, where and how we shall die is uncertain; but that one day our soul will depart from our body, and that our body will then return to the dust of earth, we are absolutely certain. The all-important question is "What will take place after death?" St. Paul tells us: "It is appointed unto men to die once but after this comes the judgment" (*Hebr. 9:27*). Our Catholic faith assures us that we shall appear before God twice to be judged for the deeds of our lifetime. The first occasion occurs the very first moment after death in the very place where we die. Then, in a single instant our entire life will be examined by the all-knowing, all-just God, and the sentence given that will determine our eternal abode. The soul will be sentenced to eternal punishment if it is defiled by the guilt of mortal sin; if it is free from all sin and from the debt of temporal punishment it will be admitted at once to the joys of heaven; if it is adorned with the supernatural life of sanctifying grace but is in venial sin or is still burdened by a debt of temporal punishment, it will go to purgatory until full satisfaction is made and it is made worthy of the presence of God. The souls in purgatory are often called the faithful departed. God punishes these souls, not in a spirit of vengeance, but because He loves them and wills that they be fully purified so that they can be admitted to His presence.

This is the particular judgment, and here the fate of the soul is determined unchangeably. But it often happens that the justice and the wisdom of God are hidden from the eyes of men in the present world. Those who lead good lives frequently have many trials to endure, while those who freely transgress God's law prosper. The question may arise in the minds of some: "How can God be just and good and wise, if He allows these things?" And so, in order that all men may see that God is all-just, and may understand that in the next life, if not in this, every one receives what is his due, there is a final or general judgment, conducted by Our Blessed Lord. He Himself describes this in an inspiring passage recorded in the twenty-fifth chapter of the Gospel according to St. Matthew, beginning with the words: "When the Son of Man shall come in his majesty, and all the angels with him, then he will sit on the throne of his glory; and before him will be gathered all the nations" (*Matthew, 25:31-32*). Before the judgment, every human being that has ever lived will rise from the dead—that is, the body of every member of the human race will be formed again from the elements of the earth into which it passed after death and will be reunited to its soul, and then in the presence of the entire human race every individual will be judged, and will hear the sentence either of eternal reward or of eternal punishment. With the aid of our body and its senses we did either good or evil; and so, our body will share our happiness or our misery for all eternity.

Every one of us therefore will spend eternity either in heaven or in hell. The most important task of life is to win heaven. To do this the one condition is that we have the state of sanctifying grace when we leave this world. We must expend every effort to avoid mortal sin. If ever we have the misfortune to commit a mortal sin, we must strive to receive pardon as soon as possible, by making an act of perfect contrition with the intention of going to confession.

RESOLUTION: Resolve to examine your conscience every night before retiring as if you were in the presence of Our Lord at the last judgment; and make an act of perfect contrition for all the sins of the day with the intention of confessing them, particularly if you have been so unfortunate as to commit mortal sin.

STUDY HELPS

A. WORD SELECTION. (*Select the word or phrase in the parentheses which most exactly and most completely fills out the sentence*):

(1) The sentence passed at the particular judgment (may be changed at the general judgment . . . will never be changed . . . may be changed in purgatory).

(2) The Blessed Virgin Mary (never died . . . died and her body corrupted in the grave . . . was taken into heaven, her glorified body united to her immaculate soul.

(3) The feast of the Assumption is celebrated on (March 25 . . . August 15 . . . December 8).

(4) A soul in sanctifying grace which has only a debt of temporal punishment will go immediately after the particular judgment to (purgatory . . . heaven . . . hell).

(5) The judgment which is passed on each individual immediately after death is called the (divine judgment . . . particular judgment . . . general judgment).

(6) After the general judgment purgatory (will continue for all eternity . . . will continue for a time . . . will cease to exist).

(7) The punishments of hell are a manifestation of God's (justice . . . mercy . . . wisdom).

(8) The chief happiness of heaven consists in (singing . . . meeting our loved ones . . . seeing God face to face).

(9) The privation of the beatific vision in hell is called (the pain of loss . . . remorse of conscience . . . the pain of sense).

(10) To win heaven we must (have the Catholic faith . . . be baptized . . . be in the state of grace when we die).

B. PROBLEMS AND EXERCISES. (*Answer the questions orally or write them as your teacher may direct*):

(1) On how many occasions after our death will God pass judgment on the deeds of our lifetime?

(2) Cordelia, a cultured college woman but utterly pagan in her morals, is extremely wealthy. She enjoys the good things of this life, often at the expense of her conscience. The society columns of the leading newspapers flatter her vanity frequently. She does not go to church. Amanda, a Catholic, is a poor laundress in her employ. Amanda is a widow with five children. The first Friday of every month sees Amanda at the Communion rail. She receives also every Sunday. She is a victim of chronic rheumatism, and barely gets along on the small pay she receives from Cordelia. Sometimes Amanda is tempted to give up the struggle to be good, the devil suggesting the thought: "How can your God be good and wise, if He allows you to suffer and your mistress to prosper? Write a short note to Amanda, cheering her, and encouraging her to continue to serve God faithfully. In your note be sure to mention a truth learned in this lesson.

(3) Write from memory the two sentences Our Lord will pronounce at the end of the general judgment.

(4) Tobias, 11 years old, is listening to Father Rex preaching at the children's Mass. Father Rex starts his sermon by asking: "What is the most important task of life?" Then he pauses. Tobias guesses an answer: "To earn a lot of money honestly and buy a nice home for my father and mother." Do you agree with Tobias? If so, tell why. If not, then give your answer to Father Rex's question.

(5) Christina is asked by her Sunday School teacher "If you hope to reach heaven, what must be in your soul when you leave this world?" Christina does not remember ever seeing that question in her Catechism. Answer it for her.

(6) Duncan, a country lad, passes a non-Catholic church where a revival is being held by a famous preacher. The sermon topic for that

night is: "The world will end within five years; make ready to meet God!" Does anyone know exactly when the world will be destroyed by fire? Has God given us any hints as to when the end is approaching? Explain your answer.

(7) Phil and his teammates on St. Pancratius' baseball team are saddened by the death of their baseball idol. They file past his corpse, all saying a short prayer for the repose of his soul. He was a Christian, but not a Catholic. Was it proper for them to pray for his soul? Why?

(8) If a soul leaves this world in mortal sin, is there any probability that God will give it an opportunity to repent in eternity?

(9) Aurelia is making a novena for the feast of the Assumption. She wonders why the priest doesn't present a relic of the Blessed Virgin Mary after every service, the same as he does after the services of the Little Flower novena, when a relic of St. Therese is venerated. Aurelia says she would very much like to kiss the reliquary containing a little piece of a bone taken from the body of our Blessed Mother. Let Aurelia know why the priest doesn't present such a relic during the Assumption novena.

(10) Two policemen shoot Valerian through the head and the heart as the gunman is staging a bank holdup. Before the horrified spectators, Valerian instantaneously topples over dead on the floor of the bank. Where does his particular judgment take place? If death claims him unrepentant in mortal sin, what is his eternal fate?

(11) Donald, a fireman, rescues three little children from a blazing building. He returns to save a fourth child, but loses his life in the attempt. Afterwards, his corpse is found in the hallway on the third floor. Where did his particular judgment take place? Donald was a good Catholic, and went to Holy Communion faithfully every month with the Holy Name men of the parish; death overtook him in the state of grace. What is his eternal fate?

(12) Adele's mother died a month ago. Daily, for two weeks afterwards, Adele went to Mass and received Holy Communion for the repose of her mother's soul. Then she stopped, thinking she had done enough to release her dear mother from purgatory. Do you think she has done enough? Give the reasons for your answer.

(13) To Belinda, a non-Catholic girl at the wake of a Catholic classmate, explain the three sections of the following prayer: "May the souls of the faithful departed . . . through the mercy of God . . . rest in peace. Amen."

(14) Gwendolin, the daughter of the local Universalist minister, is playing bridge with three Catholic girl friends. Between games a discussion arises, during which Gwendolin tries to convince her Catholic friends that although some souls go to hell after death, nevertheless, all of them will eventually be purified and reach heaven. All of the Catholic girls hold steadfastly to the true Catholic doctrine. What is that doctrine concerning the damned in hell, and the saved in heaven?

(15) Veronica, one of the three, narrates a well-known parable of Our Lord to prove the Catholic belief about the fire of hell. What is the name of that parable? Show how it proves that there is fire in hell

110

PART TWO — THE COMMANDMENTS

LESSON 15

The Two Great Commandments

188. Besides believing what God has revealed, what else must we do to be saved?

Besides believing what God has revealed, we must keep His law.

(a) God has clearly revealed that we must keep His law to attain eternal salvation. The revealed doctrines, which we must believe, give us the reasons for obeying the law.

(b) The law of God is an expression of divine wisdom guiding man to his end and regulating man's relations to his Creator and to his fellow men. Some actions are good in themselves; others are good because they are commanded. Some actions are evil in themselves; others are evil because they are forbidden. Good actions are in conformity with human nature as created by God; evil actions are contrary to it. The law of God presupposes the divine will and also divine wisdom.

(c) Every rational creature must obey the law of God as made known through human reason and divine revelation.

SCRIPTURE:

"If you love me, keep my commandments" (*John 14:15*).

"He who has my commandments and keeps them, he it is who loves me" (*John 14:21*).

"But if thou wilt enter into life, keep the commandments" (*Matthew 19:17*).

189. Which are the two great commandments that contain the whole law of God?

The two great commandments that contain the whole law of God are:

first, Thou shalt love the Lord thy God with thy whole heart, and with thy whole soul, and with thy whole mind, and with thy whole strength;

second, Thou shalt love thy neighbor as thyself.

(a) The whole law of God can be reduced to the commandment of love of God, because the proper motive of love of neighbor and love of self is God.

(b) The first three commandments of the Decalogue refer directly to the commandment of love of God; the last seven regard the love of neighbor and imply love of oneself.

(c) Every person who has received or is capable of receiving sanctifying grace and eternal happiness is our neighbor. Only the devils and the souls of the damned are excluded from our love. [13]

---

13. See question 124 (c).

111

SCRIPTURE:
"And one of them, a doctor of the Law, putting him to the test, asked him, 'Master, which is the great commandment in the Law?' Jesus said to him, ' "Thou shalt love the Lord thy God
with thy whole heart,
and with thy whole soul,
and with thy whole mind."
This is the greatest and the first commandment.
And the second is like it,
"Thou shalt love thy neighbor as thyself."
On these two commandments depend the whole Law and the Prophets' "
(*Matthew 22:35-40*).

190. What must we do to love God, our neighbor, and ourselves?

To love God, our neighbor, and ourselves we must keep the commandments of God and of the Church, and perform the spiritual and corporal works of mercy.

(a) Just as the commandments of God determine in detail what we must do in order to love God, our neighbor, and ourselves, so the commandments of the Church and the spiritual and corporal works of mercy show us how to apply practically the commandments of God.

(b) God, through His Divine Son Jesus Christ, empowered and directed the Catholic Church to make necessary and useful laws for its, members to help them attain their eternal salvation.

(c) We prove our true love for our fellow man by performing the corporal and spiritual works of mercy, which should have as their motive the love of God and not merely humanitarian or natural reasons.

SCRIPTURE:
"Give alms out of thy substance, and turn not away thy face from any poor person: for so it shall come to pass that the face of the Lord shall not be turned from thee" (*Tobias 4:7*).

"Let love be without pretense. Hate what is evil, hold to what is good. Love one another with fraternal charity, anticipating one another with honor. Be not slothful in zeal; be fervent in spirit, serving the Lord, rejoicing in hope. Be patient in tribulation, persevering in prayer. Share the needs of the saints, practicing hospitality. Bless those who persecute you; bless and do not curse. Rejoice with those who rejoice; weep with those who weep. Be of one mind towards one another. Do not set your mind on high things but condescend to the lowly. Be not wise in your own conceits. To no man render evil for evil but provide good things not only in the sight of God, but also in the sight of all men. If it be possible, as far as in you lies, be at peace with all men. Do not avenge yourselves, beloved, but give place to the wrath, for it is written, 'Vengeance is mine; I will repay, says the Lord' " (*Romans 12:9-19*).

"Brethren, even if a person is caught doing something wrong, you who are spiritual instruct such a one in a spirit of meekness, considering thyself, lest thou also be tempted. Bear one another's burdens, and so you will fulfill the law of Christ" (*Galatians 6:1-2*).

"And we exhort you, brethren, reprove the irregular, comfort the fainthearted, support the weak, be patient towards all men. See that no one renders evil for evil to any man; but always strive after good towards one another and towards all men" (*I Thessalonians 5:14-15*).

112

"I urge therefore, first of all, that supplications, prayers, intercessions and thanksgivings be made for all men" (*I Timothy 2:1*).

"Religion pure and undefiled before God the Father is this: to give aid to orphans and widows in their tribulation, and to keep oneself unspotted from this world" (*James 1:27*).

"My brethren, if any one of you strays from the truth and someone brings him back, he ought to know that he who causes a sinner to be brought back from his misguided way, will save his soul from death, and will cover a multitude of sins" (*James 5:19-20*).

"My dear children, let us not love in word, neither with the tongue, but in deed and in truth" (*I John 3:18*).

See Scripture, question 124, I Corinthians 13:1-7; question 174, Matthew 25:34-40.

191. Which are the chief corporal works of mercy?

The chief corporal works of mercy are seven:
1. To feed the hungry.
2. To give drink to the thirsty.
3. To clothe the naked.
4. To visit the imprisoned.
5. To shelter the homeless.
6. To visit the sick.
7. To bury the dead.

(a) Our Lord taught explicitly that one can earn the eternal reward of heaven by performing the corporal works of mercy and that those who deliberately refuse to perform such works will be barred from heaven.

(b) One can feed the hungry, give drink to the thirsty, clothe the naked, and shelter the homeless not only by actually providing the necessities of life but also by working to correct economic abuses which cause unnecessary unemployment and poverty. Those who work to provide comfortable and sanitary housing for the poor perform a corporal work of mercy.

(c) One can visit the sick by paying a social call or by providing the necessary medical care as far as means and circumstances permit. Those who help support hospitals for the poor and home-nursing organizations also perform this work of mercy. Doctors and nurses who attend the sick can gain the reward promised by Our Lord if they perform their duties for the love of God and not merely for money or for humanitarian reasons.

(d) That Almighty God is pleased to reward those who bury the dead is distinctly taught in the book of Tobias. To visit a house of mourning or to attend a funeral is a mark of respect to the dead and a consolation to the relatives of the deceased person.

(e) The Church has forbidden cremation not because it is wrong in itself nor because it is contrary to divine law but because it is in opposition to the Jewish and Christian tradition and has been advocated by anti-Christians with the express purpose of destroying belief in the immortality of the soul and the resurrection of the body. The Fathers of the Church defended the custom of burial by reason of the doctrine of the resurrection of the body and the respect due to it as the temple of the Holy Ghost.

113

(f) During great pestilences when it is impossible to bury the dead in time to prevent the spread of contagion, the Church permits mass cremation because it is neither wrong in itself nor expressly forbidden by the divine law.

192. Which are the chief spiritual works of mercy?

The chief spiritual works of mercy are seven:

1. To admonish the sinner.
2. To instruct the ignorant.
3. To counsel the doubtful.
4. To comfort the sorrowful.
5. To bear wrongs patiently.
6. To forgive all injuries.
7. To pray for the living and the dead.

(a) The spiritual works of mercy by their very nature excel the corporal works. They refer directly to the soul of man and to his eternal welfare. They are aids in healing the soul and in preserving it from spiritual disease; they help to foster the true happiness of mankind and are the most perfect fulfillment of the command to love our neighbor.

(b) We are obliged to admonish the sinner and to try to persuade him to turn from evil and to practice virtue whenever prudence dictates. We are not obliged to do so when, for example, we judge that our words will not be heeded or that greater harm will follow. Persons in authority, for example, parents and teachers, have a greater obligation than others in this regard. Sinners may be admonished not only by kind words but also by good example.

(c) Teachers in Catholic schools, missionaries, catechists, confessors, and Cathlolic writers perform in an excellent manner the spiritual work of instructing the ignorant. Those who help to support Catholic schools, colleges, and missions, as well as those who teach merely secular subjects, perform this spiritual work of mercy provided the motive of their actions is love of God and neighbor.

(d) Whenever their words are likely to be heeded, Christians must be ready to give helpful advice to those who need it.

(e) To console those who are in sorrow because of the death or sickness of loved ones or because of some other spiritual or temporal affliction is an act of Christian charity.

(f) The true Christian imitates the example of Christ by bearing wrongs patiently and by forgiving all injuries because of love of God. While dying on the cross, Christ prayed to His heavenly Father to forgive His executioners "for they do not know what they are doing" (*Luke 23:34*). The true Christain loves all men, even those who reproach and persecute him.

(g) The sublime doctrines of the Communion of Saints and the Mystical Body of Christ should make us pray for all our brothers in Christ.

114

193. Is everyone obliged to perform the works of mercy?

Everyone is obliged to perform the works of mercy, according to his own ability and the need of his neighbor.

(a) The obligation to perform the works of mercy varies with one's vocation and condition of life and the degree of the neighbor's need.

194. Are all the ordinary deeds done every day to relieve the corporal or spiritual needs of others true works of mercy?

All the ordinary deeds done every day to relieve the corporal or spiritual needs of others are true works of mercy, if done in the name of Christ.

(a) We can make all the good works done for our neighbor supernatural by doing them in the name of Christ and for the love of God.

SCRIPTURE:
"For whoever gives you a cup of water to drink in my name, because you are Christ's, amen I say to you, he shall not lose his reward" (*Mark 9:40*).

"Therefore, whether you eat or drink, or do anything else, do all for the glory of God" (*I Corinthians 10:31*).

195. Which are the commandments of God?

The commandments of God are these ten:

1. I am the Lord thy God; thou shalt not have strange gods before Me.
2. Thou shalt not take the name of the Lord thy God in vain.
3. Remember thou keep holy the Lord's day.
4. Honor thy father and thy mother.
5. Thou shalt not kill.
6. Thou shalt not commit adultery.
7. Thou shalt not steal.
8. Thou shalt not bear false witness against thy neighbor.
9. Thou shalt not covet thy neighbor's wife.
10. Thou shalt not covet thy neighbor's goods.

(a) These commandments, engraven on two tablets of stone, were given by God to Moses on Mount Sinai. In giving these commandments God made plain and determined the obligations which arise from man's very nature.

SCRIPTURE:
"And the Lord spoke all these words:

"I am the Lord thy God, who brought thee out of the land of Egypt, out of the house of bondage.

"Thou shalt not have strange gods before me.

"Thou shalt not make to thyself a graven thing, nor the likeness of anything that is in heaven above, or in the earth beneath, nor of those things that are in the waters under the earth.

"Thou shalt not adore them, nor serve *them:* I am the Lord thy God, mighty, jealous, visiting the iniquity of the fathers upon the children, unto the third and fourth generation of them that hate me:

"And showing mercy unto thousands to them that love me, and keep my commandments.

115

"Thou shalt not take the name of the Lord thy God in vain: for the Lord will not hold him guiltless that shall take the name of the Lord his God in vain.

"Remember that thou keep holy the sabbath day.

"Six days shalt thou labor, and shalt do all thy works.

"But on the seventh day is the sabbath of the Lord thy God: thou shalt do no work on it, thou nor thy son, nor thy daughter, nor thy man-servant, nor thy maid-servant, nor thy beast, nor the stranger that is within thy gates.

"For in six days the Lord made heaven and earth, and the sea, and all things that are in them, and rested on the seventh day: therefore the Lord blessed the seventh day, and sanctified it.

"Honor thy father and thy mother, that thou mayest be long-lived upon the land which the Lord thy God will give thee.

"Thou shalt not kill.

"Thou shalt not commit adultery.

"Thou shalt not steal.

"Thou shalt not bear false witness against thy neighbor.

"Thou shalt not covet thy neighbor's house: neither shalt thou desire his wife, nor his servant, nor his handmaid, nor his ox, nor his ass, nor anything that is his" (*Exodus 20:1-17*).

"Do not think that I have come to destroy the Law or the Prophets. I have not come to destroy, but to fulfill. For amen I say to you, till heaven and earth pass away, not one jot or one tittle shall be lost from the Law till all things have been accomplished. Therefore whoever does away with one of these least commandments, and so teaches men, shall be called least in the kingdom of heaven; but whoever carries them out and teaches them, he shall be called great in the kingdom of heaven" (*Matthew 5:17-19*).

196. Should we be satisfied merely to keep the commandments of God?

We should not be satisfied merely to keep the commandments of God, but should always be ready to do good deeds, even when they are not commanded.

(a) The commandments of God state the minimum requirements for salvation. They should be kept not merely according to the letter but also according to the spirit, which obliges us to strive for greater perfection.

SCRIPTURE:

"And behold, a certain man came to him and said, 'Good Master, what good work shall I do to have eternal life?' He said to him, 'Why dost thou ask me about what is good? One there is who is good, and he is God. But if thou wilt enter into life, keep the commandments.' He said to him, 'Which?' And Jesus said,

' "Thou shalt not kill,
Thou shalt not commit adultery,
Thou shalt not steal,
Thou shalt not bear false witness,
Honor thy father and mother,
and, Thou shalt love thy neighbor as thyself." '

The young man said to him, 'All these I have kept; what is yet wanting to me?' Jesus said to him, 'If thou wilt be perfect, go, sell what thou hast, and give to the poor, and thou shalt have treasure in heaven; and come, follow me.' But when the young man heard the saying, he went away sad, for he had great possessions" (*Matthew 19:16-22*).

116

197. What does Our Saviour especially recommend that is not strictly commanded by the law of God?

Our Saviour especially recommends the observance of the Evangelical Counsels — voluntary poverty, perpetual chastity, and perfect obedience.

(a) These recommendations are called counsels because, although they extend an invitation to all, the obligation to practice them is assumed voluntarily. They are called evangelical because they are recommended in the Gospel.

(b) The Evangelical Counsels are the most perfect of the many counsels recommended in the Gospel; they remove impediments to sanctity and are positive helps to greater holiness. The observance of voluntary poverty enables a person to overcome the inclinations of greed; the observance of perpetual chastity helps in conquering the flesh; the observance of perfect obedience demands the entire subjection of the will.

(c) The obligations of the Evangelical Counsels are assumed by the vows of the religious life, which is called the life of perfection. Those who make these vows do not thereby become perfect but they assume the obligation of tending toward perfection in a special way.

(d) Any Catholic may voluntarily seek admission to the religious life who is free from legal impediments, has the right intention, and is fitted to discharge the duties of the particular institute of his choice. Married persons, and persons under fifteen years of age, as well as those whose parents need their help, are prevented by legal impediments from embracing the religious state. A person who wishes to please God, to save his soul, or to help his neighbor has a right intention in seeking admission to the religious state. The novitiate of the religious life is a period during which a vocation is tested and superiors and subjects are enabled to decide freely on the mutual obligations that are assumed by public profession in the religious state. By profession, members of the religious life publicly assume the obligations of their state through the vows of poverty, chastity, and obedience. These obligations are assumed for a definite period or for life.

(e) Persons who do not embrace the religious life can tend toward perfection in their particular state by observing the spirit of the Evangelical Counsels. The spirit of poverty will make them freely give up many needless things in order to help the poor. Married persons will strive to govern their lives by marital chastity, realizing that they can place limitation of their family only through virtuous living. The spirit of obedience will make them docile to legitimate superiors, in whom they will see the representatives of God.

SCRIPTURE:

"You therefore are to be perfect, even as your heavenly Father is perfect" (*Matthew 5:48*).

"And Peter said, 'Behold, we have left all and followed thee.' And he said to them, 'Amen I say to you, there is no one who has left house, or parents, or brothers, or wife, or children, for the sake of the kingdom of God, who shall not receive much more in the present time, and in the age to come life everlasting' " (*Luke 18:28-30*).

117

Poverty — See Scripture, question 196, *Matthew 19:16-22*.

Chastity — "He who is unmarried is concerned about the things of the Lord, how he may please God" (*I Corinthians 7:32*).

Obedience — "For obedience is better than sacrifices" (*I Kings 15:22*).

IMPORTANT TRUTHS ABOUT THE TWO GREAT COMMANDMENTS

"Faith without works is dead" (*James 2:26*), says the apostle, St. James. This same lesson was taught by Our Lord when He said "Not every one who says to me, 'Lord, Lord' shall enter the kingdom of heaven; but he who does the will of my Father in heaven shall enter the kingdom of heaven" (*Matthew 7:21*). In other words, we are obliged not only to believe all that God has revealed, but also to obey all that He commands.

Our reason tells us that certain things are good and obligatory, such as worshiping God and obeying our parents, while other things are bad and sinful, such as theft or murder. These obligations and prohibitions make up the natural law. To know this we need no revelation; yet, because human beings through ignorance and malice are apt to go astray even in this law, God gave the Israelites the ten commandments, which explicitly contain the chief obligations of the natural law, and implicitly contain all the rest. Thus, the fourth commandment explicitly commands children to honor their parents; yet it surely implies other obligations, such as love, respect and obedience, as also the duties of parents toward their children. God also laid down certain other laws for the people of Israel in addition to the natural law, such as the prohibition to eat certain kinds of food (*Leviticus 11*). These constitute what we call the positive law. It is evident that God, Creator and Lord of all mankind, has a right to make any laws He wills, and men have the obligation to obey them.

It should be noted that the enumeration of the ten commandments differs in the Catholic Church from that followed by most Protestants. What is the first commandment for Catholics is divided into two commandments by Protestants, while the ninth and tenth commandments of Catholics form only one commandment for Protestants, so that our commandments from the second to the ninth are numbered one higher by Protestants.

Our Lord emphasized the necessity of obeying the natural law. He Himself also added some positive laws for all mankind, such as the obligation to enter His Church. He did away with the ceremonial laws of the Jewish people, such as the laws regarding the types of food that were forbidden and the observance of the Sabbath Day. In His law the prominent feature is love — love for God and love for our fellow men. That is why He said that all the laws of God could be summed up in the two commandments, to love God and to love our neighbor. For this same reason He wills that His followers shall not content themselves with merely obeying laws. He wishes them to do more than what is commanded. In the Christian religion the works of mercy, which are deeds of charity toward one's neighbor in his bodily or spiritual needs, are recommended to all. And to those who wish to practice Christian virtue in its highest forms our Saviour gave the counsels of perfection: poverty, chastity and obedience.

These counsels are the basis of the religious state. There are hundreds of different orders and congregations, each doing its own particular work for God's glory, but all leading their members nearer to God by the constant practice of Christian virtue. Some female religious teach, others care for the sick and the aged and orphans, others devote themselves entirely to prayer in the seclusion of their convents. Some male religious are priests; others are brothers. And the Church is ever holding the religious life before Catholic boys and girls as the most perfect way in which one may serve God and our neighbor and the surest way of winning the happiness of heaven.

118

Sometimes young folks feel a desire for the life of holiness which the religious state offers, but they fear that they have no vocation to this sublime state. It is possible that they entertain a false notion about a vocation. They seem to imagine that those who are called to the religious life receive a clear internal inspiration, inviting them to the monastery or the convent. On this point they are entirely mistaken. The very fact that a person has the requisite qualities of body and of soul to fulfil the duties of the religious life and feels an inclination toward this form of life can be regarded as an indication that he has a vocation and that he may lawfully seek admission to an order or congregation. During the noviciate he will have a sufficient opportunity to judge whether or not he is called to the religious state.

Today there is great need of candidates for the religious life, especially of those who will devote themselves to works of charity, such as the care of the sick and the education of children. The spirit of the age, so eager for material wealth and pleasures and honors, is indeed the very opposite of the religious spirit of poverty and self-denial and humility. But the very fact that there is so great a difference between the world and the cloister reflects great credit and merit on those who enter the religious life.

Young folks who think that they may have a religious vocation should pray fervently for divine guidance, read good books on the religious state, and consult an experienced confessor.

RESOLUTION: Resolve to perform at least once a day a work of corporal or spiritual mercy.

STUDY HELPS

A. TRUE OR FALSE. (*Check each of the following statements as either true or false. The correct answer can be found in the preceding portions of this lesson.*)

	TRUE	FALSE
(1) The Catholic Church commands us to keep holy the Sabbath day.	. . . . .	. . . . .
(2) We must love every person who has received or is capable of receiving sanctifying grace.	. . . . .	. . . . .
(3) The corporal works of mercy are superior to the spiritual works.	. . . . .	. . . . .
(4) If we perform the works of mercy for humanitarian reasons we are fulfilling our Lord's commandment to love our neighbor as ourselves.	. . . . .	. . . . .
(5) A person can tend to perfection only in the religious life.	. . . . .	. . . . :
(6) A person must be at least sixteen years old before he may enter the novitiate of a religious order.	. . . . .	. . . . .
(7) Our Lord did away with the ceremonial laws of the Jewish people.	. . . . .	. . . . .
(8) We are obliged to follow the counsels as well as obey the commandments.	. . . . .	. . . . .
(9) All male religious are either priests or candidates for the priesthood.	. . . . .	. . . . .
(10) God gave the ten commandments to Moses on Mount Sinai.	. . . . .	. . . . .

9. PROBLEMS AND EXERCISES. (*Answer the questions orally or write them as your teacher may direct*):

(1) Before the arrival of the early Catholic missionaries, could the Indians of our country have known anything about any of the ten commandments? Explain your answer.

(2) Try to condense the entire Law of God into as few as five words.

(3) In a short paragraph of three or four sentences show that obedience and service are the best expressions of this love.

(4) Restaurants, cafeterias and lunch-rooms feed the hungry. Saloons, soda counters, and tea-rooms give drink to the thirsty. Haberdasheries, dressmakers, and clothiers supply clothing to their customers. Are they performing corporal works of mercy? Explain your answer.

(5) Daniel goes to St. Hope's Hospital to have a chat with his classmate Edward, who is very sick, and at the same time, very discouraged and sad. At the end of his visit, Dan has Eddie in good humor and resigned to God's will. On the way out of the hospital, Dan drops into the hospital chapel to recite five Our Fathers and five Hail Marys for his friend Eddie. How many works of mercy has he performed? Specify them.

(6) Frances and Genevieve are good friends. Frances has great influence over her friend. She knows that Genevieve has been reading immodest publications and going with questionable companions. What spiritual work of mercy should Frances perform in Genevieve's regard?

(7) Suppose Frances objects: "I'd prefer to mind my own business!" What answer should be given her? Explain why Frances is perhaps obliged to perform this particular work of mercy.

(8) Nicholas, a Catholic Boy Scout, a very faithful fellow, seldom, if ever, misses his morning and night prayers. He is very charitably inclined, and a very willing helper. Tell him how to make doubly sure of being credited with his many daily good deeds.

(9) In a general way, explain to Jacob, a Jewish lad of your acquaintance, what you have learned about the ten commandments, mentioning the points of difference that now exist between Jews and Christians in their regard.

(10) Sophie, now in the graduating class at St. Mamertus', recently got the idea she would like to become a nun. Up to the present time she has been pretty lazy around the house, doing only those things she is compelled to do. Her constitution is weak. When asked why she wants to become a Sister she replies: "Because I like Sister Alphonsina, and I'm just crazy about the habit she wears!" Do you think Sophie has a vocation? What are the reasons for your answer?

(11) Myles, an altar boy and daily communicant, would like to become a priest. He is in the eighth grade. Raymond, his chum, would like to join an order of teaching brothers. Both have confided their ambitions to each other, but to no one else. In six months they are to graduate. What should they do promptly?

(12) Cite some words of Our Saviour Himself proving that more than faith alone is necessary to work out our salvation.

(13) If a Protestant friend speaks to you about the fifth commandment, to which commandment is he probably referring according to the Catholic enumeration?

LESSON 16

The First Commandment of God

198. What is the first commandment of God?

The first commandment of God is: I am the Lord thy God; thou shalt not have strange gods before Me.

(a) The first commandment forbids idolatry, that is, offering to a creature the supreme worship due to God alone. Idolatry is sinful because God alone has a right to supreme worship as the Creator and Preserver of all things. The first commandment also forbids us to ascribe to a creature any of the attributes that belong to God alone.

> SCRIPTURE:
> "Thou shalt not have strange gods before me. Thou shalt not make to thyself a graven thing, nor the likeness of anything that is in heaven above, or in the earth beneath, nor of those things that are in the waters under the earth" (*Exodus 20:3-4*).

199. What are we commanded by the first commandment?

By the first commandment we are commanded to offer to God alone the supreme worship that is due Him.

> SCRIPTURE:
> "And Jesus answered and said to him, 'It is written, "The Lord thy God shalt thou worship, and him only shalt thou serve" ' " (*Luke 4:8*).
> "For from him and through him and unto him are all things. To him be the glory forever, amen" (*Romans 11:36*).

200. How do we worship God?

We worship God by acts of faith, hope, and charity, and by adoring Him and praying to Him.

(a) We worship God by an act of faith when we firmly assent to the truth of God's revelation, on the word of God revealing, who can neither deceive nor be deceived.

(b) We worship God by an act of hope when we firmly trust that God who is all-powerful and faithful to His promises, will in His mercy give us eternal happiness and the means to obtain it.

(c) We worship God by an act of charity when we love God above all things for His own sake and our neighbor as ourselves for the love of God.

(d) We adore God by acknowledging His infinite excellence, our complete dependence upon Him, and our total subjection to His will.

(e) We pray to God by lifting up our minds and hearts to Him.[14]

(f) Acts of faith, hope, charity, adoration, and prayer may be internal or external. They are internal when they are only in our mind or heart; they are external when they are manifested outwardly by signs or words.

---

14. See questions 122, 123, 124 on acts of faith, hope, and charity; see lesson 37 on prayer.

121

(g) External worship is of no value unless it is joined with internal worship and is an outward manifestation of our internal convictions and sentiments.

(h) External worship is necessary because we are bound to render to God the homage of our bodies and because it serves to preserve, increase, and express internal worship. Man is composed of body and soul, and the body can and does aid the soul in its operations. We are moved to be more devout in our internal acts of worship by sacred music, art, public and private recitation of prayers, and the ceremonies of the liturgy.

201. What does faith oblige us to do?

Faith obliges us:

first, to make efforts to find out what God has revealed;
second, to believe firmly what God has revealed;
third, to profess our faith openly whenever necessary.

(a) God, whose power and knowledge are infinite, can reveal supernatural truths to man. Every man who knows or suspects that he does not profess the religion revealed by God is under the obligation of seeking it and, when he has found it, of embracing it.

(b) Whoever has attained the use of reason must make an interior act of faith:

first, when he comes to the knowledge of divine revelation or becomes certain of a dogma of the Church;
second, when he, having rejected the errors of infidelity or heresy, recognizes the obligation of believing the Catholic religion;
third, when an act of faith is necessary to resist temptations against faith, or another virtue;
fourth, often during life.

(c) A Catholic is bound to profess his faith openly:

first, whenever the honor due to God requires it; for example, when his failure to profess his faith openly would be equivalent to a denial of faith;
second, when the good of his neighbor requires it.

SCRIPTURE:

"Therefore, everyone who acknowledges me before men, I also will acknowledge him before my Father in heaven. But whoever disowns me before men, I in turn will disown him before my Father in heaven" (*Matthew 10:32-33*).

"For whoever is ashamed of me and my words, of him will the Son of Man be ashamed when he comes in his glory and that of the Father and of the holy angels" (*Luke 9:26*).

"He who believes in the Son has everlasting life; he who is unbelieving towards the Son shall not see life, but the wrath of God rests upon him" (*John 3:36*).

"This is 'The stone that was rejected by you, the builders, which has become the cornerstone.' Neither is there salvation in any other. For there is no other name under heaven given to men by which we must be saved" (*Acts 4:11-12*).

"For with the heart a man believes unto justice, and with the mouth profession of faith is made unto salvation" (*Romans 10:10*).

"For we in the Spirit wait for the hope of justice in virtue of faith. For in Christ Jesus neither circumcision is of any avail, nor uncircumcision, but faith which works through charity" (*Galatians 5:5-6*).

"For by grace you have been saved through faith; and that not from yourselves, for it is the gift of God" (*Ephesians 2:8*).

"And without faith it is impossible to please God. For he who comes to God must believe that God exists and is a rewarder to those who seek him" (*Hebrews 11:6*).

See Scripture, question 77, John 3:16; question 158, Mark 16:15-16.

202. What does hope oblige us to do?

Hope obliges us to trust firmly that God will give us eternal life and the means to obtain it.

(a) An act of hope must be made:

first, when a person comes to a knowledge of God's existence and his own destiny, namely, eternal happiness in heaven;

second, when it is necessary to resist temptations against the virtue of hope or some other virtue;

third, after the virtue of hope is lost by a sin opposed to it, that is, by despair or presumption;

fourth, often during life.

SCRIPTURE:

"Paul, a servant of God and apostle of Jesus Christ, in accordance with the faith of God's elect and the full knowledge of the truth which is according to piety, in the hope of life everlasting which God, who does not lie, promised before the ages began — " (*Titus 1:1-2*).

203. What does charity oblige us to do?

Charity obliges us to love God above all things because He is infinitely good, and to love our neighbor as ourselves for the love of God.

(a) An act of charity must be made:

first, when a person comes to the realization of the duty of loving God above all things and his neighbor as himself for the love of God;

second, when temptation can be overcome only by an act of charity;

third, at the hour of death;

fourth, often during life.

SCRIPTURE: *See Scripture, question 189, Matthew 22:35-40.*

204. How can a Catholic best safeguard his faith?

A Catholic can best safeguard his faith by making frequent acts of faith, by praying for a strong faith, by studying his religion very earnestly, by living a good life, by good reading, by refusing to associate with the enemies of the Church, and by not reading books and papers opposed to the Church and her teaching.

205. How does a Catholic sin against faith?

A Catholic sins against faith by apostasy, heresy, indifferentism, and by taking part in non-Catholic worship.

(a) Apostasy is the complete abandonment of the Christian faith by those who have been baptized.

(b) Heresy is the refusal of baptized persons, retaining the name Christian, to accept one or more of the truths revealed by God and taught by the Catholic Church. If this refusal is voluntary and obstinate, it is formal heresy; if it is involuntary, it is material heresy.

(c) Indifferentism is the error of those who hold that one religion is as good as another and that all religions are equally true and pleasing to God, or that one is free to accept or reject any or all religions.

(d) Those take part in the worship of non-Catholics who join in their religious services. Attendance at non-Catholic religious services, provided no part is taken in such worship, is allowed for a sufficiently grave reason, for example, presence at a non-Catholic funeral or a marriage ceremony for social reasons.

(e) Infidelity is also a sin against faith. It is the unbelief of those to whom the truths of faith have been sufficiently proposed but who nevertheless deliberately refuse to accept them.

SCRIPTURE:
Apostasy — *See Scripture, question 201, Matthew 10:32-33.*

Heresy — "I know that after my departure fierce wolves will get in among you, and will not spare the flock. And from among your own selves men will rise speaking perverse things, to draw away the disciples after them" (*Acts 20:29-30*).

Infidelity—*See Scripture, question 107, John 3:5; question 158, Mark 16:15-16.*

206. Why does a Catholic sin against faith by taking part in non-Catholic worship?

A Catholic sins against faith by taking part in non-Catholic worship because he thus professes belief in a religion he knows is false.

SCRIPTURE:
"Jesus said to him, 'I am the way, and the truth, and the life' " (*John 14:6*).

"Pilate therefore said to him, 'Thou art then a king?' Jesus answered, 'Thou sayest it; I am a king. This is why I was born, and why I have come into the world, to bear witness to the truth. Everyone who is of the truth hears my voice' " (*John 18:37*).

207. What are the sins against hope?

The sins against hope are presumption and despair.

208. When does a person sin by presumption?

A person sins by presumption when he trusts that he can be saved by his own efforts without God's help, or by God's help without his own efforts.

SCRIPTURE:
"Nay I do not even judge my own self. For I have nothing on my conscience, yet I am not thereby justified" (*I Corinthians 4:4*).

"Therefore let him who thinks he stands take heed lest he fall" (*I Corinthians 10:12*).

"For he is not approved who commends himself, but he whom the Lord commends" (*II Corinthians 10:18*).

209. When does a person sin by despair?

A person sins by despair when he deliberately refuses to trust that God will give him the necessary help to save his soul.

SCRIPTURE:

"Then Judas, who betrayed him, when he saw that he was condemned, repented and brought back the thirty pieces of silver to the chief priests and the elders, saying, 'I have sinned in betraying innocent blood. . . .' And he flung the pieces of silver into the temple, and withdrew; and went away and hanged himself with a halter" (*Matthew 27:3-5*).

"My dear children, these things I write to you in order that you may not sin. But if anyone sins, we have an advocate with the Father, Jesus Christ the just; and he is a propitiation for our sins, not for ours only but also for those of the whole world" (*I John 2:1-2*).

"May no temptation take hold of you but such as man is equal to. God is faithful and will not permit you to be tempted beyond your strength, but with the temptation will also give you a way out that you may be able to bear it" (*I Corinthians 10:13*).

210. What are the chief sins against charity?

The chief sins against charity are hatred of God and of our neighbor, envy, sloth, and scandal.

(a) When a person hates another, he wishes him evil or rejoices in his misfortune.

(b) One who hates God wishes evil to befall Him, if that were possible, or wishes grievous sins to be committed, or rejoices in sin as an insult to God. Hatred of God is the most grievous offense against Him and is always a mortal sin.

(c) A person who hates his neighbor wishes him harm or rejoices when evil befalls him. To wish a neighbor serious harm is a mortal sin; for example, to wish another's damnation. To wish a neighbor a slight evil or to hold a slight aversion for him is a venial sin. It is not a sin to wish some temporal misfortune to overtake another in order that he may be converted or cease to do harm. Nor is it sinful to wish another's death, under the condition that it be in accord with God's will; for example, to wish a person's death so that he will be relieved of great suffering, or because he is a menace to society or is likely to inflict grave harm on an innocent person, or because he deserves death by reason of crime.

(d) Envy is sadness at another's good fortune which is considered to be detracting from one's own excellence. Sadness at another's prosperity is not envy when it is caused by a neighbor's using his advantage to harm us, or when another is unreasonably and unjustly preferred to us.[15]

(e) Sloth is distaste for spiritual things because their attainment requires much labor.[16]

(f) Scandal is any word, act, or omission that is in itself evil or has the appearance of evil and which can be the occasion of another's sin. Scandal

---

15. See question 74 (f).
16. See question 74 (g).

125

may be given even though no sin follows. A person who has already determined to sin or a person who cannot be led into sin cannot be scandalized. Scandal is direct when a word, act, or omission is intended to lead another to sin. Scandal is indirect when it is foreseen that one's word, act, or omission is likely to be the occasion of another's sin, even though such is not intended.

SCRIPTURE:
Envy — "Charity does not envy" (*I Corinthians 13:4*).

Sloth — "But we want every one of you to show to the very end the same earnestness for the fulfillment of your hopes; so that you may become not sluggish but imitators of those who by faith and patience will inherit the promises" (*Hebrews 6:11-12*).

"Be not slothful in zeal; be fervent in spirit, serving the Lord" (*Romans 12:11*).

Scandal — "Woe to the world because of scandals! For it must needs be that scandals come, but woe to the man through whom scandal does come!" (*Matthew 18:7*).

211. Besides the sins against faith, hope, and charity, what other sins does the first commandment forbid?

Besides the sins against faith, hope, and charity, the first commandment forbids also superstition and sacrilege.

212. When does a person sin by superstition?

A person sins by superstition when he attributes to a creature a power that belongs to God alone, as when he makes use of charms or spells, believes in dreams or fortune-telling, or goes to spiritists.

(a) Superstition is by its nature a mortal sin, but it may be venial either when the matter is slight or when there is a lack of full consent to the act. Often this sin is not mortal when there is question of certain popular superstitions, for example, belief in unlucky days and numbers, or when superstitious acts are performed as a joke without any serious thought of attributing divine powers to a creature, or when these acts are performed for amusement.

SCRIPTURE:
"Neither let there be found among you any one that ... consulteth soothsayers, or observeth dreams and omens. Neither let there be any wizard, nor charmer, nor any one that consulteth pythonic spirits, or fortune tellers: or that seeketh the truth from the dead. For the Lord abhorreth all these things: and for these abominations he will destroy them" (*Deuteronomy 18:10-12*).
See Scripture, question 198, Exodus 20:3-4.

213. When does a person sin by sacrilege?

A person sins by sacrilege when he mistreats sacred persons, places, or things.

(a) To mistreat a person consecrated to God in the clerical or religious state of life is a *personal* sacrilege. The violation of places dedicated to divine worship by the public authority of the Church, for example, churches and chapels, is a *local* sacrilege. The misuse or violation of sacred things, for example, the sacraments, the Holy Scriptures, or objects consecrated or blessed for divine worship or devotion, as chalices and statues, etc., is a *real* sacrilege.

(b) Sacrilege, of its nature, is a grievous sin, but it may be venial either because the matter is slight or because there is lack of full consent to the act.

SCRIPTURE:
"They have set thy sanctuary ablaze, they have profaned the dwelling of thy name on the earth. They said in their heart: 'Let us destroy them all together; burn ye all God's sanctuaries in the land' " *(Psalm 73:7-8).*

IMPORTANT TRUTHS ABOUT THE 1st COMMANDMENT OF GOD

Many persons believe that in order to lead a good life one has only to act justly and charitably toward his fellow men. Such persons do not realize that the most important of man's obligations are those toward his Creator. The chief of these obligations are those laid down in the first three commandments. The first commandment prescribes our fundamental duty as creatures — the adoration of God—and forbids those things that are opposed to it.

To obey the first commandment we must especially practice those virtues which have God Himself as their immediate object, the theological virtues. We should frequently make acts of these virtues. Although every practical Catholic, without thinking expressly of these virtues, makes acts of faith, hope and charity when he performs his religious duties, such as attendance at Mass, the reception of the sacraments, prayer, etc., it is advisable for every one to make acts of the theological virtues in a more express manner at certain times. The most convenient occasion is when we say our night prayers.

Sins against the first commandment are very common nowadays. Besides the great multitude of persons who deliberately reject belief in God and Christ, there are many who will not accept the Catholic religion, even though they see the force of the arguments the Catholic Church presents to show that it is the true Church of Jesus Christ, the Son of God. Many of these persons are moved by the thought of the difficulties and the sacrifices that are connected with the Catholic religion, such as the stricter observance of the moral code, confession, and the laws of fast and abstinence. These persons often try to justify themselves with the statement that one religion is as good as another; but this is ridiculous, because there can be only one true religion, and surely false religions cannot be as good as that which is true.

Unfortunately, there are even Catholics who violate the first commandment — some by sins against hope and charity, some even by sins against faith. It is true, there are few Catholics who after being instructed in their religion, go so far as to doubt or deny any of the Church's teachings. Even those unfortunate persons who leave the Catholic Church are generally led to make this decision, not by difficulties concerning the faith but by desire of worldly success or the intention of marrying a divorced person, or some other unworthy material motive. But there are Catholics who are more or less seriously addicted to superstitious practices, such as avoiding thirteen at table, reading tea-leaves, knocking on wood, etc. Some even engage in more serious superstitious practices, such as consulting fortune tellers or spiritistic mediums. These practices are a violation of the first commandment of God, inasmuch as they attribute to created things powers that God reserves to Himself.

The most important truths of revelation, which every one should know explicitly as a means of salvation, are these four: (1) God exists; (2) God rewards the good and punishes the wicked; (3) God is one in nature and three in Persons; (4) The second Person of the Holy Trinity became man and died for our salvation, rose from the dead and ascended into heaven, whence He shall come to judge the living and the dead.

127

Catholics should be on their guard against the sin of sacrilege, such as the lack of proper reverence in church, jokes concerning the Bible or other sacred things, disrespectful use of holy water or blessed medals, etc. Generally such sins are only venial; but a person is guilty of the mortal sin of sacrilege when there is a question of the unworthy reception of a sacrament. By far the worst example of this kind is the unworthy reception of the Holy Eucharist.

RESOLUTION: Resolve to avoid carefully anything which would involve even a slight sin of superstition or sacrilege.

STUDY HELPS

A. COLUMN SELECTION. (*Join correctly the parts of the sentences in Columns I and II, by placing the right key letter in the proper parentheses*):

I

(1) Apostasy is (. .).

(2) Heresy is (. .).

(3) Infidelity is (. .).

(4) To wish one's neighbor serious harm (. .).

(5) A slight irreverence in church (. .).

(6) A Catholic is never allowed (. .).

(7) External worship is of no value (. .).

(8) A Catholic must profess his faith (. .).

(9) Idolatry is sinful (. .).

(10) We make an act of faith when we believe revealed truth (. .).

II

(A) to take active part in non-Catholic religious services.

(B) because God who revealed it can neither deceive nor be deceived.

(C) the complete abandonment of the Christian faith by a baptized person.

(D) is a venial sin.

(E) the refusal of a baptized person, retaining the name of Christian, to accept one or more of the truths revealed by God and taught by the Catholic Church.

(F) the unbelief of one to whom the faith has been sufficiently proposed.

(G) because the true God alone has the right to supreme worship.

(H) is a mortal sin.

(I) when the good of his neighbor requires it.

(J) is a mortal sin.

B. PROBLEMS AND EXERCISES. (*Answer the questions orally or write them as your teacher may direct*):

(1) Titus, a fallen-away Catholic, is urged by his wife Lulu to make the parish mission. He angrily replies: "I don't need the mission! I'm okay as I am. I don't harm or injure anyone, I'm a sober and honest man, and I mind my own business! Let me alone!" What important obligations are being neglected by Titus? In what commandments are they contained?

(2) As creatures, what is our most fundamental duty? Which of the commandments orders us to fulfill that duty?

(3) Joseph's night prayer is generally very short. Tired out from the work and the play of each day, he kneels alongside his bed, blesses himself, says one Our Father and one Hail Mary, then goes to bed. What recommendation would you make to him that will becomingly lengthen his night prayer and help him more perfectly fulfill the duty placed on him by the first commandment?

(4) Benjamin, a Jewish boy, Aquinas, a Catholic boy, and Adrian, a Protestant boy are sitting around their campfire discussing religion. Benjamin goes to his synagogue four or five times a year; Aquinas never misses Mass of obligation; Adrian's attendance at Sunday service is about 50%. "After all, we all worship the same God," says Bennie, "so it doesn't make much difference to what church we belong!" "That's what I think, too!" chimes in Adrian. Should Aquinas be "liberal" and agree with his two companions? Why not?

(5) Eduarda, Diana, and Maude sing in the choir at High Mass. Before Mass they talk pretty freely among themselves about worldly matters; sometimes they disturb the priest while he is reading the Gospel, making the announcements, or preaching his sermon. Occasionally they annoy members of the congregation by their silly antics. Lately the organist reprimanded Maude for reading the Sunday comics during the sermon. Express your opinion about these improprieties.

(6) Brendan, fourteen years old, spending the summer at a camp with his brother Tommy, aged ten, misses Mass on Sunday through laziness, realizing at the same time that because of his bad example, Tommy will also miss Mass. How many and what sins has Brendan committed?

(7) Ronald, a good friend of yours, but an indifferentist all his life, has only five minutes to live. No priest is available. He asks you to make a Catholic out of him before he dies. Tell us what instruction you will give him before you baptize him, and what prayer, or prayers, you will say with him, after your hurried instruction is completed.

(8) Jonathan thinks that if a person reads the "Sunday Visitor" or the diocesan paper regularly such a person will be a well instructed practical Catholic. His sister Hannah claims that it is better to listen in regularly to the Catholic programs over the radio, especially the Catholic Hour on Sunday evenings. In a paragraph of from 100 to 125 words tell us what you think of both opinions, and add your own.

(9) Bertram, a Catholic, is visiting New York City for the first time. On a sightseeing trip he goes to the Episcopalian Cathedral of St. John the Divine. Although a service is going on, he moves about quietly, looking at the various objects of interest. Has he committed a sin against faith? Explain your answer.

(10) Flora, a member of the Book-of-the-Month Club, reads each book as it is delivered to her home. Some of these books are most unfavorably reviewed by our Catholic publications as endangering faith and morals. Advise Flora as to whether or not she should renew her membership.

(11) Jasper is an infidel; Launcelot, an apostate; Algernon, a heretic. What has each done to incur such a title. Against what virtue, and against what commandment has each one sinned?

129

LESSON 17

Honoring the Saints, Relics, and Images

214. Does the first commandment forbid us to honor the saints in heaven?

The first commandment does not forbid us to honor the saints in heaven, provided we do not give them the honor that belongs to God alone.

(a) A saint, in the strict sense of the word, is a person who is declared officially by the Church to be in heaven and who may be publicly venerated.

(b) The veneration paid to the saints in heaven differs essentially from the adoration of God. The saints are creatures and are not to be given the supreme worship due to the Creator alone. The supreme honor given to God only is adoration in the full and strict sense of the word. The veneration given to the Blessed Mother and to the saints is an act of respect and honor of an entirely different nature. The veneration given to the Blessed Mother of God surpasses that given to the saints and angels.

SCRIPTURE:

"Behold I will send my angel. . . . Take notice of him and hear his voice, and do not think him one to be contemned" (*Exodus 23:20-21*).

"And he answered: No: but I am prince of the host of the Lord, and now I am come. Josue fell on his face to the ground. And worshipping, said: What saith my Lord to his servant?" (*Josue 5:14-15*).

"Let us now praise men of renown, and our fathers in their generation" (*Ecclesiasticus 44:1*).

"Then Jesus said to him, 'Begone, Satan! for it is written, "The Lord thy God shalt thou worship and him only shalt thou serve" ' " (*Matthew 4:10*).

"For, behold, henceforth all generations shall call me blessed" (*Luke 1:48*).

215. Why do we honor the saints in heaven?

We honor the saints in heaven because they practiced great virtue when they were on earth, and because in honoring those who are the chosen friends of God we honor God Himself.

216. How can we honor the saints?

We can honor the saints:

first, by imitating their holy lives;

second, by praying to them;

third, by showing respect to their relics and images.

SCRIPTURE:

"And Eliseus died, and they buried him. And the rovers from Moab came into the land the same year. And some that were burying a man, saw the rovers, and cast the body into the sepulchre of Eliseus. And when it had touched the bones of Eliseus, the man came to life, and stood upon his feet" (*4 Kings 13:20-21*).

130

"Go to my servant Job. . . . And my servant Job shall pray for you. His face I will accept" (*Job 42:8*).

"And God worked more than the usual miracles by the hand of Paul; so that even handkerchiefs and aprons were carried from his body to the sick, and the diseases left them and the evil spirits went out" (*Acts 19:11-12*).

"Brethren, be imitators of me, and mark those who walk after the pattern you have in us" (*Philippians 3:17*).

217. When we pray to the saints what do we ask them to do?

When we pray to the saints we ask them to offer their prayers to God for us.

218. How do we know that the saints will pray for us?

We know that the saints will pray for use because they are with God and have great love for us.

219. Why do we honor relics?

We honor relics because they are the bodies of the saints or objects connected with the saints or with Our Lord.

(a) The honor given to a relic does not stop at the sacred object itself but is directed to the person whose relic is venerated.

SCRIPTURE: *See Scripture, question 216, 4 Kings 13:20-21; Acts 19:11-12.*

220. When does the first commandment forbid the making or the use of statues and pictures?

The first commandment forbids the making or the use of statues and pictures only when they promote false worship.

SCRIPTURE:

"'Thou shalt not make to thyself a graven thing, nor the likeness of anything that is in heaven above, or in the earth beneath, nor of those things that are in the waters under the earth. Thou shalt not adore them, nor serve them" (*Exodus 20:4-5*).

"Keep therefore your souls carefully. You saw not any similitude in the day that the Lord God spoke to you in Horeb from the midst of the fire: lest perhaps being deceived you might make you a graven similitude, or image of male or female, the similitude of any beasts, that are upon the earth, or of birds, that fly under heaven, or of creeping things, that move on the earth, or of fishes, that abide in the waters under the earth: lest perhaps lifting up thy eyes to heaven, thou see the sun and the moon, and all the stars of heaven, and being deceived by error thou adore and serve them, which the Lord thy God created for the service of all the nations, that are under heaven" (*Deuteronomy 4:15-19*).

221. Is it right to show respect to the statues and pictures of Christ and of the saints?

It is right to show respect to the statues and pictures of Christ and of the saints, just as it is right to show respect to the images of those whom we honor or love on earth.

222. Do we honor Christ and the saints when we pray before the crucifix, relics, and sacred images?

We honor Christ and the saints when we pray before the crucifix, relics, and sacred images because we honor the persons they represent; we adore Christ and venerate the saints.

223. Do we pray to the crucifix or to the images and relics of the saints?

We do not pray to the crucifix or to the images and relics of the saints, but to the persons they represent.

(a) In venerating relics, statues, and pictures of Our Lord and the saints we must not believe that any divine power resides in them, nor should we put our trust in them as though they had the power of themselves to bestow favors. We place our trust in God and the intercessory power of the saints.

IMPORTANT TRUTHS ABOUT HONORING THE SAINTS, RELICS AND IMAGES

Devotion to the saints is one of the Catholic practices most misunderstood and most opposed by non-Catholics. Yet, it is a most reasonable devotion. If we truly love God, we shall love those who are dear to Him; and the saints in heaven are the souls most dear to God, united to Him for all eternity. Since they are so near to Him, their prayers are most effective, so we ask them to pray for us. We can have a particular devotion to certain saints, whose condition in life was similar to our own, or who we believe will show a special interest in us. Thus, the members of a religious order whose founder is among the canonized saints will naturally have a special devotion to this saint. All Catholics should have a special devotion to the Queen of Saints, the Blessed Virgin Mary.

In the liturgy of the Catholic Church seven general classes of saints are distinguished—apostles. martyrs, popes, confessors who were bishops, confessors who were not bishops, virgins, and women who were not virgins. Thus, everyone can find saints whose state in life was like his own. It should be noted here that when we speak of a saint as a confessor we mean, not that he heard confessions, but that he openly confessed himself a follower of Christ.

Naturally we cherish and venerate the images of the saints and their relics, just as the citizens of a nation respect and honor the images of the country's heroes and the articles they used in life. Catholics know full well that pictures and relics in themselves are only material things, incapable of helping us in our needs; but we find in them a means of inspiring us with pious affections, of reminding us of the saints, and of helping us to pray more devoutly. That is why every truly Catholic home bears holy pictures on the walls or sacred images among the furnishings. Only lukewarm, cowardly Catholics are afraid to have such representations in their homes out of fear lest their non-Catholic friends may laugh at them.

Of all holy images, the most sacred is the representation of Christ's death on the cross, the crucifix. This should find a place in every Catholic home, especially in every bedroom, so that the occupants may say their morning and night prayers before this reminder of God's great love for us. The most venerated relic of the Church is the Cross on which our Saviour died. The largest portion of this is kept in the Church of the Holy Cross in Rome, and small pieces are distributed to different churches throughout the world. Frequently a bishop carries a relic of the true Cross in the pectoral cross which he wears on his breast.

The Church does not permit the public veneration of a relic unless it is properly encased and sealed and its authenticity supported by a document, signed by a bishop or other ecclesiastical dignitary. This does not mean necessarily that it is absolutely certain that the relic is genuine; but it means that reasonable care has been taken to establish the fact that the relic is a true one.

There are three classes of relics—first-class relics, which are the bodies or portions of the bodies of the saints; second-class relics, which are articles used by a saint, such as his clothing or books; third-class relics, which are articles that have touched a first or second-class relic, such as the coffin in which the saint was buried.

We honor the saints best by imitating their virtues. Every Catholic should be familiar with the lives of some of the saints, and especially of the saints whose names were given him or her in Baptism. Sometimes, indeed the saints performed extraordinary deeds, or actions which were not in accord with ordinary prudence. In these things we must not try to imitate them, for on those occasions they were especially inspired by God. But we can all imitate the spirit that animated the saints, especially their love for God and for their fellow-men. They were human beings like ourselves, subject to temptation; some of them had sinned gravely before they became saints. We are all called to be saints; for to all of us Our Lord said: "You therefore are to be perfect, even as your heavenly Father is perfect" (*Matt. 5:48*).

RESOLUTION: Resolve to choose certain saints, pray to them, in particular, and try to imitate their lives.

STUDY HELPS

A. WORD SELECTION. (*Select the word or phrase which most exactly and most completely fills out the sentence.*)

(1) The honor we give to a relic is directed toward (the relic itself . . . God . . . the person whose relic it is).

(2) A saint in the strict sense of the word is (anyone in sanctifying grace . . . one who has been canonized . . . one who has been beatified).

(3) When we pray to the saints we ask them (to offer their prayers to God for us . . . to enlighten our minds . . . to confer grace on us).

(4) We give Jesus Christ (the honor due to a great man . . . the honor due to a great saint . . . the honor due to God).

(5) All Catholics should have a special devotion to (St. Theresa of the Child Jesus . . . the Blessed Virgin Mary . . . St. Joseph).

(6) The most sacred of all images is (the crucifix . . . the statue of the Blessed Virgin . . . the statue of the Sacred Heart).

(7) The largest portion of the true cross is kept in (St. Peter's church in Rome . . . the church of the Holy Cross in Rome . . . Jerusalem).

(8) A person who has sinned gravely (can never be a canonized saint . . . can be beatified but not canonized . . . can become a canonized saint).

(9) When a relic has a document in support of its authenticity (we can be absolutely sure that the relic is genuine . . . we know that reasonable care has been taken to establish the fact that it is genuine . . . the document proves nothing).

(10) When we call St. Gerard Majella a confessor we mean that (he heard confessions . . . he frequently went to confession . . . he openly confessed himself a follower of Christ).

B. PROBLEMS AND EXERCISES. (*Answer the questions orally or write them as your teacher may direct*):

(1) Jay, a politician and a Presbyterian without much religion, ridicules the idea of Catholics honoring the saints. Write him a short letter asking

133

him in a friendly way if he condemns patriotic Americans who pay their respects to George Washington, Thomas Jefferson, and Abraham Lincoln at the respective monuments to those outstanding citizens in Washington, D. C., and at other shrines erected to their memory throughout the nation. In a polite way, show him the reasonableness of our Catholic custom.

(2) Judith, a poorly-instructed Catholic, has great devotion to St. Anthony of Padua. She visits his shrine every day, rain or shine, even though on Sundays she sometimes misses Mass without a good excuse. She will spend from fifteen to forty-five minutes before St. Anthony's shrine, paying little or no attention to Our Lord in His Real Presence beyond a sort of curtsey as she enters or leaves the church. Is that well-regulated devotion? What advice would you give Judith?

(3) What do you consider well-regulated devotion towards the saints? Arrange the following saints in the order of your preference: St. Aloysius, St. Agnes, The Blessed Virgin Mary, the Little Flower, St. Anthony, St. Joseph, St. Patrick, St. Boniface, St. Francis Xavier, St. Francis of Assisi.

(4) Now from the foregoing list select three only, naming them in the order of your preference, together with a short reason why you rank them first, second, and third. If your favorite saint is not listed, you may supply that saint's name.

(5) Ambrose wants to know how to honor his patron saint. Can you tell him ways in which he can honor his great patron? How can he secure information about Saint Ambrose?

(6) St. Rose of Lima did some rather extraordinary things, such as cutting off her beautiful hair, observing an extremely rigorous Lenten fast, torturing her innocent flesh with sharp instruments of penance. Rose, a schoolgirl of 11, would like to know if she should do the things her illustrious patron did. What answer are you going to give her?

(7) Eric inquires whether or not the prayers he offers to St. Ann eventually reach God. What is your reply to Eric? Explain it.

(8) Anna has a tiny bone relic of the Little Flower of Jesus; Winifred has a piece of her Carmelite habit; Vivian, a small square of linen that was touched to one of the Saint's prayerbooks. Classify each relic.

(9) Jeremiah's family are moving into a new house. They leave behind them many old and wornout things, among them a picture of the Holy Family. They take with them the frame, but the picture itself is thrown in with the rubbish. Write three or four sentences to Jerry telling him what you think about the treatment of the discarded picture, and what you would have done under the same circumstances.

(10) On your own person do you habitually carry any religious image? Give at least two reasons why you think it is a good practice.

(11) What religious image is appropriate in the bedrooms of our homes?

(12) Marcella, a newlywed, says it is fashionable nowadays not to ornament the walls of one's home with pictures of any kind. What reply can be made to Marcella?

(13) What relic is generally found in the bishop's pectoral cross? Where is the largest portion of this relic kept at the present time?

The Second and Third Commandments of God

224. What is the second commandment of God?

The second commandment of God is: Thou shalt not take the name of the Lord thy God in vain.

SCRIPTURE:

"Thou shalt not take the name of the Lord thy God in vain: for the Lord will not hold him guiltless that shall take the name of the Lord his God in vain" (*Exodus 20:7*).

225. What are we commanded by the second commandment?

By the second commandment we are commanded always to speak with reverence of God, of the saints, and of holy things, and to be truthful in taking oaths and faithful to them and to our vows.

(a) When we honor a name, we actually honor the person or thing related to the name.

(b) We reverence God's name:

first, by using it reverently in prayer;

second, by bowing the head or tipping the hat at the name of Jesus;

third, by speaking reverently of the Blessed Virgin Mary, the angels, the saints, the Church, and persons, places, or things dedicated to the service of God;

fourth, by public manifestations of reverence, such as rallies, parades, and processions proclaiming the divinity of Christ, devotion to His Blessed Mother, and the recitation of the Divine Praises.

SCRIPTURE:

"Blessed be the name of the Lord both now and forever. From the rising of the sun unto its going down, may the name of the Lord be praised" (*Psalm 112:2-3*).

226. What is an oath?

An oath is the calling on God to witness to the truth of what we say.

SCRIPTURE:

"Thou shalt fear the Lord thy God, and shalt serve him only: and thou shalt swear by his name" (*Deuteronomy 6:13*).

"Now in what I am writing to you, behold, before God, I do not lie" (*Galatians 1:20*).

"For men swear by one greater than themselves, and an oath given as a guarantee is the final settlement of all their disagreement" (*Hebrews 6:16*).

227. What things are necessary to make an oath lawful?

To make an oath lawful, three things are necessary:

first, we must have a good reason for taking an oath;

135

second, we must be convinced that what we say under oath is true;

third, we must not swear, that is, take an oath to do what is wrong.

(a) An oath reverently taken is a meritorious act of divine worship; otherwise it is sinful. It is lawful to take an oath, that is, to swear, because an oath is a guarantee of truthfulness; it is useful in having our word accepted in matters which concern the glory of God or the good of our neighbor or of ourselves. An oath, at times, is prescribed by civil or ecclesiastical authority. To take an oath without sufficient reason, or to swear rashly, is ordinarily a venial sin but can be a mortal sin if it is the occasion of perjury or scandal.

(b) The binding force of an oath arises from the virtues of veracity and religion. The obligation to fulfill a promise made under oath is grave or light, depending on the gravity of that which is promised.

(c) If we take an oath to do that which is wrong, useless, or impossible, we are obliged not to keep it.

(d) A promissory oath ceases to bind:
first, if it is relaxed by the one to whom the promise was given;
second, if the object of the promise changes substantially;
third, if the object becomes sinful or useless;
fourth, if the reason for making the oath ceases to exist;
fifth, if a condition under which the oath was given ceases;
sixth, if it is legitimately annulled, dispensed, or commuted.

(e) An oath to observe civil constitutions does not oblige us to obey laws which are opposed to divine or ecclesiastical right. We are not permitted to swear unconditional obedience to a constitution containing laws against justice or the divine law. One cannot, for example, swear to observe a civil constitution which prohibits the teaching of the religion of Christ.

SCRIPTURE:
"By my own self have I sworn, saith the Lord: Because thou hast done this thing, and hast not spared thy only begotten son for my sake" (*Genesis 22:16*).
"And thou shalt swear: As the Lord liveth, in truth and in judgment and in justice" (*Jeremias 4:2*).

228. What great sin does a person commit who deliberately calls on God to bear witness to a lie?

A person who deliberately calls on God to bear witness to a lie commits the very grievous sin of perjury.

SCRIPTURE:
"The person that sweareth, and uttereth with his lips, that he would do either evil or good, and bindeth the same with an oath, and his word: and having forgotten it afterwards understandeth his offence, Let him do penance for his sin" (*Leviticus 5:4-5*).

"Thou shalt not swear falsely by my name, nor profane the name of thy God" (*Leviticus 19:12*).

"Neither shalt thou bear false witness against thy neighbor" (*Deuteronomy 5:20*).

136

229. What is a vow?

A vow is a deliberate promise made to God by which a person binds himself under pain of sin to do something that is especially pleasing to God.

(a) In making a vow, a person must act with freedom, knowledge, and deliberation, and with the intention of binding himself under pain of sin. What is promised by the vow must be possible, morally good, and better than its contrary. We make vows to God alone, but we may make them to God in honor of the saints in order to have greater assurance of obtaining the favor which we seek. A vow, therefore, is an act of divine worship by which we acknowledge God's supreme dominion. Any act that pertains to a vow is an act of divine worship.

(b) Vows may be public or private. A public vow is one made before a legitimate ecclesiastical superior and accepted in the name of the Church. A private vow is made to God immediately without the intervention of an ecclesiastical superior authorized to receive it.

(c) A vow should never be made without due reflection and the advice of a prudent spiritual director. In making a vow a person should avoid haste and levity and should seriously consider the responsibility to be assumed.

(d) The obligation of a vow depends upon the gravity of the object of the vow and the intention of the person making it.

SCRIPTURE:
"When thou hast made a vow to the Lord thy God, thou shalt not delay to pay it: because the Lord thy God will require it. And if thou delay, it shall be imputed to thee for a sin" (*Deuteronomy 23:21*).

"If thou hast vowed anything to God, defer not to pay it. For an unfaithful and foolish promise displeaseth him: but whatsoever thou hast vowed, pay it. And it is much better not to vow than after a vow not to perform the things promised" (*Ecclesiastes 5:3-4*).

See Scripture, question 224, Exodus 20:7.

230. What is meant by taking God's name in vain?

By taking God's name in vain is meant that the name of God or the holy name of Jesus Christ is used without reverence: for example, to express surprise or anger.

SCRIPTURE:
"Bless the Lord, O my soul, and let all that is within me bless his holy name" (*Psalm 102:1*).

"And let not the naming of God be usual in thy mouth, and meddle not with the names of saints: for thou shalt not escape free from them" (*Ecclesiasticus 23:10*).

231. Is it a sin to take God's name in vain?

It is a sin to take God's name in vain; ordinarily, it is a venial sin.

(a) To take God's name in vain is a mortal sin when it is done out of deliberate contempt for God, or when serious scandal may be given.

137

232. What is cursing?

Cursing is the calling down of some evil on a person, place, or thing.

(a) Cursing is a mortal sin when a grave evil is deliberately willed. Cursing is a venial sin when it is done thoughtlessly or when only a slight evil is willed or when it is directed to animals or inanimate things.

SCRIPTURE:

"He that curseth his father, or mother, shall die the death" (*Exodus 21:17*).

"And he loved cursing: may it come upon him; he would not have blessings: be it far from him. And may he be clothed with cursing as with a garment" (*Psalm 108:17-18*).

"Bless those who persecute you; bless and do not curse" (*Romans 12:14*).

"Out of the same mouth proceed blessing and cursing. These things, my brethren, ought not to be so" (*James 3:10*).

233. What is blasphemy?

Blasphemy is insulting language which expresses contempt for God, either directly or through His saints and holy things.

(a) Blasphemy is a grievous sin. It can become venial only through lack of reflection or consent.

(b) Blasphemy is heretical when it contains a denial of faith, for example, a denial of God's existence, His mercy, providence, or justice.

SCRIPTURE:

"And thou shalt speak to the children of Israel: The man that curseth his God, shall bear his sin: And he that blasphemeth the name of the Lord, dying let him die. All the multitude shall stone him, whether he be a native or a stranger. He that blasphemeth the name of the Lord, dying let him die" (*Leviticus 24:15-16*).

" 'Amen I say to you, that all sins shall be forgiven to the sons of men, and the blasphemies wherewith they may blaspheme; but whoever blasphemes against the Holy Spirit never has forgiveness, but will be guilty of an everlasting sin.' For they said, 'He has an unclean spirit' " (*Mark 3:28-30*).

234. What is the third commandment of God?

The third commandment of God is: Remember thou keep holy the Lord's day.

(a) The obligation to worship God is imposed on all men by the natural law. Man is obliged to adore and to thank God for His continuous blessings. Since the nature of man makes it impossible for him actually to express his adoration and his thanks continuously, reason dictates that certain times be specified for this purpose. God defined more exactly how man is to fulfill this obligation by His divine precept given in the Old Testament.

SCRIPTURE:

"And on the seventh day God ended his work which he had made: and he rested on the seventh day from all his work which he had done. And he blessed the seventh day, and sanctified it: because in it he had rested from all his work which God created and made" (*Genesis 2:2-3*).

"Remember that thou keep holy the sabbath day. Six days shalt thou labor, and shalt do all thy works. But on the seventh day is the sabbath of the Lord thy God: thou shalt do no work on it, thou nor thy son, nor thy daughter, nor thy man-servant, nor thy maid-servant, nor thy beast, nor the stranger that is within thy gates. For in six days the Lord made heaven and earth, and the sea, and all things that are in them, and rested on the seventh day: therefore the Lord blessed the seventh day, and sanctified it" (*Exodus 20:8-11*).

"Observe the day of the sabbath, to sanctify it, as the Lord thy God hath commanded thee. Six days shalt thou labor, and shalt do all thy works. The seventh is the day of the sabbath, that is, the rest of the Lord thy God" (*Deuteronomy 5:12-14*).

235. Why does the Church command us to keep Sunday as the Lord's day?

The Church commands us to keep Sunday as the Lord's day, because on Sunday Christ rose from the dead, and on Sunday the Holy Ghost descended upon the apostles.

(a) The early Church changed the day of worship from Saturday to Sunday on the authority given to it by Christ. The New Testament makes no explicit mention that the apostles changed the day of worship, but we know it from Tradition.

236. What are we commanded by the third commandment?

By the third commandment we are commanded to worship God in a special manner on Sunday, the Lord's day.

SCRIPTURE:
"Keep you my sabbath: for it is holy unto you. He that shall profane it, shall be put to death: he that shall do any work in it, his soul shall perish out of the midst of his people. Six days shall you do work: in the seventh day is the sabbath, the rest holy to the Lord" (*Exodus 31:14-15*).

237. How does the Church command us to worship God on Sunday?

The Church commands us to worship God on Sunday by assisting at the Holy Sacrifice of the Mass.

(a) Catholics who have reached the age of seven years and have sufficient use of reason are bound under pain of mortal sin to hear Mass on Sunday.

(b) To satisfy the obligation to assist at Mass on Sunday a person must actually be present at the place where Mass is celebrated. If he cannot enter the church because it is overcrowded, he can still hear Mass provided he is part of the assembly assisting at the Holy Sacrifice. A person who is a notable distance from the worshipers certainly is not bodily present at Mass.

(c) A person should be present for the entire Mass, from the beginning to the last Gospel. It is a venial sin to miss even a slight part of a Mass of obligation deliberately and a mortal sin to miss a notable part. The obligation to assist at Mass is not fulfilled if the Consecration or the Communion is missed. The obligation can be fulfilled by hearing parts of two or more Masses in succession, provided one is present for both the Consecration and the Communion of the same Mass.

139

(d) To fulfill the obligation to assist at Mass a person must have at least an implicit intention of hearing Mass and must advert, at least in a vague way, to the celebration of the Mass. It would be a mortal sin if he paid no attention at all to the principal parts of the Mass at which he assisted on Sunday. A person is obliged under pain of venial sin to avoid deliberate distractions during Mass and to take ordinary care to assist attentively and in a becoming manner.

(e) The Mass offers us an opportunity to gain great spiritual benefits, and the more frequently and more devoutly we hear Mass, the more grace we can obtain. Ordinarily the best way to hear Mass is to unite with the priest and follow him in reciting the prayers of the Mass.

(f) A grave inconvenience to oneself or to another excuses one from the obligation to hear Mass on Sundays and holydays.

238. What is forbidden by the third commandment of God?

By the third commandment of God all unnecessary servile work on Sunday is forbidden.

239. What is servile work?

Servile work is that which requires labor of body rather than of mind.

(a) Farming, mechanical and industrial labor, and business transactions are forbidden even though one does them for pleasure and without any gain. Reading, writing, typewriting, studying, drawing, painting, embroidering, playing music, traveling, hunting, fishing, and the like are not servile works even though they may require considerable bodily exertion.

(b) The obligation to avoid servile work on Sunday is grave, and therefore, its violation is a mortal sin if one works for a notable time.

240. When is servile work allowed on Sunday?

Servile work is allowed on Sunday when the honor of God, our own need, or that of our neighbor requires it.

(a) It is permissible on Sunday to do work directly concerned with divine worship; to perform necessary household duties which cannot conveniently be anticipated or deferred; to take personal care of the sick; and to do work required for the common good or necessary for one's own livelihood.

IMPORTANT TRUTHS ABOUT THE 2nd AND 3rd COMMANDMENTS

Like the first commandment, the second and third commandments of God are concerned with man's duties toward his Creator. The second regards his duties in the matter of speech, the third in the matter of external worship.

It is indeed sad to realize that many persons use one of God's greatest gifts, the gift of speech, to insult God Himself. Nowadays, the use of the name of God and of the holy name of Jesus as an interjection to mark any form of feeling or emotion has become common. Even children, barely able to speak, are thus using God's name in vain—often because they have heard it from their parents. Cursing and even blasphemy are also frequent. In the courtroom perjury is something often committed with little or no qualm of conscience. Truly, the world today has forgotten the commandment: "Thou shalt not take the name of the Lord thy God in vain".

Catholics should set an example of reverence toward the holy name of God and of His Incarnate Son. To incite Catholic men toward such reverence and to wage warfare on all evil talk, the Holy Name Society has been organized for Catholic men, and branches are established in almost every parish. It is a commendable practice of Catholics to bow reverently whenever they use or hear the name of Jesus.

A vow is an act of religion most pleasing to God. It is a deliberate promise made to God whereby a person binds himself under pain of sin to do something that is especially pleasing to God. The most common vows in the Catholic Church are the public vows of poverty, chastity and obedience taken by members of religious orders and religious congregations. By the vow of poverty a religious promises to live frugally and not to use money or other material goods except in accordance with the rules of his or her order and with proper permission; by the vow of chastity he or she promises not to marry or in any way violate the sixth or the ninth commandment; by the vow of obedience he or she promises to obey the Pope and the lawful superiors of his or her order.

The third commandment, as God gave it to the Jewish people, designated the seventh day of the week, the Sabbath, as the special day of worship of the Most High. God Himself laid down detailed rules as to the manner in which the Jews were to observe this day. Under the Christian law the first day of the week, Sunday, is the day set aside for the special worship of God. The Church does not impose the many restrictions that were prescribed for the Sabbath among the ancient Jews; but all Catholics are obliged to attend Mass and to abstain from servile work. It makes no difference whether the work is performed for wages or not. On the other hand, the Church does not forbid lawful amusement, such as athletics, nor work that is of a literary, artistic, or intellectual nature. Sometimes it is not easy to distinguish between prohibited work and lawful occupation. Thus, to paint a house is servile work, to paint a picture is liberal. In doubt, Catholics should consult their confessor before commencing the work.

Finally we should remember that while the Church obliges us to no other religious service on Sunday but Mass, it is advisable to devote more time to the worship of God, particularly by attendance at Benediction of the Blessed Sacrament. Sunday is also an appropriate day for reading some good Catholic literature, especially the diocesan Catholic paper, and for tuning in on Catholic radio programs.

RESOLUTION: Resolve to bow reverently every time you hear or pronounce the Holy Name of Jesus; and if you hear this Holy Name taken irreverently, say in your heart: "Blessed be the name of Jesus".

STUDY HELPS

A. TRUE OR FALSE. (*Check each of the following statements as either true or false. The correct answers can be found in the preceding portions of this lesson.*)

TRUE   FALSE

(1) To call on God to bear witness to a lie is a venial sin, if it is only a slight lie.   . . . .

(2) A person may not swear obedience to a civil constitution which forbids the teaching of Christ's religion.   . . . .

(3) A person can make a vow to the Blessed Virgin.   . . . .

(4) It is usually a mortal sin to take God's name in vain.   . . . .

(5) Cursing is usually a venial sin when it is directed against animals.   . . . .

141

TRUE   FALSE

(6) The change of the Sabbath day to Sunday was explicitly commanded by Christ.   ....

(7) A child who has reached the age of reason but is not yet seven years old is strictly not obliged to attend Mass on Sunday.   ....

(8) Typewriting is a servile work.   ....

(9) A person can fulfil his obligation of Sunday Mass if he sees the Mass by television from a distance.   ....

(10) It is a mortal sin if a person deliberately pays no attention to the consecration in a Mass of obligation.   ....

B. PROBLEMS AND EXERCISES. (*Answer the questions orally or write them as your teacher may direct*):

(1) When our gift of speech treats of things divine, what commandment governs its use?

(2) Which of the commandments regulates our external worship?

(3) Which vows are most commonly made by Catholics? Explain them.

(4) Hugo is a member of the parish Holy Name Society. He tries to induce Julian to become a member. Julian in the meantime asks you what is the real purpose of the Holy Name Society. Tell him.

(5) Julian has been, for many years, an extremely profane fellow. He wants to know if the Holy Name Society will be satisfied if he reveres the Holy Name, or must he also give up his profanity. Answer him.

(6) What practice is recommended to you when you use the Holy Name, or hear others use It?

(7) In certain Catholic countries many boys receive in Baptism the name of Jesus. Does this lesson suggest to you a reason why it is not customary in the United States to confer this Holy Name in Baptism?

(8) Urban, a boy with a fiery disposition, frequently takes the Holy Name irreverently. What resolution would you suggest he take, and what penance should he impose on himself every time he slips?

(9) Father Elias, giving a children's mission, suggests to them that if they offend God by irreverent and profane speech they should make the sign of the cross over their lips, and say an ejaculation. Would you agree that this is a good practice? Why?

(10) On Sunday morning after Mass, Cornelius was prevented from overhauling his motor boat by the reminder of his mother that he should not do servile work on Sunday. That afternoon he pitched a fifteen-inning ballgame. At supper, he tells his mother that he is more tired out than he would have been had he worked the whole day on his motorboat. Why was he allowed to play baseball, and forbidden to work on his motorboat?

(11) Letitia, a schoolgirl, spends over an hour every Sunday reading the newspaper and the funnies. The diocesan paper comes to her home every week, but she seldom glances at it. Her sister, Antoinette, spends almost as much time on the Sunday papers, but she also reads regularly the youth section of the "Sunday Visitor", and the "Sacred Heart Messenger." In a paragraph of four or five short sentences tell us why you consider Antoinette's practice more commendable.

142

The Fourth, Fifth, and Sixth Commandments of God

241. What is the fourth commandment of God?

The fourth commandment of God is: Honor thy father and thy mother.

(a) This commandment deals explicitly with the duties of children toward their parents, implicitly with the obligation of parents toward their children. Parents should make themselves worthy of the honor which this commandment imposes.

(b) All true authority of superiors comes from God. Subjects must therefore respect their legitimate superiors and obey their just commands. Superiors in turn must exercise their authority in full conformity with the laws of nature and of God.

SCRIPTURE:
"Honor thy father and thy mother, that thou mayest be long-lived upon the land which the Lord thy God will give thee" (*Exodus 20:12*).

242. What are we commanded by the fourth commandment?

By the fourth commandment we are commanded to respect and love our parents, to obey them in all that is not sinful, and to help them when they are in need.

(a) Children respect their parents when they pay them due reverence, speak and act with proper deference, accept their corrections readily, seek their advice regarding important decisions, and bear with charity their parents' faults.

(b) Children love their parents when they wish them well, show them a spirit of gratitude, try to please and help them, and pray for them.

(c) Children should obey the lawful commands of their parents as long as they live under parental authority. Parents must not command their children to sin. Children must obey the laws of God rather than the commands of men—even of their parents, when such commands are against the law of God.

(d) Children should ordinarily consult their parents about the choice of a state of life, but they are not strictly obliged to follow their advice.

(e) Parents must not command a son or a daughter to marry. One may exercise one's natural right to live singly if one so desires; moreover, the state of virginity or celibacy, embraced for the love of God, is higher than the married state. Parents must not command their children to marry a certain person. Ordinarily children should consult their parents before definitely deciding to marry. They are not always obliged to follow their parents' advice.

(f) Children are obliged to aid their parents in bodily or spiritual need, when they can do so. Children must provide for parents who are not able to support themselves.

143

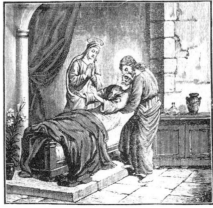

143a

The Holy Family

At the top, the Child Jesus is helping the Blessed Virgin Mary in her housework and St. Joseph in his craft.

At the bottom left, in the presence of the angel Raphael, the young Tobias is restoring the sight of his father by anointing his eyes with the fish gall that he brought back from his journey.

On the right, Our Savior is assisting St. Joseph, his foster-father, in his last moments, pressing him affectionately against His Sacred Heart.

143c

Our Lord and the Centurion

This picture offers two touching examples of the duties of masters towards their servants. The first is that of the centurion of the Gospel:

"Now when He had entered Capharnaum, there came to Him a centurion who entreated Him, saying, 'Lord, my servant is lying sick in the house, paralyzed, and is grievously afflicted.' Jesus said to him, 'I will come and cure him.' But in answer the centurion said, 'Lord, I am not worthy that thou shouldst come under my roof; but only say the word, and my servant shall be healed. For I too am a man subject to authority, and have soldiers subject to me; and I say to one, 'Go,' and he goes; and to another, 'Come,' and he comes; and to my servant, 'Do this,' and he does it.' And when Jesus heard this, He marvelled, and said to those who were following Him, 'Amen I say to you, I have not found such great faith in Israel. And I tell you that many will come from the east and from the west, and will feast with Abraham and Isaac and Jacob in the kingdom of heaven, but the children of the kingdom will be put forth into the darkness outside; there will be the weeping, and the gnashing of teeth.' Then Jesus said to the centurion, 'Go thy way; as thou hast believed, so be it done to thee.' And the servant was healed in that hour." (St. Matthew 8:5-13)

At the top, this centurion is shown on his knees at the feet of Jesus, surrounded by His apostles. Two servants who accompanied him stand respectfully behind their master.

The second example, shown at the bottom left, is that of St. Elzear, count of Sabran, in Provence. Having drawn up a rule of life for his servants, St. Elzear has it displayed in one of the most beautiful rooms of his palace, and gathers his servants there to explain it to them. Here are the chief provisions:

1. Morning and evening prayers
2. Assistance at the Holy Mass
3. Frequent reception of the sacraments
4. Devotion to the Holy Virgin and to St. Joseph
5. To avoid idleness
6. To flee bad company
7. To avoid quarrels, etc.

St. Elzear is standing at a chair, facing his servants to whom he is showing the rule. A crucifix and a statue of the Holy Virgin adorn the room. St. Delphine, his wife, helps with the instructions and forms, with her servants and daughters of honor, the little group to the right of her husband.

We are obliged: (1) to respect our superiors, (2) to serve them with fidelity, (3) to obey them in all that is not contrary to the law of God. We must regard our superiors as the representatives of God and obey them as God Himself.

At the bottom right, Eliezer, the servant of Abraham, offers to us a remarkable example of the fidelity that we owe to our superiors. He embarks on a long journey and goes to Mesopotamia to look for a wife for Isaac, his young master. Laden with gifts, he is near a well with his camels. Rebecca, daughter of Nachor, brother of Abraham, is there with a few companions to draw water. She presents some to Eliezer, who, recognizing in this a sign of the will of the Lord, offers her in exchange the lavish gifts from his master.

143d

"He that honoreth his mother is as one that layeth up a treasure. He that honoreth his father shall have joy in *his own* children: and in the day of his prayer he shall be heard. He that honoreth his father shall enjoy a long life: and he that obeyeth the father shall be comfort to his mother. He that feareth the Lord honoreth his parents and will serve them as his masters that brought him into the world. Honor thy father, in work and word, and all patience: That a blessing may come upon thee from him, and his blessing may remain in the latter end" *(Ecclesiasticus 3:5-10).*

"Support the old age of thy father: and grieve him not in his life; And if his understanding fail, have patience with him, and despise him not when thou art in thy strength: for the relieving of the father shall not be forgotten" *(Ecclesiasticus 3:14-15).*

"Children, obey your parents in the Lord, for that is right. 'Honor thy father and thy mother' — such is the first commandment with a promise — 'that it may be well with thee, and that thou mayest be long-lived upon the earth' " *(Ephesians 6:1-3).*

243. Does the fourth commandment oblige us to respect and to obey others besides our parents?

Besides our parents, the fourth commandment obliges us to respect and to obey all our lawful superiors.

(a) All are obliged to respect and to obey legitimate civil and ecclesiastical authorities when they discharge lawfully their official duties.

(b) Children must obey their teachers and other persons in whose charge they have been placed by their parents.

SCRIPTURE:
"And he said to them, 'Render, therefore, to Caesar the things that are Caesar's, and to God the things that are God's' " *(Luke 20:25).*

"Let everyone be subject to the higher authorities, for there exists no authority except from God, and those who exist have been appointed by God. Therefore he who resists the authority resists the ordinance of God; and they that resist bring on themselves condemnation. For rulers are a terror not to the good work but to the evil. Dost thou wish, then, not to fear the authority? Do what is good and thou wilt have praise from it. For it is God's minister to thee for good. But if thou dost what is evil, fear, for not without reason does it carry the sword. For it is God's minister, an avenger to execute wrath on him who does evil. Wherefore you must needs be subject, not only because of the wrath, but also for conscience' sake. For this is also why you pay tribute, for they are the ministers of God, serving unto this very end. Render to all men whatever is their due; tribute to whom tribute is due; taxes to whom taxes are due; fear to whom fear is due; honor to whom honor is due" *(Romans 13:1-7).*

244. What duty have parents toward their children and superiors toward those under their care?

Parents must provide for the spiritual and bodily welfare of their children; superiors, according to their varying degrees of responsibility, must care for those entrusted to them.

(a) Parents must manifest their love for their children in a reasonable manner. They must be on guard lest they spoil their children by granting them unreasonable requests; they must not neglect to correct their faults.

144

(b) It is the duty of parents to care for the spiritual welfare of their children, by having them baptized as soon as possible, by having them well instructed in the truths of religion; by training them in the practice of the Christian virtues, both by word and example; by counselling them to choose good companions; by directing their reading and recreation; and by urging them to fulfill their obligations to assist at Mass on Sundays and holydays, and to receive the sacraments regularly, even frequently.

(c) The Church forbids parents to send their children to non-Catholic or secular schools in which the Catholic religion is not taught, unless the bishop of a diocese grants permission because of particular circumstances.

(d) Parents are responsible for the physical and social well-being of their children. They must provide the necessary food, clothing, shelter, and medical care insofar as they are able. Parents are equally responsible for the intellectual and religious instruction and moral training of their children. They should rear them to be useful, self-supporting, patriotic citizens and informed, practical members of the Church.

SCRIPTURE:
"He that spareth the rod hateth his son: but he that loveth him correcteth him betimes" (*Proverbs 13:24*).

"Hast thou children? Instruct them, and bow down their neck from their childhood" (*Ecclesiasticus 7:25*).

"And you, fathers, do not provoke your children to anger, but rear them in the discipline and admonition of the Lord" (*Ephesians 6:4*).

245. What are the duties of a citizen toward his country?

A citizen must love his country, be sincerely interested in its welfare, and respect and obey its lawful authority.

(a) A person who plots against his country or rebels against its legitimate government commits a grave sin. Citizens, however, have a right to defend themselves against tyranny when there is no other way to secure the exercise of their fundamental human rights.

SCRIPTURE: *See Scripture, question 243, Romans 13:1-7.*

246. How does a citizen show a sincere interest in his country's welfare?

A citizen shows a sincere interest in his country's welfare by voting honestly and without selfish motives, by paying just taxes, and by defending his country's rights when necessary.

(a) Citizens should exercise their right to vote. This is a moral obligation when the common good of the state or the good of religion, especially in serious matters, can be promoted.

(b) Citizens should vote for the candidates who in their judgment are best qualified to discharge the duties of public office. Mere personal gain or friendship does not justify one's voting for a candidate. It would be sinful to cast a ballot for one who, in the judgment of the voters, would do grave public harm.

(c) Citizens of a country as well as aliens should obey the law of paying just taxes in order to contribute their fair share to the lawful expenses of good government and public security.

(d) Citizens are obliged to help their country wage a just war. They must serve in the armed forces if the government commands them to do so unless they are convinced from adequate and unquestionable evidence that the war is unjust.

247. Why must we respect and obey the lawful authority of our country?

We must respect and obey the lawful authority of our country because it comes from God, the Source of all authority.

(a) Citizens may accept any form of government that does not claim for itself rights that belong to God alone or those that are proper to the individual, to the family, or to the Church. The state exists for the common good of men, and not men for the state. A government may not infringe on the right of an individual or of a family to worship God and to live according to His laws; nor may it forbid parents to instruct their children in the truths of God and to train them in virtuous living. A government may not prohibit the Church from preaching the Gospel, administering the sacraments, and legislating in all those matters that pertain to the worship of God and the salvation of souls.

(b) If a government commands citizens to violate the law of God they must refuse to obey, for, according to Saint Luke, "We must obey God rather than men" (Acts 5:29).

SCRIPTURE: *See Scripture, question 243.*

248. Why are we obliged to take an active part in works of good citizenship?

We are obliged to take an active part in works of good citizenship because right reason requires citizens to work together for the public welfare of the country.

249. What are the chief duties of those who hold public office?

The chief duties of those who hold public office are to be just to all in exercising their authority and to promote the general welfare.

SCRIPTURE:
"Give ear, you that rule the people, and that please yourselves in multitudes of nations: For power is given you by the Lord, and strength by the most High. Who will examine your works, and search out your thoughts" (*Wisdom 6:3-4*).

250. What does the fourth commandment forbid?

The fourth commandment forbids disrespect, unkindness, and disobedience to our parents and lawful superiors.

(a) Children sin mortally when they fail to give the respect and love due to their parents by hating them, unjustly threatening them, or striking them, by seriously insulting or ridiculing them, by wishing them serious evil, by treating them heartlessly, by disregarding them when they are in grave need, by cursing them, by causing them great sorrow, or by provoking them to serious anger.

146

(b) Children still subject to parental authority sin mortally by disobeying the just commands of their parents in serious matters. The command of parents to avoid bad companions, sinful reading or immoral amusements, to receive the sacraments and religious instruction, to assist according to the law of the Church at Mass on Sundays and holydays of obligation, and to preserve the necessary order and peace of the home, must be considered as ordinarily binding under serious obligation. The disobedience of young children is frequently not sinful because of inadvertence, levity, or lack of seriousness on the part of parents who do not insist on their children obeying their commands under pain of sin.

(c) Disobedience of children and of other subjects, even in slight matters, can become a grave sin when the motive of the disobedience is serious contempt for the authority of parents and legitimate superiors.

SCRIPTURE:
"Cursed be he that honoreth not his father and mother. And all the people shall say: Amen" (*Deuteronomy 27:16*).

"Render to all men whatever is their due; tribute to whom tribute is due; taxes to whom taxes are due; fear to whom fear is due; honor to whom honor is due" (*Romans 13:7*).

251. What is the fifth commandment of God?

The fifth commandment of God is: Thou shalt not kill.

(a) Killing, which is forbidden by this commandment, means taking the life of a human being unjustly. Animals may be killed for man's reasonable need or convenience. Hunting, fishing, and using animals for scientific purposes are permissible. To kill or injure animals without a good reason is sinful but it is not a violation of this commandment.

SCRIPTURE:
"Thou shalt not kill" (*Exodus 20:13*).

252. What are we commanded by the fifth commandment?

By the fifth commandment we are commanded to take proper care of our own spiritual and bodily well-being and that of our neighbor.

(a) Man does not have supreme dominion over his own life; he was not the cause of its beginning nor may he be the deliberate cause of its end. Man must use the ordinary means to preserve life. He is not, however, obliged to use extraordinary means which would involve relatively great expense or intolerable pain or shame.

(b) Man is obliged to use prudent means in order to preserve his health and the health of those under his care.

253. What does the fifth commandment forbid?

The fifth commandment forbids murder and suicide, and also fighting, anger, hatred, revenge, drunkenness, and bad example.

(a) Murder is the voluntary and unjust killing of a human being. It is a serious crime because it is an infringement on the right of God's dominion over human life and is an irreparable injustice to the victim, to his family, and to society.

147

ESAÜ & JACOB

MARTIR S: CYPRIEN

147a

The Martyrdom of St. Stephen

The top picture shows St. Stephen, deacon and first martyr, giving the admirable example of the pardon of his enemies. Kneeling with his eyes lifted up to heaven, he addresses to God his touching prayer for the Jews who are stoning him, "Lord, do not lay this sin against them." (Acts 7:60) Suddenly, Heaven opens before him. God looks at him with pleasure with His arms extended towards him. An angel offers him the palm of martyrdom, and another shows him the crown that awaits him.

At the bottom of this plate on the left are Esau and Jacob being reconciled to each other, while on the right, St. Cyprian is about to be beheaded. His friends are paying the executioner twenty-five gold pieces, having been ordered to do so by the Saint. St. Cyprian was a bishop, and he shares the feastday of September 16 with St. Cornelius, Pope and Martyr. The two martyrs are mentioned together in the Canon of the Mass.

All the scenes of this plate relate to the commandment, "Thou shalt not kill."

(b) The life of another person may lawfully be taken:

first, in order to protect one's own life or that of a neighbor, or a serious amount of possessions from an unjust aggressor, provided no other means of protection is effective;

second, by a soldier fighting a just war;

third, by a duly appointed executioner of the state when he metes out a just punishment for a crime.

(c) War is an armed conflict between sovereign states which is undertaken by public sanction. A nation may wage a just war under the following conditions:

first, if it is necessary to defend the rights of the state in a grave matter,

second, if it is undertaken only as a last resort after all other means have failed;

third, if it is conducted justly in accordance with natural and international law;

fourth, if it is not continued after due satisfaction has been offered or given by the unjust aggressor nation.

(d) The direct intention to kill an innocent person is never permissible, either by public or private authority. The state does not have the right to take the life of a sick person, even at his own request, in order to relieve him of pain. An unborn child has the same right to life as any other person and may never be directly killed, even to save the life of the mother.

(e) The human body may not be mutilated unless there is no other way to preserve the health or to save the life of a person.

(f) It is sinful to risk one's life without a sufficiently good reason. To risk one's life in order to save the life of another person is permissible and in certain cases obligatory.

(g) It is the law of the Church that the bodies of those who have knowingly and deliberately committed suicide shall not be given Christian burial.

(h) One may never take part in a duel, which is a prearranged contest between two persons with deadly weapons. The Church punishes with excommunication not only those who engage in a duel, but also those who assist them and even those who are deliberately present at a duel and do not, as far as they can, try to prevent it.

(i) Unjust anger leads to hatred, revenge, fighting, and other grave sins.

(j) Excessive eating and drinking are sinful because they injure the health of a person and often lead to other sins. A person commits a mortal sin when by excessive use of alcoholic drink he deliberately deprives himself of the use of reason without a just cause, or when by habitual drinking he seriously injures his health, neglects to provide for his family or gives scandal, or when, as a result of excessive drinking, he violates a grave obligation arising from the law of God, the Church, or the state.

SCRIPTURE:

"You have heard that it was said to the ancients, 'Thou shalt not kill'; and that whoever shall kill shall be liable to judgment. But I say to you that everyone who is angry with his brother shall be liable to judgment; and whoever says

148

to his brother, 'Raca,' shall be liable to the Sanhedrin; and whoever says, 'Thou fool!', shall be liable to the fire of Gehenna. Therefore, if thou art offering thy gift at the altar, and there rememberest that thy brother has anything against thee, leave thy gift before the altar and go first to be reconciled to thy brother, and then come and offer thy gift" (*Matthew 5:21-24*).

"Woe to the world because of scandals! For it must needs be that scandals come, but woe to the man through whom scandal does come! And if thy hand or thy foot is an occasion of sin to thee, cut it off and cast it from thee! It is better for thee to enter life maimed or lame, than, having two hands or two feet, to be cast into the everlasting fire. And if thy eye is an occasion of sin to thee, pluck it out and cast it from thee! It is better for thee to enter into life with one eye, than, having two eyes, to be cast into hell-fire" (*Matthew 18:7-9*).

"The works of the flesh are manifest, which are . . . enmities, contentions . . . anger, quarrels . . . murders, drunkenness, carousings, and suchlike. And concerning these I warn you, as I have warned you, that they who do such things will not attain the kingdom of God" (*Galatians 5:19-21*).

"But let every man be swift to hear, slow to speak, and slow to wrath. For the wrath of man does not work the justice of God" (*James 1:19-20*).

"Everyone who hates his brother is a murderer. And you know that no murderer has eternal life abiding in him" (*I John 3:15*).

254. What is the sixth commandment of God?

The sixth commandment of God is: Thou shalt not commit adultery.

SCRIPTURE:
"Thou shalt not commit adultery" (*Exodus 20:14*).

255. What are we commanded by the sixth commandment?

By the sixth commandment we are commanded to be pure and modest in our behavior.

(a) Purity is a moral virtue which rightly regulates all voluntary expression of sexual pleasure in marriage and excludes it altogether outside the married state. Purity, moreover, is necessary to preserve and to strengthen the other virtues.

(b) Modesty inclines one to refrain from any action or word that might lead oneself or others to an unlawful incitement of the sexual appetite. Modesty is necessary for safeguarding purity.

SCRIPTURE:
"I exhort you therefore, brethren, by the mercy of God, to present your bodies as a sacrifice, living, holy, pleasing to God — your spiritual service" (*Romans 12:1*).

"Or do you not know that your members are the temple of the Holy Spirit, who is in you, whom you have from God, and that you are not your own? For you have been bought at a great price. Glorify God and bear him in your body" (*I Corinthians 6:19-20*).

256. What does the sixth commandment forbid?

The sixth commandment forbids all impurity and immodesty in words, looks, and actions, whether alone or with others.

(a) Impurity is any deliberate thought, word, look, or deed with oneself or another by which the sexual appetite is aroused outside of marriage,

149a

Our Lord and the Woman Caught in Adultery

At the top is Our Lord and, at His feet, a woman who was guilty of the sin of adultery. We read in the Gospel:

"Now the Scribes and Pharisees brought a woman caught in adultery, and setting her in the midst, said to Him, 'Master, this woman has just now been caught in adultery. And in the Law Moses commanded us to stone such persons. What, therefore, dost thou say?' Now they were saying this to test Him, in order that they might be able to accuse him. But Jesus, stooping down, began to write with His finger on the ground.

"But when they continued asking him, he raised Himself and said to them, 'Let him who is without sin among you be the first to cast a stone at her.' And again stooping down, he began to write on the ground. But hearing this, they went away, one by one, beginning with the eldest. And Jesus remained alone, with the woman standing in the midst.

"And Jesus, raising Himself, said to her, 'Woman, where are they? Has no one condemned thee?' She said, 'No one, Lord.' Then Jesus said, 'Neither will I condemn thee. Go thy way, and from now on sin no more.'" (St. John 8:3-11)

At the bottom right is king David, and before him the prophet Nathan. He is reproaching David for the adultery which he committed with Bethsabee and for the murder of her husband Urias.

On the left is shown the story which Nathan told to make David realize the enormity of his crime. "There were," he told him, "two men in one city, the one rich and the other poor. The rich man had exceeding many sheep and oxen. But the poor man had nothing at all but one little ewe lamb, which he had bought and nourished up, and which had grown up in his house together with his children, eating of his bread, and drinking of his cup, and sleeping in his bosom: and it was unto him as a daughter. And when a certain stranger was come to the rich man, he spared to take of his own sheep and oxen, to make a feast for that stranger, who was come to him: but took the poor man's ewe, and dressed it for the man that was come to him.

"And David's anger being exceedingly kindled against that man, he said to Nathan, 'As the Lord liveth, the man that hath done this is a child of death.'"

"Thou art the man," replied the prophet. "Thus saith the Lord, 'I anointed thee king over Israel; and I delivered thee from the hand of Saul, and gave thee thy master's house and all his goods, and I was to add far greater things to thee. Why therefore hast thou despised the word of the Lord, to commit sin by causing Urias the Hethite to perish by the sword and by marrying his wife? In punishment for thy double crime, it is from thy own family that the Lord will raise up ministers of His vengeance. Thy family will become for thee a source of unhappiness.'

"The king was astounded, and was seized with repentance in the depths of his soul and uttered this saving cry of penitence that God will never despise, 'I have sinned against the Lord.'" (2 Kings 12)

149b

and even in marriage when contrary to the purpose for which God instituted the married state.

(b) Some of the chief sins against purity are:

first, adultery, by which one violates the sexual rights of the married state. This sin is also committed by one who lives as the legal husband or wife of another after one or both parties have secured a civil divorce;

second, fornication, by which an unmarried person usurps the marriage right by sexual intercourse with another unmarried person;

third, deliberate actions with oneself or others performed to arouse the sexual appetite.

(c) Immodesty is any deliberate thought, word, or action that tends toward impurity.

(d) When there is full deliberation in any sin of impurity it is a mortal sin Immodesty may be either a mortal or venial sin depending on the greater or less danger of impurity to which it tends, the degree of scandal, and the intention of the sinner.

(e) Sins of impurity and immodesty are extremely dangerous because human nature is strongly inclined toward them, and because they quickly develop into habits which are most difficult to eradicate.

SCRIPTURE:

"You have heard that it was said to the ancients, 'Thou shalt not commit adultery.' But I say to you that anyone who so much as looks with lust at a woman has already committed adultery with her in his heart" (*Matthew 5:27-28*).

"But immorality and every uncleanness or covetousness, let it not even be named among you, as becomes saints; or obscenity or foolish talk or scurrility, which are out of place; but rather thanksgiving. For know this and understand, that no fornicator, or unclean person, or covetous one (for that is idolatry) has any inheritance in the kingdom of Christ and God. Let no one lead you astray with empty words; for because of these things the wrath of God comes upon the children of disobedience" (*Ephesians 5:3-7*).

"For this is the will of God, your sanctification; that you abstain from immorality; that every one of you learn how to possess his vessel in holiness and honor, not in the passion of lust like the Gentiles who do not know God" (*I Thessalonians 4:3-5*).

257. What are the chief dangers to the virtue of chastity?

The chief dangers to the virtue of chastity are: idleness, sinful curiosity, bad companions, drinking, immodest dress, and indecent books, plays, and motion pictures.

(a) We must avoid as far as possible any person, place, or thing that is likely to tempt us to immodesty and impurity. Special care must be taken to avoid the near occasions of these sins.

(b) Unmarried persons may not carry on a courtship with those who are not free to marry. They should avoid receiving any attention from them. Familiarity with such persons can readily lead to many sins of impurity and to an invalid marriage.

SCRIPTURE:

"Idleness hath taught much evil" (*Ecclesiasticus 33:29*).

150

258. What are the chief means of preserving the virtue of chastity?

The chief means of preserving the virtue of chastity are to avoid carefully all unnecessary dangers, to seek God's help through prayer, frequent confession, Holy Communion, and assistance at Holy Mass, and to have a special devotion to the Blessed Virgin.

SCRIPTURE:

"Watch and pray, that you may not enter into temptation. The spirit indeed is willing, but the flesh is weak" (*Mark 14:38*).

"Be sober, be watchful! For your adversary the devil, as a roaring lion, goes about seeking someone to devour. Resist him, steadfast in the faith, knowing that the same suffering befalls your brethren all over the world" (*I Peter 5:8-9*).

IMPORTANT TRUTHS ABOUT THE 4th, 5th and 6th COMMANDMENTS

After the first three commandments prescribing man's duties toward God come seven others laying down man's obligations toward himself and his fellow-men. There is first a special commandment regarding the important duties of children toward their parents, and of parents toward their children. This is the fourth of the ten commandments. In a general way, the others are concerned with actions (5, 6, 7), and words (8), and desires (9, 10).

It is important to remember that the commandments imply much more than they expressly command. For example, the fourth commandment explicity prescribes only honor for one's parents, but under this heading are included love, obedience and service. Moreover, as the Church interprets it, this same commandment refers to the duties of all those in any position of subordination toward lawful superiors; it also imposes on those who rule others, particularly parents, the obligation to provide for the welfare of those in their charge. Similarly, the fifth commandment, though it explicitly forbids only killing, is to be extended to the prohibition of any unjust injury to the body, and even to the soul, whether of oneself or of other human beings. The sixth commandment is explicitly directed against adultery—the gravest sin of impurity that can be committed by or against a married person. Yet, it really forbids every external act against the noble virtues of chastity and modesty.

Many persons in public office seem to forget that they are strictly bound to provide for the welfare of the citizens and to protect their rights; they are guilty of sin if they neglect to perform the duties demanded of them or if they exercise their authority for their own personal advantage rather than for the benefit of their fellow citizens. A public official must always remember that the authority he possesses comes to him from God and that he must employ that authority in the way that God wills. It is unfortunate that there are many public officials nowadays who, while they may be conscientious in their duties as private citizens and perhaps even faithful in their religious practices, frequently transgress the fourth commandment in their public life.

It should be our concern to regard the commandments of God, not as merely forbidding what is bad but also as commanding what is good. Of the commandments considered in this lesson, the one which demands the most effort for its observance and entails the most exalted holiness on the part of those who obey it perfectly is the sixth commandment. Nowadays there is much in the world that incites people to sins of impurity. We must be constantly on our guard lest we fall into this degrading sin. To mention only a few of the sources of danger to chastity in our own land, there are obscene motion pictures, magazines filled with lewd pictures, a great laxity in the matter of dress. Catholics should be mindful of the admonitions of recent Popes regarding these dangers. If Catholics follow those admonitions of the Church, and make use

151

of the means at their disposal to gain spiritual strength—particularly the frequent reception of Holy Communion, nourishing us with the immaculate flesh of Our Divine Saviour—they can avoid the dangers that surround them and practice perfectly the virtue of purity, known as the angelic virtue, because it makes us like the pure angels who surround the throne of God in heaven.

RESOLUTION: Resolve that you will carefully avoid anything that may endanger your purity, such as bad companions, dangerous reading, unchaste conversation, and suggestive motion pictures.

STUDY HELPS

A. COLUMN SELECTION. (*Join correctly the parts of the sentences in Columns I and II, by placing the right key letter in the proper parenthesis.*)

I

(1) Ordinarily children should consult their parents (. .).

(2) Parents must have their children baptized (. .).

(3) A citizen is obliged to vote (. .).

(4) Disobedience even in slight matters can become a grave sin (. .).

(5) A public official is guilty of sin (. .).

(6) A person may lawfully kill an unjust aggressor (. .).

(7) It is a mortal sin to deprive oneself of the use of reason without a just cause (. .).

(8) It is sinful for a person to carry on a courtship (. .).

(9) A fully deliberate act of impurity (. .).

(10) Sins of impurity and immodesty are extremely dangerous (. .).

II

(A) by the excessive use of alcoholic drink.

(B) because human nature is strongly inclined toward them.

(C) as soon as possible.

(D) if it is the only way in which he can protect his own life.

(E) before definitely deciding to marry.

(F) when the common good of the state or the good of religion demands it.

(G) with one who is not free to marry.

(H) is always a mortal sin.

(I) if he employs his authority for his personal advantage rather than for the benefit of the citizens.

(J) when the motive is contempt for the authority of those who command.

B. PROBLEMS AND EXERCISES. (*Answer the questions orally or write them as your teacher may direct*):

(1) Silvanus, a skilled pickpocket, is teaching his son Quintin to follow his dishonest mode of life. He sends the lad to the church bazaar to try his skill for the first time. Is Quintin bound to obey his father?

(2) Ella and her brother Lyle, both over 21 and still living at home with their parents, consider their parents old-fashioned. Father and mother demand that all the children be in the house by eleven o'clock each night. Ella and Lyle refuse to abide by that regulation. Are they guilty of any sin? Why?

(3) John, a married man and a wealthy contractor, seldom visits his widowed mother. She lives in the poorer section of the same town and

152

barely manages to get along on her limited income. What obligations, if any, has John toward his mother?

(4) Ida, eighteen years old, would like to join the Sisters after her graduation from High School. Her mother strongly objects to her ambition; she wants the girl to get married to Orlando, a young Protestant lawyer with lots of money. Must Ida obey her mother? Explain.

(5) Jonas, a Catholic, has been keeping company with Rania, the daughter of a Protestant minister in the neighboring town. He plans to be married in three weeks. Both of his parents are still ignorant of the whole affair. Has Jonas acted correctly toward them? Explain.

(6) Audrey in the seventh grade dislikes being reminded by her mother that it is time to go to confession and Communion with the Sodality girls. Has Audrey a just complaint against her mother? Explain your reply.

(7) Paul is a very sick boy; the doctor has ordered certain tablets to be taken every three hours. Has Paul an obligation to take the doctor's prescription? What commandment imposes the obligation?

(8) If Fido is run over by a bus, a policeman usually shoots the dog to end its misery. If you were to meet with the same accident may a doctor or a surgeon end your misery by an easy death (euthanasia)? Explain.

(9) Leon, an honest and thrifty young man, saved his money to buy furniture for the home he planned after his marriage with Teresa, a devout Catholic girl. A few days before the wedding he drew $1200 out of the bank and kept it in his room, so that he could buy the furniture the next day. That night he awoke to see a robber leaving the room with his money. Leon seized a knife, pursued the robber, and grappled with him. The robber drew a gun, and Leon stabbed him in the heart, killing him. Was Leon allowed to do this? What difference would it make if the robber had no gun? If Leon had a gun would he have been allowed to shoot the robber?

(10) What virtue are we commanded to practice by the sixth commandment?

(11) The sixth beatitude encourages us to the practise of the same virtue. What is that beatitude? Who proclaimed it?

(12) What girl saint is the patroness of holy purity? In the same virtue, who is the model saint for the boys?

(13) In a paragraph of five or six sentences explain three practices of devotion that preserve and cultivate modesty and purity.

(14) Ethelbert is accustomed to buy magazines which have indecent pictures, and he not only looks at them himself but he displays them to his companions. What sins does Ethelbert commit?

(15) George and Rebecca, students in the sophomore class in High School and each sixteen years of age, are keeping company with each other steadily, and have even mutually promised that they will marry each other in six or seven years. Are they allowed to do these things? Explain your answer, and tell what you think about steady company-keeping by High School boys and girls.

153

The Seventh, Eighth, Ninth, and Tenth Commandments of God

259. What is the seventh commandment of God?

The seventh commandment of God is: Thou shalt not steal.

(a) To steal is to take or to retain voluntarily something belonging to another, for gain, against his reasonable will. To steal secretly is *theft;* to steal violently is *robbery.*

(b) Theft and robbery are contrary to the natural law and are opposed to justice. They are considered mortal sins unless that which is stolen is of little value. Even in the case of slight value, the violence attached to robbery may make it a mortal sin.

(c) When the thing stolen is of great value, solely from its own intrinsic worth, it is said to constitute absolutely grave matter. Theft or robbery of something which in itself is grave matter may not impose a hardship on the owner but it is a mortal sin because it is a serious attack on society, on the public peace of a community, and on its security. Dishonesty which seriously disturbs the public order is always a mortal sin. The amount that constitutes absolutely grave matter in theft or robbery varies in different countries, owing to the special conditions and circumstances of the countries.

(d) When the thing stolen is of relatively greater value, that is, not from its own intrinsic worth, but considering the condition of the owner and the injury suffered, it is said to constitute relatively grave matter. The theft, for example, from a poor man of an amount that is required for one day's support of himself and his family would constitute, at least, relatively grave matter and would be a mortal sin.

(e) One who frequently steals things of small value from one or different persons within a short period (a month of two), the total of which is of serious value, commits a mortal sin in the last act of the series of stealing, because the small amounts stolen go together to constitute grave matter.

SCRIPTURE:
"Thou shalt not steal" (*Exodus 20:15*).

260. What are we commanded by the seventh commandment?

By the seventh commandment we are commanded to respect what belongs to others, to live up to our business agreements, and to pay our just debts.

(a) These obligations are imposed on us in the court of conscience even though the civil law may not oblige us.

(b) It is sinful to incur willfully debts beyond one's ability to pay. The desire for pleasure and social and political ambition do not justify living beyond one's means, an abuse which has become a prevalent vice.

154

"The beginning of a good way is to do justice; and this is more acceptable with God than to offer sacrifices. . . . Better is a little with justice, than great revenues with iniquity" (*Proverbs 16:5, 8*).

"The wicked man borrows and does not repay" (*Psalm 36:21*).

"Render to all men whatever is their due; tribute to whom tribute is due; taxes to whom taxes are due . . . " (*Romans 13:7*).

261. What does the seventh commandment forbid?

Besides stealing, the seventh commandment forbids cheating, unjust keeping of what belongs to others, unjust damage to the property of others, and the accepting of bribes by public officials.

(a) The seventh commandment is violated by merchants who use false weights and measures, make exorbitant profits, or lie about the essential qualities of their goods; by those who obtain money from others by persuading them to make unsound investments with the assurance of gain; and by those who knowingly pass counterfeit money or take undue advantage of the ignorance or necessity of another.

(b) Employers who defraud laborers by not paying them a just, living wage keep what belongs to others and are guilty of grave injustice not only to the employee but also to members of his family. This injustice can cause serious sins in the domestic life as well as in the social life of a community. Employees who waste time during working hours, do careless work, or neglect to take reasonable care of the property of their employers violate the seventh commandment.

(c) Public officials are obliged to make appointments on merit; they sin against the seventh commandment when they demand money or its equivalent for such appointments. If these appointees do not render a just service for the tax payments of a community, a further injustice is done to the citizens. Public officials sin mortally by taking bribes for allowing persons to violate the law in serious matters. The guilt of these officials is all the greater when they violate their oath to uphold the law.

SCRIPTURE:
"Do not any unjust thing in judgment, in rule, in weight, or in measure. Let the balance be just and the weights equal, the bushel just, and the sextary equal" (*Leviticus 19:35-36*).

262. Are we obliged to restore to the owner stolen goods, or their value?

We are obliged to restore to the owner stolen goods, or their value, whenever we are able.

(a) If the owner is dead, stolen goods must be restored to the heirs. If the owner or heir of stolen goods cannot be determined, the goods or their value are to be given to the poor or pious causes. A person who has obtained goods unjustly, but who no longer possesses them, must sincerely intend to make due restitution as soon as he can; otherwise his sin cannot be forgiven.

(b) A person who deliberately assists another in stealing, even though he receives none of the loot, must make restitution if the other person does not do so. Stolen goods that have been bought or received as a gift must be restored to their rightful owner. Compensation may be demanded from the person who stole the goods, but not from their owner. In some places, civil law makes provisions for the owner in such cases.

(c) Lost goods that are found may be kept only after every reasonable effort has been made to find the owner and to restore the goods.

SCRIPTURE:
"If any man steal an ox or a sheep, and kill or sell it: he shall restore five oxen for one ox, and four sheep for one sheep" (*Exodus 22:1*).

263. Are we obliged to repair damage unjustly done to the property of others?

We are obliged to repair damage unjustly done to the property of others, or to pay the amount of the damage, as far as we are able.

(a) A person who has accidentally damaged the property of another through no fault of his own is not obliged to repair the damage unless required to do so by civil law.

SCRIPTURE:
"If any man hurt a field or a vineyard, and put in his beast to feed upon that which is other men's: he shall restore the best of whatsoever he hath in his own field, or in his vineyard, according to the estimation of the damage" (*Exodus 22:5*).

264. What is the eighth commandment of God?

The eighth commandment of God is: Thou shalt not bear false witness against thy neighbor.

SCRIPTURE:
"Thou shalt not bear false witness against thy neighbor" (*Exodus 20:16*).

265. What are we commanded by the eighth commandment?

By the eighth commandment we are commanded to speak the truth in all things, but especially in what concerns the good name and honor of others.

(a) This commandment concerns the practice of the virtue of truthfulness which promotes the general welfare of society, the orderly function of which depends, in large measure, on its members speaking the truth.

(b) A good name is a most precious possession. The eighth commandment obliges us to respect the good name of our neighbor by not making known his faults when we have no right to do so and by not making false accusations against him.

SCRIPTURE:
"Speak ye truth every one to his neighbor" (*Zacharias 8:16*).

"Wherefore, put away lying and speak truth each one with his neighbor, because we are members of one another" (*Ephesians 4:25*).

266. What does the eighth commandment forbid?

The eighth commandment forbids lies, rash judgment, detraction, calumny, and the telling of secrets we are bound to keep.

156

(a) A lie expresses opposition between one's word and one's thought; it implies the intention to deceive by stating what is false. A lie is intrinsically wrong and is opposed to the natural law. It undermines mutual trust among men.

(b) Ordinarily, a lie told in jest or for someone's benefit is a venial sin; a deliberate lie which causes serious harm is a mortal sin. A lie told under oath is perjury and is always a mortal sin.

(c) It is permissible to give an evasive answer to a question when there is no obligation to answer. In this case, the hearer is permitted to deceive himself by his own interpretation.

(d) Cheating in examinations is wrong because one thereby acquires unearned credits in studies. If by cheating one wins a prize, one really steals and is obliged to restitution.

SCRIPTURE:
"Thou shalt fly lying" (*Exodus 23:7*).
"Lying lips are an abomination to the Lord" (*Proverbs 12:22*).

267. When does a person commit the sin of rash judgment?

A person commits the sin of rash judgment when, without sufficient reason, he believes something harmful to another's character.

(a) We rightly prize the favorable judgment of others about our character. We may not, without certain knowledge, believe things that undermine or destroy the character of another. Rash judgment is a sin against justice; it is a mortal sin if grave injustice is done deliberately. To suspend judgment about a person's character until suspicion or doubt can be settled is not sinful.

SCRIPTURE:
"Before thou inquire, blame no man" (*Ecclesiasticus 11:7*).
"Do not judge, that you may not be judged. For with what judgment you judge, you shall be judged; and with what measure you measure, it shall be measured to you. But why dost thou see the speck in thy brother's eye, and yet dost not consider the beam in thy own eye?" (*Matthew 7:1-3*).

268. When does a person commit the sin of detraction?

A person commits the sin of detraction when, without a good reason, he makes known the hidden faults of another.

(a) There must be a sufficiently grave reason to reveal the hidden faults of others, for example, the defense of one's self or others; the correction of others by their parents or superiors; the welfare of society, as when one is obliged to inform public authorities of another's secret crimes. A person who has been found guilty in court has lost his good name owing to the charge proved against him. It is not detraction to speak of this court action to others, nor is it against the eighth commandment to speak of faults that are generally known in a community. It is, however, more charitable not to do so.

(b) Detraction is a mortal sin if it unjustly does great harm to a person's reputation.

157

(c) We should avoid unkind remarks about others, and talebearing which needlessly causes misunderstanding, distrust, and enmity.

(d) Contumely or insult dishonors a person unjustly in his presence by refusing to show him the signs of honor due him, or by not noticing him, or by making known his faults, without sufficient reason. The same harm can be done by any means of communication, as by letter, telephone, radio, motion picture, or television. Contumely is a sin against justice and charity and its gravity depends on the extent of the dishonor shown.

SCRIPTURE:

"The slanderer of his neighbor in secret: him I will destroy" (*Psalm 100:5*).

"A good name is better than great riches: and good favor is above silver and gold" (*Proverbs 22:1*).

"The whisperer and the double tongued is accursed: for he hath troubled many that were at peace" (*Ecclesiasticus 28:15*).

"Take care of a good name: for this shall continue with thee, more than a thousand treasures precious and great" (*Ecclesiasticus 41:15*).

"Admonish them ... speaking evil of none" (*Titus 3:1-2*).

269. **When does a person commit the sin of calumny or slander?**

A person commits the sin of calumny or slander when by lying he injures the good name of another.

(a) We are guilty of calumny or slander when we falsely charge another with defects or sins. Calumny is opposed to truth, justice, and charity. It is a mortal sin if serious harm is deliberately done.

(b) To listen with pleasure to calumny, slander, or detraction is a mortal sin against justice and against charity when prompted by hatred; it is a venial sin when the motive is curiosity or levity. We should try to change a conversation that seriously deals with calumny, slander, or detraction, or we should show that we are not interested in such conversation.

SCRIPTURE:

"Thou shalt not calumniate thy neighbor" (*Leviticus 19:13*).

"Devise not a lie against thy brother: neither do the like against thy friend" (*Ecclesiasticus 7:13*).

"Plunder no one, accuse no one falsely" (*Luke 3:14*).

270. **When are we obliged to keep a secret?**

We are obliged to keep a secret when we have promised to do so, when our office requires it, or when the good of another demands it.

(a) A person who violates a secret commits a mortal sin if he foresees that it will reasonably give greater offense or cause grave harm to another, or if the fact made known under secrecy is serious; otherwise it is a venial sin.

(b) It is permissible to reveal a secret if consent to do so can be reasonably presumed. A secret should be revealed to prevent some grave harm to the general welfare of a community or to an innocent party. Secrets of the confessional may never be revealed, no matter what the consequence, even if it be death.

158

(c) It is sinful to read a letter addressed to another without his permission, or to eavesdrop on private conversation, unless done in order to prevent some grave harm.

271. What must a person do who has sinned by detraction or calumny, or has told a secret he is bound to keep?

A person who has sinned by detraction or calumny, or who has told a secret he is bound to keep must repair the harm he has done to his neighbor, as far as he is able.

(a) This reparation, like the restoration of stolen goods, is necessary because a person's good name and honor are more precious than his material possessions. This obligation is serious when grave harm is done. It is binding even if the one who must retract thereby suffers some harm. If a person insults someone publicly, he is obliged to apologize publicly; if the insult is in private, the apology may be made privately.

272. What is the ninth commandment of God?

The ninth commandment of God is: Thou shalt not covet thy neighbor's wife.

SCRIPTURE:
"Thou shalt not covet thy neighbor's wife: nor his house" (*Deuteronomy 5:21*).

273. What are we commanded by the ninth commandment?

By the ninth commandment we are commanded to be pure in thought and desire.

SCRIPTURE:
"Evil thoughts are an abomination to the Lord: and pure words most beautiful shall be confirmed by him" (*Proverbs 15:26*).

"Blessed are the clean of heart, for they shall see God" (*Matthew 5:8*).

"For out of the heart come evil thoughts, murders, adulteries, immorality, thefts, false witness, blasphemies. These are the things that defile a man" (*Matthew 15:19-20*).

"Therefore mortify your members, which are on earth: immorality, uncleanness, lust, evil desire and covetousness (which is a form of idol-worship). Because of these things the wrath of God comes upon the unbelievers" (*Colossians 3:5-6*).

"Beloved, I exhort you as strangers and pilgrims to abstain from carnal desires which war against the soul" (*I Peter 2:11*).

See Scripture, question 256, Matthew 5:27-28).

274. Are mere thoughts about impure things always sinful in themselves?

Mere thoughts about impure things are not always sinful in themselves, but such thoughts are dangerous.

275. When do thoughts about impure things become sinful?

Thoughts about impure things become sinful when a person thinks of an unchaste act and deliberately takes pleasure in so thinking, or when unchaste desire or passion is aroused and consent is given to it.

159

276. What is forbidden by the ninth commandment?

The ninth commandment forbids all thoughts and desires contrary to chastity.

(a) We should form the habit of praying immediately when we are beset by impure thoughts, desires, or imaginations. It is well to know by heart many ejaculations addressed to Our Lord and His Blessed Mother which we should repeat in time of such temptations.

(b) In confessing deliberate impure desires, one must tell the confessor their object, for example, a married or single person, of the same or the opposite sex, because such circumstances change the nature of the sin.

277. What is the tenth commandment of God?

The tenth commandment of God is: Thou shalt not covet thy neighbor's goods.

SCRIPTURE: *See Scripture, question 272, Deuteronomy 5:21.*

278. What does the tenth commandment forbid?

The tenth commandment forbids all desire to take or to keep unjustly what belongs to others, and also forbids envy at their success.

(a) It is permissible to seek material prosperity if we do so honestly and do not expose ourselves to the proximate dangers of sin.

SCRIPTURE:

"The eye of the envious is wicked" (*Ecclesiasticus 14:8*).

"Take heed and guard yourself from all covetousness, for a man's life does not consist in the abundance of his possessions" (*Luke 12:15*).

"For covetousness is the root of all evils, and some in their eagerness to get rich have strayed from the faith and have involved themselves in many troubles" (*I Timothy 6:10*).

"Let your manner of life be without avarice; be content with what you have, for he himself has said,

'I will not leave thee, neither will I forsake thee' " (*Hebrew 13:5*).

IMPORTANT POINTS ABOUT THE 7th, 8th, 9th and 10th COMMANDMENTS

The seventh and eighth commandments are concerned primarily with our duties toward two possessions of our neighbor—his material goods and his good reputation. Because human beings are inclined to be selfish and neglectful of the rights of others, God considered it necessary to lay down the explicit commands: "Thou shalt not steal" ... "Thou shalt not bear false witness against thy neighbor". Like the other commandments, these two commandments actually prescribe more obligations than those which they explicitly assert. The seventh commandment forbids not only stealing but every type of dishonest dealing; the eighth forbids not only falsehood but also many other sins of the tongue such as gossiping, the unlawful revelation of secrets, etc.

The ninth and tenth commandments are related to the sixth and seventh—the ninth forbidding interior sins regarding matters of purity, while the sixth forbids external acts; the tenth forbidding those internal sins the external performance of which is forbidden by the seventh commandment.

In our days there is much dishonesty, due largely to the excessive desire of people for riches and luxuries. In business, in politics, even in the home, many

160

people are so anxious to enrich themselves that they are entirely unconcerned with the rights of their fellow men. Moreover, crimes of theft and robbery, often accompanied by violence or even murder, are becoming more and more common.

Sometimes people buy stolen goods knowingly, and apparently do not realize that they have no claim to them but that they must give them back to the real owner. Indeed, even if a person buys stolen goods without realizing that they have been stolen, he may not keep them when he finds out that they were stolen if he knows the owner. If the owner appears and proves his right to the goods, the man who has bought them must restore them, even though the owner makes no recompense for the price the recipient has paid; but the latter has a right to get his money back from the thief who sold him the goods.

The civil law is unable to accomplish much toward preventing these violations of the seventh commandment. True, people are sent to prison for theft when they are captured. But many escape the law; many others commit sins of dishonesty in so clever a way that there is no civil law to cover their case. But they do not escape the all-seeing eye of God. And no matter how successfully a person may have acquired dishonest gain, no matter how prosperous he may have made himself at the expense of his fellow men, death will come in a few brief years to separate him from his riches and to summon him to judgment before the throne of an all-just God.

Many persons, by not paying their just debts, are guilty of sins against the seventh commandment. Some claim that they are unable to pay, yet they continue to buy luxuries, a fact which shows that they are not sincere. There are even some who deliberately refuse to pay a debt even though they know it was contracted, if the creditor has no written proof of his claim. God's law of justice is not limited to what can be proved in a civil court.

Sins of the tongue which injure others are also prevalent. Without the least qualm of conscience men lie to their fellow men. There are many who gravely injure the reputation of their fellows by their uncharitable, often false, remarks and stories. Backbiting, tale-bearing, the violation of secrets that one should keep, rash judgments—how common these are today!

Catholics, followers of Our Lord who was so attentive to the rights of others, should try to lead men to observe these commandments—and the best way is to inspire them by good example. We must be strictly honest in our dealings with others. Even when there is a question of something of slight value, we must never take it or keep it if it belongs to another. How many, for example, seem to think that if they find something on the street they are entitled to keep it without an attempt to find the owner! Similarly, we must watch over our speech, rejecting every form of falsehood, carefully avoiding anything that might wound our neighbor's character, shunning rash and harsh judgments about our neighbor. "Do not judge, that you may not be judged" (*Matt. 7:1*).

RESOLUTION: Resolve to be strictly honest both in deed and in word.

STUDY HELPS

A. TRUE OR FALSE. (*Check each of the following statements as either true or false. The correct answers can be found in the preceding portions of this lesson*).

TRUE   FALSE

(1) A person who has damaged another's property through no fault of his own is bound in conscience to make reparation for the damage, even when the civil law does not require it.   . . . .

161

(2) Even a slight lie told under oath is a mortal sin. . . . .

(3) If the owner of stolen goods or his heir cannot be found, the thief may keep them. . . . .

(4) We are always allowed to tell the hidden faults of others as long as what we say is true. . . . .

(5) To speak about the publicly known faults of others is not against justice. . . . .

(6) To judge a person rashly is against justice even if we say or do nothing unjust to him. . . . .

(7) When a person deliberately takes pleasure in an impure thought he is guilty of grave sin, even though he does not commit any bad action. . . . .

(8) When we find something we may keep it without making any further investigation. . . . .

(9) If a creditor cannot prove by a written document that his debtor owes him money, the debtor has no obligation to pay. . . . .

(10) If a person finds out after buying an article that it was really stolen, and the owner appears and demands it, he must return it, and has no right to receive any payment from the owner. . . . .

B. PROBLEMS AND EXERCISES. (*Answer the questions orally or write them as your teacher may direct*):

(1) Myron has stolen $3.00 from a rich man. Is that a mortal sin or a venial sin? Give the reason for your answer.

(2) Sibyl is in a department store buying clothespins for her mother. On her way out she stops at the jewelry counter to admire the display. Yielding to temptation, she steals a brooch priced at $50. What commandment has she broken? Is her sin mortal or venial? Why?

(3) Siegfried is living in a furnished room on an old-age pension. The pension is not enough to pay his expenses every month, so the parish St. Vincent de Paul Society helps him out regularly. Laurinda runs his errands. He gives her a $5.00 bill, erroneously thinking it is $1.00. She doesn't correct his mistake. Her purchase amounted to 95 cents. The old man tells the child to keep the change. Has she committed any sin? What kind of sin? Why?

(4) Elmer confesses he has stolen an expensive bicycle from the sporting-goods store in his neighborhood. Is God's justice satisfied when Elmer tells the sin he has committed? Is there anything else Elmer must do, in addition to telling the sin with sorrow? What is that obligation?

(5) Two years ago Myrna stole 50 cents from the pocketbook of a playmate's mother. She told her sin in confession, but forgot that her obligation did not end with the mere telling of the sin. She is now willing to do her duty, but that family has moved to another State. What is she to do about it, since she doesn't know the present whereabouts of the family?

162

(6) Millicent buys a very fine camera from an acquaintance for $5, thinking she is getting a good bargain. That afternoon a boy comes to her house and proves that it is his camera which was stolen by Millicent's acquaintance. Must Millicent give it to the boy? May she demand $5 from him to make up for the price she paid? May she demand that amount from her dishonest acquaintance?

(7) Every now and then a child is heard to say: "Findings is keepings!" If you find a lost article is it yours? Explain your answer.

(8) One who is wilfully destructive of beautiful or expensive things not his own may be called a vandal. What do you think of children who ruin or disfigure buildings, monuments, even churches with paint, indelible crayons, knives and other sharp instruments of destruction? Do they offend against the seventh commandment? Suppose they do these things "just for fun!" Does that change your conviction?

(9) Rhoda, with a rating of 95% wins the four years' High School scholarship worth $500. Priscilla, her nearest competitor, received 93%. Priscilla was thoroughly honest in her examination; but Rhoda cheated on only one answer that gave her 5% credit. Which of the ten commandments did Rhoda break? How can she make her peace with God?

(10) Tabitha, an extremely inquisitive schoolgirl, makes it a practice to listen to the conversations on her telephone, a party line. Is that permissible in ordinary circumstances? What commandment is violated?

(11) Gustave, a janitor in a stylish apartment house, now and then opens the tenants' mail out of sheer curiosity. Does he commit sin in acting that way? What personal right of the tenants is violated? What commandment safeguards that right of the tenants?

(12) Chrysostom, a choir boy, with ambitions to become a priest, is sometimes upset in conscience because filthy thoughts and vile imaginations assail him. As soon as he notices their presence, he utters the ejaculation: "Jesus and Mary, help me!" What do you think about his custom? Explain your answer in two or three short sentences.

(13) Sophronia, endowed by God with an exceptionally beautiful voice, hopes some day to become a famous singer. She has ambitions to own a beautiful home and to earn plenty of money with which to help her father and mother, her brothers and sisters. Is Sophronia breaking any of God's commandments by having such high hopes and ambitions? Explain.

(14) John, a rich man, employs Harvey as handy man on his estate. Harvey works faithfully for eight hours a day, but John gives him only $25 a week — a sum that is entirely insufficient for the needs of Harvey and his wife and five children. Does John sin against the seventh commandment? Explain.

(15) Mrs. Jones, suffering from a bad headache, tells her daughter Helen to inform anyone who may visit her that afternoon that she is not at home. Do you think that Helen is allowed to say this without breaking the eighth commandment?

163

The Commandments of the Church;
The First and Second Commandments

279. Whence has the Catholic Church the right to make laws?

The Catholic Church has the right to make laws from Jesus Christ, who said to the apostles, the first bishops of His Church: "Whatever you bind on earth shall be bound also in heaven."

(a) The power of the Church to bind and to loose is known as "the power of the keys" and includes everything necessary for the government of the Church and for the direction of the faithful in order that they may attain their eternal destiny. The primary purpose of Church laws is the eternal salvation of men.

(b) The Church has power from Christ to make laws and to enforce their observance.

(c) It is a mortal sin to disobey a law of the Church in a serious matter, a venial sin in a slight matter.

(d) The Church has indirect power over those temporal matters which are necessary or useful for the salvation of men.

SCRIPTURE:
"Amen I say to you, whatever you bind on earth shall be bound also in heaven; and whatever you loose on earth shall be loosed also in heaven" (*Matthew 18:18*).

"He therefore said to them again, 'Peace be to you! As the Father has sent me, I also send you' " (*John 20:21*).

280. By whom is this right to make laws exercised?

This right to make laws is exercised by the bishops, the successors of the apostles, and especially by the Pope, who as the successor of the chief of the apostles, Saint Peter, has the right to make laws for the universal Church.

(a) The Roman Pontiff has full, supreme, ordinary (that is, in virtue of his office), and immediate jurisdiction over the universal Church.

(b) All the bishops of the Church assembled in a general council in union with the Pope can make laws for the universal Church.

(c) A residential bishop or one who is empowered by the Holy See as an Ordinary, whether invested with the episcopal character or not, has immediate jurisdiction over his own diocese or territory.

SCRIPTURE: *See Scripture, question 137, Matthew 28:18-20; question 147, Matthew 16:17-19.*

281. Which are the chief commandments, or laws, of the Church?

The chief commandments, or laws, of the Church are these six:

1. To assist at Mass on all Sundays and holydays of obligation.

2. To fast and to abstain on the days appointed.
3. To confess our sins at least once a year.
4. To receive Holy Communion during the Easter time.
5. To contribute to the support of the Church.
6. To observe the laws of the Church concerning marriage.

(a) Besides these six commandments there are many other laws regulating the government of the Church and the administration of its affairs.

(b) The collection of laws binding the Latin Church is contained in an official book called the *Code of Canon Law*.

282. What sin does a Catholic commit who through his own fault misses Mass on a Sunday or holyday of obligation?

A Catholic who through his own fault misses Mass on a Sunday or holyday of obligation commits a mortal sin. [17]

(a) The grave obligation to hear Mass on Sunday and holydays of obligation does not bind the following:

first, those who must care for the sick;

second, those whose illness does not permit them to go outdoors;

third, those who live a considerable distance from a church;

fourth, those who must give immediate attention to urgent work.

(b) A person in doubt about this obligation should consult a priest.

SCRIPTURE: *See Scripture, question 236.*

283. Which are the holydays of obligation in the United States?

The holydays of obligation in the United States are these six:
Christmas Day (December 25)
The Circumcision (January 1)
Ascension Thursday (40 days after Easter)
The Assumption (August 15)
All Saints' Day (November 1)
The Immaculate Conception (December 8)

(a) There are four other holydays of obligation in the universal Church: the Feasts of Epiphany, Corpus Christi, Saint Joseph, and Saints Peter and Paul. With the approval of the Holy See, these four feasts are not holydays of obligation in the United States.

284. What else does the Church oblige us to do on holydays of obligation?

The Church obliges us to abstain from servile work on holydays of obligation, just as on Sundays, as far as we are able. [18]

(a) Catholics who must work on holydays are obliged to hear Mass unless excused by a reasonably grave cause.

---

17. See question 237.
18. For causes permitting servile work on holydays of obligation, see questions 239, 240.

165

285. Why were holydays instituted by the Church?

Holydays were instituted by the Church to remind us of the mysteries of our religion and of the important events in the lives of Christ and of His Blessed Mother, and to recall to us the virtues and the rewards of the saints.

286. What is a fast day?

A fast day is a day on which only one full meal is allowed, but in the morning and evening some food may be taken, the quantity and quality of which are determined by approved local custom.

(a) The one full meal may be taken either at noontime or in the evening. At this meal only may meat be taken.

(b) To take liquid does not break one's fast, provided it is not equivalent to food. Malted milk or cream, for example, is equivalent to food.

287. Who are obliged to observe the fast days of the Church?

All baptized persons between the ages of twenty-one and fifty-nine are obliged to observe the fast days of the Church, unless they are excused or dispensed.

(a) The sick and those who do extremely hard labor are excused from fasting. A person who is in doubt regarding the obligation to fast should consult a priest.

288. What is a day of abstinence?

A day of abstinence is a day on which we are not allowed the use of meat.

289. Who are obliged to observe the abstinence days of the Church?

All baptized persons seven years of age or over who have attained the use of reason are obliged to observe the abstinence days of the Church, unless they are excused or dispensed.

(a) The sick who need meat, persons who do extremely hard work, and those who would otherwise be deprived of sufficient food are excused from the law of abstinence.

(b) For a just cause, a parish priest can dispense his subjects from the law of fast or of abstinence, or of both, in particular cases. He can dispense individuals or particular families of his parish. He can grant this dispensation to his subjects even when they are outside the limits of his parish, and also to visitors who are, at the time, in his parish. A bishop enjoys the same power with respect to his diocese.

(c) Furthermore, the bishop of a diocese, when there is a gathering of many people, or when there is question of public health, can dispense a particular locality, or even the whole diocese, from the law of fast or of abstinence, or of both. The bishop can give faculties to dispense from the law of fast and abstinence to particular priests or to the confessors of the diocese.

290. Why does the Church command us to fast and to abstain?

The Church commands us to fast and to abstain in order that we may control the desires of the flesh, raise our minds more freely to God, and make satisfaction for sin.

(a) It is not because meat and other foods are evil in themselves that the Church prescribes days of fast and abstinence. The Church commands us to deny ourselves for the glory of God and the good of our souls.

SCRIPTURE:

"Prayer is good with fasting and alms: more than to lay up treasures of gold" (*Tobias 12:8*).

"Now therefore saith the Lord: 'Be converted to me with all your heart, in fasting . . .' " (*Joel 2:12*).

"Then Jesus was led into the desert by the Spirit, to be tempted by the devil. And after fasting forty days and forty nights, he was hungry" (*Matthew 4:1-2*).

"And when you fast, do not look gloomy like the hypocrites, who disfigure their faces in order to appear to men as fasting. Amen I say to you, they have received their reward. But thou, when thou dost fast, anoint thy head and wash thy face, so that thou mayest not be seen fasting by men, but by thy Father, who is in secret; and thy Father, who sees in secret, will reward thee" (*Matthew 6:16-18*).

291. Why does the Church make Friday a day of abstinence?

The Church makes Friday a day of abstinence to remind us of Our Lord's death on Good Friday.

292. How can we know the days appointed for fast or abstinence?

We can know the days appointed for fast or abstinence from the instructions of our bishops and priests. See page 302.

(a) From the general laws of the Church, we know the following regulations: *first, abstinence* binds on all Fridays; *second, fast* and *abstinence* bind on Ash Wednesday, the Fridays and Saturdays of Lent, the Ember Days, and the vigils of Pentecost, the Immaculate Conception, All Saints (see footnote, p. 302), and Christmas. The Ember Days are twelve in number, three in each season, namely, the Wednesday, Friday, and Saturday after December 13; after the first Sunday of Lent; after Pentecost; and after September 14; *third, fast* binds on all the other days of Lent.

(b) There is no obligation of fast or of abstinence on Sundays and holydays of obligation except when the holydays are in the season of Lent.

(c) In the United States at present, most dioceses have special rules regarding fast and abstinence. These are explained on page 302.

IMPORTANT TRUTHS ABOUT THE 1st AND 2nd COMMANDMENTS OF THE CHURCH

As is customary in every organized society, in the Church the lawful rulers have the authority to make laws for the other members. Christ Himself explicitly gave this power to the first bishops, the apostles, and from them it has been passed down through the centuries to the bishops of the present day. The fullest measure of this authority resides in the Pope, the chief bishop of the entire Church who can make laws for all its members, whereas other bishops can legislate for their respective dioceses only.

The laws of the Church are all directed to one great purpose—to bring men to eternal salvation. For more than nineteen centuries the Church has had experience in making laws; in her legislative action she is guided by the Holy Ghost. Indeed, on account of the infallibility of the Church it would be impossible for her to pass any general law that would be harmful to the faith or morals of Christians. Like a good mother, the Church is not too severe in her laws. She knows the inclinations of human nature and human frailty; she is ready to dispense from her laws when there is good reason for a dispensation. Moreover, the Church is always ready to adapt her legislation to local conditions and to the customs of different nations.

What are known as the six commandments of the Church are in reality certain laws selected from the body of the Church's legislative enactments, stating the more urgent duties of the practical Catholic. The two commandments considered in this lesson concern the two important virtues of religion and temperance. In order that her children may practice religion, the Church prescribes that they assist at the sacrifice of the Mass, the most sublime act of Christianship, at least on every Sunday and on certain great feasts. In order that they may practice temperance the Church prescribes fast and abstinence at certain times —some days being days of both fast and abstinence, others imposing only one of these forms of self-denial.

These laws, like all the laws of the Church, are reasonable and easy to observe. The first of these two commandments calls for only one hour of our time every Sunday and on six other days in the course of the year. This is a grave precept, so that one who misses Mass, or a considerable portion of it, on a Sunday or holyday by his own fault is guilty of a mortal sin. If a person failed to come before the Offertory but was present from the Offertory to the end of the Mass, he would substantially fulfil his obligation but he would guilty of a venial sin, in the supposition that the omission was culpable. But a person would not substantially satisfy his obligation if he were present only from the beginning of the Offertory through the Communion. It is permitted to fulfil the obligation by hearing successively portions of two Masses which together constitute an entire Mass, as long as one is present at both the Consecration and the Communion of one of the Masses.

In former centuries there were many more holydays of obligation than at present. In fact, even today Catholics in the United States are dispensed from the observance of four of the ten holydays that are prescribed for the universal Church. Similarly, our present-day laws regarding fast and abstinence are much easier than those of the early Church, when the precept of fasting forbade a person to touch food until late in the afternoon. Even at the present day among the Catholics of the Oriental rites the laws of fasting are much stricter than those binding Latin Catholics. And the Church is quite lenient in granting dispensations when there is a good reason. Thus, in the United States the laws of fast and abstinence have been considerably mitigated. For example, besides the points mentioned in the lesson, the soldiers and sailors of our country are dispensed from fast and abstinence on all days except Ash Wednesday, Good Friday, the Vigil of Christmas, and all of Holy Saturday, and if the soldier or sailor lives with his family, all the members share in this privilege.

Generally speaking, the laws of the Church begin to bind only when a Catholic has passed his seventh birthday and has attained the use of reason. This rule holds in regard to the law of abstinence and of attendance at Mass on

168

Sundays and holydays. However, the law of fasting binds only those who have passed their twenty-first birthday and have not yet passed their fifty-ninth birthday. On the other hand, a child who has attained the use of reason but is not yet seven years old is obliged to obey the law of annual Holy Communion.

The two commandments we have considered in this lesson are a good test of a Catholic's loyalty to his religion. Catholics who observe them faithfully are usually practical Catholics, while those who habitually neglect Mass and the laws of fast and abstinence—particularly the Friday abstinence—are Catholics only in name and are in grave danger of losing their souls.

RESOLUTION: Resolve never to miss Mass on a Sunday or a holyday of obligation, and never to eat meat on a Friday without a very grave reason.

STUDY HELPS

A. WORD SELECTION. (*Select the word or phrase in the parentheses which most exactly and most completely fills out the sentence*).

(1) The Church has received the power to make laws from (the apostles . . . St. Peter . . . Christ).

(2) The primary purpose of the Church's laws is (to procure the eternal salvation of souls . . . to increase the power of the Church . . . to test the virtue of Catholics).

(3) The collection of laws binding the Latin church is called (the digest of law . . . the Code of Canon Law . . . the summary of ecclesiastical law).

(4) There are (six . . . ten . . . twelve) holydays of obligation according to the general law of the Church.

(5) There are (eight . . . ten . . . twelve) Ember Days in the course of the year.

(6) On Sundays of Lent (there is neither fast nor abstinence . . . there is an obligation to abstain but not to fast . . . there is an obligation to fast but not to abstain).

(7) On a fast day a person who is obliged to fast (may not eat meat at all . . . may eat meat at all meals . . . may eat meat at the principal meal only).

(8) A Friday in Lent is (a day of fast and abstinence . . . a day of abstinence only . . . a day of fast only).

(9) For a just reason a parish priest can dispense his subjects from (the laws of fast and abstinence . . . from the law of fast only . . . from the law of abstinence only).

(10) The Pope can make laws for the entire Church (only with the consent of the bishops . . . only with the consent of the cardinals . . . by his own authority without asking the consent of anyone else).

B. PROBLEMS AND EXERCISES. (*Answer the questions orally or write them as your teacher may direct*):

(1) Whose authority does the Church exercise when she makes laws for us? Is disobedience to Church laws always a serious sin? Explain.

(2) Near the church, before the children's Mass on Sunday, Mark and Linus are playing marbles. Knowing that the Mass has started, they continue to play. When they enter the church, the priest is reading the Epistle. Are they guilty of sin? Explain your reply.

169

(3) Clare and her sister Assunta are awakened promptly by their mother on Sunday morning. Carelessly, they delay their rising, are tardy in dressing, and idle on their way to the church. When they arrive the priest has already finished the Gospel, made the announcements, and is nearing the end of his sermon. Of what kind of sin are these girls guilty? Why? If they remain for the next Mass and supply the part they have missed will they be guilty of the sin of missing a part of the Mass?

(4) Norbert and his sister Monica are anxious to go on an automobile trip with their uncle Otto. Carelessly, they enter the church late for Mass, the priest having just finished the "Credo." When the priest drains the chalice of the Precious Blood, Norbert nudges Monica and says: "C'mon, let's go; we've heard the three principal parts of Mass!" What do you say of their conduct? Explain your answer.

(5) Sheila, a precocious child of 5½ has been admitted to her First Holy Communion. Her big sister Pauline wants to know if Sheila is obliged to go to Mass next Sunday. What is your opinion?

(6) Herbert and Oliver, High School boys, buy a second-hand car for $25.00. All day Thursday they are busy cleaning it. On Friday, a holyday of obligation, after they hear Mass, they continue the work of overhauling the car, and have the job finished by 8:00 o'clock that night. What comment have you to make about their observance of the holyday?

(7) Xavier and his sister Harriet are on a motor tour of the Rockies. On Friday, August 15th, they hear Mass at Our Lady of the Snows. In a nearby roadway lunchroom they ask for a breakfast of scrambled eggs and toast; the proprietor prevails on them to breakfast on some New England sausages. What do you think about the propriety of their breakfast that Friday morning? Why do you think so?

(8) What general commandment of Christ is obeyed through the faithful observance of Church laws governing fast and abstinence?

(9) Imogen, "fat and forty", is taking treatments at a gymnasium for reduction of weight. In Lent she continues the treatments, but two or three times a week she takes a double portion of ice cream and a piece of cake. Her breakfast, dinner and supper satisfy the requirements of the Church and of the gymnasium director. Is she observing the Lenton fast? Explain your reply.

(10) Jim and Jack are going for a fishing trip on Sunday, and they want to start about 6 o'clock in the morning. The first Mass in the parish church is at 6:30; if they attend Mass, they will not be able to start until about 7 o'clock. Jim says that they will commit a mortal sin if they miss Mass, but Jack says that they have a sufficient reason to be excused. Which of the two do you think is right?

(11) Mrs. Aylward's baby daughter is very sick. On Sunday morning her older daughter, ten years old, offers to take care of the baby while her mother goes to Mass. Should Mrs. Aylward trust the baby to the little girl's care and go to Mass, or should she stay away from Mass to take care of the sick baby?

(12) On Christmas Eve Eunice, a healthy college student, 22 years old, who has eaten a big dinner at noon, goes to a party in the evening, and there consumes a large number of turkey sandwiches with several glasses of malted milk. Which laws of the Church has Eunice violated?

170

The Third, Fourth, Fifth, and Sixth Commandments of the Church

293. What is meant by the commandment to confess our sins at least once a year?

By the commandment to confess our sins at least once a year is meant that we are strictly obliged to make a good confession within the year, if we have a mortal sin to confess.

(a) This commandment binds all Catholics who have attained the use of reason.

(b) One who commits a mortal sin after Baptism is obliged by divine law to receive the sacrament of Penance. If this is impossible, one must make an act of perfect contrition and have the desire to receive the sacrament.

(c) Baptized persons in the state of mortal sin who are in danger of death are obliged to receive the sacrament of Penance.

(d) Owing to the obligation to receive Holy Communion at Easter time, it is customary to discharge the duty of annual confession at the same time.

(e) One guilty of mortal sin who does not fulfill the precept of annual confession commits another mortal sin.

SCRIPTURE:
"He therefore said to them again, 'Peace be to you! As the Father has sent me, I also send you.' When he had said this, he breathed upon them, and said to them, 'Receive the Holy Spirit; whose sins you shall forgive, they are forgiven them; and whose sins you shall retain, they are retained' " (*John 20:21-23*).

"Confess, therefore, your sins to one another" (*James 5:16*).

"If we say that we have no sin, we deceive ourselves, and the truth is not in us. If we acknowledge our sins, he is faithful and just to forgive us our sins and to cleanse us from all iniquity. If we say that we have not sinned, we make him a liar, and his word is not in us" (*I John 1:8-10*).

294. Why should we go to confession frequently?

We should go to confession frequently because frequent confession greatly helps us to overcome temptation, to keep in the state of grace, and to grow in virtue.

(a) It is not necessary to go to confession before every Communion, provided one has not sinned mortally. One can best be guided about frequent confession by one's confessor.

295. What sin does a Catholic commit who neglects to receive Holy Communion worthily during the Easter time?

A Catholic who neglects to receive Holy Communion worthily during the Easter time commits a mortal sin.

(a) This commandment obliges all Catholics who have the use of reason. Children who have completed seven years of age are presumed to have the use of reason.

(b) One does not fulfill this commandment of the Church by a sacrilegious Communion.

(c) One who has failed to receive Holy Communion within the appointed time is obliged to receive the Holy Eucharist as soon as possible.

SCRIPTURE:
"Jesus therefore said to them, 'Amen, amen, I say to you, unless you eat the flesh of the Son of Man, and drink his blood, you shall not have life in you. He who eats my flesh and drinks my blood has life everlasting and I will raise him up on the last day. For my flesh is food indeed, and my blood is drink indeed' " (*John 6:54-56*).

296. What is the Easter time in the United States?

The Easter time in the United States begins on the first Sunday of Lent and ends on Trinity Sunday.

(a) Trinity Sunday, or the Sunday after Pentecost, is eight weeks after Easter.

297. What is meant by the commandment to contribute to the support of the Church?

By the commandment to contribute to the support of the Church is meant that each of us is obliged to bear his fair share of the financial burden of the Holy See, of the diocese, and of the parish.

(a) The Church instituted by Christ has the right to all the means it needs for the fulfillment of its divine commission, for divine worship, and for the support of the clergy. The Church has the right to determine how to secure the necessary means without civil interference.

(b) Mass stipends are given to the priest, not in payment for the spiritual benefits received, but as a means of his support.

SCRIPTURE:
"When thou shalt take the sum of the children of Israel according to their number, every one of them shall give a price for their souls to the Lord: and there shall be no scourge among them, when they shall be reckoned. And this shall every one give that passeth at the naming, half a sicle according to the standard of the temple" (*Exodus 30:12-13*).

"The priests and Levites, and all that are of the same tribe, shall have no part nor inheritance with the rest of Israel: because they shall eat the sacrifices of the Lord, and his oblation. And they shall receive nothing else of the possession of their brethren: for the Lord himself is their inheritance, as he hath said to them. This shall be the priest's due from the people, and from them that offer victims. Whether they sacrifice an ox, or a sheep, they shall give to the priest the shoulder and the breast: The first fruits *also* of corn, of wine, and of oil, and a part of the wool from the shearing of their sheep. For the Lord thy God hath chosen him of all thy tribes, to stand and to minister to the name of the Lord: him and his sons for ever. If a Levite go out of any one of the cities throughout all Israel, in which he dwelleth, and have a longing mind to come to the place which the Lord shall choose: he shall minister in the name of the Lord his God, as all his brethren the Levites *do,* that shall stand at that time before the Lord. He shall receive the same portion of food that the rest do: besides that which is due to him in his own city, by succession from his fathers" *(Deuteronomy 18:1-8).*

"Do not keep gold, or silver, or money in your girdles, no wallet for your journey, nor two tunics, nor sandals, nor staff; for the laborer deserves his living" *(Matthew 10:9-10).*

"So also the Lord directed that those who preach the gospel should have their living from the gospel" *(I Corinthians 9:14).*

298. What is the ordinary law of the Church to be observed at the wedding of a Catholic?

The ordinary law of the Church to be observed at the wedding of a Catholic is this: A Catholic can contract a true marriage only in the presence of an authorized priest and two witnesses. [19]

(a) Before marriage the contracting parties have a serious obligation to answer truthfully all questions asked by the priest concerning their freedom to marry. These questions are asked for the protection of the sacrament and the parties concerned.

299. Does the Church forbid Catholics to contract marriage with certain persons?

The Church does forbid Catholics to contract marriage with certain persons, and the following are examples:

first, a marriage with a non-Catholic; this is a mixed marriage

second, a marriage with a second cousin, or any relative closer than a second cousin.

(a) Some other examples of marriages forbidden by the Church are:

first, marriage of a boy who is not sixteen years old or of a girl who is not fourteen years of age;

second, marriage between a godparent and a godchild;

third, marriage between a widow or a widower and the near relatives of the deceased spouse.

300. Why does the Church forbid Catholics to marry non-Catholics?

The Church forbids Catholics to marry non-Catholics because mixed marriages often bring about family discord, loss of faith on the part of the Catholic, and neglect of the religious training of the children.

SCRIPTURE:

"And it is better to die without children, than to leave ungodly children" *(Ecclesiasticus 16:4).*

"You therefore, brethren, since you know this beforehand, be on your guard lest, carried away by the error of the foolish, you fall away from your own steadfastness" *(II Peter 3:17).*

19. See questions 462-465.

301. Does the Church ever permit mixed marriages or marriages between close relatives?

For grave reasons the Church sometimes permits mixed marriages or marriages between close relatives; such a permission is called a dispensation.

(a) The divine law forbids mixed marriages as long as there is danger to the faith of the Catholic party or of the offspring.

(b) The Church, before granting the dispensation for a mixed marriage, demands that this danger be removed and asks that guarantees to that effect be given by explicit promises made before a representative of ecclesiastical authority.

(c) The non-Catholic party must promise not to endanger the faith of the Catholic; both parties must promise that the children born of the marriage will be baptized in the Catholic Church alone and educated solely in the Catholic religion. The Catholic party, moreover, must promise to strive for the conversion of the non-Catholic party by prayer and good example.

(d) Those who do not understand that marriage is a sacrament divinely instituted and that only one Church was established by the Lord Christ are apt to consider these regulations of the Church rigorous and unreasonable. The Church is the divine guardian of faith and of the religion established by Christ. It is opposed to mixed marriages and does all that is possible to discourage them.

302. Does the Church allow Catholics to marry during Lent and Advent?

The Church allows Catholics to marry during Lent and Advent, provided they do so quietly and without much ceremony; a Nuptial Mass is forbidden during these seasons.

303. What is a Nuptial Mass?

A Nuptial Mass is a Mass which has special prayers to beg God's blessing on the married couple.

IMPORTANT TRUTHS ABOUT THE 3rd, 4th, 5th AND 6th COMMANDMENTS OF THE CHURCH

The third and fourth commandments of the Church are concerned with the reception of the two sacraments that are the principal sources of supernatural strength in the Christian life—Penance and the Holy Eucharist. One would think that every Catholic, realizing the great benefits given to his soul by these two sacraments, would need no special law obliging him to confess his sins and to nourish himself with the body and blood of Our Blessed Saviour. In the early days of the Church, it is true, no such legislation was needed; Christians made frequent use of these sacraments, particularly the Holy Eucharist, without the necessity of compulsion. But when fervor cooled, the Church was obliged to make laws in the matter. For a time Catholics were bound to go to confession and to receive Holy Communion three times a year—at Christmas, Easter and Pentecost. Later, at the Fourth Council of the Lateran in the year 1215, the law was mitigated to its present form, prescribing the reception of these sacraments at least once a year, the Holy Communion being received in the Easter season. For this reason the obligatory reception of Holy Eucharist is known as the "Easter Duty." According to the general law of the Church the period for receiving the Easter communion lasts only two weeks, from Palm

174

Sunday to Low Sunday; but by special privilege this period is extended in the United States to fourteen weeks, from the first Sunday in Lent to Trinity Sunday. If a person has no mortal sin to confess he is not bound to receive the sacrament of Penance even once a year either by the law of God or by any general law of the Church. However, it is surely advisable to go to confession regularly even though one has no mortal sins to confess. Needless to say, annual confession and Communion represent the very least that can be expected of any member of the Church. We know, of course, that the other occasion when these sacraments must be received—the Holy Eucharist by all, Penance by those who have mortal sin to confess—is when a sick or very old person is in danger of death. Holy Communion on this occasion is called the Viaticum, which means "Food for a journey", the long journey into eternity.

The fifth commandment of the Church imposes on Catholics the obligation of doing their part toward supplying the material needs of religion. Catholics share in the benefits of their churches and schools; hence they must share in the expense of building and maintaining them. Catholics benefit by the services of their clergy and religious; hence they must contribute toward their support. In the Old Law God obliged the Jewish people to give a substantial portion of their possessions to the service of religion; Our Lord Himself spoke of a similar obligation toward those preaching the Gospel in His name, when He said, on sending His disciples to announce His message "The laborer deserves his living" (Matt., 10:10). The laws of the Church in former ages imposed on Catholics in some places the obligation of giving tithes—that is, one tenth of their earnings. Nowadays, very few Catholics give anything near this proportion of their income to religion. But all should give generously, with the conviction that they are giving to God, rather than to their fellow-men.

The sixth commandment of the Church refers to the sacrament of Matrimony. The Church has laid down a number of laws regulating marriage, because it is so important and holy a state, and the happiness of individuals and of the human race depends so much on the ideals and the conduct of married persons. Some of the more important Church laws have been mentioned in this lesson: but there are many others. One of the laws which all Catholics should seriously consider at the present day is that which forbids the marriage of Catholics with those who are not members of their Church. It is true, such marriages sometimes turn out successfully; sometimes they even serve as the occasion of the conversion of the non-Catholic to the true faith. But more frequently they injure the faith of the Catholic and of the children. Hence, the Church's first advice to young people thinking of marriage is: Marry those of your own religion. Even when the Church permits a mixed marriage, it demands that only a Catholic ceremony be used.

According to the law of the Church, a Catholic cannot be married validly, whether he marries another Catholic or a non-Catholic, except in the presence of an authorized priest and two witnesses. By an authorized priest is meant a bishop (or a vicar general) within his diocese, a pastor within his parish, or a priest deputed by any of these within his respective territory. A Catholic who attempts to contract marriage before a non-Catholic clergyman not only commits a grave sin but also incurs the penalty of excommunication. However, when an authorized priest cannot be had or approached without grave inconvenience, there are two exceptional cases in which a Catholic can validly and lawfully marry without a priest: *first*, when one, at least, of the parties of the marriage is in danger of death; *second*, when it can be prudently foreseen that an authorized priest cannot be had for a month. In these two cases Catholics can contract a marriage validly and lawfully in the presence of two witnesses.

RESOLUTION: Resolve to go to confession and receive Holy Communion at least once a month during your entire lifetime.

175

STUDY HELPS

A. COLUMN SELECTION. (*Join correctly the parts of the sentences in Columns I and II, by placing the right key letter in the proper parentheses*).

I	II
(1) A Catholic is bound to receive Holy Communion as Viaticum (. .).	(A) at least once a year.
(2) A person who has mortal sins to confess must receive the sacrament of Penance (. .).	(B) only in the presence of an authorized priest and two witnesses.
(3) All Catholics who have reached the use of reason must receive Holy Communion (. .).	(C) if there is danger to the faith of the children.
(4) According to the general law of the Church, the Easter season lasts (. .).	(D) when he is in danger of death.
(5) In the United States the Easter season lasts (. .).	(E) from Palm Sunday to Low Sunday.
(6) A Mass stipend is given to a priest (. .).	(F) to strive for the conversion of the non-Catholic.
(7) The Church forbids marriage (. .).	(G) in the Easter season.
(8) The law of God forbids a mixed marriage (. .).	(H) between a godparent and a godchild.
(9) The Catholic party of a mixed marriage is obliged (. .).	(I) not in payment for the spiritual benefits received but for his support.
(10) A Catholic can contract marriage (. .).	(J) from the first Sunday of Lent to Trinity Sunday.

B. PROBLEMS AND EXERCISES. (*Answer the questions orally or write them as your teacher may direct*):

(1) The civil year begins with January 1st,—the ecclesiastical year with the first Sunday of Advent. How is the year generally reckoned within which the precept of annual confession must be fulfilled?

(2) Barnabas made a good confession on the vigil of Trinity Sunday. He received his Easter duty Communion the next day. Three days later, unfortunately, he committed a mortal sin. Two days after that he was seriously injured in a railroad wreck and was in danger of death. Is he bound to go to confession by the general law of the Church? By God's law? Explain your answers.

(3) His sister Rita is also seriously injured in the same accident. She is a daily communicant. She is in the state of grace. Is she compelled by any law of God or of the Church to go to confession?

(4) Isidore is an eccentric lad with a pronounced 'bump of contradiction.' Last year he went to Communion every Sunday, up to and including Quinquagesima Sunday. For no good reason at all he remained away from the Communion railing until the second Sunday after Pentecost. Did he satisfy the precept of Easter duty? Explain your answer.

176

(5) Ludmilla is a very bright little girl in the second grade of elementary school. She is only six years old. May she receive her First Holy Communion? Give a brief explanation of your answer.

(6) Polycarp, in mortal sin, has been putting off his annual confession and Easter duty from week to week. Finally, he lets the Easter duty season pass by without complying with these precepts. Trinity Sunday night he says to himself: "Well, I missed my Easter duty this year; now all the worry is over until next year!" Has Polycarp rid himself of the two obligations for the present year? What comment have you to make about the correctness or incorrectness of his conclusion?

(7) Are Barnabas and Rita, mentioned above in the railroad wreck, obliged to receive Viaticum?

(8) Gilbert's mother hands him $2.00 "for a Mass to be said by Father Roger." What is the customary name of that offering? For what is it given? Explain the answer.

(9) Angela, of St. Luke's parish, is going to marry Regis of St. Gemma's parish. Angela's brother Damian, a priest in a neighboring diocese, is to perform the marriage ceremony. Does Father Damian need special authorization to perform the service in his sister's parish? Explain your decision.

(10) What two sacraments are the principal sources of strength in the Christian life?

(11) In former times, the support of religion took a tithe of one's earnings. What percentage of one's income is that? Theophilus, a local storekeeper, is earning $50.00 a week. If religion were to receive a tithe of his annual income, how much would he contribute to the various collections, drives, charitable institutions, and other works of a religious character during the course of the year?

(12) Basil, a Catholic, 23 years of age, meets Vesta, a Congregationalist Sunday School teacher, and falls in love with her at first sight. His parents make strenuous objections to his company-keeping with Vesta. Are the parents correct in this attitude? Why? Should Basil discontinue the company-keeping? Why?

(13) Lorenzo and Concetta are working for a year with an oil company in the Near East. The nearest Catholic church is 100 miles distant; and a priest comes to their camp only once every two months to say Mass and to administer the sacraments. The young couple decide to marry. They cannot get a car to journey to the church; and they know that the priest is not due to visit them for five weeks. May they marry even without the presence of a priest? Explain how this can be done.

(14) Howard, an earnest Methodist, tells his fiancee Martha, a Catholic, that the Catholic Church is unjust in laying down the conditions it requires for a mixed marriage. He claims that the fair thing is to have two ceremonies, one in his church and one in the Catholic church. Moreover, he says, as far as the children of the marriage are concerned, while he is willing that the girls be brought up as Catholics, he demands that the boys accept the Methodist religion. What should Martha reply, and what should she do if Howard persists in his demands?

177

PART THREE — THE SACRAMENTS AND PRAYER

LESSON 23

The Sacraments

304. What is a sacrament?

A sacrament is an outward sign instituted by Christ to give grace.

(a) Man, composed of body and soul, lives in the midst of visible things, deals with them constantly, and gains his knowledge from them. His knowledge of spiritual things depends on the use of his senses. It was fitting, therefore, that the sacraments, which were to bring man the supernatural, spiritual gifts of grace, be instituted by Christ as visible signs which could be perceived by man.

(b) In each of the sacraments there is an outward sign, that is, some external thing or action called the *matter*, and a set formula of words known as the *form*. The *matter* and the *form* together make up the sign of each sacrament. In the sacrament of Baptism, for example, the *matter* consists in the water and in its application to the person being baptized; the *form* is the sentence: "I baptize thee in the name of the Father and of the Son and of the Holy Ghost," which is said while the water is being poured.

(c) When the sign is applied to the one who receives the sacrament, it signifies inward grace and has the power of producing it in the soul. The external action performed by the minister of the sacrament is called a sign of the inward grace because it signifies and represents outwardly what is produced inwardly and invisibly in the soul. The sacramental signs actually effect what they represent. In Baptism, for example, the application of the water and the pronouncing of the words are a sign which both represents the cleansing of the soul from sin and actually effects that cleansing.

(d) The sacramental signs were instituted by Christ. Our Lord is the Author of all the sacraments. Only God can give to material things or to outward signs the power of producing grace in the soul

(e) Although Christ instituted all seven sacraments before ascending into heaven, He did not completely specify the matter and form of all the sacraments as clearly and definitely as He did for Baptism and the Eucharist. Christ gave His Church the power to make certain determinations in the matter and form of some of the sacraments.

305. How many sacraments are there?

There are seven sacraments: Baptism, Confirmation, Holy Eucharist, Penance, Extreme Unction, Holy Orders, and Matrimony.

(a) Christ instituted seven sacraments to supply the various needs of the spiritual life of man. Baptism is the sacrament of spiritual rebirth; Con-

178

firmation is the sacrament of spiritual strength and maturity; the Holy Eucharist gives us food for spiritual nourishment; Penance is the cure for the spiritual sickness of sin committed after Baptism; Extreme Unction strengthens us when dying; Holy Orders provides for the work of the Church; and Matrimony provides for the social needs of the Church.

(b) Christ instituted the seven sacraments during His public ministry and after His Resurrection before ascending into heaven.

306. From whom do the sacraments receive their power to give grace?

The sacraments receive their power to give grace from God, through the merits of Jesus Christ.

(a) All grace, including the grace of the sacraments, comes from God through Jesus Christ, who merited it for all men by His life, His passion, and His death.

(b) God uses the seven sacraments as instruments to produce grace in our souls.

(c) Christ willed that the sacraments be administered by men who act in His name.

(d) Although faith and sanctity of life should characterize the minister, they are not required for the valid administration of the sacraments. That the minister validly confer the sacraments it is necessary:

first, that he have the power of administering them;

second, that he have jurisdiction for those sacraments which require it;

third, that he perform all the essential ceremonies;

fourth, that he have the intention of at least "doing what the Church does," that is, of performing the sacred ceremony that is usual among Catholics.

SCRIPTURE:

"They are justified freely by his grace through the redemption which is in Christ Jesus, whom God has set forth as a propitiation by his blood through faith" (*Romans 3:24-25*).

"Let a man so account us, as servants of Christ and stewards of the mysteries of God" (*I Corinthians 4:1*).

307. Do the sacraments give sanctifying grace?

The sacraments do give sanctifying grace.

SCRIPTURE:

"Amen, amen, I say to you, unless you eat the flesh of the Son of Man, and drink his blood, you shall not have life in you. He who eats my flesh and drinks my blood has life everlasting and I will raise him up on the last day" (*John 6:54-55*).

"Receive the Holy Spirit; whose sins you shall forgive, they are forgiven them; and whose sins you shall retain, they are retained" (*John 20:22-23*).

"Now when the apostles in Jerusalem heard that Samaria had received the word of God, they sent to them Peter and John. On their arrival they prayed for them, that they might receive the Holy Spirit; for as yet he had not come upon any of them, but they had only been baptized in the name of the Lord Jesus. Then they laid their hands on them and they received the Holy Spirit" (*Acts 8:14-17*).

179

"For all you who have been baptized into Christ, have put on Christ" (*Galatians 3:27*).

"For this reason I admonish thee to stir up the grace of God which is in thee by the laying on of my hands" (*II Timothy 1:6*).

"He saved us through the bath of regeneration and renewal by the Holy Spirit" (*Titus 3:5*).

308. Does each of the sacraments also give a special grace?

Each of the sacraments also gives a special grace, called sacramental grace, which helps one to carry out the particular purpose of that sacrament.

(a) The sacramental grace of Baptism is a regenerative grace which helps us to live well the new supernatural life we have begun; the sacramental grace of Confirmation is a strengthening grace which helps us to profess our faith openly; the sacramental grace of Holy Eucharist is a nourishing and unitive grace which helps us to be united more closely to God and to one another by supernatural charity; the sacramental grace of Penance is a curative grace which helps us to detest sin effectively, to satisfy for sin committed, and to avoid future sin; the sacramental grace of Extreme Unction is an alleviating grace which comforts us in our last agony, and helps us to overcome final temptations; the sacramental grace of Holy Orders is a consecrating grace which helps bishops and priests to discharge the duties of the sacred ministry faithfully; the sacramental grace of Matrimony is a grace which helps the married couple to live chastely and to fulfill their duties to each other and to their children.

309. Do the sacraments always give grace?

The sacraments always give grace if we receive them with the right dispositions.

(a) The sacraments, validly administered, always give grace to those who receive them with the right dispositions, because the power of the sacraments does not depend on anything human but solely on the will of God as expressed by Christ when He instituted them. The right dispositions do not produce the grace; they merely remove the obstacles which would prevent the reception of grace. The right dispositions, or the acts and habits required as conditions in order that the sacraments have their effect, vary with the different sacraments.

(b) It is important to prepare fervently for the reception of the sacraments, because ordinarily they confer grace in proportion to our dispositions.

SCRIPTURE:

"Therefore whoever eats this bread or drinks the cup of the Lord unworthily, will be guilty of the body and the blood of the Lord" (*I Corinthians 11:27*).

"Is any one among you sick? Let him bring in the presbyters of the Church, and let them pray over him, anointing him with oil in the name of the Lord. And the prayer of faith will save the sick man, and the Lord will raise him up, and if he be in sins, they shall be forgiven him" (*James 5:14-15*).

310. Why are Baptism and Penance called sacraments of the dead?

Baptism and Penance are called sacraments of the dead because their chief purpose is to give the supernatural life of sanctifying grace to souls spiritually dead through sin.

(a) The sacraments of the dead increase sanctifying grace when they are received by one who is already in the state of grace. Thus when a person who has only venial sins to confess receives absolution in the sacrament of Penance, he receives an increase of sanctifying grace.

SCRIPTURE:
"Amen, amen, I say to thee, unless a man be born again of water and the Spirit, he cannot enter into the kingdom of God" (*John 3:5*).

See also Scripture, question 307, John 20:22-23.

311. Why are Confirmation, Holy Eucharist, Extreme Unction, Holy Orders, and Matrimony called sacraments of the living?

Confirmation, Holy Eucharist, Extreme Unction, Holy Orders, and Matrimony are called sacraments of the living because their chief purpose is to give more grace to souls already spiritually alive through sanctifying grace.

312. What sin does one commit who knowingly receives a sacrament of the living in mortal sin?

He who knowingly receives a sacrament of the living in mortal sin commits a mortal sin of sacrilege, because he treats a sacred thing with grave irreverence.

SCRIPTURE: *See Scripture, question 309, I Corinthians 11:27.*

313. Which are the sacraments that can be received only once?

The sacraments that can be received only once are Baptism, Confirmation, and Holy Orders.

314. Why can Baptism, Confirmation, and Holy Orders be received only once?

Baptism, Confirmation, and Holy Orders can be received only once because they imprint on the soul a spiritual mark, called a character, which lasts forever.

(a) A character is a spiritual quality enabling a person to discharge the duty of worshiping God according to the laws of Christ and His Church. The character places on the soul the sign of Christ, the Eternal Priest, and gives the one who receives it a special position in the service of Christ. The indelible character received in Baptism enables one to receive the other sacraments; in Confirmation, the character enables one to profess the Christian faith before its enemies; in Holy Orders, the character enables one to consecrate oneself to the work of administering the sacraments to other persons.

(b) The character imprinted on the soul by Baptism and Confirmation imposes the obligation of being a lay apostle, that is, of bringing the faith and the grace of Christ to others under the leadership and the guidance of the Pope and bishops.

181

(c) Persons who have received a sacramental character are forever distinguished from those who have not received it. Thus it will forever be a mark of glory for those who are saved, but a mark of shame for those who are lost.

SCRIPTURE:

"Now it is God who is warrant for us and for you in Christ, who has anointed us, who has also stamped us with his seal and has given us the Spirit as a pledge in our hearts" (*II Corinthians 1:21-22*).

"And in him you too, when you had heard the word of truth, the good news of your salvation, and believed in it, were sealed with the Holy Spirit, ... for a redemption of possession, for the praise of his glory" (*Ephesians 1:13-14*).

"And do not grieve the Holy Spirit of God, in whom you were sealed for the day of redemption" (*Ephesians 4:30*).

IMPORTANT TRUTHS ABOUT THE SACRAMENTS

Before He ascended into heaven Our Blessed Lord decided to establish means of communicating to the souls of men the graces He had merited by His life and death. For this purpose Our Saviour willed to use external ceremonies, signs which could be perceived by men through their bodily senses. Human beings derive their knowledge by the use of their senses, and what appeals to their senses makes a greater impression than something that is perceived by the intellect alone; hence, Our Lord decided to suit His means of grace to man's nature. Accordingly, He instituted seven signs, or external ceremonies, capable of giving grace. He chose the particular signs to satisfy the most urgent spiritual needs of men. And, as will become more apparent in the lessons to follow, He adapted the sacraments to a plan of the spiritual life very similar to the course of man's natural life from the cradle to the grave.

A sacrament is an instrument of God's power and goodness. Just as an artist, using his brush as an instrument, paints a beautiful picture, so God through the sacraments draws His own image on the soul of man. However, the sacraments give grace dependently on man's cooperation. It is true, when a child who has not reached the age of reason receives a sacrament, God gives him the graces of the sacrament without demanding any dispositions. But when a person has once reached the use of reason, he must do his part in order to be sanctified. Such a person cannot receive a sacrament *validly*—that is, really—unless he has at least a general intention of receiving it. The external rite could indeed be forced on him, but it would not be a real sacrament unless he consented to receive it. Moreover, one who has attained the age of reason cannot receive a sacrament *fruitfully*—that is, with its graces—unless he has in his soul suitable dispositions as a becoming preparation. Generally speaking, the disposition required of an adult for the reception of a sacrament of the dead—that is Baptism or Penance—is sorrow for sin based on faith; and the essential disposition for a worthy reception of one of the sacraments of the living is the possession of the state of sanctifying grace.

However, it is generally believed that if a person in mortal sin receives a sacrament of the living, unaware of his unworthiness and with imperfect contrition for his mortal sins, he will receive the state of grace. This is certain in regard to Extreme Unction, for St. James says, of the sick person who receives this sacrament, "If he be in sins, they shall be forgiven him" (*James 5:15*).

Most of the sacraments can be administered only by a priest or a bishop. However, two of them—Baptism and Matrimony—can be administered by laymen, as we shall see in the lessons on these sacraments. The Holy Eucharist can be consecrated by no one except a priest; but after it is consecrated, one who is not a priest can administer it. Ordinarily the Church allows only priests

182

and (under certain conditions) deacons to give Holy Communion, but in extraordinary circumstances even a lay-person would be permitted to administer the Blessed Sacrament. Thus, any Catholic could consume the Holy Eucharist or give it to another Catholic, if this were necessary to prevent it from being profaned; and if no priest could be had, and the Blessed Sacrament were available, a layman would be allowed to administer Holy Communion as Viaticum to one in danger of death.

Sometimes a priest administers a sacrament conditionally—that is, with the intention of conferring it only on condition that certain circumstances of which he is uncertain, are present. Thus, if a priest, baptizing a baby, is not certain whether or not the child has been previously baptized, he administers the sacrament with the condition: "If you are not baptized." If a priest, called to a person who has been seriously injured, is not sure whether or not the person is still living, he gives Extreme Unction with the condition: "If you are alive."

Our Lord Himself instituted the seven sacraments for our sanctification, but the Church has instituted various rites and ceremonies for the administration of the sacraments, to manifest more clearly their significance and to impress us more deeply with their holiness.

RESOLUTION: Resolve to be reverent and devout toward the sacraments, and never to receive them carelessly or through routine; above all, resolve never to be guilty of the grave sacrilege of receiving a sacrament unworthily.

STUDY HELPS

A. **WORD SELECTION.** (*Select the word or phrase in the parentheses which most exactly and most completely fills out the sentence*).

(1) The words used by the person who administers a sacrament are called (the matter . . . the form . . . the character).

(2) For a priest to administer the sacraments validly he needs (the intention of doing what the Church does . . . faith . . . sanctity of life).

(3) Christ instituted all the sacraments (before He began His public ministry . . . before His death . . . before His ascension).

(4) Penance is called a sacrament of the dead because (only a person whose soul is dead in sin can receive it . . . it must be received by everyone in danger of death . . . it is intended chiefly to give the life of sanctifying grace to souls dead in mortal sin).

(5) The sacramental grace of Confirmation helps us (to profess our faith openly . . . to avoid sin in future . . . to be united more closely with God).

(6) A person who knowingly receives a sacrament of the living in mortal sin commits a sin of (blasphemy . . . sacrilege . . . perjury).

(7) The sacramental character of Baptism (endures forever in all who have received it . . . passes away with death . . . remains in the saints but not in the souls condemned to hell).

(8) To receive the sacrament of Baptism validly a person having the use of reason must have (faith . . . sorrow for sin . . . the intention of receiving it).

(9) A person is made capable of receiving the other sacraments besides Baptism by (the character of Baptism . . . the grace of Baptism . . . the profession of the Catholic faith).

(10) A person who receives a sacrament of the living in mortal sin but unaware of his unworthiness will receive sanctifying grace if he has (faith . . . the use of reason . . . imperfect contrition).

183

B. PROBLEMS AND EXERCISES. (*Answer the questions orally or write them as your teacher may direct*):

(1) Why are external ceremonies, namely, the sacraments, properly used for transmitting God's grace to our souls?

(2) Explain to Myrtle in the eighth grade, why Our Lord decided to suit His means of grace to our human nature.

(3) Describe in your own words the sacramental grace of each of the seven sacraments.

(4) In the commentary, references are made to an artist, his brush, and a beautiful picture. What point is brought out by these references?

(5) At what stage in life do the sacraments begin to require dispositions on our part in order that we may receive their benefits?

(6) Glenn, an unbeliever, is anxious to marry Claudia, a good Catholic. Accordingly, he takes instructions, receives Baptism and Holy Communion, and marries Claudia at a nuptial Mass. He willingly receives these sacred rites, but he does not believe in them. Has he received these sacraments validly? Has he received them fruitfully?

(7) What is meant by the expressions: "to receive a sacrament fruitfully . . . to receive a sacrament validly"?

(8) Generally speaking, what is the disposition required in one who has attained the use of reason, for the fruitful reception of the sacraments of the dead?

(9) What is the essential disposition for a worthy reception of one of the sacraments of the living?

(10) Which of the sacraments may be administered by lay persons?

(11) Julia, a novice, is kneeling before the Blessed Sacrament in a convent chapel of an obscure town in Eastern Europe. All the nuns and novices are in lay disguise on account of the persecution raging there. The convent is in a private house. At 3:00 o'clock one afternoon a friendly warning is given them that their presence has been discovered. There is no time to lose. Mother Superior asks the fervent novice, Julia, remarkable for her devotion to the Blessed Sacrament, to open the Tabernacle, and to distribute the Communions reserved in the Ciborium to the members of the community, including herself. Each of the Sisters and novices receives four of the Sacred Particles. Write a paragraph of comment on the episode,—a paragraph of from five to seven sentences.

(12) What can the sacramental grace of Baptism do for you?

(13) Silas, a happy-go-lucky lad in the seventh grade, wants to know what is the use of going to confession every two weeks, as Brother St. Lawrence O'Toole advises. Silas rightly claims he doesn't commit mortal sins. Tell Silas why the Brother recommends confession fortnightly.

(14) The night before her wedding, Viola is so thoroughly concerned with her appearance and her appointment at the hairdresser's that she completely forgets to go to confession. Unhappily, she is in mortal sin at the time of the ceremony, but she doesn't realize it until after the honeymoon. Now she is greatly upset about the whole matter and does not want to risk her salvation. Was her marriage sacrilegious? Is she really married? Add a reason to both answers.

(15) Father Tugwell enjoys a rare distinction. He has received during the past 73 years all of the seven sacraments. Explain how that is possible.

184

Baptism

315. What is Baptism?

Baptism is the sacrament that gives our souls the new life of sanctifying grace by which we become children of God and heirs of heaven.

(a) Our adoption as sons of God through sanctifying grace is more perfect than human adoption whereby children are adopted by foster parents. In human adoption nothing is given to the foster son that makes him similar to the foster parent. Into the souls of the adopted sons of God, however, sanctifying grace is infused, which gives them supernaturally a likeness to God. In human adoption the foster son succeeds to his inheritance only after the death of the father; in God's adoption the eternally living Father lets us share in our inheritance at the time of the adoption, that is, when the sacrament of Baptism is administered. By means of sanctifying grace received in Baptism we are spiritually reborn; we become members of the family of God, who becomes our Father in the supernatural order.

(b) The Baptism preached by Saint John did not have the same power as the Baptism instituted by Christ. The Baptism instituted by Christ directly produces grace; the Baptism preached by Saint John was intended to arouse in souls sorrow for sin. The Baptism of St. John prepared the way for the Baptism of Christ.

(c) After His Resurrection, Christ commanded all to receive Baptism as a necessary condition for salvation.

SCRIPTURE:

"All power in heaven and on earth has been given to me. Go, therefore, and make disciples of all nations, baptizing them in the name of the Father, and of the Son, and of the Holy Spirit, teaching them to observe all that I have commanded you; and behold, I am with you all days, even unto the consummation of the world" (*Matthew 28:18-20*).

"And he preached, saying, 'One mightier than I is coming after me, the strap of whose sandals I am not worthy to stoop down and loose. I have baptized you with water, but he will baptize you with the Holy Spirit'" (*Mark 1:6-8*).

"Go into the whole world and preach the gospel to every creature. He who believes and is baptized shall be saved, but he who does not believe shall be condemned" (*Mark 16:15-16*).

"But to as many as received him he gave the power of becoming sons of God" (*John 1:12*).

"Amen, amen, I say to thee, unless a man be born again of water and the Spirit, he cannot enter into the kingdom of God" (*John 3:5*).

"Repent and be baptized every one of you in the name of Jesus Christ for the forgiveness of your sins; and you will receive the gift of the Holy Spirit" (*Acts 2:38*).

"For whoever are led by the Spirit of God, they are the sons of God. Now you have not received a spirit of bondage so as to be again in fear, but you

185a

Baptism

The baptism of Jesus Christ, which is shown in the middle, demonstrates the effect that baptism produces in us. When Our Lord was baptized by St. John the Baptist in the waters of the Jordan, the voice of God the Father was heard, saying, "This is my beloved Son, in whom I am well pleased." (St. Matthew 3:17) The Holy Spirit descended upon Him in the form of a dove, and the heavens were opened. When we are baptized, God adopts us as His children. The Holy Spirit descends upon us by His grace, and we become heirs of the kingdom of heaven.

At the bottom is a priest baptizing an infant. An angel is holding the white robe with which the baptized child is being clothed. This garment signifies that his soul is adorned with grace and innocence that makes him beautiful and pleasing in the eyes of God.

A child who dies as soon as he is baptized goes immediately to heaven. This is shown at the top right, where the soul of a child who died after baptism is carried to heaven by angels.

Baptism is so necessary for salvation that even children cannot enter heaven if they are unbaptized. This is why, at the top on the left, the soul of a dead unbaptized child heads for a place where it will be deprived of celestial happiness forever. The child will, however, enjoy a natural state of happiness since it was never guilty of actual sin.

have received a spirit of adoption as sons, by virtue of which we cry, 'Abba! Father!' The Spirit himself gives testimony to our spirit that we are sons of God. But if we are sons, we are heirs also: heirs indeed of God and joint heirs with Christ, provided, however, we suffer with him that we may also be glorified with him" (*Romans 8:14-17*).

"But when the goodness and kindness of God our Savior appeared, then not by reason of good works that we did ourselves, but according to his mercy, he saved us through the bath of regeneration and renewal by the Holy Spirit; whom he has abundantly poured out upon us through Jesus Christ our Savior, in order that, justified by his grace, we may be heirs in the hope of life ever- lasting" (*Titus 3:4-7*).

316. What sins does Baptism take away?

Baptism takes away original sin; and also actual sins and all the punishment due to them, if the person baptized be guilty of any actual sins and truly sorry for them.

(a) Baptism takes away both the eternal punishment of hell due to un- forgiven mortal sin, and the temporal punishment on earth or in purgatory due to venial sin or to forgiven mortal sin.

(b) Though Baptism takes away original sin and restores sanctifying grace to the soul, it does not take away all the consequences of original sin. For example, it does not take away death, suffering, ignorance, and a strong inclination to sin.

SCRIPTURE:

"Get up and be baptized and wash away thy sins, calling on his name" (*Acts 22:16*).

"Do you not know that all we who have been baptized into Christ Jesus have been baptized into his death? . . . for he who is dead is acquitted of sin. But if we have died with Christ, we believe that we shall also live together with Christ" (*Romans 6:3, 7-8*).

"There is therefore now no condemnation for those who are in Christ Jesus" (*Romans 8:1*).

See Scripture, question 315, John 3:5; Acts 2:38.

317. What are the effects of the character imprinted on the soul by Baptism?

The effects of the character imprinted on the soul by Baptism are that we become members of the Church, subject to its laws, and capable of receiving the other sacraments.

(a) Baptized persons remain *members* of the Church as long as they are united to it by profession of the same faith and have not broken the bonds of communion with it.

(b) All validly baptized persons are *subjects* of the Church, even if they are not members. Hence they are obliged to obey the laws of the Church unless exempted. If, however, they are invincibly ignorant of their obligation to obey the laws of the Church, they do not sin by not obeying them.

(c) An unbaptized person cannot validly receive the other sacraments.

186

(d) A baptized person renounces Satan, his works, and his pomps, and has the obligation of leading a Christian life by following Christ and by obeying the legitimate pastors of the Church, especially the Roman Pontiff.

SCRIPTURE:
See Scripture, question 314, II Corinthians 1:21-22; question 315, John 1:12, 3:5.

318. Who can administer Baptism?

The priest is the usual minister of Baptism, but if there is danger that someone will die without Baptism, anyone else may and should baptize.

(a) In case of necessity even a heretic or an unbaptized person can validly and licitly baptize. He must, however, perform the ceremony correctly and have the intention of "doing what the Church does," namely, of performing the ceremony that is usual among Catholics.

319. How would you give Baptism?

I would give Baptism by pouring ordinary water on the forehead of the person to be baptized, saying while pouring it: "I baptize thee in the name of the Father, and of the Son, and of the Holy Ghost."

(a) By the command of Christ, real water must be used in Baptism. Thus, anything that is not water in the usual sense of the word cannot be used.

(b) In solemn Baptism, baptismal water, blessed for the purpose, must be used under penalty of grave sin.

(c) In Baptism conferred at home by necessity, it is best to use ordinary water. Holy water, however, may be used. If for any reason the ceremonies of Baptism are omitted, these ceremonies are to be later supplied in church.

(d) The sacrament of Baptism may be validly administered:
first, by immersion;
second, by pouring;
third, by sprinkling.
Christ commanded Baptism by water; He did not prescribe the manner of applying water. According to Church law, however, it is not now licit to confer Baptism by the method of sprinkling.

(e) In conferring Baptism by pouring, care must be taken that the water flows over the skin of the person's head, and that the words are clearly and exactly spoken *while* the water is being poured, not before or after the water is poured.

(f) In Baptism, the pouring of the water and the saying of the words must be done by the same person.

(g) If in case of necessity a person's head cannot be baptized, the water may be poured on another part of the body, preferably the chest or shoulders, since this Baptism is probably valid. If a person baptized in one of these ways can later be baptized on the forehead, this should be done, with the condition, "If you are not baptized, I baptize," etc.

"Now they who received his word were baptized, and there were added that day about three thousand souls" (*Acts 2:41*).

"These in times past had been disobedient when the patience of God waited in the days of Noe while the ark was building. In that ark a few, that is, eight souls were saved through water. Its counterpart, Baptism, now saves you also" (*I Peter 3:20-21*).

See Scripture, question 315, Matthew 28:18-20; John 3:5.

320. Why is Baptism necessary for the salvation of all men?

Baptism is necessary for the salvation of all men because Christ has said: "Unless a man be born again of water and the Spirit, he cannot enter into the kingdom of God."

(a) Today, many of the sects, renewing the ancient heresy of the Pelagians, reject Christ's words concerning the necessity of Baptism and seek to establish their own norms of salvation.

SCRIPTURE: *See Scripture, question 315, John 3:5; Mark 16:15-16.*

321. How can those be saved who through no fault of their own have not received the sacrament of Baptism?

Those who through no fault of their own have not received the sacrament of Baptism can be saved through what is called baptism of blood or baptism of desire.

322. How does an unbaptized person receive the baptism of blood?

An unbaptized person receives the baptism of blood when he suffers martyrdom for the faith of Christ.

(a) Baptism of blood does not imprint a character on the soul, nor does it give one the right to receive the other sacraments. It does, however, confer grace and take away sin, original and actual, and the punishment due to sin.

(b) Martyrdom is the suffering, from a supernatural motive, of death or a mortal wound inflicted out of hatred for Christ, His religion, or a Christian virtue. In sinners guilty of mortal sin, at least attrition is also required in order to secure the effects of baptism of blood.

SCRIPTURE:
"He who finds his life will lose it, and he who loses his life for my sake, will find it" (*Matthew 10:39*).

"For he who would save his life will lose it; but he who loses his life for my sake and for the gospel's sake will save it" (*Mark 8:35*).

"And I say to you, everyone who acknowledges me before men, him will the Son of Man also acknowledge before the angels of God" (*Luke 12:8*).

"Greater love than this no one has, that one lay down his life for his friends" (*John 15:13*).

323. How does an unbaptized person receive the baptism of desire?

An unbaptized person receives the baptism of desire when he loves God above all things and desires to do all that is necessary for his salvation.

(a) Baptism of desire takes away all sin, original and actual, and the eternal punishment due to sin. It does not, however, imprint a character on the soul, nor does it necessarily take away all the temporal punishment due to actual sins.

(b) In baptism of desire there need not always be an *explicit* desire to receive baptism of water.

SCRIPTURE:

"And behold, a certain lawyer got up to test him, saying, 'Master, what must I do to gain eternal life?' But he said to him, 'What is written in the Law? How dost thou read?' He answered and said,

'Thou shalt love the Lord thy God
    with thy whole heart,
    and with thy whole soul,
    and with thy whole strength,
    and with thy whole mind;
And thy neighbor as thyself.'

And he said to him, 'Thou hast answered rightly; do this and thou shalt live' " (*Luke 10:25-28*).

"He who has my commandments and keeps them, he it is who loves me. But he who loves me will be loved by my Father, and I will love him and manifest myself to him" (*John 14:21*).

"If anyone love me, he will keep my word, and my Father will love him, and we will come to him and make our abode with him" (*John 14:23*).

324. When should children be baptized?

Children should be baptized as soon as possible after birth.

(a) Children should be baptized as soon as possible because Baptism is necessary for salvation. Infants who die without baptism of any kind do not suffer the punishments of those who die in mortal sin. They may enjoy a certain natural happiness, but they will not enjoy the supernatural happiness of heaven.

(b) Except in danger of death, Baptism may not be administered to a child who has not attained the use of reason and whose non-Catholic parents are unwilling to have it baptized.

325. What sin do Catholic parents commit who put off for a long time, or entirely neglect, the Baptism of their children?

Catholic parents who put off for a long time, or entirely neglect, the Baptism of their children, commit a mortal sin.

326. What do we promise through our godparents in Baptism?

We promise through our godparents in Baptism to renounce the devil and to live according to the teachings of Christ and of His Church.

327. Why is the name of a saint given in Baptism?

The name of a saint is given in Baptism in order that the person baptized may imitate his virtues and have him for a protector.

189

328. What is the duty of a godparent after Baptism?

The duty of a godparent after Baptism is to see that the child is brought up a good Catholic, if this is not done by the parents.

(a) Godparents contract a spiritual relationship, not with each other, but with their godchildren. Godparents cannot marry their godchildren without a dispensation.

329. Who should be chosen as godparents for Baptism?

Only Catholics who know their faith and live up to the duties of their religion should be chosen as godparents for Baptism.

(a) Godparents should be at least thirteen years of age.

(b) Non-Catholics cannot be godparents, nor can the father, the mother, the husband, or the wife of the person to be baptized.

IMPORTANT TRUTHS ABOUT BAPTISM

The beginning of man's earthly life takes place at birth; the beginning of his spiritual life takes place at Baptism. It was under the figure of a spiritual birth that Our Lord spoke of Baptism, when He said: "Unless a man be born again of water and the Spirit he cannot enter into the kingdom of God" (*John 3, 5*). Through Baptism one begins to live the divine life of a child of God.

Our Lord Himself received a baptism from St. John the Baptist, but this ceremony was not a sacrament. It was only a foreshadowing of the sacrament. However, it was probably about this time that Our Saviour instituted the sacrament; and perhaps administered it to the apostles with His own hands. At any rate, they must have been baptized before the Last Supper, for they then became priests, and the character of the priesthood can be given only to one who possesses the character of Baptism. Before His Ascension into heaven Christ deputed the apostles to go and baptize all men; and on Pentecost Sunday the apostles began the task, telling those who heard the Gospel and were converted: "Repent and be baptized every one of you in the name of Jesus Christ for the forgiveness of your sins; and you will receive the gift of the Holy Spirit" (*Acts, 2, 38*). As the apostles went to various lands and made converts, they announced the reception of Baptism as the chief condition of becoming a follower of Christ and a member of His Church. In the words of St. Paul: "All you who have been baptized into Christ, have put on Christ" (*Gal., 3, 27*) . . . "We were all baptized into one body" (*I Cor., 12, 13*).

The Catholic Church has always emphasized the importance of Baptism, and has always taken the greatest care that no child depart from this world without receiving this sacrament. The children of non-Catholics can lawfully be baptized even against the wishes of their parents, if they are in danger of death, for this sacrament is necessary for salvation, and in such a case the right of the child to eternal salvation takes precedence over parental rights.

The child of Catholic parents should be baptized soon after birth—if possible, within two weeks. In the event that the child is in danger of death, it should be baptized immediately, in the way described in this lesson. A lay person who baptizes a child in such circumstances should not make the validity of the sacrament depend on a future condition—for example, he should not intend to give the sacrament only on condition that the priest does not come in time—but should have the intention of baptizing absolutely and unconditionally. When a child has been baptized privately, it should afterward be brought to the church in order that the various ceremonies of solemn Baptism may be supplied.

190

The essential ceremony of Baptism is the washing of the recipient with water. Our Saviour prescribed this washing in a general way, but He did not designate the particular mode in which it is to be performed. Hence at different times the Church has used different modes. In the beginning complete immersion was practiced, and this is still used in the Oriental rites. The Latin Church commonly employs the method of pouring, or infusion; and even sprinkling the baptismal water is a valid way of baptizing, provided the water touches the skin of the recipient's head and flows over it. The words required for Baptism, pronounced by the minister, explain what is being done—"I baptize thee"—then the words assert that the power of the sacrament comes from the three divine Persons—"in the name of the Father, and of the Son, and of the Holy Ghost". To these divinely established elements of the sacrament the Church has added many beautiful ceremonies for the solemn administration of Baptism, which can be performed only by a priest or (as an extraordinary minister) a deacon, such as the anointing of the breast and shoulders with oil and the giving of a lighted candle. Catholics should study the meaning of these ceremonies, particularly if they are invited to serve as godparents at Baptism.

RESOLUTION: Resolve to find out the date of your Baptism and to celebrate it each year as your spiritual birthday, especially by receiving Holy Communion in thanksgiving to God for the grace of Baptism, and by renewing the promises made in your name at Baptism, to be faithful to Christ and to His Church.

STUDY HELPS

A. TRUE OR FALSE. (*Check each of the following statements as either true or false. The correct answers can be found in previous portions of this lesson*).

	TRUE	FALSE
(1) Baptism by St. John the Baptist was a sacrament.	....	....
(2) Baptism takes away all the temporal punishment due to actual sins.	....	....
(3) A person who bears the character of Baptism on his soul is subject to the laws of the Church, whether he is a Catholic or not.	....	....
(4) A person who is not himself baptized cannot confer the sacrament of Baptism.	....	....
(5) Baptism cannot be given validly by sprinkling.	....	....
(6) Baptism of blood does not imprint a character on the soul.	....	....
(7) Baptism of desire takes away all the temporal punishment due to actual sins.	....	....
(8) Godparents at the same baptism cannot marry each other without a special dispensation.	....	....
(9) A person should be at least thirteen years old to be a godparent.	....	....
(10) An infant in danger of death may be baptized even against the will of its parents.	....	....

B. PROBLEMS AND EXERCISES. (*Answer the questions orally or write them as your teacher may direct*):

(1) What are the words of Our Lord commanding the reception of the sacrament of Baptism? Did He give this command before Holy Week, during it, or afterwards?

191

(2) Terence, an infant, has just been baptized by Father Tracy. What has Baptism given his soul?

(3) Who baptized Our Lord? Was that baptism a sacrament or a mere ceremony? Did that baptism give grace of itself?

(4) Spenser unfortunately commits a sacrilege by receiving Holy Communion unworthily. Is that a mortal sin? Spenser now repents and makes a good confession. Do any penalties still remain? Explain.

(5) Before God, Warren and Sigismund, eighteen years old have about an equal amount of guilt on their souls as the result of many mortal and venial sins. Both receive a sacrament of the dead,—Warren, Baptism; Sigismund, Penance. Warren died immediately after his Baptism this morning. In another city, almost at the same hour, Sigismund died of a heart attack in the confessional just as the priest completed the words of absolution. Did Warren and Sigismund both enter heaven immediately? Did one or both of them go to purgatory? Explain your answer.

(6) This morning, at the request of the child's Anglican parents, Dr. Saul, a Jewish doctor, baptized a frail, new-born infant boy. Doctor Saul does not believe in Christian baptism, but he does what the parents ask him to do, pours the water correctly, and says the words of Baptism accurately. The child is baptized David, the Jewish doctor's first name. Now is the infant David subject to the laws of the Catholic church, or to the laws of the Anglican church, or to the laws of the synagogue? Why?

(7) Why do the Sisters, Brothers, Priests and Bishops demand a baptismal certificate before the reception of First Holy Communion, Confirmation, marriage, and Holy Orders?

(8) It is a cold wintry Sunday afternoon. The parish priest is about to baptize Cornelia, a baby ten days old. Why does he ask the godmother to remove Cornelia's cap, and to loosen its little dress at the neck?

(9) The Holy Innocents martyred by cruel Herod shortly after Jesus was born are honored by the Church as saints. Did some priest baptize them before they died? How was original sin removed from their souls?

(10) Giles is murdered by a Communist just as he leaves the church after his confession. Giles had been away from the church for 28 years. He just about satisfied the requirements for a good confession, having only imperfect contrition, aroused during this week's mission. The Communist demanded to know if Giles was a Catholic, threatening to kill him if he was. Fearlessly, Giles said: "Yes, thank God!" Did Giles go immediately to heaven, or did he go to purgatory for a while? Give a reason for your answer.

(11) Where now are the countless millions of infants who have died without Baptism? Are they happy or unhappy?

(12) Estelle, in the eighth grade of St. Venantius' school, has a very healthy new baby sister now six weeks old. She is to be baptized Joan. Her parents are waiting for the godparents to come up from South America three months from now. Estelle wants to know if the delay in Joan's Baptism is justified. Tell her, and add a reason to your reply.

(13) When does the priest consecrate baptismal water?

(14) Leonard, an infant, is baptized by the doctor an hour after his birth. The Baptism is true, that is, valid. A month later, Leonard is completely out of danger. To what must Leonard's parents now attend?

Confirmation

330. What is Confirmation?

Confirmation is the sacrament through which the Holy Ghost comes to us in a special way and enables us to profess our faith as strong and perfect Christians and soldiers of Jesus Christ.

(a) The word "confirmation" means "a strengthening."

(b) We are not certain from Sacred Scripture of the exact time and circumstances of the institution of Confirmation. We do know, however, that Christ instituted the sacrament before He ascended into heaven, because it is clearly evident in the New Testament that the apostles administered this sacrament.

(c) A confirmed person is called a soldier of Christ because, through Confirmation, he is especially deputed to profess the faith strongly and to fight for it.

SCRIPTURE:

" 'He who believes in me, as the Scripture says, "From within him there shall flow rivers of living water." ' He said this, however, of the Spirit whom they who believed in him were to receive; for the Spirit had not yet been given, since Jesus had not yet been glorified" (*John 7:38-39*).

"But I speak the truth to you; it is expedient for you that I depart. For if I do not go, the Advocate will not come to you; but if I go, I will send him to you" *(John 16:7).*

"And when the days of Pentecost were drawing to a close, they were all together in one place. And suddenly there came a sound from heaven, as of a violent wind blowing, and it filled the whole house where they were sitting. And there appeared to them parted tongues as of fire, which settled upon each of them. And they were all filled with the Holy Spirit and began to speak in foreign tongues, even as the Holy Spirit prompted them to speak" (*Acts 2:1-4*).

"Now when the apostles in Jerusalem heard that Samaria had received the word of God, they sent to them Peter and John. On their arrival they prayed for them, that they might receive the Holy Spirit; for as yet he had not come upon any of them, but they had only been baptized in the name of the Lord Jesus" (*Acts 8:14-16*).

"On hearing this they were baptized in the name of the Lord Jesus; and when Paul laid his hands on them, the Holy Spirit came upon them, and they began to speak in tongues and to prophesy" (*Acts 19:5-6*).

331. Who is the usual minister of Confirmation?

The bishop is the usual minister of Confirmation.

(a) Pastors and administrators of parishes, in virtue of a decreee that became effective January 1, 1947, are granted the faculty of confirming, as extraordinary ministers, those among their faithful and others in their territory who are in danger of death from sickness, accident, or old age.

(b) Priests, especially those in missionary lands, are sometimes delegated by the Holy Father to administer Confirmation. Most priests of the Oriental Church have this privilege.

SCRIPTURE: *See Scripture, question 330, Acts 8:14-16.*

332. What does the bishop do when he gives Confirmation?

The bishop extends his hands over those who are to be confirmed, prays that they may receive the Holy Ghost, and, while laying his hand on the head of each person, anoints the forehead with holy chrism in the form of a cross.

SCRIPTURE: *See Scripture, question 330, Acts 8:14-16; Acts 19:5-6.*

333. What does the bishop say in anointing the person he confirms?

In anointing the person he confirms, the bishop says: "I sign thee with the sign of the cross and I confirm thee with the chrism of salvation, in the name of the Father, and of the Son, and of the Holy Ghost."

(a) The words, "I sign thee with the sign of the cross," designate the character by which the confirmed person becomes a soldier of Christ. The words, "I confirm thee," etc., designate the gift of strength received in this sacrament.

SCRIPTURE: *See Scripture, question 330, Acts 8:14-16.*

334. What is holy chrism?

Holy chrism is a mixture of olive oil and balm, blessed by the bishop on Holy Thursday.

(a) Olive oil was formerly used to condition and strengthen the limbs of athletes. The olive oil in holy chrism signifies the strengthening grace of the Holy Spirit received in the sacrament.

(b) Balm, sometimes used as a preservative, is a fragrant substance derived from the balsam tree. In holy chrism it signifies the sweetness of virtue and freedom from the corruption of sin.

335. What does the anointing of the forehead with chrism in the form of a cross signify?

The anointing of the forehead with chrism in the form of a cross signifies that the Catholic who is confirmed must always be ready to profess his faith openly and to practice it fearlessly.

336. Why does the bishop give the person he confirms a slight blow on the cheek?

The bishop gives the person he confirms a slight blow on the cheek to remind him that he must be ready to suffer everything, even death, for the sake of Christ.

337. What are the effects of Confirmation?

Confirmation increases sanctifying grace, gives its special sacramental grace, and imprints a lasting character on the soul.

SCRIPTURE:
See Scripture, question 315, Acts 2:38; question 330, Acts 8:14-16; Acts 19:5-6.

338. What does the sacramental grace of Confirmation help us to do?

The sacramental grace of Confirmation helps us to live our faith loyally and to profess it courageously.

(a) The sacramental grace of Confirmation also gives us a right to the actual graces we need when tempted against faith.

339. What is the character of Confirmation?

The character of Confirmation is a spiritual and indelible sign which marks the Christian as a soldier in the army of Christ.

(a) The character of Confirmation is a quality impressed on the soul that enables us to fight spiritual battles against the enemies of the faith after the example of the apostles, who, upon receiving the Holy Spirit at Pentecost, were not afraid to profess and preach the faith to the entire world.

340. What is necessary to receive Confirmation properly?

To receive Confirmation properly it is necessary to be in the state of grace, and to know well the chief truths and duties of our religion.

(a) A non-baptized person cannot receive validly the sacrament of Confirmation.

(b) In the Latin Church it is proper for children to receive Confirmation at about the age of seven. The sacrament, however, may be given at an earlier age either by reason of danger of death or for any other cause which the minister considers grave and just. In the Eastern Church, children usually receive Confirmation immediately after Baptism.

(c) A baptized person cannot without sin neglect to receive Confirmation when the opportunity offers itself. Further, if the neglect to receive Confirmation arises from contempt for the sacrament, the sin is grave.

(d) A baptized person who receives Confirmation knowing that he is in the state of mortal sin, commits a grave sin of sacrilege and receives no grace. He does, however, receive the sacrament validly. If, therefore, he regains the state of grace, he will then receive the graces of Confirmation.

(e) The candidate for Confirmation should have a sponsor of his own sex who was not his godparent in Baptism. The sponsor must be a baptized Catholic who is confirmed. The other conditions of sponsorship are in general the same as those for godparents in Baptism.

(f) A spiritual relationship is contracted between the confirmed person and the sponsor. The sponsor, moreover, has the obligation of considering the confirmed person as placed under his special care and of providing, if

195

195a

Confirmation

At the top left, a soldier fights against a dragon with seven heads. This signifies that in confirmation we receive the strength necessary to conquer the seven capital sins.

On the right is a child, faithful to the lessons of his mother, declaring himself Christian in front of a pagan judge who wanted to make him renounce the faith of Jesus Christ. This scene shows that confirmation gives us the strength to remain faithful to Jesus Christ amidst persecutions.

In the middle, St. Peter and St. John are bestowing confirmation upon the faithful of Samaria. They impose their hands upon them and pray for them that they might receive the Holy Spirit. On the right of St. Peter, approaching from a distance, is a man who is holding a purse in his hand. This is Simon the Magician, who came to ask the Apostle to sell the power to give the Holy Spirit. St. Peter reproved him severely for wanting to buy the gift of God with money.

The Holy Spirit is shown hovering above those who are confirmed and pouring out all His gifts upon them.

At the bottom is a bishop who is administering confirmation to first communicants. He is preceded by his vicar-general, who gives him, one by one, the names of those who are to be confirmed. He is followed by another priest holding a tray on which is the container of the Holy Chrism. A third priest wearing a surplice and stole wipes with balls of cotton the foreheads of those who have just been confirmed.

necessary, for his Christian education. This spiritual relationship does not constitute an impediment to Matrimony.

SCRIPTURE: *See Scripture, question 330, Acts 8:14-16; Acts 19:5-6.*

341. After we have been confirmed, why should we continue to study our religion even more earnestly than before?

After we have been confirmed, we should continue to study our religion even more earnestly than before, so that we may be able to explain and defend our faith, and thus co-operate with the grace of Confirmation.

342. Why should all Catholics be confirmed?

All Catholics should be confirmed in order to be strengthened against the dangers to salvation and to be prepared better to defend their Catholic faith.

IMPORTANT TRUTHS ABOUT CONFIRMATION

In the normal course of nature every one who is born eventually comes to maturity—the fulness of bodily strength and vigor. So too, God wills that every one who has been born to the spiritual life by Baptism shall come to spiritual maturity and to the fulness of spiritual strength; and for this purpose Our Divine Lord instituted a special sacrament, Confirmation. During His lifetime, and particularly at the Last Supper, Christ promised to send the Holy Ghost for the enlightenment and the strengthening of His followers. This promise was fulfilled for the apostles and the disciples on Pentecost, when the Holy Ghost descended on them in the form of fiery tongues. But the means which our Lord chose to confer this privilege on the other members of the Church was a sacrament. We find reference to this sacrament in the Acts of the Apostles which relate that Peter and John went to Samaria to give the Holy Ghost to the newly baptized converts of that city: "Then they laid their hands on them and they received the Holy Spirit" (*Acts, 8:17*). Similarly, it is related that when St. Paul converted some of the people of Ephesus: "They were baptized in the name of the Lord Jesus; and when Paul laid his hands on them, the Holy Spirit came upon them" (*Acts, 19:6*).

In the beginning, this sacrament may have been conferred only by the laying on of hands; but at any rate, anointing was in use in the third or fourth century. Even today there are some differences in the manner of confirming between the Latin Church and the Oriental churches. Thus, in the former only one anointing is given, on the forehead, whereas in the latter the anointing is given on several parts of the body. Moreover, in the Oriental rites infants are usually confirmed immediately after Baptism, whereas in the Latin Church it is considered preferable to wait until children have reached the use of reason.

In connection with the sacrament of Confirmation it is appropriate to describe the various holy oils used in the liturgical ceremonies of the Church. These oils are three in number—the oil of catechumens, holy chrism, and the oil of the sick. These are blessed by the bishop at the Solemn Mass on Holy Thursday and are then distributed as soon as possible to the pastors throughout the diocese, because the law of the Church prescribes that in the administration of the sacraments and the other sacred functions in which blessed oil is used the oil which has been blessed on the preceding Holy Thursday shall be employed. Thus, in the blessing of the baptismal water on Holy Saturday the priest must use the oil of catechumens and the chrism blessed two days before.

The holy oils are used in the administration of four sacraments—Baptism, Confirmation, Holy Orders and Extreme Unction. In conferring Baptism the priest anoints the breast and the back of the recipient with oil of catechumens before the pouring of the water, and his head with chrism afterward. In Confirmation, as was described in this lesson, the bishop anoints the brow of the person being confirmed with holy chrism. When a man is being ordained to the priesthood his hands are anointed with the oil of catechumens; and when a priest is being consecrated a bishop his head and hands are anointed with chrism. The oil of the sick is used for the administration of Extreme Unction.

We cannot value too highly the importance of Confirmation in the supernatural life. It is a great source of strength in the warfare we must wage against the three great enemies of our salvation, the world, the flesh and the devil. The character of Confirmation remains on the soul forever, marking one who has been confirmed as a soldier of Christ, with the right and the duty of proclaiming and defending the Christian faith before the world. Nowadays there is a great need of those who will explain and uphold the true religion of Christ, even though it demands personal sacrifice; and this task belongs not merely to the priests and bishops but also to the laity—of course, always with due subordination to their ecclesiastical rulers. And when a lay-person, according to his capacities and position, defends and explains the faith of Christ, he is living up to the task committed to him through Confirmation and is contributing his share toward Catholic Action.

It is evident that every Catholic should receive Confirmation in order to partake of the strengthening graces of this great sacrament. It sometimes happens that a person who, through no fault of his own, was not confirmed in his earlier years comes to maturity without having received Confirmation. Such a person should ask his pastor to arrange for his Confirmation. Even though he may not be guilty of mortal sin if he fails to receive this sacrament, he is surely depriving himself of a most effective means of spiritual light and strength.

RESOLUTION: If you have not yet received Confirmation resolve to prepare for this great sacrament most devoutly in the spirit of the apostles when they awaited the coming of the Holy Ghost. If you have been confirmed, resolve to make use of every opportunity in which you can prudently and effectively explain and defend your faith. Write the dates of your Baptism, your Confirmation and your First Communion in your prayerbook.

STUDY HELPS

A. WORD SELECTIONS. (*Select the word or phrase in each parenthesis which most exactly and most completely fills out the sentence*).

(1) Holy chrism is blessed on (Holy Thursday...Good Friday...Easter Sunday).

(2) Confirmation can be conferred (only by a bishop...by any priest... by a bishop or by a priest specially delegated to confer it).

(3) A person who knowingly receives Confirmation in mortal sin (does not receive the sacrament validly...receives it validly and will receive the grace of Confirmation when he returns to the state of sanctifying grace... will never receive the grace of Confirmation).

(4) The bishop gives the person confirmed a light blow on the cheek to remind him (that he deserves punishment for his sins...that he must be ready to suffer everything for the sake of Christ...that he must be obedient to the authorities of the Church).

(5) The hands of a man being ordained a priest are anointed with (oil of catechumens...holy chrism...oil of the sick).

(6) The hands of a priest being consecrated a bishop are anointed with (oil of catechumens...holy chrism...oil of the sick).

(7) The head of a person who has just been baptized is anointed with (oil of catechumens...holy chrism...oil of the sick).

(8) In the Latin Church a child should be confirmed (immediately after Baptism...after his first Communion...at about the age of seven).

(9) To be a sponsor at Confirmation a person should be at least (seven... thirteen...twenty-one) years old.

(10) In Confirmation a person should have (one sponsor of the same sex...two sponsors...one sponsor of the opposite sex.

B. PROBLEMS AND EXERCISES. (*Answer the questions orally or write them as your teacher may direct*):

(1) Bella, a prospective convert to our faith, would like to know who are our spiritual enemies referred to in this lesson? Write her three or four sentences of explanation.

(2) Nina, in the fifth grade got a letter yesterday from her brother, a missionary priest in the East Indies. Among other news items, Nina's brother wrote that he had confirmed 175 natives on his last missionary tour. Nina is studying Catechism No. 2, and it seems to her that only a bishop can give Confirmation. But her brother, Pius, is just a missionary priest, and not a bishop. Please clear up Nina's difficulty.

(3) On Holy Thursday afternoon Fr. Cletus informed Andrew, one of the altar-boys, that he was driving to the cathedral, forty miles distant, to get the holy oils. Andrew asked why Fr. Cletus could not wait until after Easter Sunday, since the roads were covered with snow. What answer do you think Fr. Cletus gave?

(4) Shirley, a non-Catholic girl, receives an invitation to attend the Confirmation of her friend Augusta. After the ceremony Shirley has many questions to ask her newly-confirmed friend. That night Shirley tries to repeat to her family everything Augusta explained. However, she cannot recall the name of the mixture used by the bishop. She remembers that some olive oil is in that mixture, and something else. She doesn't remember the symbolism of the two substances in the mixture. Supply the information Shirley has forgotten.

(5) Six months ago, Bishop James, for the first time in his life, received the last rites of the Church. He has now recovered his health. How many of the sacred oils has he received up to now? In which Sacraments were they used? Have any of these oils been used in more than one Sacrament? Explain.

(6) Little Stephen, two years old, is very sick, and the doctor says that he is sure to die within several days. His good Catholic parents would like to have Stephen confirmed before his death, so that he may have additional glory in heaven. But it is impossible to bring the sick child to the Bishop, whose residence is more than a hundred miles distant; and it would be unreasonable to expect the Bishop to make the long journey. Can you tell Stephen's parents how they can procure Confirmation for their little boy through an extraordinary privilege granted by Pope Pius XII, which began to be effective on January 1, 1947?

(7) Colin, when a boy in the sixth grade, received Confirmation unfortunately in a state of mortal sin. Now he is about to graduate. The bishop is to confirm another group of children the week before graduation.

198

Should Colin ask to be included in the new group, so as to receive Confirmation worthily this time? Explain your answer.

(8) Dominic, a Catholic boy in the sixth grade of public school receives the Sacrament of Confirmation. But after that he stops going to Sunday School and to religious instructions. Cajetan, a Catholic boy in the same grade, also receives Confirmation, but continues to attend religious instruction classes. Whose action do you approve? Why?

(9) Jolanda, a girl in the same class, also receives Confirmation. She tells Walberga she doesn't have to go to Sunday School any more because she is confirmed. Walberga disagrees with her and says that Jolanda should go to the Sunday School and religious instruction classes at least until she graduates from Junior High School. What do you think of Walberga's suggestion? What is your opinion of Jolanda's statement?

(10) Lawrence, twelve years of age, was very sick when Confirmation was administered in his parish and hence could not receive it. In the course of the next few years his parents changed their abode several times, so that it was not until Lawrence was eighteen years old that he heard the announcement of an approaching Confirmation in his parish church. Lawrence is now embarrassed at the thought of receiving Confirmation with little boys and girls, for he is a tall, robust young man. Will he commit a mortal sin if he refuses to be confirmed? What arguments can you give him to induce him to put aside his fears?

(11) Were the apostles themselves confirmed? Were they confirmed by bishops? Please explain your answers.

(12) Eudora, a little girl of five, a child of Greek Catholic parents, is admitted into the kindergarten of St. Ferdinand's parish school. Although she has never made her first confession, the youngster has already received two of the Sacraments. Explain.

(13) Hyacinth and his sister Lydia, confirmed ten years ago, are visiting some non-Catholic friends on a day of fast and abstinence. Neither of them is lawfully excused from its observance. Can the sacrament of Confirmation help them as they are put to the test? How? Both of them ate the fried chicken that was served. Account for their failure.

(14) Muriel, an office worker, is a girl of angelic purity. Many of her associates, even Catholics among them, have vile tongues, and still viler imaginations. Muriel never joins in their obscene conversations, and pays no attention to the offensive remarks that are hurled at her from time to time. Even those who pass such indelicate remarks secretly admire the girl's courage. Do you think the sacrament of Confirmation she received years ago is helping her? Is she cooperating with the Holy Ghost? Add a short explanation to each answer.

(15) Alexander has great devotion to the Holy Ghost. Frequently during the day he utters aspirations such as these: "Come, Holy Ghost!"—"God, the Holy Ghost, have mercy on me!" Among his daily Mass prayers he has the following neatly written on a piece of paper: "O Holy Spirit, sweet Guest of my soul, remain with me, and grant that I may ever remain with Thee!" Would you encourage Alexander to continue these devotional practices. For what reason?

199

The Holy Eucharist

343. What is the Holy Eucharist?

The Holy Eucharist is a sacrament and a sacrifice. In the Holy Eucharist, under the appearances of bread and wine, the Lord Christ is contained, offered, and received.

(a) The whole Christ is really, truly, and substantially present in the Holy Eucharist. We use the words "really, truly, and substantially" to describe Christ's presence in the Holy Eucharist in order to distinguish Our Lord's teaching from that of mere men who falsely teach that the Holy Eucharist is only a sign or figure of Christ, or that He is present only by His power.

(b) All Christians, with but few minor exceptions, held the true doctrine of the Real Presence from the time of Christ until the Protestant Revolution in the sixteenth century.

(c) The word "Eucharist" means "Thanksgiving."

344. When did Christ institute the Holy Eucharist?

Christ instituted the Holy Eucharist at the Last Supper, the night before He died.

(a) About a year before the Last Supper Our Lord promised to give us the Holy Eucharist. This promise is related in the sixth chapter of the Gospel according to Saint John. The fulfillment of this promise took place at the Last Supper.

SCRIPTURE:

I: The Promise

" 'I am the bread of life. Your fathers ate the manna in the desert, and have died. This is the bread that comes down from heaven, so that if anyone eat of it he will not die. I am the living bread that has come down from heaven. If anyone eat of this bread he shall live forever; and the bread that I will give is my flesh for the life of the world.'

"The Jews on that account argued with one another, saying, 'How can this man give us his flesh to eat?'

"Jesus therefore said to them, 'Amen, amen, I say to you, unless you eat the flesh of the Son of Man, and drink his blood, you shall not have life in you. He who eats my flesh and drinks my blood has life everlasting and I will raise him up on the last day. For my flesh is food indeed, and my blood is drink indeed. He who eats my flesh, and drinks my blood, abides in me and I in him. As the living Father has sent me, and as I live because of the Father, so he who eats me, he also shall live because of me. This is the bread that has come down from heaven; not as your fathers ate the manna, and died. He who eats this bread shall live forever' " (*John 6:48-59*).

II: The Institution

"And while they were at supper, Jesus took bread, and blessed and broke, and gave it to his disciples, and said, 'Take and eat; this is my body.' And taking a cup, he gave thanks and gave it to them, saying, 'All of you drink of this; for this is my blood of the new covenant, which is being shed for many unto the forgiveness of sins' " (*Matthew 26:26-28*).

"And while they were eating, Jesus took bread, and blessing it, he broke and gave it to them, and said, 'Take; this is my body.' And taking a cup and giving thanks, he gave it to them, and they all drank of it; and he said to them, 'This is my blood of the new covenant, which is being shed for many' " (*Mark 14:22-24*).

"And having taken bread, he gave thanks and broke, and gave it to them, saying, 'This is my body, which is being given for you; do this in remembrance of me.' In like manner he took also the cup after the supper, saying, 'This cup is the new covenant in my blood, which shall be shed for you' " (*Luke 22:19-20*).

"For I myself have received from the Lord (what I also delivered to you), that the Lord Jesus, on the night in which he was betrayed, took bread, and giving thanks broke, and said, 'This is my body which shall be given up for you; do this in remembrance of me.' In like manner also the cup, after he had supped, saying, 'This cup is the new covenant in my blood; do this as often as you drink it, in remembrance of me. For as often as you shall eat this bread and drink the cup, you proclaim the death of the Lord, until he comes.' Therefore whoever eats this bread or drinks the cup of the Lord unworthily, will be guilty of the body and the blood of the Lord. But let a man prove himself, and so let him eat of that bread and drink of the cup; for he who eats and drinks unworthily, without distinguishing the body, eats and drinks judgment to himself" (*I Corinthians 11:23-29*).

345. Who were present when Our Lord instituted the Holy Eucharist?

When Our Lord instituted the Holy Eucharist the apostles were present.

SCRIPTURE:

"Now when evening arrived, he reclined at table with the twelve disciples" (*Matthew 26:20*).

"Now when evening arrived, he came with the Twelve" (*Mark 14:17*).

"And when the hour had come, he reclined at table, and the twelve apostles with him" (*Luke 22:14*).

346. How did Christ institute the Holy Eucharist?

Christ instituted the Holy Eucharist in this way: He took bread, blessed and broke it, and giving it to His apostles, said: "Take and eat; this is My body;" then He took a cup of wine, blessed it, and giving it to them, said: "All of you drink of this; for this is My blood of the new covenant which is being shed for many unto the forgiveness of sins;" finally, He gave His apostles the commission: "Do this in remembrance of Me."

347. What happened when Our Lord said: "This is My body ... this is My blood"?

When Our Lord said, "This is My body," the entire substance of the bread was changed into His body; and when He said, "This is My blood," the entire substance of the wine was changed into His blood.

(a) Christ could not have used clearer, more explicit words than "This is My body." He did not say, "This is a sign of My body," or "This

201

201a

Holy Eucharist

In the center, Our Lord is instituting the Eucharist on Holy Thursday, the eve of His death, in the Cenacle in Jerusalem. At the top left, the treacherous apostle hangs himself from a tree after making a sacrilegious communion.

At the bottom, a priest distributes Holy Communion to the faithful during the Mass.

The principal effect of Communion, which is to nourish our souls spiritually, is shown at the top right in the person of the prophet Elias. An angel gives him a hearth cake and a vessel of water, saying to him, "Arise and eat, for thou hast yet a great way to go." (3 Kings 19:7) St. Elias got up, ate, and drank. Strengthened by this nourishment, he walked forty days and forty nights to Horeb, the mountain of God. The bread of St. Elias is a figure of the Eucharist which strengthens our souls, helps us to live a holy life, and brings us to the happiness of heaven.

represents My body," but, "This *is* My body." Catholics take Christ at His word because He is the omnipotent God. On His word they know that the Holy Eucharist *is* the body and blood of Christ.

SCRIPTURE:
See Scripture, question 344, Matthew 26:26-28; Mark 14:22-24; Luke 22:19-20; I Corinthians 11:23-29.

348. Did anything of the bread and wine remain after their substance had been changed into Our Lord's body and blood?

After the substance of the bread and wine had been changed into Our Lord's body and blood, there remained only the appearances of bread and wine.

(a) Because the appearances of bread and wine remain in the Holy Eucharist, we cannot see Christ with our bodily eyes in this sacrament. We do see Him, however, with the eyes of faith. Our bodily eyes, moreover, do not deceive us when they see the *appearances* of bread and wine, for these *appearances* really remain after the Consecration of the Mass.

349. What do we mean by the appearances of bread and wine?

By the appearances of bread and wine we mean their color, taste, weight, shape, and whatever else appears to the senses.

350. What is the change of the entire substance of the bread and wine into the body and blood of Christ called?

The change of the entire substance of the bread and wine into the body and blood of Christ is called Transubstantiation.

351. Is Jesus Christ whole and entire both under the appearances of bread and under the appearances of wine?

Jesus Christ is whole and entire both under the appearances of bread and under the appearances of wine.

(a) We know that Christ is whole and entire under both appearances because, "Christ having risen from the dead, dies now no more" (*Romans 6:9*). Because Christ cannot die, His blood must remain united always to His body, and His soul to both. The divinity of Christ, moreover, always remains united to His body and blood and soul because He is God made man.

(b) The whole Christ is present under each part of the sacred appearances and remains present as long as the sacred appearances remain.

SCRIPTURE:
See Scripture, question 344, Matthew 26:26-28; Mark 14:22-24. Luke 22:19-20; I Corinthians 11:23-29.

352. How was Our Lord able to change bread and wine into His body and blood?

Our Lord was able to change bread and wine into His body and blood by His almighty power.

(a) God, who created all things from nothing, who fed the five thousand with five loaves, who changed water into wine instantaneously, who raised

202

the dead to life, can change bread and wine into the body and blood of Christ. Although the Holy Eucharist is a great mystery, and consequently beyond human understanding, the principles of sound reason can show that this great gift is not impossible by the power of God.

SCRIPTURE:

"And looking upon them, Jesus said to them, 'With men this is impossible, but with God all things are possible' " (*Matthew 19:26*).

"All power in heaven and on earth has been given to me" (*Matthew 28:18*).

353. Does this change of bread and wine into the body and blood of Christ continue to be made in the Church?

This change of bread and wine into the body and blood of Christ continues to be made in the Church by Jesus Christ, through the ministry of His priests.

(a) Only ordained priests have the power of changing bread and wine into the body and blood of Christ. When they consecrate, they act in the person of Christ, through the power received in the sacrament of Holy Orders.

SCRIPTURE: *See Scripture, question 344, Luke 22:19-20; I Corinthians 11:23-29.*

354. When did Christ give His priests the power to change bread and wine into His body and blood?

Christ gave His priests the power to change bread and wine into His body and blood when He made the apostles priests at the Last Supper by saying to them: "Do this in remembrance of Me."

355. How do priests exercise their power to change bread and wine into the body and blood of Christ?

Priests exercise their power to change bread and wine into the body and blood of Christ by repeating at the Consecration of the Mass the words of Christ: "This is My body . . . this is My blood."

356. Why does Christ give us His own body and blood in the Holy Eucharist?

Christ gives us His own body and blood in the Holy Eucharist:

first, to be offered as a sacrifice commemorating and renewing for all time the sacrifice of the cross;

second, to be received by the faithful in Holy Communion;

third, to remain ever on our altars as the proof of His love for us, and to be worshiped by us.

IMPORTANT TRUTHS ABOUT THE HOLY EUCHARIST

When we love someone very much, we desire to be constantly in his company. Our Divine Lord had an immeasurable love for every member of the human race, and gave proof of this by shedding His blood for the salvation of all mankind. However, after His task on earth was completed, He was destined to ascend into heaven to take His place at the right hand of His Father; and so it would seem that He could no longer associate intimately with men. But His love and power devised a means whereby He could still remain on earth, not merely in one place but in every church, and thus be the intimate companion of every one of His faithful followers. This means is the Blessed Sacrament, the Holy Eucharist, wherein Our Lord remains truly present under the appearances of bread and wine.

The Catholic doctrine of the Holy Eucharist contains many mysteries. It is beyond our comprehension how the same living Christ who is in heaven should also be on earth, in every place where the Holy Eucharist is consecrated. We cannot understand how the body of our Saviour with its full stature can be present beneath the small host. We cannot attempt to explain how our Divine Redeemer can be present, whole and entire, in the smallest portions of the consecrated species of bread and wine, although we have some resemblance to this miracle in the presence of our entire soul in every portion of our body. But we have the statement of Our Lord Himself for the truth of these mysteries, and hence it is our duty to believe them without hesitation. When Our Saviour first announced the doctrine of the Holy Eucharist to His followers, some of them would not believe. They said: "This is a hard saying, who can listen to it?" (*John, 6, 62*), and some of them even left Him forever. Today there are many persons in the world who say that the doctrine of the Real Presence is too hard to believe, and claim that the Eucharist is only bread and wine representing Christ. But Catholics accept the words of Our Lord Himself who said: "This is my body . . . this is my blood," and adore Him as truly present in the Holy Eucharist.

The Holy Eucharist is the very center of Catholic worship, the heart of Catholic life. Because the Church believes that the Son of God is truly present in the Blessed Sacrament, she erects beautiful cathedrals and adorns them with exquisite sculpture and priceless paintings. The most magnificent liturgical ceremonies of the Catholic Church are directed toward honoring the King of kings, who for the love of mankind dwells beneath the appearances of bread and wine. Music and lights and incense and flowers the Church uses lavishly in her desire to show fitting honor to the Son of God, dwelling in our midst. Twice a year the Church celebrates in a special manner the great privilege of the Real Presence of Jesus Christ in the Holy Eucharist. On Holy Thursday the Church recalls to our minds the institution of the Blessed Sacrament by Our Divine Lord on the night before His death. But since our predominant sentiment in Holy Week is sorrow, the Church has assigned another day, the Thursday after Trinity Sunday, to be the Feast of Corpus Christi, when with sentiments of unrestrained joy we thank Our Saviour for the wonderful gift of the Holy Eucharist. Moreover, it is customary to have annually in every parish church the Forty Hours' Devotion, when Our Lord is enthroned in the monstrance for a period of almost three days. The purpose of Eucharistic Congresses, bringing together Catholics from all parts of the earth, is to give glory and praise to Christ in the Holy Eucharist.

Every loyal Catholic should be in harmony with the Church in expressing his devotion toward the Holy Eucharist in a fitting manner. The first sentiment of our hearts toward Our Lord in the Blessed Sacrament should be profound adoration, for even in His human nature Jesus Christ is a divine person, worthy of the highest form of worship. Our next sentiment should be ardent love. It was out of love for us that He established this wondrous sacrament; in return He asks our love. We can testify our love for the Holy Eucharist in many ways— Mass, Holy Communion, visits to Our Lord in the tabernacle. Whenever we enter a church in which the Blessed Sacrament is kept our first thought should be: "Our loving Lord is present here just as truly as He was present in the little house of Nazareth when He dwelt on earth nineteen centuries ago."

RESOLUTION: Resolve to learn and to use some short prayers in honor of the Holy Eucharist, such as: "O Sacrament most holy, O Sacrament divine, all praise and all thanksgiving be every moment thine" and "May the Heart of Jesus, in the Most Blessed Sacrament be praised, adored and loved with grateful affection at every moment in all the tabernacles of the world even to the end of time. Amen."

STUDY HELPS

A. COLUMN SELECTION. (*Join correctly the parts of the sentences in Columns I and II, by placing the right key letter in the proper parenthesis*).

I

(1) We do not see Our Lord in the Blessed Sacrament (. .)

(2) Our Lord promised the Blessed Sacrament (. .)

(3) Our Lord remains present in the Blessed Sacrament (. .)

(4) Our Blessed Redeemer instituted the Holy Eucharist (. .)

(5) We commemorate the institution of the Blessed Sacrament (. .).

(6) Some persons falsely teach that (. .).

(7) Christ gave His priests the power to change bread and wine into His body and blood when He said (. .).

(8) The priest uses his power to change bread into the body of Christ when he says (. .).

(9) We joyfully thank Our Saviour for the gift of the Blessed Sacrament (. .).

(10) We give Our Lord in the Blessed Sacrament (. .).

II

(A) on Holy Thursday.

(B) on the Feast of Corpus Christi.

(C) with our bodily eyes.

(D) the highest form of worship.

(E) as long as the appearance of bread and wine remain.

(F) This is My body.

(G) the Eucharist is only a sign or figure of Christ.

(H) Do this in remembrance of me.

(I) the night before He died.

(J) about a year before His death

B. PROBLEMS AND EXERCISES. (*Answer the questions orally or write them as your teacher may direct*):

(1) Gertrude, on her way to the children's Mass, at which she intends to receive Holy Communion, passes a Protestant Church. The bulletin board in front of the church advertises the Lord's Supper service at 11:00 A.M. every Sunday morning. Is Gertrude on her way to "The Lord's Supper" in her church?

(2) Jessie, a Protestant neighbor of Gertrude, goes to that "Lord's Supper" service at 11:00 A.M. the same morning. Have Gertrude and Jessie both received the same great Gift? Explain the difference, if any.

(3) Hubert notices that the Church celebrates two special feasts of the Blessed Sacrament during the year, and neither of them falls on a Sunday. What are those feasts, and what do they commemorate? On what day of the week do they occur? Why?

205

(4) Hilary is passing through a strange town on Sunday morning. He enters what appears to be a Catholic Church. He looks for the sign that customarily indicates the Real Presence. What is that sign? What is the Real Presence?

(5) Felix, a new altar-boy, is instructed by the pastor to hold the Communion paten (plate) level—in a horizontal position—and to be careful not to tilt it, or touch it to the chins or clothing of the communicants. Why does the pastor instruct Felix in this way? Felix notices a small, tiny piece of a Sacred Host on the plate he is carrying. The priest afterwards carefully brushes It into the chalice. Why?

(6) Gladys would like to know when the apostles received their First Holy Communion.

(7) At the Consecration in the Mass, the priest leans on the altar and speaks certain words over the bread in his hands and, again over the wine in the chalice he is holding; next, he bends his right knee to the ground, then elevates, first the Host, and next the Chalice, and finally repeats the genuflection. Which of the above enumerated actions are the most important? Why?

(8) Lucille, a cultured little pagan girl, whose parents are not church-goers, learned from Joyce, her Catholic playmate, that Our Lord is present within our tabernacles. She seems pleased with her newly-acquired knowledge, but is a bit mystified to know how Our Lord can be in thousands of tabernacles throughout the United States, and all over the world at one and the same time. Joyce tells Lucille that we cannot understand how that can be; we take Our Lord's word for it that it is so; but she gives an illustration from the modern wonders of world-wide hookups over the radio and television that helps Lucille in her difficulty. How would you express the same illustration?

(9) Bernard has the habit of burying his head in his left arm at the elevations in the Mass, while he thumps his breast resoundingly with his right fist as the altar-boy rings the bells. Make a comment of not less than 15 words and not more than 30 on this particular habit of Bernard.

(10) Does Our Lord ask us to understand HOW He can be present in the Blessed Sacrament, or to believe THAT He is present therein? Explain your answer in three or four sentences.

(11) To pay honor to the Blessed Eucharist, periodically the faithful assemble in devotional gatherings that are sometimes regional in character, at others, national, and still others, international. What are these meetings called? Where was the last international one held? When?

(12) What annual devotion, extending usually over three days, is conducted in every parish of our country as a tribute of love and reparation to the Blessed Eucharist?

(13) What is the center of Catholic worship, the heart of Catholic life?

(14) Name three ways of showing appreciation for the immense treasure we have in the Blessed Sacrament.

(15) Write out from memory three ejaculations honoring Our Lord in the Blessed Sacrament. Say each of them ten times—slowly and thoughtfully—in your next thanksgiving after Communion.

206

The Sacrifice of the Mass

357. What is the Mass?

The Mass is the Sacrifice of the New Law in which Christ, through the ministry of the priest, offers Himself to God in an unbloody manner under the appearances of bread and wine.

(a) The name "Mass" comes from the Latin word *Missa* meaning dismissal. In the early days of the Church the catechumens were asked to leave after the gospel and sermon were finished. The faithful, however, remained until they were dismissed after the sacrifice was completed. Then, as now, this was done by saying or singing *Ite Missa Est*. In the course of time the word *Missa*, or dismissal, was used to designate the entire sacrifice.

SCRIPTURE:

"I have no pleasure in you, saith the Lord of hosts: and I will not receive a gift of your hand. For from the rising of the sun even to the going down, my name is great among the Gentiles: and in every place there is sacrifice and there is offered to my name a clean oblation" (*Malachias 1:10-11*).

"Therefore, beloved, flee from the worship of idols. I am speaking as to men of sense; judge for yourselves what I say. The cup of blessing that we bless, is it not the sharing of the blood of Christ? And the bread that we break, is it not the partaking of the body of the Lord? Because the bread is one, we though many, are one body, all of us who partake of the one bread. Behold Israel according to the flesh, are not they who eat of the sacrifices partakers of the altar? What then do I say? That what is sacrificed to idols is anything, or that an idol is anything? No; but I say that what the Gentiles sacrifice, 'they sacrifice to devils and not to God'; and I would not have you become associates of devils. You cannot drink the cup of the Lord and the cup of devils; you cannot be partakers of the table of the Lord and of the table of devils. Or are we provoking the Lord to jealousy? Are we stronger than he?" (*I Corinthians 10:14-22*).

"We have an altar, from which they have no right to eat who serve the tabernacle" (*Hebrews 13:10*).

See Scripture, question 344, Matthew 26:26-28; Mark 14:22-24; Luke 22:19-20; I Corinthians 11:23-29.

358. What is a sacrifice?

A sacrifice is the offering of a victim by a priest to God alone, and the destruction of it in some way to acknowledge that He is the Creator of all things.

(a) By his very nature man wants to adore and thank his Creator. Men mistaken at times about the nature of the true God have offered false worship; but they have always recognized the obligation of adoring the Supreme Being. As far back as the history of man is recorded, there is evidence that men acknowledged their dependence on the Supreme Being by offering sacrifices to Him.

(b) Before the coming of Christ, sacrifices were offered to God in many different ways. The patriarchs and Jewish priests at the command of God offered fruits, wine, or animals as victims. Cain, for example, offered fruits; Abel offered some sheep of his flock; Melchisedech offered bread and wine. The destruction of these offerings removed them from man's use and thereby signified that God is the Supreme Lord and Master of the entire created universe and that man is wholly dependent upon Him for everything. Sacrifice, therefore, is the most perfect way for man to worship God.

(c) All these different sacrifices of the Old Law were only figures of the sacrifice which Christ was to make of Himself. His offering of Himself on the cross was the greatest sacrifice ever offered to God. All the sacrifices of the Old Law derived their efficacy, or value, from the sacrifice which Christ was to offer on the cross.

SCRIPTURE: *See Scripture, question 357, Malachias 1:10-11.*

359. Who is the principal priest in every Mass?

The principal priest in every Mass is Jesus Christ, who offers to His heavenly Father, through the ministry of His ordained priest, His body and blood which were sacrificed on the cross.

(a) The Mass is the same sacrifice as the sacrifice of the cross. It is now, in the New Law, the sacrifice that is acceptable to God.

SCRIPTURE: *See Scripture, question 344, Matthew 26:26-28; Luke 22:19-20.*

360. Why is the Mass the same sacrifice as the sacrifice of the cross?

The Mass is the same sacrifice as the sacrifice of the cross because in the Mass the victim is the same, and the principal priest is the same, Jesus Christ.

(a) Christ, though invisible, is the principal minister, offering Himself in the Mass. The priest is the visible and secondary minister, offering Christ in the Mass.

(b) The most important part of the Mass is the Consecration. In the Consecration bread and wine are changed into the body and blood of Christ, who then is really present on the altar. Through the priest He offers Himself to God in commemoration of His death on the cross.

(c) The other most important parts of the Mass are the Offertory and the Communion. In the Offertory the priest offers to God the bread and wine that will be changed into the body and blood of Christ. In the Communion the priest and the people receive the body and blood of Our Lord under the appearances of bread and wine.

SCRIPTURE:
"And Jesus cried out with a loud voice and said, 'Father, into thy hands I commend my spirit.' And having said this, he expired" (*Luke 23:46*).
See Scripture, question 344, Luke 22:19-20.

361. What are the purposes for which the Mass is offered?

The purposes for which the Mass is offered are:
first, to adore God as our Creator and Lord;
second, to thank God for His many favors;
third, to ask God to bestow His blessings on all men;
fourth, to satisfy the justice of God for the sins committed against Him.

(a) In every Mass adoration, praise, and thanksgiving are given to God, and reparation is made to Him.

(b) Besides the purpose for which the Mass is offered and the effects that it produces, there are also special fruits of the Mass. The fruits of the Mass are the blessings that God bestows through the Mass upon the celebrant, upon those who serve or assist at it, upon the person or persons for whom it is offered, and also upon all mankind, especially the members of the Church and the souls in purgatory.

(c) The measure of these blessings depends especially on the dispositions of those to whom they are given.

SCRIPTURE: *See Scripture, question 360, Luke 23:46.*

362. Is there any difference between the sacrifice of the cross and the Sacrifice of the Mass?

The manner in which the sacrifice is offered is different. On the cross Christ physically shed His blood and was physically slain, while in the Mass there is no physical shedding of blood nor physical death, because Christ can die no more; on the cross Christ gained merit and satisfied for us, while in the Mass He applies to us the merits and satisfaction of His death on the cross.

(a) On the cross Christ was offered in a bloody manner; in the Mass He is offered in an unbloody manner. On the cross Christ alone offered Himself directly; in the Mass He offers Himself through the priest, who is the secondary but true minister, dependent upon Christ.

(b) On the cross Christ suffered and died; in the Mass He can no longer suffer or die. On the cross He paid the price of our redemption; in the Mass He applies to us the merits of His Sacrifice on the cross.

(c) There are various kinds of Masses:
first, a Solemn Mass, which is celebrated by a priest who is immediately assisted by a deacon and a sub-deacon;
second, a High Mass, in which the celebrating priest sings certain parts of the Mass;
third, a Low Mass, in which the priest reads all the parts of the Mass;
fourth, a Pontifical Mass, which is celebrated by a bishop and by certain other prelates.

Any of these kinds of Masses can be a Requiem Mass, which is one offered for the dead. In a Requiem Mass the celebrating priest wears black vestments and reads or chants special prayers for the dead.

(d) Some prayers make up the "Ordinary" of the Mass and are pract.

cally always the same; others make up the "Proper" of the Mass and differ according to the seasons and the feasts of the ecclesiastical calendar.

(e) Ordinarily Mass must be offered on an altar stone consecrated by a bishop or by his delegate.

(f) The priest wears the following vestments during Mass:

first, the amice, a white linen cloth placed over the shoulders and about the neck;

second, the alb, a long white linen garment covering the body;

third, the cincture, a cord tied about the waist;

fourth, the maniple, a short band of cloth hanging from the left arm;

fifth, the stole, a long narrow band of cloth worn over the shoulders and crossed in front of the body; and

sixth, the chasuble, an outer garment covering the greater part of the body.

These vestments have an ancient origin, and most of them resemble the garments worn by the apostles.

(g) The colors of the outer vestments worn during Mass are: white, which signifies purity of soul and holiness; red, which signifies the shedding of blood and burning love; green, which signifies hope; violet, which signifies penance; black, which signifies mourning; rose, which signifies joy in the midst of penance; and gold, which is used on solemn occasions in place of white, red, or green vestments.

White vestments are worn on feasts of Our Lord, the Blessed Virgin, saints who were not martyrs, and during the Easter season; red is used on the feasts of the Holy Ghost, the passion of Our Lord, and martyrs; green is used on the Sundays outside of Advent, Lent, and the Christmas and Easter season; violet is worn in Lent, Advent, and on penitential days; black is worn in Masses for the dead; rose may be used instead of violet on the third Sunday of Advent and on the fourth Sunday of Lent.

(h) Some of the important articles used during Mass are: the chalice, or gold-lined cup, in which the wine is consecrated; the paten, or gold-covered plate, on which the host is placed; the purificator, or cloth, for wiping the chalice; the pall, or linen-covered card, used to cover the chalice; the corporal, or square linen cloth, on which the host is placed; the missal, or book, from which the priest reads the prayers of the Mass; the beeswax candles; the crucifix over the altar; and the three linen cloths that cover the altar.

SCRIPTURE:

"For we know that Christ, having risen from the dead, dies now no more, death shall no longer have dominion over him. For the death that he died, he died to sin once for all, but the life that he lives, he lives unto God" (*Romans 6:9-10*).

"For Jesus has not entered into a Holies made by hands, a mere copy of the true, but into heaven itself, to appear now before the face of God on our behalf; nor yet has he entered to offer himself often, as the high priest enters into the Holies year after year with blood not his own; for in that case he must

210

have suffered often since the beginning of the world" (*Hebrews 9:24-26*). "Because Christ also died once for sins, the Just for the unjust, that he might bring us to God. Put to death indeed in the flesh, he was brought to life in the spirit" (*I Peter 3:18*).

363. How should we assist at Mass?

We should assist at Mass with reverence, attention, and devotion.

(a) There are different ways of assisting at Mass devoutly: using the missal to follow the priest, saying the Mass prayers as found in a prayer book, reciting the Rosary, or singing hymns.

364. What is the best method of assisting at Mass?

The best method of assisting at Mass is to unite with the priest in offering the Holy Sacrifice, and to receive Holy Communion.

(a) It is evident from the words of the priest himself that we do unite with him in offering up the Holy Sacrifice. After the Offertory he turns to the people and says: "Pray, brethren, that *my* sacrifice and *yours* may be acceptable to God the Father Almighty." In the second commemoration of the Canon of the Mass he says: "Remember, O Lord, Thy servants . . ., for whom we offer, or *who offer up to Thee*, this sacrifice of praise . . . ."

365. Who said the first Mass?

Our divine Saviour said the first Mass, at the Last Supper, the night before He died.

SCRIPTURE: *See Scripture, question 344.*

IMPORTANT TRUTHS ABOUT THE SACRIFICE OF THE MASS

Man naturally seeks some way of showing externally his adoration and gratitude toward His Creator. From the beginning of time the method by which men most clearly manifested their reverence toward God has been by the ceremony of sacrifice. By this ceremony man takes a creature—for example, an animal, or a cup of wine—and makes a gift of it to God. This is an expressive way of saying that God is the Lord of all created things. Also implied in this offering is man's acknowledgement that God gives him everything he has, and so he thanks the Almighty for His favors in the past and begs Him to continue His favors in the future. Then the offering is destroyed—for example, the animal is killed, or the wine is poured out. This too has a symbolic meaning. It signifies that man confesses that he has sinned, and deserves to be punished by God, and by this ceremony he implores pardon. Thus, the purposes of every sacrifice are four—adoration, gratitude, petition, and atonement for sin and for its punishments. Sacrifice is a public act—that is, it is offered by a group or society, through their representative, an official known as a priest.

There are many references to sacrifices in the Old Testament. Cain and Abel, the sons of our first parents offered sacrifices, the former of the fruits of the earth, the latter some of the sheep of his flock. Noe offered a sacrifice on leaving the Ark. Melchisedech offered a sacrifice of bread and wine on meeting Abraham. God Himself prescribed many forms of sacrifice for the Jewish people. However, all these sacrifices were but preparations for the great sacrifice that was to be offered on Calvary, the sacrifice of Jesus Christ, the sacrifice of which He was both priest and victim. As St. Paul says: "At the end of the ages. He has appeared for the destruction of sin by the sacrifice of Himself" (*Hebr., 9, 26*)

The sacrifice of Himself which Our Lord offered was of infinite worth, because of the infinite dignity of the priest and victim, and so it gave infinite praise and adoration to God, and was capable of satisfying for the sins of all mankind.

However, Our Lord wished that the sacrifice of Calvary should not be limited to one place or one time. He willed that all men should have an opportunity of assisting at the sacrifice of His body and blood. And so, on the night before His death He established the Sacrifice of the Mass. This was to be a renewal of Calvary, in the sense that the same body and blood that were offered on the cross were to be offered again. There was to be no new death of Our Saviour; but His death was to be represented vividly by the twofold consecration of the bread into His body and the wine into His blood, typifying the separation of body and blood that actually took place on Calvary. This sacrifice was to apply to the souls of men the merits and satisfaction which Our Saviour earned by His death. It was this sacrifice, the Mass, which God through the prophet Malachias announced, more than four centuries before Christ: "From the rising of the sun even to the going down, my name is great among the Gentiles: and in every place there is sacrifice, and there is offered to my name a clean oblation" (*Mal., 1, 11*).

The Sacrifice of the Mass is therefore the greatest possible act of divine worship. It is the only form of sacrifice now acceptable to God. The power to offer Mass is the greatest power of the Catholic priest. However, the members of the laity should remember that they too have a share in the offering of this divine sacrifice. It is in their name that the priest officiates; they offer the body and blood of Our Saviour to His eternal Father through the hands of the priest. And the more fervently they participate in the offering of the Mass, the more benefits they will receive from this precious sacrifice by which the death of our Redeemer on Calvary is daily represented and its benefits applied on thousands of altars throughout the Catholic Church.

The more actively and intimately a person participates in the offering of the Mass, the greater benefits will he derive. Thus, a boy who serves Mass or a person who sings in the choir will partake more abundantly of the fruits of the Holy Sacrifice, other things being equal, than one who merely assists as a member of the congregation.

RESOLUTION: Resolve to become familiar with the ceremonies of the Mass, the vestments, the sacred vessels, and especially the prayers of the Mass, so that you can follow intelligently the Holy Sacrifice with the Missal.

STUDY HELPS

A. TRUE OR FALSE. (*Check each of the following statements as either true or false. The correct answers will be found in the preceding portions of the lesson*).

	TRUE	FALSE
(1) The most important part of the sacrifice of the Mass is the Communion.	.....	.....
(2) The measure of the fruits of the Mass depends especially on the dispositions of those to whom they are given.	.....	.....
(3) Christ is the principal priest in every Mass.	.....	.....
(4) Gold vestments can take the place of violet vestments.	.....	.....
(5) In every Mass Our Lord gains new merit and satisfaction for us.	.....	.....
(6) The Mass is offered for the same purposes as the sacrifice of the Cross.	.....	.....

212

	TRUE	FALSE
(7) The altar should be covered with four linen cloths.	. . . . .	. . . . .
(8) The pall is the linen cloth for wiping the chalice.	. . . . .	. . . . .
(9) The first Mass was said on Calvary.	. . . . .	. . . . .
(10) The people unite with the priest in offering the sacrifice of the Mass.	. . . . .	. . . .

B. PROBLEMS AND EXERCISES. (*Answer the questions orally or write them as your teacher may direct*):

(1) What is the earliest sacrifice acceptable to God, of which we have a record?

(2) What gave value to the sacrifices of the Old Law?

(3) Are modern religious sacrifices, other than the Mass, acceptable to God? Explain your answer.

(4) Gabriel, who hopes some day to become an outstanding journalist, finds it hard to write from six to nine sentences that will explain what the priest does at the three principal parts of the Mass. You try it.

(5) Sum up in four words the purposes for which the Mass is offered.

(6) Richard, an altar-boy, and his twin brother Anthony, go to the children's Mass. Richard serves the Mass; Anthony kneels in the first pew. Supposing their fervor is the same, and all other considerations being equal, how do they share in the fruits of the Mass? Does one get more than the other, or do they get the same amount? Explain the answer.

(7) Father Bronislaus, vesting for Mass, is interrupted by a parishioner just before he puts on the final vestment for Mass. The interview with the parishioner being ended in two or three minutes, Father Bronislaus takes the chalice, and starts for the sanctuary. "Father, you forgot to put on that thing" said the vigilant altar-boy Quintus as he pointed to the vestment that had been overlooked. What is the proper name of the "thing" referred to by Quintus? Name the other garments the priest wears at the celebration of Holy Mass. There are six garments in all.

(8) On the following days, what color of vestments does the priest wear during Mass: December 8th and 25th, Ash Wednesday, Easter, Pentecost, November 1st, November 2nd, March 17th, and August 15th?

(9) Name the liturgical articles the priest carries in his hands as he approaches the altar to celebrate Mass.

(10) What is the name of the large book the priest uses in the celebration of Mass? In what language is it written?

(11) When James assists at Mass he follows the priest, reading the prayers from an English Missal. His brother John recites the rosary. Which method do you think is preferable, and why?

(12) One Sunday morning Fr. John announces that the following Sunday a bishop will celebrate a pontifical Mass. Explain what is meant.

(13) Explain in your own words, with examples, the difference between the Ordinary and the Proper of the Mass.

(14) Was the first Mass celebrated on a Sunday morning? If not, when was it celebrated? In what city? In what country? On what continent? By whom? Was it celebrated in a church, a temple, a synagogue, or a private dwelling?

213

Holy Communion

366. What is Holy Communion?

Holy Communion is the receiving of Jesus Christ in the sacrament of the Holy Eucharist.

(a) Just as it is necessary to nourish our bodies with material food, so also it is necessary to nourish our souls with spiritual food. Our Divine Saviour so loved us that He gave us Himself in the sacrament of the Holy Eucharist; He gave us His own body and blood as food for our souls.

(b) It is not necessary that we receive Our Lord's body and blood under the appearances of both bread and wine. Christ is entirely present under the appearances of bread, and also entirely present under the appearances of wine. Therefore, we receive Him whole and entire under the appearances of bread alone or of wine alone.

(c) In some Eastern Churches the faithful receive Holy Communion under the appearances of both bread and wine. In the Western Church the faithful receive Communion only under the appearances of bread.

SCRIPTURE:
"Jesus therefore said to them, 'Amen, amen, I say to you, unless you eat the flesh of the Son of Man, and drink his blood, you shall not have life in you. He who eats my flesh and drinks my blood has life everlasting and I will raise him up on the last day. For my flesh is food indeed, and my blood is drink indeed. He who eats my flesh, and drinks my blood, abides in me and I in him. As the living Father has sent me, and as I live because of the Father, so he who eats me, he also shall live because of me. This is the bread that has come down from heaven; not as your fathers ate the manna, and died. He who eats this bread shall live forever' " (*John 6:54-59*).
"And they continued steadfastly in the teaching of the apostles and in the communion of the breaking of the bread and in the prayers" (*Acts 2:42*).
See Scripture, question 344, Luke 22:19-20.

367. What is necessary to receive Holy Communion worthily?

To receive Holy Communion worthily it is necessary to be free from mortal sin, to have a right intention and to obey the Church's laws on the fast required before Holy Communion out of reverence for the body and blood of Our Divine Lord. However, these are some cases in which Holy Communion may be received without fasting.

(a) Venial sin does not make us unworthy of receiving Holy Communion; but it does prevent us from receiving the more abundant graces and blessings which we would otherwise receive from Holy Communion.

SCRIPTURE:
"For I myself have received from the Lord (what I also delivered to you), that the Lord Jesus, on the night in which he was betrayed, took bread, and giving thanks broke, and said, 'This is my body which shall be given up for you; do this in remembrance of me.' In like manner also the cup, after he had supped, saying, 'This cup is the new covenant in my blood; do this as often as you drink it, in remembrance of me. For as often as you shall eat this bread and drink the cup, you proclaim the death of the Lord, until he comes.'

Therefore whoever eats this bread or drinks the cup of the Lord unworthily, will be guilty of the body and the blood of the Lord. But let a man prove himself, and so let him eat of that bread and drink of the cup; for he who eats and drinks unworthily, without distinguishing the body, eats and drinks judgment to himself. This is why many among you are infirm and weak, and many sleep. But if we judged ourselves, we should not thus be judged. But when we are judged, we are being chastised by the Lord that we may not be condemned with this world. Wherefore, my brethren, when you come together to eat, wait for one another. If anyone is hungry, let him eat at home, lest you come together unto judgment. The rest I shall set in order when I come" (*I Corinthians 11:23-34*).

368. Does he who knowingly receives Holy Communion in mortal sin receive the body and blood of Christ and His graces?

He who knowingly receives Holy Communion in mortal sin receives the body and blood of Christ, but he does not receive His graces and commits a grave sin of sacrilege.

(a) To receive Holy Communion unworthily is a serious abuse of the sacred body and blood of the Lord, and therefore a sacrilege.[20]

See Scripture, question 367, I Corinthians 11:23-34.

369. What should we do to receive more abundantly the graces of Holy Communion?

To receive more abundantly the graces of Holy Communion we should strive to be most fervent and to free ourselves from deliberate venial sin.

370. Does the Church now command us to fast from midnight before Holy Communion?

The Church does not now command us to fast from midnight before Holy Communion, as it did formerly. The laws enacted by Pope Pius XII now regulate this matter by the number of hours we must fast.

(a) For many centuries the Church commanded a strict fast from midnight before one could receive Holy Communion. However, in 1953 Pope Pius XII introduced a much more lenient form of fasting before Holy Communion, and in 1957 the same Pope granted greater concessions, in order to give Catholics an opportunity to receive Holy Communion more frequently.

(b) Pope Pius XII also allowed the celebration of afternoon and evening Masses every day, when the spiritual good of a considerable number of the faithful requires it. It is the right of the bishop of each diocese to decide when such Masses may be offered in his diocese.

371. When may Holy Communion be received without fasting?

Holy Communion may be received without fasting when one is in danger of death, or when it is necessary to save the Blessed Sacrament from insult or injury.

(a) Ordinarily the danger of death comes from sickness or injury. But it is not necessary that a person be in danger of death from sickness in order to receive Holy Communion without fasting. The danger of death

20. For the definition of sacrilege see question 213.

215

may come from some other cause. A soldier, for example, who is about to go into battle or a person about to be executed may receive Holy Communion without fasting.

372. What are the laws enacted by Pope Pius XII regarding the fast required before Holy Communion?

The laws enacted by Pope Pius XII regarding the fast required before Holy Communion are the following:

1. Water may be taken at any time before Holy Communion without breaking the fast.
2. Sick persons, though not confined to bed, may receive Holy Communion after taking medicine or non-alcoholic drinks. A priest's permission is not necessary.
3. All Catholics may receive Holy Communion after fasting three hours from food and alcoholic drinks and one hour from non-alcoholic drinks. This applies to Holy Communion at midnight Mass as well as at Masses celebrated in the morning, afternoon or evening. A priest's permission is not necessary.
4. Catholics are urged to observe the eucharistic fast from midnight as formerly, and also to compensate for the use of the new privileges by works of charity and penance, but these practices are not obligatory. One who has already received Holy Communion may not receive the Blessed Sacrament again on the same day, except in danger of death.

373. How should we prepare ourselves for Holy Communion?

We should prepare ourselves for Holy Communion by thinking of Our Divine Redeemer whom we are about to receive, and by making fervent acts of faith, hope, love, and contrition.

(a) We should be neat, clean, and modest in our appearance, and respectful and reverent in our manner.

(b) Each time we receive Holy Communion we should try to be as devout and fervent as if it were the only Communion of our lives.

(c) When actually receiving Communion we should raise the head and extend the tongue. We should swallow the sacred host as soon as possible, not allowing it to dissolve in the mouth.

SCRIPTURE:
"Lord, I am not worthy that thou shouldst come under my roof; but only say the word, and my servant will be healed" (*Matthew 8:8*).
"Behold, the lamb of God, who takes away the sin of the world" (*John 1:29*).
See Scripture, question 366, John 6:54-59.

374. What should we do after Holy Communion?

After Holy Communion we should spend some time adoring Our Lord, thanking Him, renewing our promises of love and of obedience to Him, and asking Him for blessings for ourselves and others.

SCRIPTURE:
"Ask, and it shall be given you; seek, and you shall find; knock, and it shall be opened to you. For everyone who asks, receives; and he who seeks, finds; and to him who knocks, it shall be opened. Or what man is there among you, who, if his son asks him for a loaf, will hand him a stone; or if he asks for a fish, will hand him a serpent? Therefore, if you, evil as you are, know how to give good gifts to your children, how much more will your Father in heaven give good things to those who ask him!" (*Matthew 7:7-11*).

375. What are the chief effects of a worthy Holy Communion?
The chief effects of a worthy Holy Communion are:
first, a closer union with Our Lord and a more fervent love of God and of our neighbor;
second, an increase of sanctifying grace;
third, preservation from mortal sin the and remission of venial sin;
fourth, the lessening of our inclinations to sin and the help to practice good works.
SCRIPTURE: *See Scripture, question 366, John 6:54-59.*

376. When are we obliged to receive Holy Communion?
We are obliged to receive Holy Communion during Easter time each year and when in danger of death.

377. Why is it well to receive Holy Communion often, even daily?
It is well to receive Holy Communion often, even daily, because this intimate union with Jesus Christ, the Source of all holiness and the Giver of all graces, is the greatest aid to a holy life.
SCRIPTURE:
"And they continued steadfastly in the teaching of the apostles and in the communion of the breaking of the bread and in the prayers" (*Acts 2:42*).
See Scripture, question 344, Luke 22:19-20; question 366, John 6:54-59.

378. How should we show our gratitude to Our Lord for remaining always on our altars in the Holy Eucharist?
We should show our gratitude to Our Lord for remaining always on our altars in the Holy Eucharist, by visiting Him often, by reverence in church, by assisting every day at Mass when this is possible, by attending parish devotions, and by being present at Benediction of the Blessed Sacrament.

(a) Benediction of the Blessed Sacrament is a ceremony in which the sacred host is exposed for a time on the altar, usually in the monstrance. During Benediction the priest blesses the people with the sacred host.

(b) The monstrance, or ostensorium, is a large vessel in which the host is exposed to view through a glass-covered opening in the center.

(c) The long cloak-like vestment worn by the priest at Benediction of the Blessed Sacrament is called a cope. The humeral veil is placed over the priest's shoulders before he gives the blessing.

IMPORTANT TRUTHS ABOUT HOLY COMMUNION

Just as the body needs food for the support of man's natural life, so the soul must be nourished for the preservation and the strengthening of its supernatural life. For this purpose Our Lord has given us a most precious food, His own body and blood. It is indeed a token of His immeasurable love for souls that He wills to come personally into our hearts in order to help and to console us in the difficulties and temptations of our journey through life. And He makes the conditions of receiving Him in Holy Communion very simple. Nothing more is necessary than that we have the proper intention and that we be in the state of sanctifying grace; venial sins do not make us unworthy. The Church, out of reverence for this great sacrament, demands that we observe the law of fasting described above, before Holy Communion, but in certain circumstances, particularly in danger of death, this law does not bind. Even though one is not sick, if there is danger of death—as in the case of a soldier going into battle—he may receive Holy Communion without fasting at any hour of the day or night.

Ordinarily it is permitted to receive Holy Communion only once a day, but there are exceptions to this rule. Thus, a person who has received Holy Communion in the morning may receive the Blessed Sacrament again as Viaticum if he falls into the danger of death in the course of the day. Again, a person who has already received Holy Communion could on the same day consume the Blessed Sacrament in order to protect It from insult or injury. Finally, a priest may receive Holy Communion more than once on the same day—namely, when he celebrates two or more Masses.

If we were permitted to receive Holy Communion only once in our lifetime we should surely prepare carefully for this great event. But we are allowed to receive this sacrament every day, except Holy Saturday, when the Easter Vigil Mass is celebrated after midnight. The frequency with which we can approach the holy table should not diminish our fervor. Each time we receive Our Lord we should prepare our souls for His coming, considering that we are to have a privilege even greater than that of Martha and Mary and the other friends of Christ who welcomed Him into their homes when He dwelt on earth.

Even when we cannot actually receive Holy Communion we can make an act of spiritual communion, which is an act of faith and love toward Our Lord in the Blessed Sacrament, with an ardent desire to receive Him.

Until comparatively recent times daily Communion was very rare in the Church. However, children were generally not admitted to their First Communion until they were about ten years old. But a great and holy Pope, Pius X, who ruled the Church from 1903 to 1914, urgently invited all Catholics to partake of the Divine Banquet frequently, even daily, telling them that the only necessary conditions are the state of grace and a right intention. He also laid down the law that children are to be admitted to Holy Communion as soon as they reach the age of reason, when they are about seven years old. Certainly Our Lord must be pleased that through the efforts of this great Pope He has the opportunity of coming so frequently into the hearts of His faithful, especially into the innocent hearts of little children.

Sometimes we hear a person say that he intends to receive Holy Communion for someone else, and we should understand correctly what is meant by this. We cannot receive Holy Communion for another in the sense that we can transfer to him the graces conferred by the sacrament, for these belong to the recipient alone. But we can receive Holy Communion for another in the sense that we can pray for him at the time of Holy Communion, when our prayers have great value, and if we receive Holy Communion for a deceased person we can offer for him any indulgences we may gain on that occasion.

No matter what difficulties we may encounter, no matter how many temptations we may have to overcome, no matter what sorrows may enter into our life, Our Lord in the Blessed Sacrament will give us the grace and the strength that we need. And we are permitted not only to receive Him in Holy Communion but also to visit Him in the tabernacle, where He remains day and night, saying to us as He said long ago to those who were in pain and sorrow: "Come to me, all you who labor and are burdened, and I will give you rest" (*Matthew 11: 28*).

218

RESOLUTION: Resolve that whenever you receive Holy Communion, you will make a worthy preparation, and will spend at least about fifteen minutes afterwards in fervent thanksgiving.

STUDY HELPS

A. WORD SELECTION. (*Select the word or phrase in each parenthesis which most exactly and most completely fills out the sentence.*)

(1) A person who is sick though not confined to bed can receive Holy Communion after taking (food . . . medicine) or (wine . . . non-alcoholic liquids).

(2) One who is to receive Holy Communion at the midnight Mass must fast (from midnight . . . 9 P. M. . . . three hours before receiving).

(3) We are bound under pain of mortal sin to receive Holy Communion (once a year at any time . . . at Christmas . . . once a year in the Easter season).

(4) The long, cloak-like vestment worn by the priest at Benediction is called the (cope . . . monstrance . . . humeral veil).

(5) We can make a spiritual communion (once a day . . . whenever we wish . . . on days when we do not receive Holy Communion actually).

(6) The Pope who permitted children to receive Holy Communion as soon as they reach the age of reason was (Leo XIII . . . Benedict XV . . . Pius X).

(7) Venial sins (do not make us unworthy of Holy Communion but prevent us from receiving more abundant graces . . . make us unworthy of Holy Communion . . . do not affect the measure of grace we receive).

(8) To receive Holy Communion knowingly in mortal sin is (a venial sin . . . a mortal sin of blasphemy . . . a mortal sin of sacrilege).

(9) The ostensorium is (the vessel in which the Blessed Sacrament is placed at Benediction . . . the vessel from which the priest distributes Holy Communion . . . the portion of the altar in which the Blessed Sacrament is reserved).

B. PROBLEMS AND EXERCISES. (*Answer the questions orally or write them as your teacher may direct*):

(1) Abie, a little Jewish fellow, wants you to explain what his Catholic friend Jude meant when he refused to eat a piece of candy this morning on his way to church: "I can't; I'm going to Communion." Tell Abie why Jude could not eat candy and what "going to Communion" is.

(2) Charity went to confession in the afternoon; at home that evening she became angry at her brother Bernardine, who was annoying her; an hour later she lied to her mother, when asked if she had done all her homework; then she went to bed without saying her night prayers. May she go to Holy Communion the following morning without going again to confession? Give the reason for your answer.

(3) Ignatius has a severe headache. At 8 o'clock Sunday morning he takes two aspirin tablets, swallowing them with a drink of milk, since he wants to go to Holy Communion that morning at the children's Mass. Does he need anyone's permission in order to receive Holy Communion?

(4) Irene is up at 6:00 o'clock, takes a cup of coffee and a buttered roll for breakfast, then goes to the church at 8:00 o'clock. Irene goes to confession. She remains for the 9:00 o'clock Mass, during which she goes to Holy Communion. Since she took nothing to eat since about 6:15 o'clock, was it all right for her to receive? Explain.

(5) It is Christmas Eve. Kenneth intends to receive Holy Communion during the midnight Mass. He decides to keep the fast from 9:00 o'clock that evening. He does so until 11:30, when knowingly and deliberately he breaks it by taking a glass of ginger ale. May he go to Communion during the midnight Mass? Explain fully.

(6) Kathryn, through forgetfulness, eats one small piece of cake on Sunday morning before she goes to Mass. Then she remembers she is going to Holy Communion, and doesn't eat any more of the cake. May she go to Communion that morning? Be sure you consider the time she ate the cake and the time of Holy Communion.

(7) Ludwig went to confession Saturday afternoon, intending to go to Communion Sunday morning. Sunday morning, on getting up at 8:00 o'clock, he is very, very hungry; knowingly and deliberately, he eats two rolls with some milk. At the Communion time of the 9:00 o'clock Mass, he remains in his pew while all the other members of his class receive Holy Communion. Did Ludwig commit any sin by breaking his fast purposely? Did he commit any sin by remaining away from Holy Communion? Because a child goes to confession one day, is he obliged to go to Communion the next day? Could he receive Holy Communion at a later Mass?

(8) Marjorie wants to know if Penance and Holy Eucharist are sacraments that must be linked together, or are they entirely separate and independent of each other? Tell her your answer.

(9) Phyllis receives Holy Communion this morning without fasting. For the past five weeks she has been a patient in the hospital. She is not in danger of death, and will not be discharged from the hospital for another week or ten days. At 7:00 o'clock this morning the nurse gave her a glass of orange juice, and some medicine; at 8:00 o'clock she enjoyed a glass of milk. The priest came with Holy Communion at 8:30 and permits her to receive without fasting. Please explain matters.

(10) A company of soldiers is ordered to the battle front at 9:00 A.M. All of them have had a good substantial breakfast. About an hour after breakfast the Catholic Chaplain is seen giving Communion to the Catholics in the company. Not one of them is fasting. Explain this situation.

(11) Jeannette has a way of her own in making thanksgiving after Communion. Returning to her pew, she buries her face in her hands for a while, then kneels in silence without reading any prayers. Afterwards she reads her prayerbook slowly and thoughtfully, taking her time about it. There are some loose pages inserted in her prayerbook. These are home-made prayers of her own. Write two or three sentences of comment on her mode of thanksgiving.

220

Penance

379. What is the sacrament of Penance?

Penance is the sacrament by which sins committed after Baptism are forgiven through the absolution of the priest.

(a) Penance is a supernatural moral virtue which prompts the sinner to detest his sins and incites him to offer satisfaction for them and to amend his life in the future.

(b) Penance is also a sacrament instituted by Our Divine Saviour in which sins committed after Baptism are forgiven through the absolution of the priest.

(c) Through mortal sin the soul is deprived of its supernatural life. The sacrament of Penance raises the soul from death to supernatural life.

380. Whence has the priest the power to forgive sins?

The priest has the power to forgive sins from Jesus Christ, who said to His apostles and to their successors in the priesthood: "Receive the Holy Spirit; whose sins you shall forgive, they are forgiven them; and whose sins you shall retain, they are retained."

(a) Our Lord spoke these words to the apostles when He appeared to them after His Resurrection.

(b) During His life on earth, Christ forgave sinners in His own name and by His own authority. Before ascending to His Father in heaven, He wanted to confer that power on His apostles and their successors in the priesthood. He knew that many persons would commit grievous sins after they had received sanctifying grace in the sacrament of Baptism.

(c) No man, by his own power and authority, could possibly forgive sins. Only God can do that because sin is an offense against Him. But the priest, as God's representative, can forgive sins because God has given him the power to do so.

SCRIPTURE:
"But if thy brother sin against thee, go and show him his fault, between thee and him alone. If he listen to thee, thou hast won thy brother. But if he do not listen to thee, take with thee one or two more so that on the word of two or three witnesses every word may be confirmed. And if he refuse to hear them, appeal to the Church, but if he refuse to hear even the Church, let him be to thee as the heathen and the publican. Amen I say to you, whatever you bind on earth shall be bound also in heaven; and whatever you loose on earth shall be loosed also in heaven" (*Matthew 18:15-18*).

381. With what words does the priest forgive sins?

The priest forgives sins with the words: "I absolve thee from thy sins in the name of the Father, and of the Son, and of the Holy Ghost. Amen."

221

221a

Penance

The large picture in the center shows Our Lord appearing to the Apostles in the Cenacle on the day of His Resurrection. "Receive the Holy Spirit; whose sins you shall forgive, they are forgiven them; and whose sins you shall retain, they are retained." (St. John 20:22-23) By these words, Our Lord instituted the sacrament of Penance, giving to the Apostles and to all priests the power to remit sins.

Jesus Christ forgave sins several times during His life. At the top right, a paralytic has been brought to Him to be cured. Our Lord says to him, "'Take courage, son; thy sins are forgiven thee.' Then, some of the scribes who were present said within themselves, 'This man blasphemes.' And Jesus, knowing their thoughts, said, 'Why do you harbor evil thoughts in your hearts? For which is easier, to say, "Thy sins are forgiven thee," or to say, "Arise, and walk"? But that you may know that the Son of Man has power on earth to forgive sins' - then he said to the paralytic - 'Arise, take up thy pallet and go to thy house.' And he arose, and went away to his house.'" (St. Matthew 9:2-7)

At the bottom right is a penitent who has gone to confession and received the pardon of his sins. On one side is his guardian angel giving him hope for heaven, and on the other side is the demon who was driven from his soul by the absolution. At bottom left is a man who has made a sacrilegious confession. He has cooperated with the demon by willfully holding back a mortal sin in confession, and, instead of obtaining pardon, he has committed another serious sin. His good angel turns away in sorrow while he is led away by the demon.

At the top left is a model of perfect contrition in the person of St. Mary Magdalen. This woman, having led an evil life, came one day to lament her sins at the feet of Jesus Christ in the hope of obtaining pardon. Our Lord, who was at table with a Pharisee named Simon, declared that many sins were forgiven Magdalen, because she had loved much. Then He said to her, "Thy sins are forgiven thee; go in peace." (St. Luke 7)

(a) The power to forgive sins by pronouncing these words of absolution is given to the priest at his ordination. In order to exercise this power the priest must have jurisdiction, or be authorized to act as a spiritual judge over the persons he absolves. This jurisdiction ordinarily is given to the priest by the bishop of the diocese where the sacrament is administered.

(b) The jurisdiction to absolve from certain serious sins and excommunications is reserved to the bishop or the Pope. Except in case of danger of death, or great urgency, a priest must have special authority to absolve these sins and excommunications.

382. What are effects of the sacrament of Penance, worthily received?

The effects of the sacrament of Penance, worthily received are:

first, the restoration or increase of sanctifying grace;

second, the forgiveness of sins;

third, the remission of the eternal punishment, if necessary, and also of part, at least, of the temporal punishment, due to our sins;

fourth, the help to avoid sin in future;

fifth, the restoration of the merits of our good works if they have been lost by mortal sin.

(a) When we receive the sacrament of Penance worthily, the merits of Christ's redemption are applied to us. Sanctifying grace is either restored or, if we are already in the state of grace, increased.

(b) The worthy reception of the sacrament of Penance also gives us a right to receive those actual graces which we will need in atoning for our past sins and avoiding sins in the future.

383. What else does the sacrament of Penance do for us?

The sacrament of Penance also gives us the opportunity to receive spiritual advice and instruction from our confessor.

(a) It is advisable to have a regular confessor, although one is free to confess to any authorized priest.

384. What must we do to receive the sacrament of Penance worthily?

To receive the sacrament of Penance worthily, we must:

first, examine our conscience;

second, be sorry for our sins;

third, have the firm purpose of not sinning again;

fourth, confess our sins to the priest;

fifth, be willing to perform the penance the priest gives us.

SCRIPTURE:

"But if the wicked do penance for all his sins which he hath committed and keep all my commandments and do judgment and justice, living he shall live, and shall not die. I will not remember all his iniquities that he hath done: in his justice which he hath wrought, he shall live. Is it my will that a sinner should die, saith the Lord God, and not that he should be converted from his ways and live?" (*Ezechiel 18:21-23*).

385. What is an examination of conscience?

An examination of conscience is a sincere effort to call to mind all the sins we have committed since our last worthy confession.

386. What should we do before our examination of conscience?

Before our examination of conscience we should ask God's help to know our sins and to confess them with sincere sorrow.

387. How can we make a good examination of conscience?

We can make a good examination of conscience by calling to mind the commandments of God and of the Church, and the particular duties of our state of life, and by asking ourselves how we may have sinned with regard to them.

(a) We should give sufficient time to an examination of conscience, making it carefully and thoughtfully, and attempting to remember all our sins.

IMPORTANT TRUTHS ABOUT PENANCE

When a person becomes sick he tries to recover his health by taking medicine. Our Blessed Lord knew that human beings are inclined to sin and thus bring on themselves sickness of soul. Indeed, mortal sin brings on spiritual death, for it deprives the soul of its supernatural life, sanctifying grace. For those who sin before being baptized, Our Saviour intended Baptism as the means of forgiveness and for the birth of the soul to the life of grace. But he knew that even after Baptism many would sin, some even grievously; and in His mercy He determined to provide these with a remedy—a sacrament that would be more potent in the spiritual order than the most effective medicine is in the physical order. For no medicine can restore a dead person to life; but the sacrament which Our Lord determined to give us is able to restore the life of grace to any soul, no matter how grievously it may be laden with sin. The sacrament is Penance. Our Lord gave some indication of His purpose to provide such a sacrament when He said to the apostles: "Whatever you bind on earth shall be bound also in heaven; and whatever you loose on earth shall be loosed also in heaven" (*Matthew 18: 18*). In these words is implied the power to loose men from the bonds of sin. But a clearer declaration of this sacrament is found in Our Lord's words to the apostles on Easter Sunday after His resurrection: "Whose sins you shall forgive, they are forgiven them; and whose sins you shall retain, they are retained" (*John 20: 23*). This power of forgiving sins, being given by Our Lord for the benefit of all mankind, has been passed down to the successors of the apostles, the bishops and the priests of the Catholic Church.

Our Saviour could indeed have decreed that men should receive the pardon of their sins by going directly to God with contrition. But a sacrament, administered by men in the name of God, is a more assuring and a more effective means. The conditions for the reception of this sacrament are very easy. The penitent confesses his sins with true contrition and the priest by the authority of God forgives him. In the early days of Christianity the Church administered this sacrament with far greater severity than nowadays. The worst sinners were sometimes obliged to perform penance publicly for a long time before receiving the pardon of their sins. But today the Church is most lenient; she receives the sinner kindly and makes his return to God as easy as possible. Every day throughout the world thousands of sinners are making use of the sacrament of Penance to have the sins of many years washed from their souls and to be restored to the life of grace and the friendship of God.

Sometimes a person is refused absolution in the confessional because the priest judges that he is not sufficiently disposed for the reception of the sacrament of Penance. This is particularly the case when the priest believes that the penitent is not truly sorry for his sins or has not a firm resolution to avoid sin and the near occasions of sin in future. A person who has been refused absolution should humbly accept the priest's decision and endeavor to dispose himself properly so that he may receive absolution when he returns to confession at the time determined by the confessor.

We can never sufficiently thank Our Blessed Saviour for the sacrament of Penance. We read in the Gospel of various occasions on which He Himself forgave sinners, such as the case of Mary Magdalen and of the penitent thief who hung beside Him on Calvary. We feel that these persons were fortunate because they received from the lips of Christ Himself the consoling assurance that their sins were forgiven. Yet, we too have a like assurance, for Our Lord Himself really administers the sacrament of Penance through the ministry of His priest; He himself says to us, when we have made a worthy confession: "Go in peace, thy sins are forgiven thee."

RESOLUTION: Resolve after every confession to thank Our Blessed Lord for the great benefit He has given us in the sacrament of Penance.

STUDY HELPS

A. COLUMN SELECTIONS. (*Join correctly the parts of the sentences in Columns I and II, by placing the right key letter in the proper parenthesis.*)

I

(1) The sacrament of Penance (..).

(2) Although it is advisable to have a regular confessor (..).

(3) Besides the power of ordination the priest needs for the administration of the sacrament of Penance (..).

(4) Only God can forgive sins (..).

(5) A person who is restored to sanctifying grace receives back (..).

(6) Jurisdiction to forgive sins is ordinarily given to a priest (..).

(7) Our Lord said to the apostles: "Whose sins you shall forgive they are forgiven them, etc." (..).

(8) In the early days of the Church sinners were sometimes obliged (..).

(9) The penitent thief was assured by Christ Himself (..).

(10) A person who has not the firm purpose of avoiding mortal sin in future cannot receive (..).

II

(A) by the bishop of the diocese in which the sacrament is administered.

(B) on Easter Sunday.

(C) the pardon of his sins in the sacrament of Penance.

(D) one is free to confess to any authorized priest.

(E) that his sins were forgiven.

(F) by His own power.

(G) to perform penance publicly

(H) the merits of his good works which were lost by sin.

(I) the power of jurisdiction.

(J) restores the soul to supernatural life.

224

B. PROBLEMS AND EXERCISES. (*Answer the questions orally or write them as your teacher may direct*):

(1) Egbert, dead in mortal sin, has his soul brought back to life by Father Reuben. Explain the terms "dead in mortal sin"—"brought back to life." What 'miraculous power' did Father Reuben use to bring about this spiritual resurrection? Who gave him that power?

(2) Mary Magdalene and the Good Thief had the consoling experience of hearing directly from Our Saviour Himself that their sins were forgiven. Have we a similar assurance that our sins are forgiven? Explain.

(3) In your own way explain the meaning of the word "penance" used in the following sentences:

(a) Do penance for your sins.

(b) Baptism was the first Sacrament received by Lucinda; Penance, the second.

(c) At home, Dinah is on penance, washing and drying the dishes, and putting them away, because she stayed out overtime last night.

(4) Write from memory the words which Our Lord spoke Easter Sunday evening when He gave the Apostles the power to forgive sins.

(5) Thornton, a Protestant boy, tells Elmer, a Catholic, that it is ridiculous to believe that the priest can forgive sins, since the priest is a mere man, and only God can forgive sin. What answer should Elmer give?

(6) Constance wants to know what the priest is saying in Latin while she is reciting her act of contrition at the end of her confession. Tell her.

(7) Dexter, in the graduating class of St. Carmela's, confides to his chum Morgan that Father Demetrius would not give him absolution today when he went to confession. Ordinarily what does this refusal indicate? What advice should Morgan give his pal, Dexter?

(8) Who authorized Father Demetrius to hear Dexter's confession? When did Father Demetrius receive the power to hear confessions? Where did this power come from?

(9) Father Tibertus is a priest of a New England diocese. He is on his way to the Pacific Coast in a train. Near the journey's end, Conrad, a fellow passenger, asks Father Tibertus to hear his confession; Father Tibertus excuses himself, explaining he has no jurisdiction to do so, being out of his own proper diocese. Yet, five minutes later, he hears the confession of Owen, another passenger, who is stricken fatally with a heart attack. Why the distinction? Explain.

(10) Theodosia, a Catholic lady in a big city, makes it a devotional hobby to go to confession to a different priest every week in the year. Do you approve of her practice? State your reason for answering that way.

(11) Adeline has made her last ten confessions to Father Hiram. At present, she is in an agony of suspense because she is ashamed to mention a certain doubt about a serious temptation she had during the past week. Advise her what to do, and give her the reason for your advice.

(12) Maureen asks her older brother, Patrick, who is studying for the priesthood why Our Lord isn't satisfied that we should go to Him directly for the pardon of our sins but demands that we confess them to the priest. What answer do you think Patrick will give his little sister?

LESSON 30

Contrition

388. What is contrition?

Contrition is sincere sorrow for having offended God, and hatred for the sins we have committed, with a firm purpose of sinning no more.

(a) It is unreasonable to expect a person to pardon us for any offense unless we are sincerely sorry for the act that has given offense and are firmly determined not to repeat the act in the future.

(b) By sin we offend and insult God. Unless we are sincerely sorry for our sins and are firmly resolved not to commit them again, we cannot reasonably expect God to forgive us.

SCRIPTURE:

"Let the wicked forsake his way and the unjust man his thoughts, and let him return to the Lord; and he will have mercy on him: and to our God; for he is bountiful to forgive" (*Isaias 55:7*).

"And when the wicked turneth himself away from his wickedness, which he hath wrought, and doeth judgment and justice, he shall save his soul alive. Because he considereth and turneth away himself from all his iniquities which he hath wrought, he shall surely live and not die" (*Ezechiel 18:27-28*).

"But when he came to himself, he said, 'How many hired men in my father's house have bread in abundance, while I am perishing here with hunger! I will get up and go to my father, and will say to him, Father, I have sinned against heaven and before thee. I am no longer worthy to be called thy son; make me as one of thy hired men.' And he arose and went to his father.

"But while he was yet a long way off, his father saw him and was moved with compassion, and ran and fell upon his neck and kissed him. And the son said to him, 'Father, I have sinned against heaven and before thee. I am no longer worthy to be called thy son.' But the father said to his servants, 'Fetch quickly the best robe and put it on him, and give him a ring for his finger and sandals for his feet; and bring out the fattened calf and kill it, and let us eat and make merry; because this my son was dead, and has come to life again; he was lost, and is found.' And they began to make merry" (*Luke 15:17-24*).

389. Will God forgive us any sin unless we have true contrition for it?

God will not forgive us any sin, whether mortal or venial, unless we have true contrition for it.

(a) Sometimes people are unwilling to pardon our offenses against them even when we are sincerely sorry for having offended them. But God will always forgive us our sins when we are sincerely sorry for them. He will not forgive us, however, unless we are sincerely sorry.

SCRIPTURE:

"Now therefore saith the Lord: Be converted to me with all your heart, in fasting and in weeping and in mourning. And rend your hearts and not your garments, and turn to the Lord your God: for he is gracious and merciful, patient and rich in mercy, and ready to repent of the evil. Who knoweth but he will return and forgive and leave a blessing behind him, sacrifice and libation to the Lord your God?" (*Joel 2:12-14*).

390. When is sorrow for sin true contrition?

Sorrow for sin is true contrition when it is interior, super natural, supreme, and universal.

SCRIPTURE:

David's sorrow for sin as expressed in Psalm 50 is true contrition:

It is *interior:*

"My sacrifice, O God, is a contrite spirit; a contrite and humbled heart, O God, thou wilt not despise" (*v. 19*).

It is *supernatural:*

"Create a pure heart for me, O God, and renew in me a steadfast spirit" (*v. 12*).

It is *supreme:*

The entire Psalm conveys David's hatred of sin and his willingness to endure anything rather than sin again.

It is *universal:*

"Turn thy face away from my sins, and blot out all my iniquities" (*v. 11*).

391. When is our sorrow interior?

Our sorrow is interior when it comes from our heart, and not merely from our lips.

(a) It is not enough merely to say that we are sorry for our sins. We must really mean it. We must sincerely detest our sins and firmly intend not to commit them again. We do not, however, have to feel our sorrow, for contrition is an act of the will, not of the feelings.

392. When is our sorrow supernatural?

Our sorrow is supernatural when, with the help of God's grace, it arises from motives which spring from faith and not merely from natural motives.

(a) "Motives which spring from faith" are truths that God has revealed. God has revealed, for example, that mortal sin will be punished in hell, venial sin in purgatory; that sin caused Christ to die; that sin is an offense against the infinite goodness of God; and that sin is hateful in itself. If we are sorry for our sins for one of these reasons, then, with God's grace, our sorrow is supernatural; it is prompted by truths which we believe because of the authority of God who revealed them.

(b) If we are sorry for our sins because they injure our health or will be punished by the civil courts or cause us to lose our friends, then our sorrow is natural. It is prompted by natural reasons. It is not wrong to be sorry for our sins because of natural motives; but this natural sorrow is not sufficient to obtain God's pardon.

393. When is our sorrow supreme?

Our sorrow is supreme when we hate sin above every other evil, and are willing to endure anything rather than offend God in the future by sin.

(a) We know that sin is the greatest of all evils because it is an offense against God, the greatest Good, and for that reason we should detest it more than we detest any other evil.

227

394. When is our sorrow universal?

Our sorrow is universal when we are sorry for every mortal sin which we may have had the misfortune to commit.

(a) When mortal sins are forgiven sanctifying grace enters the soul, and it is impossible for sanctifying grace to enter the soul if a single mortal sin remains there. All our mortal sins, therefore, must be forgiven, or none of them is forgiven.

395. Should we always try to have sorrow for all our venial sins when receiving the sacrament of Penance?

We should try to have sorrow for all our venial sins when receiving the sacrament of Penance, and, when we have only venial sins to confess, we must have sorrow for at least one of them or for some sin of our past life which we confess.

396. Why should we have contrition for mortal sin?

We should have contrition for mortal sin because it is the greatest of all evils, gravely offends God, keeps us out of heaven, and condemns us forever to hell.

SCRIPTURE:

"Turn to the Lord: and forsake thy sins. . . . Return to the Lord, and turn away from thy injustice: and greatly hate abomination" (*Ecclesiasticus 17:21, 23*).

"If anyone does not abide in me, he shall be cast outside as the branch and wither; and they shall gather them up and cast them into the fire, and they shall burn" (*John 15:6*).

"Or do you not know that the unjust will not possess the kingdom of God?" (*I Corinthians 6:9*).

"But when sin has matured, it begets death" (*James 1:15*).

397. Why should we have contrition for venial sin?

We should have contrition for venial sin because it is displeasing to God, merits temporal punishment, and may lead to mortal sin.

(a) As long as a person has mortal sin on his soul he cannot be pardoned for his venial sins. Mortal sin makes man an enemy of God. He cannot, therefore, receive pardon for his slighter offenses if he does not receive pardon for the serious offenses which make him an enemy of God.

(b) A person having only venial sins on his soul can obtain pardon for those for which he is sincerely sorry, even though other venial sins remain unforgiven because he is not sorry for them.

398. How many kinds of contrition are there?

There are two kinds of contrition: perfect contrition and imperfect contrition.

399. When is our contrition perfect?

Our contrition is perfect when we are sorry for our sins because sin offends God, whom we love above all things for His own sake.

(a) We love God because He is the supreme Good. Sin is the greatest evil because it is an offense against God, the supreme Good. Our sorrow for sin is perfect, therefore, when we detest sin because it offends God, whom we love above all things.

SCRIPTURE: *See Scripture, question 390, Psalm 50.*

400. When is our contrition imperfect?

Our contrition is imperfect when we are sorry for our sins because they are hateful in themselves or because we fear God's punishment.

(a) Imperfect contrition is sometimes called attrition.

SCRIPTURE:
"And the children of Israel said to the Lord: We have sinned: do thou unto us whatsoever pleaseth thee. Only deliver us this time" (*Judges 10:15*).

401. To receive the sacrament of Penance worthily, what kind of contrition is sufficient?

To receive the sacrament of Penance worthily, imperfect contrition is sufficient.

402. Should we always try to have perfect contrition in the sacrament of Penance?

We should always try to have perfect contrition in the sacrament of Penance because perfect contrition is more pleasing to God, and because with His help we can always have it.

403. How can a person in mortal sin regain the state of grace before receiving the sacrament of Penance?

A person in mortal sin can regain the state of grace before receiving the sacrament of Penance by making an act of perfect contrition with the sincere purpose of going to confession.

(a) It is not true that we can regain the state of grace by perfect contrition only when we are in danger of death or when it is impossible to go to confession.

(b) In order to regain sanctifying grace by perfect contrition, it is sufficient that we intend to go to confession the next time we are obliged to do so.

SCRIPTURE:
"Is it my will that a sinner should die, saith the Lord God, and not that he should be converted from his ways and live?" (*Ezechiel 18:23*).

404. What should we do if we have the misfortune to commit a mortal sin?

If we have the misfortune to commit a mortal sin, we should ask God's pardon and grace at once, make an act of perfect contrition, and go to confession as soon as we can.

405. May we receive Holy Communion after committing a mortal sin, if we merely make an act of perfect contrition?

We may not receive Holy Communion after committing a

mortal sin, if we merely make an act of perfect contrition; one who has sinned grievously must go to confession before receiving Holy Communion.

406. What is the firm purpose of sinning no more?

The firm purpose of sinning no more is the sincere resolve not only to avoid sin but to avoid as far as possible the near occasions of sin.

(a) This firm purpose of amendment does not necessarily exclude the fear that a person may repeat his sin in the future. It does mean that, at the time, a person, relying fully upon God's grace, sincerely intends never to commit this sin again.

(b) The firm purpose of amendment includes also the intention to remain away from persons, places, or things that may easily lead him to sin.

(c) The firm purpose of amendment must include not only those mortal sins which the person has committed in the past and confessed, but also all mortal sins.

SCRIPTURE:
"He that loveth danger shall perish in it" (*Ecclesiasticus 3:27*).

"My son, hast thou sinned? Do so no more: but for thy former sins also pray that they may be forgiven thee. Flee from sins as from the face of a serpent: for if thou comest near them, they will take hold of thee" (*Ecclesiasticus 21:1-2*).

"Watch and pray, that you may not enter into temptation" (*Mark 14:38*).

"Then Jesus said, 'Neither will I condemn thee. Go thy way, and from now on sin no more' " (*John 8:11*).

"Do not be led astray, 'evil companionships corrupt good morals' " (*I Corinthians 15:33*).

407. What purpose of amendment must a person have if he has only venial sins to confess?

If a person has only venial sins to confess, he must have the purpose of avoiding at least one of them.

IMPORTANT TRUTHS ABOUT CONTRITION

If we insult a friend, it is our duty to ask his pardon, to tell him we are sorry, to promise that we shall not repeat the offense. We must do the same toward God when we offend Him by sin. We cannot expect Him to forgive us unless we turn to Him with true sorrow of soul, or contrition. On the other hand, if we turn to Him with the necessary contrition, He will forgive us. In this, His mercy is greater than that of creatures. Sometimes we ask a human being to pardon the wrong we have done, but he refuses. But God is always ready to forgive the sinner, however wicked he has been, if he returns to his heavenly Father with true sorrow of heart. Naturally, this sorrow must be based on motives of faith, not on merely natural motives. It must extend to all mortal sins, it must include a firm purpose of not sinning, at least mortally, in future; it must contain the will to endure any suffering rather than offend God by grievous sin in the time to come. Such an act of contrition is not difficult for any one who knows from the principles of the Catholic faith how terrible an evil is sin. One must remember also that God is always ready to give the grace to make an act of contrition to any one who sincerely begs His assistance.

When we say that God will not forgive any sin without contrition, we are speaking only of actual sin, not of original sin. We cannot have contrition for original sin since we did not contract it by our own free will; hence, infants who have only original sin are cleansed of that sin by Baptism, without making any act of contrition.

In the sacrament of Penance, contrition based on any supernatural motive suffices, even though it arises merely from the fear of God's punishments, of which He has spoken to us frequently in revelation. It is true, contrition based on fear alone is not very noble. Indeed, it might be called selfish. Yet, Our Lord proposed this as a good motive of contrition when He said: "Be afraid of him who, after He was killed, has power to cast into hell" (*Luke, 12: 5*). Other reasons for contrition, sufficient to obtain the forgiveness of sins in the sacrament of Penance, are the realization of the ingratitude to God that every sin contains, the hatefulness of sin as opposed to the supernatural virtues, the injustice to our Creator included in every transgression of His law.

The most noble type of contrition is that which arises from the love of God for His own sake, or because of His own goodness. This is called perfect contrition, and it has the power to procure the forgiveness of all mortal sins that may be on the soul of the person who detests his sins from this motive. It was of this contrition that Our Lord spoke when He said, pointing to the repentant sinner, Mary Magdalen, "Her sins, many as they are, shall be forgiven her, because she has loved much" (*Luke, 7: 47*). It is indeed unfortunate that Catholics are often unaware of the wonderful power of perfect contrition. Some think it remits sin only when one is in danger of death and cannot get to confession. The truth is that an act of perfect contrition will always take away mortal sin; one has only to have the intention of going to confession when he is next obliged to do so—that is, within the year or when in danger of death—and telling the mortal sins which have been remitted by perfect contrition. One who has had his sins forgiven by perfect contrition may not go to Communion until he has been to confession; nevertheless he can enjoy the advantages of being in the state of grace and of gaining merit for his good works.

A person can have at the same time both perfect and imperfect contrition for his sins. One does not exclude the other. For this reason we say in our act of contrition: "I detest all my sins because of thy just punishments" thus expressing imperfect contrition, and then we add our expression of perfect contrition, when we say: "But most of all because they offend Thee, my God, who art all-good and deserving of all my love."

RESOLUTION: Resolve that if ever you are so unfortunate as to fall into mortal sin, you will immediately make an act of perfect contrition and thus regain the state of sanctifying grace.

STUDY HELPS

A. TRUE OR FALSE. (*Check each of the statements given below as either true or false. The correct answer will be found in the preceding portions of the lesson.*)

	TRUE	FALSE
(1) A person can have both perfect and imperfect contrition at the same time.	.....	.....
(2) An act of perfect contrition will take away a person's mortal sins even when he is not in danger of death and can go to confession.	.....	.....
(3) A person cannot have true contrition unless he is sure that he will never sin mortally again.	.....	.....

231

(4) We may not receive Holy Communion after committing a mortal sin until we have gone to confession, even though we have received the pardon of the sin by perfect contrition.   . . . .

(5) The purpose of amendment need not include any sins except the kind which the penitent has confessed.   . . . .

(6) If we have only venial sins to confess we can receive the sacrament of Penance fruitfully even though we are not sorry for any of them, provided we confess some sin of the past for which we are truly sorry.   . . . .

(7) We do not have to feel our sorrow, as long as it is in our will.   . . . .

(8) If we are sorry for some of our mortal sins but not for all of them, we can receive the pardon of those for which we are sorry.   . . . .

(9) A person in mortal sin can receive the pardon of the venial sins for which he is sorry.   . . . .

(10) A person who has only venial sins on his soul can obtain the pardon of those for which he has contrition, even though he is not sorry for the others.   . . . .

B. PROBLEMS AND EXERCISES. (*Answer the questions orally or write them as your teacher may direct*):

(1) Alvin asks, can we be sorry for original sin? Answer him, giving the reason for your answer.

(2) Bede, a highly sensitive lad, is wondering has he true sorrow for his sins. That wonder is occasioned by his inability to be emotional during the recitation of the act of contrition. Give your comment on this problem of Bede—in three or four sentences.

(3) Enumerate at least five motives for contrition that spring from faith.

(4) Ivan, a prisoner in the State Prison, is in a death cell, with only two more weeks to live. His crimes were robbery and murder. He is grieving over the shame and sorrow he is causing his devout Catholic parents. He is dreading the ordeal of execution. He is afraid of God's punishments in the next life. Is he disposed to receive absolution? Which of the foregoing motives for sorrow is sufficient for his worthy reception of the sacrament of Penance? Why?

(5) Through shame, Cynthia keeps back in confession one of her five mortal sins. How many mortal sins are on her soul as she leaves the confessional? Explain your answer.

(6) Ulysses thinks he can get rid of his venial sins by his prayers and by using sacramentals; he is not sorry for some of his mortal sins. Is his opinion correct about the pardon of his venial sins under these circumstances? Give the reason for your answer.

(7) Olga, a daily communicant, is sorry for her venial sins of anger, but not much concerned about her numerous petty lies. She confesses only her sins of anger, but purposely does not confess her many small lies. Is her confession good? Why? Are both classes of venial sin forgiven, or only one? If only one, which one? Explain the answer.

(8) In a Catechism quiz Dennis lost first prize because he could not give the definition of attrition. What is it? Give a complete definition of it.

(9) Wilhelmina in the third grade is listening closely to the catechists's vivid portrayal of Our Lord's sufferings. After a while the catechist notices tears glistening in her innocent eyes. Would you say that natural or supernatural contrition in the soul of Wilhelmina has given rise to those tears? What is the reason for your answer?

(10) Write from memory the act of contrition that you say when you make your confession. Analyze it, pointing out whether it is perfect, imperfect, or a combination of both kinds of contrition. If a combination of both, mark a single line under the expression of imperfect contrition, and a double line under that of perfect contrition.

(11) Arnold is not convinced that fear of God's punishments is a wholesome religious motive for sorrow. Tell him why he is wrong.

(12) Remy, a boy of 9, is unfortunately led to commit his first mortal sin by Quincy, a vicious companion of 11. That night Remy is afraid to go to sleep. He knows that if he dies during the night in mortal sin he will be lost forever in the fire of hell. What should he try to do? When should he do it?

(13) Callistus and Melba are on their honeymoon trip—a cruise of twelve days. There is no priest aboard the ship. Through human respect, both of them eat a meat dinner on Friday, the first day of their trip. Both are soon ashamed of their moral cowardice. How long will they have to wait before they get back into the state of grace? Explain your answer.

(14) Pulcheria is unusually fond of dancing. Of late, she has been frequenting a disreputable dance hall, chiefly because she meets there a very skillful dancing partner, Ethan. The place has affected her morals quite seriously. The last ten times she has been there, she has broken God's laws seriously. She makes a very truthful confession of her wickedness, but is very disappointed when the priest insists that she stay away from the place altogether. Pulcheria promises to avoid the sins and asks the priest's permission to keep going to the dance hall. The priest firmly, but kindly, refuses to grant her request. Write a paragraph of comment on the situation—a paragraph of about four sentences.

(15) Hans has 15 venial sins to confess: 5 small lies, 5 slight outbursts of anger, and 5 acts of disobedience to his parents. His purpose of amendment covers only the sins of disobedience. Does he make a good confession? How could he make it better?

(16) Merlin, staying at a camp for the summer, committed a mortal sin; but that same evening made an act of perfect contrition. The following Sunday he attended Mass, celebrated by a visiting priest in the dining hall of the camp. The priest explained to the congregation that he could not hear confessions because he came from another diocese and did not have jurisdiction for administering the sacrament of Penance in the diocese where the camp was situated. "However," he added, "those who have committed no mortal sin since their last confession may receive Holy Communion, if they wish." Merlin concluded that, even though he had committed a mortal sin since his last confession, he was now in the state of grace through his act of perfect contrition; hence, he received Holy Communion. Did he reason correctly?

233

LESSON 31

Confession

408. What is confession?

Confession is the telling of our sins to an authorized priest for the purpose of obtaining forgiveness.

(a) An authorized priest is one who has not only the power to forgive sins by reason of his ordination to the priesthood, but also the power of jurisdiction over the persons who come to him. He has this jurisdiction ordinarily from his bishop, or by reason of his office. [22]

SCRIPTURE:

"I have confessed my sin to thee, and my fault I have not concealed; I said: 'I confess my iniquity to the Lord,' and thou didst forgive the guilt of my sin" (*Psalm 31:5*).

"He that hideth his sins shall not prosper: but he that shall confess and forsake them shall obtain mercy" (*Proverbs 28:13*).

"And this became known to all the Jews and Gentiles living in Ephesus, and fear fell on them all, and the name of the Lord Jesus came to be held in high honor. And many of those who believed kept coming, and openly confessed their practices" (*Acts 19: 17-18*).

409. Why must we confess our sins?

We must confess our sins because Jesus Christ obliges us to do so in these words, spoken to the apostles and to their successors in the priesthood: "Whose sins you shall forgive, they are forgiven them; and whose sins you shall retain, they are retained."

SCRIPTURE: *See Scripture, questions 380 and 384.*

410. How do these words of Christ oblige us to confess our sins?

These words of Christ oblige us to confess our sins because the priest cannot know whether he should forgive or retain our sins unless we tell them to him.

(a) The priest must judge the penitent. In order to act as judge the priest must know whether to forgive or to retain the penitent's sins. It would be impossible for the priest to decide, that is, to judge, whether or not the penitent should be forgiven unless the penitent made known the extent of his guilt and his sorrow.

(b) In the sacrament of Penance the priest acts also as the physician of the soul. He tells the penitent how to avoid sin and how to amend his life. Just as we tell a doctor about our bodily aches and pains in order that he can cure us, so also we tell our sins to the priest in order that he can suggest spiritual remedies.

(c) Since God has commanded us to confess our sins to the priest, as His representative, we should not let shame prevent us from doing so. The

---

22. See question 381.

234

priest, as God's representative, will advise and encourage us, help us solve our doubts, guide our future conduct, and forgive our sins in the name of Christ. He will never, under any circumstances, not even to save his own life, make our sins known to anyone else. Priests, bishops, and even the Pope must also confess their sins to a priest.

411. Is it necessary to confess every sin?

It is necessary to confess every mortal sin which has not yet been confessed and forgiven; it is not necessary to confess our venial sins, but it is better to do so.

(a) It is not necessary to confess venial sins because they do not deprive the soul of sanctifying grace.

(b) It is better to confess our venial sins because when we do so, we have more assurance that they are forgiven and because we receive from the sacrament of Penance special graces to help us avoid them in the future.

SCRIPTURE: *See Scripture, question 408, Proverbs 28:13.*

412. What are the chief qualities of a good confession?

The chief qualities of a good confession are three: it must be humble, sincere, and entire.

413. When is our confession humble?

Our confession is humble when we accuse ourselves of our sins with a conviction of guilt for having offended God.
SCRIPTURE:
"And the son said to him, 'Father, I have sinned against heaven and before thee. I am no longer worthy to be called thy son' " (*Luke 15:21*).
"O God, be merciful to me the sinner!" (*Luke 18:13*).

414. When is our confession sincere?

Our confession is sincere when we tell our sins honestly and frankly.

(a) We must manifest our humility and sincerity in confession by telling our sins clearly and distinctly so that the priest can understand them.

(b) Persons who lack the power of speech may, if they wish, write a list of their sins for the priest.

(c) Persons who are hard of hearing should confess in places set aside for them so that neither they nor the priest will be overheard.

415. When is our confession entire?

Our confession is entire when we confess at least all our mortal sins, telling their kind, the number of times we have committed each sin, and any circumstances changing their nature.

(a) By the kind of sins is meant the class to which they belong, such as blasphemy, missing Mass, disobedience, theft. The best way to determine the different kinds of sin is to determine the virtue that has been violated or the commandment that has been broken. We must confess whether the sin was in thought. word, or deed.

(b) In most prayerbooks there are lists of sins which help us to determine the kinds of sins we have committed.

(c) Circumstances that change the nature of a sin are those which add some new kind of wickedness to the act we have done. For example, if a person kills another, he commits a sin of murder; but the killing of a cleric is a circumstance that adds a new wickedness to his act and makes it also a sin of sacrilege.

SCRIPTURE:
"And the Lord spoke to Moses, saying: Say to the children of Israel: When a man or woman shall have committed any of all the sins that men are wont to commit, and by negligence shall have transgressed the commandment of the Lord, and offended: they shall confess their sin . . . " (Numbers 5:5-7).

416. What are we to do if without our fault we forget to confess a mortal sin?

If without our fault we forget to confess a mortal sin, we may receive Holy Communion, because we have made a good Confession and the sin is forgiven; but we must tell the sin in confession if it again comes to our mind.

(a) There are times when a person can receive the sacrament of Penance without telling the nature and number of all his sins. A dying person, for example, or a large number of soldiers going into battle may not have time for a detailed confession. Before receiving absolution they must admit that they have sinned, that they are sorry, and that they want to be absolved. Those who have confessed in this general way must, in their next confession, tell all their sins according to their nature, number, and circumstances that change their nature.

417. What happens if we knowingly conceal a mortal sin in confession?

If we knowingly conceal a mortal sin in confession, the sins we confess are not forgiven; moreover, we commit a mortal sin of sacrilege.

(a) Deliberately to conceal a mortal sin in confession is a sacrilege, because it is a grievous abuse of the sacrament of Penance, a sacred institution of Christ.

SCRIPTURE: See Scripture, question 408, Proverbs 28:13.

418. What must a person do who has knowingly concealed a mortal sin in confession?

A person who has knowingly concealed a mortal sin in confession must confess that he has made a bad confession, tell the sin he has concealed, mention the sacraments he has received since that time, and confess all the other mortal sins he has committed since his last good confession.

419. Why should a sense of shame and fear of telling our sins to the priest never lead us to conceal a mortal sin in confession?

A sense of shame and fear of telling our sins to the priest should never lead us to conceal a mortal sin in confession because the priest, who represents Christ Himself, is bound by the seal of the sacrament of Penance never to reveal anything that has been confessed to him.

(a) The priest may not speak about anything he has heard in confession even to the penitent who told it to him, unless the penitent himself willingly permits it.

(b) If any person overhears something that is told in confession by another, he may not speak of it to anyone.

(c) A person ordinarily should not mention to others what he has told in confession.

SCRIPTURE:
"Be not ashamed to confess thy sins" (Ecclesiasticus 4:31).

"He who hears you, hears me; and he who rejects you, rejects me; and he who rejects me, rejects him who sent me" (*Luke 10:16*).

420. Why does the priest give us a penance after confession?

The priest gives us a penance after confession that we may make some atonement to God for our sins, receive help to avoid them in the future, and make some satisfaction for the temporal punishment due to them.

(a) It is a sin deliberately to omit the penance received in confession, a mortal sin if the penance is grave and imposed for a grave sin, a venial sin if the penance is slight.

(b) If a person intended to perform the penance at the time he received it, the sins he told in confession are forgiven; but he is guilty of a new sin afterward when he deliberately omits the penance.

(c) A person should follow exactly the instructions of the priest as to the manner and time of performing the penance. If the priest does not give such instructions it is best to perform the penance immediately, or as soon as possible.

SCRIPTURE: "And David said to Nathan: I have sinned against the Lord. And Nathan said to David: The Lord also hath taken away thy sin. Thou shalt not die. Nevertheless, because thou hast given occasion to the enemies of the Lord to blaspheme, for this thing, the child that is born to thee, shall surely die" (*II Kings 12:13-14*).

"Wherefore, O king, let my counsel be acceptable to thee, and redeem thou thy sins with alms and thy iniquities with works of mercy to the poor: perhaps he will forgive thy offenses" (*Daniel 4-24*).

"Now therefore saith the Lord: Be converted to me with all your heart, in fasting and in weeping and in mourning" (*Joel 2:12*).

421. What kinds of punishment are due to sin?

Two kinds of punishment are due to sin: the eternal punishment of hell, due to unforgiven mortal sins, and temporal punishment, lasting only for a time, due to venial sins and also to mortal sins after they have been forgiven.

(a) We know that God demands temporal punishment for mortal sins even after they have been forgiven, because God Himself has made this known by divine revelation.

237

(b) Christ, by His death on the cross, made more than adequate satisfaction to atone for all the temporal punishment due to all the sins of
mankind; but God wants us to perform works of penance ourselves in
order to receive all the benefits of the satisfaction of Christ.

SCRIPTURE: "If anyone does not abide in me, he shall be cast outside as the
branch and wither; and they shall gather them up and cast them into the fire,
and they shall burn" (*John 15:6*).

"But if anyone build upon this foundation, gold, silver, precious stones, wood,
hay, straw—the work of each will be made manifest, for the day the Lord will
declare it, since the day is to be revealed in fire. The fire will assay the quality
of everyone's work: if his work abides which he has built thereon, he will
receive reward; if his work burns he will lose his reward, but himself will be
saved, yet so as through fire" (*I Corinthians 3:12-15*).

"But as for the cowardly and unbelieving, and abominable and murderers, and
fornicators and sorcerers, and idolaters and all liars, their portion shall be in
the pool that burns with fire and brimstone, which is the second death"
(*Apocalypse 21:8*).

422. Does the sacrament of Penance, worthily received, always take away all punishment?

The sacrament of Penance, worthily received, always takes
away all eternal punishment; but it does not always take
away all temporal punishment.

(a) The sacrament of Baptism takes away all punishment, temporal as
well as eternal, due not only to original sin but also to all actual sins
committed before Baptism.

(b) The sacrament of Penance, however, does not always take away all
temporal punishment due to sins committed after Baptism. The dispositions with which one receives the sacrament of Penance determine the
amount of temporal punishment which will be taken away.

SCRIPTURE: *See Scripture, question 420.*

423. Why does God require temporal punishment for sin?

God requires temporal punishment for sin to satisfy His
justice, to teach us the great evil of sin, and to warn us not
to sin again.

424. Where do we pay the debt of our temporal punishment?

We pay the debt of our temporal punishment either in this
life or in purgatory.

(a) We should do as much penance as we can in this life for our sins. Our
works of satisfaction in this life help us to merit greater glory in heaven.

(b) The debt of temporal punishment is paid in this life according to the
penance imposed and the devotion with which it is performed. The priest
is obliged to impose greater or less penance in proportion to the gravity
and number of the sins confessed.

SCRIPTURE: *See Scripture, question 421, I Corinthians 3:12-15.*

425. What are the chief means of satisfying the debt of our temporal punishment, besides the penance imposed after confession?

Besides the penance imposed after confession, the chief means of satisfying the debt of our temporal punishment are: prayer, attending Mass, fasting, almsgiving, the works of mercy, the patient endurance of sufferings, and indulgences.

SCRIPTURE: "Prayer is good with fasting and alms: more than to lay up treasures of gold. For alms delivereth from death: and the same is that which purgeth away sins, and maketh to find mercy and life everlasting" (*Tobias 12:8-9*).

See Scripture, question 420.

IMPORTANT TRUTHS ABOUT CONFESSION

Most persons outside the Catholic Church think that it is a very difficult thing to go to confession. The truth is that confession is one of the most consoling features of the Catholic religion. Catholics go to confession with the conviction that they are really telling their sins to God. The priest is present as God's representative, to give advice and encouragement, to settle doubts of conscience, to guide the penitent's future conduct, above all to forgive sins in the name of Christ Himself. Never, under any circumstances, even to save his own life, may he reveal a single sin of the penitent.

Sometimes we hear people say that it is enough to confess our sins to God, without having to tell them to another human being. To these persons we answer that since God Himself has commanded us to confess our sins to the priest, as His representative, we must obey God if we wish to receive the pardon of our sins.

With all these considerations before them, Catholics should not find it difficult to make a worthy confession, especially in view of the fact that they are always free to confess to a priest who does not know them. Surely, it is most unreasonable to conceal a mortal sin in confession. Such an act renders the confession useless. The sinner leaves the confessional still burdened with all the sins with which he entered and in addition with a new sin of sacrilege. He has the obligation of telling all the sins again; and if he has the misfortune of leaving this world without receiving the forgiveness of his transgressions, the sin which he was afraid to reveal to one person in private will be revealed to the whole world to his shame at the last judgment.

In the early centuries it was not unusual for Christians to make their confession publicly, before the entire congregation. Moreover, a very severe penance was often imposed in those times, sometimes lasting for several years. Nowadays the Church is far more lenient. The modern penance is generally a few prayers that can be said in a short time. Hence, we see the necessity of supplying for our debt of temporal punishment by works of self-denial over and above the sacramental penance. We need not practice the extraordinary deeds of mortification performed by the great saints; even the smallest deeds of self-denial, when we are in the state of grace, possess satisfactory value toward atoning for our debt of temporal punishment. And we can perform such works of satisfaction not only for ourselves but also for others, whether living or dead.

When a person realizes that he has been guilty of many sins and doubtless has a great debt of temporal punishment to pay, it is always better for him to make as much satisfaction as he can in the present life instead of deferring it to purgatory. For our satisfactory works in the present life, unlike our sufferings in purgatory, not only pay our debt of temporal punishment but also merit greater glory for us in heaven.

We should be very careful in preparing for confession to know exactly what sins we have committed, their particular nature, any circumstances changing their nature, and especially the number of times each has been committed. If we do not know the exact number of times, we should strive to know it as nearly as possible; or at least get an average number by the week or the day. Of course, strictly speaking, we are obliged to tell the number of our *mortal* sins only; *venial* sins can be confessed merely by specifying their nature without mentioning their number. Indeed, venial sins need not be confessed at all. Yet, it is advisable to inform our confessor how frequently we have failed even by venial sins.

RESOLUTION: Resolve never to keep back anything serious in confession; and if the temptation to do so enters your mind, remember that when confessing your sins in the sacrament of Penance you are speaking to God rather than to the priest.

STUDY HELPS

A. WORD SELECTION. (*Select the word or phrase in each parenthesis which most exactly and most completely fills out the sentence.*)

(1) If a person kills a priest he commits, in addition to the sin of murder, a sin of (sacrilege . . . perjury . . . blasphemy).

(2) An authorized priest for the sacrament of Penance is one who possesses not only the power of orders but also the power of (teaching . . . ruling . . . jurisdiction).

(3) The obligation of confessing our sins comes from (the law of Moses, the law of Christ . . . the law of the Church).

(4) If a person has forgotten a mortal sin in confession (he may not go to Holy Communion until he has confessed it . . . he need not worry about it any more . . . he may go to Holy Communion but he must confess it the next time he goes to confession).

(5) If a person overhears something said in another's confession (he may not speak of it to anyone . . . he may speak of it to the person who confessed it but not to others . . . he may speak of it to anyone).

(6) If a person neglects a light penance (he commits a mortal sin . . . he commits no sin . . . he commits a venial sin).

(7) A confessor (may reveal venial sins he has heard in confession but not mortal sins . . . may not reveal either venial or mortal sins under any circumstances . . . may reveal a penitent's sins to save his own life).

(8) In confessing venial sins (it is better not to mention the number . . . it is necessary to confess the number . . . it is advisable but not necessary to mention the number).

(9) The sacrament of Baptism received by one who has attained the use of reason (takes away all the debt of temporal punishment . . . takes away no temporal punishment . . . takes away some temporal punishment according to the dispositions of the recipient).

(10) If a person deliberately neglects to perform a penance received for mortal sins, though at the time he received it he intended to perform it (his mortal sins return to his soul . . . he commits a mortal sin but his forgiven sins do not return . . . he commits a venial sin

240

B. PROBLEMS AND EXERCISES. (*Answer the questions orally or write them as your teacher may direct*):

(1) Father Geoffrey, a priest from the Los Angeles Archdiocese, is visiting his relatives in Philadelphia for a few days. Ralph, the altar-boy who is to serve his Mass asks Father Geoffrey to hear his confession. Father Geoffrey excuses himself by saying that he is from another diocese and may not hear confessions in Philadelphia. During the Mass he is serving, Ralph is asking himself how it is that this visiting priest may say Mass in Philadelphia and yet not hear confessions. Explain the case to Ralph.

(2) Pierpont, a Unitarian Sunday School pupil, tells his Catholic friend Clarence that it is not necessary to tell his sins to the priest. Pierpont suggests that it is nicer and easier to tell them directly to God in the privacy of one's own home. What reply should Clarence make to his friend Pierpont? Does God need to be informed about our sins?

(3) By God's grace, Annuntiata, now in the graduating class of St. Bruno's school, has preserved her baptismal innocence. Venial sins and imperfections have been the only things she has had to confess in the years gone by. In her examination of conscience she has always been very exact; she was likewise been very exact in telling her sins by their names and the number of times she has committed them. In three or four sentences, please tell us whether or not you approve of Annuntiata's exactness. Give reasons for the statements you make.

(4) Cosmas is a deaf-mute. Generally he makes his confession to Father Thaddeus by means of the sign language. But Father Thaddeus is absent at the present time—in Europe. There is no other priest available, who understands the sign language. Write a short note to Cosmas telling him what to do.

(5) Wesley, a lad of 12, has lost his angelic innocence by wicked companionships with members of a bad gang down on the waterfront. His conscience has been bothering him for a long time. His mother keeps urging him to go to confession. Finally he decides to go, not to one of the parish priests, but to a foreign-language priest downtown. He will confess his sins in waterfront slang that he feels pretty sure the priest will not really understand. Has Wesley the right idea about the sincerity that is required for confession? Explain your answer.

(6) Sergius, a town bully, gives his own father a terrible beating, breaking his jaw, and knocking out four of his teeth. It happened when his father was trying to get him up for Mass on Sunday morning. Six months later Sergius goes to confession during a Mission. In telling this particular sin how must he confess it? Add an explanation to your answer.

(7) Rhea, an elderly lady, is burned seriously in a fire that destroyed her home. For 35 years she has been a careless Catholic, neglectful of the Sacraments and attendance at Mass. The chaplain at the hospital gives her the Last Rites. Because of her serious condition, and inability to speak much, the priest suggests, in a general way, that she be sorry for all the sins of her life, especially neglect of religion. He asks her to repeat in her heart the act of contrition he says aloud, he presses the crucifix to her lips that she may kiss it as an expression of her sorrow. After several weeks of careful nursing, Rhea emerges from the danger of death. Since her last

241

confession she has been guilty of only three venial sins—three acts of impatience. Is it enough if she confess only those three sins? Explain.

(8) Nine weeks ago, while making his confession, through fear Ernest kept back a mortal sin. He goes to confession every week with the members of his class. In the next seven confessions Ernest told truthfully and accurately all the new sins he committed each week, but said nothing about the sin concealed, the bad confession, or the unworthy Communion that followed both. Yesterday in his confession again he told truthfully all the new sins committed last week. Then he "slipped in" the big sin he concealed nine weeks ago, but he did not tell that he had kept it back in confession. Can a concealed sin of this kind be "slipped into" a later confession in this way? How is Ernest to straighten out things?

(9) There may be in hell Catholics who made worthy confessions during their lifetime but who unfortunately died as enemies of God. In eternity are they better off than they would have been had they never made those worthy confessions? Why?

(10) Evans, a Protestant boy, wants to know may a priest tell what he has heard in confession if thereby the priest could save his own life. What answer is to be given to Evans?

(11) Miranda, a girl in Junior High School, and all her classmates are brought to the church for their weekly confession. Miranda is assigned to Father April's confessional. She doesn't want to go to confession to him, but is afraid to attract notice by leaving her place to go to another priest. When her turn comes she says; "Father, please give me your blessing; I don't want to go to confession today." What do you think of her solution of the difficulty?

(12) During the school year, Ariel and his classmates, are taken over to the church regularly every week to make their confession. Ariel is in the seventh grade. Each Summer, during the ten weeks' vacation, Ariel also takes "a vacation from the Sacraments." Once Ariel graduates from the parish school, do you think he will be a 'regular' at the confessional and at the Communion rail? What is the reason for your opinion? What remedy for his ailment would you suggest?

(13) Clifton has a serious sin to confess, but he is very friendly with the priest, and is ashamed to tell him about it. That priest is the only priest in Clifton's home town. Saturday afternoon Clifton takes the bus to the next town and there makes his confession. Do you approve or disapprove of what he did? Give the reason for your answer.

(14) Alfred was a soldier in World War II, and several times before going into battle he received, together with the other Catholic soldiers of his regiment, absolution in a general way from the chaplain, after merely reciting the act of contrition, without confessing his sins according to their number and nature. Since returning from the war Alfred has been going to confession every month, but he never told the sins he had on his soul when he received general absolution from the chaplain, because, he says: "Since these sins were forgiven by the priest, why do I have to worry about them any more?" Can you enlighten Alfred regarding the obligation he still has to confess any mortal sins that were forgiven by the chaplain's general absolution?

242

How To Make a Good Confession

426. Before entering the confessional, how should we prepare ourselves for a good confession?

Before entering the confessional, we should prepare ourselves for a good confession by taking sufficient time not only to examine our conscience but, especially, to excite in our hearts sincere sorrow for our sins and a firm purpose not to commit them again.

(a) Respect for the sacrament of Penance requires serious preparation for its reception. Reverence in church, a careful examination of conscience, exciting sincere sorrow for our sins, and patience in awaiting one's turn to approach the confessional, are marks of respect for the sacrament.

427. How should we begin our confession?

We should begin our confession in this manner: Entering the confessional, we kneel, and making the sign of the cross we say to the priest: "Bless me, Father, for I have sinned"; and then we tell how long it has been since our last confession.

428. After telling the time of our last confession, what do we confess?

After telling the time of our last confession, if we have committed any mortal sins since that time, we must confess them and also any that we have forgotten in previous confessions, telling the nature and number of each; we may also confess any venial sins we wish to mention.

(a) In the confessional it is necessary to speak distinctly and loud enough to be heard by the priest, but not so loud that other persons standing or kneeling near the confessional can hear.

(b) A person should not attempt to offer excuses for himself; but he should mention those conditions or circumstances that increase or decrease his guilt.

(c) It is not necessary to mention acts that are not sins. It is not necessary, for example, to mention that one has eaten meat on a day of abstinence unless it was eaten deliberately with the knowledge that it was a day of abstinence. Nor is it necessary to mention that one has missed Mass on Sunday if one was seriously ill and could not go to Mass.

(d) Other persons should not be mentioned in confession unless it is necessary to indicate the species of sin. The faults or sins of others should not be mentioned. When it is necessary to refer to others in confession, their names must never be mentioned.

429. What should we do if we cannot remember the exact number of our mortal sins?

If we cannot remember the exact number of our mortal sins, we should tell the number as nearly as possible, or say how often we have committed the sins in a day, a week, a month, or a year.

(a) If we discover, after confession, that we have unintentionally accused ourselves of more sins than were committed, there is no need to make any further mention of it.

(b) If we discover, after confession, that we unintentionally omitted some mortal sins, or failed to state the exact species, or mentioned a smaller number than were actually committed, we must mention the fact in our next confession.

430. What should we do when we have committed no mortal sin since our last confession?

When we have committed no mortal sin since our last confession, we should confess our venial sins or some sin told in a previous confession, for which we are again sorry, in order that the priest may give us absolution.

(a) Even though we have already confessed a sin of our past life in a previous confession, we can again be sincerely sorry for it, especially if it is a mortal sin. This sincere sorrow is sufficient to enable the priest to give us absolution even if we confess only slight sins for which we do not have sufficient sorrow.

SCRIPTURE:
"Remember not the sins of my youth nor my offenses. According to thy mercy remember thou me, for thy goodness' sake, O Lord" (*Psalm 24:7*).

431. How should we end our confession?

We should end our confession by saying: "I am sorry for these and all the sins of my past life, especially for . . . "; and then it is well to tell one or several of the sins which we have previously confessed and for which we are particularly sorry.

(a) A general confession is one in which all sins told in previous confessions, either of our whole life or of a part of our life, are repeated.

(b) Sometimes it is necessary to make a general confession. If a person has made a bad confession, or several of them, he must repeat all mortal sins committed since his last good confession, even though he has told them in previous confessions.

(c) Sometimes it is advisable to make a general confession, for example, when a person is about to enter a different state of life, such as the married state, or the priesthood, or the religious life. A person should consult his confessor before making a general confession.

432. What should we do after confessing our sins?

After confessing our sins, we should answer truthfully any question the priest asks, seek advice if we feel that we need any, listen carefully to the spiritual instruction and counsel of the priest, and accept the penance he gives us.

(a) If, for some reason, it would be impossible or too difficult for us to perform the penance given by the priest, we should ask him to give us some other penance.

(b) If there is any matter of a spiritual nature that is bothering us, we should not hesitate to ask the priest for his advice.

433. What should we do when the priest is giving us absolution?

When the priest is giving us absolution, we should say from our heart the act of contrition in a tone to be heard by him.

SCRIPTURE: *Psalm 50 contains all the requisites of an act of perfect contrition.*

434. What should we do after leaving the confessional?

After leaving the confessional we should return thanks to God for the sacrament we have received, beg Our Lord to supply for the imperfections of our confession, and promptly and devoutly perform our penance.

SCRIPTURE: *Psalm 17 is a model prayer of thanksgiving.*

IMPORTANT TRUTHS ABOUT THE MANNER OF MAKING A GOOD CONFESSION

Well-bred persons are most exact in observing the rules of politeness. When they are in the company of others they are always careful to act according to the customs approved by society. Catholics too have certain rules of politeness which they are expected to observe in the performance of religious functions. However, there is a great difference between these rules and those adopted by people of the world. For the sole object of the courtesies of the world is to please human beings, while the purpose of the acts of politeness we practice in performing our religious duties is to please God. Whenever we take part in any function of the Church—whether it be assistance at Mass, or the reception of the sacraments, or participation in a procession or a special devotion—we should remember that we are in the presence of the King of kings, to do homage to Him; and this thought should inspire us to be most observant of all the rules of deportment that the particular function imposes on us.

There is no occasion better suited for testing our Catholic courtesy than the reception of the sacrament of Penance. Sad to say, there are some Catholics who show a great lack of respect and seriousness in the reception of this sublime sacrament. They walk into church, gazing around as if it were a theater. Instead of a reverent genuflection, they make a slight inclination and slouch into a pew. A minute or two suffices for preparation; then they approach the confessional, perhaps forcing their way ahead of others who had the first right. They make their confession in a careless, slipshod way, rendering if necessary for the priest to put a number of questions regarding the nature and number of their sins. The act of contrition is hastily mumbled; when they leave the confessional they say their penance as fast as possible and hasten from the church. Strange to say, many of these persons are most careful in obeying the rules of politeness when they are at some social function in a parlor or dining-room; but in the house of God they are ill-mannered and disrespectful.

The well-mannered Catholic shows from the moment he enters the church that he realizes he is in the presence of Our Divine Saviour. His genuflection is performed properly, the knee touching the floor. His preparation for confession is careful and exact, without being scrupulous. He makes a fervent act of contrition, and waits his turn to enter the confessional. He confesses his sins exactly and sincerely but without unnecessary details. The confessor has no difficulty with his confession; he gives him some advice, which is attentively received, and imparts absolution while the penitent humbly and fervently repeats his act of contrition. On leaving the confessional he not only recites his penance but also spends some time in thanking God for having received the pardon of his sins and in begging strength to avoid sin in future. Such a Catholic

245

is conscious that in approaching the confessional he is really kneeling before Our Lord Himself to hear from His lips the words: "Thy sins are forgiven."

It may happen that after confession a person will forget what penance he has received. In that event he should return to the confessor and ask him to repeat it, if he can do so without much inconvenience. If, however, he would have to wait a considerable length of time or suffer some other grave inconvenience before he could again get to the confessor, he can consider himself free from the penance, though it would be advisable for him to say some prayers in satisfaction for his debt of temporal punishment.

RESOLUTION: Resolve that in going to confession you will carefully observe all the points brought out in this lesson.

STUDY HELPS

A. COLUMN SELECTION. *(Join correctly the parts of the sentences in Columns I and II, by placing the right key letter in the proper parenthesis.)*

I

(1) To await one's turn patiently in approaching the confessional (..).

(2) Other persons should not be mentioned in our confession (..).

(3) If a person unintentionally confesses more sins than he actually committed (..).

(4) If a person unintentionally confesses a smaller number of sins than he actually committed (..).

(5) If a person has made a bad confession or several of them (..).

(6) If a person is about to enter a new state of life (..).

(7) It is advisable (..).

(8) If a person thinks it too difficult to perform the penance imposed on him (..).

(9) If a penitent has difficulties of a spiritual nature (..).

(10) If a person cannot remember the exact number of his sins (..).

II

(A) there is no need to make any further mention of the matter.

(B) to perform our penance promptly after confession.

(C) he should tell the number as nearly as possible.

(D) he should seek advice from the confessor.

(E) he should ask the priest for another penance.

(F) he must make known the fact in his next confession.

(G) a general confession is necessary.

(H) a general confession is advisable.

(I) is a mark of respect for the sacrament of Penance.

(J) unless this is necessary to indicate the nature of a sin.

B. PROBLEMS AND EXERCISES. *(Answer the questions orally or write them as your teacher may direct)*:

(1) Justin, 12 years old, is playing in front of the church. Suddenly, he gets the bright idea to go to confession. He hasn't been there for more than three months. Discontinuing the play, he enters the church hurriedly, and out of breath, genuflects quickly, and goes straight into the confessional. What do you think about Justin's preparation for confession?

(2) Thecla has recovered from a serious heart ailment. She goes to confession after an absence of five weeks. While a patient in the Jewish hospital she missed Mass on four Sundays. Among her sins she accuses herself of missing Mass. What have you to say concerning her confession.

246

(3) Wallace, a careless Catholic, attending public school, has been away from the sacraments for nine months. He is making the confession for his Easter Duty Communion. In telling his sins he accuses himself this way: "I missed Mass lots of times; I ate meat on Friday many times etc." Point out the serious defect in Wallace's manner of confessing.

(4) Pearl is worried about the confession she made three days ago. She told the priest she stole two expensive rings and a valuable necklace; but she forgot to mention that she missed her Easter Duty. Is the sin of missing Easter Duty still on her soul? Explain your reply.

(5) Louis, who formerly was a very careless Catholic, is now changed for the better. He is somewhat upset on discovering that he did not tell the exact truth in his last confession. He confessed that he missed Mass twelve times; but it was only ten times. Advise him how to act.

(6) Annabelle is earnestly striving to be a saint. At her weekly confession she can't find any sin of the past week to confess. The nearest thing to sin that she remembers is that she spoke in church to an old man who asked her a question. So she confesses: "I spoke in church once. That's all, Father." Did she commit a sin in answering the old man? What do you suggest that penitents add to their confession when they have no new sins to tell, or only imperfections? Why?

(7) Vincent is about to enter an order of teaching brothers. He is making his confession before taking the habit. Must he make a general confession, or is a general confession only advisable.

(8) Next Saturday, Hedwig is going to be married to Innocent at a Nuptial Mass. Friday night both of them are going to confession. What kind of a confession do you advise them to make, their regular monthly confession, or a general confession? Why?

(9) Lester is a very nervous lad of fourteen. The thought of going to confession tortures him, yet he goes two or three times a week just the same. Nearly everything he thinks, says and does he considers as sinful. He goes from church to church, from priest to priest, seeking peace of mind. Most of the priests will not allow him to make a general confession. How can Lester get over this nervousness? Should he make general confessions? Give a reason for your answer.

(10) After every confession, Hilda, 11 years of age, goes directly to the Communion railing, and there before Our Lord in the Blessed Sacrament she recites her penance. Then she tells Our Lord how thankful she is for His kindness and forgiveness. Before leaving the church, Hilda kneels before the image of Our Lady, asking her to help Hilda stay good. Tell us what you think of Hilda's custom after confession.

(11) Seumas had to confess a long list of mortal sins. He thinks the priest has given him too difficult a penance,—the Stations of the Cross every day for a month. Afterwards, Seumas takes matters in his own hands and changes tne penance to one decade of the beads each day for that month. Is Seumas allowed to do that? Explain your answer.

(12) Sinon thinks the priest gave him a penance of only three Hail Marys. But he isn't sure. A large number of penitents are awaiting their turn to go to confession. Sinon must hurry home to run an important errand for his mother. So he decides to say 5 Our Fathers and 5 Hail Marys as his penance. What have you to say about his decision?

Temporal Punishment and Indulgences

435. What is an indulgence?

An indulgence is the remission granted by the Church of the temporal punishment due to sins already forgiven.

(a) An indulgence does not take away sin. Neither does it take away the eternal punishment due to mortal sins. An indulgence can produce its effects in the soul only after sins are forgiven and, in the case of mortal sins, only after their eternal punishment is taken away. Many who are not Catholic wrongly understand an indulgence to be a permission to commit sin, or a pardon for future sin, or a guarantee against temptation. By an indulgence the Church merely wipes out or lessens the temporal punishment due to sins already forgiven.

(b) The Church from the beginning has granted indulgences. Up to the sixth century indulgences generally took the form of a lessening of the public penances imposed for sins. In the early centuries it was customary for those who were to be martyred to ask that indulgences be granted to certain individuals.

SCRIPTURE:
"And I will give thee the keys of the kingdom of heaven; and whatever thou shalt bind on earth shall be bound in heaven, and whatever thou shalt loose on earth shall be loosed in heaven" (*Matthew 16:19-20*).
Also, read II Kings 24:1-25.

436. How many kinds of indulgences are there?

There are two kinds of indulgences, plenary and partial.

437. What is a plenary indulgence?

A plenary indulgence is the remission of all the temporal punishment due to our sins.

(a) A plenary indulgence is understood to be so granted that if a person should be unable to gain it fully, he will nevertheless gain it partially, in keeping with the disposition that he has.

(b) A plenary indulgence, unless it be otherwise expressly stated, can be gained only once a day, even though the prescribed work be performed several times.

(c) The conditions ordinarily prescribed for gaining the plenary indulgence and designated by the familiar phrase, "under the usual conditions," are the following: confession, Communion, a visit to a church or public oratory, or even a semi-public oratory in certain cases, and prayer for the intentions of the Supreme Pontiff.

(d) The confession which may be required for gaining any particular indulgences can be made within the eight days which immediately precede the day to which the indulgences are appointed; and the Communion may take place on the previous day; or both conditions may be satisfied on the day itself or within the following octave.

(e) The following are several examples of plenary indulgences that can be gained by all the faithful:

Those who piously recite a third part of the Rosary (five decades) in the presence of the Blessed Sacrament, publicly exposed or even reserved in the tabernacle, may gain a plenary indulgence, on condition of confession and Communion (*The Raccolta, No. 395, c*).

The faithful who with at least a contrite heart, whether singly or in company, perform the pious exercises of the Way of the Cross, when the latter has been legitimately erected according to the prescriptions of the Holy See, may gain a plenary indulgence as often as they perform the same, and another plenary indulgence if they receive Holy Communion on the same day, or even within a month after having made the Stations ten times (*The Raccolta, No. 194*).

The faithful who recite devoutly the prayer, "Behold, O good and sweetest Jesus" before an image of Jesus Christ Crucified, may gain a plenary indulgence under the usual conditions (*The Raccolta, No. 201*).

438. What is a partial indulgence?

A partial indulgence is the remission of part of the temporal punishment due to our sins.

(a) A partial indulgence, unless the contrary be expressly stated, can be gained frequently throughout the day, whenever the prescribed work is repeated.

(b) To say that an indulgence of so many days or years is granted means that the amount of temporal punishment is remitted which, in the sight of God, would have been remitted by so many days or years of penance in the early Church.

(c) God alone knows exactly how much of the temporal punishment is actually taken away by an indulgence.

(d) The following are some ejaculations and invocations to which partial indulgences are attached:

An indulgence of 500 days for saying the ejaculation: "Holy, Holy, Holy, Lord God of hosts: the heavens and the earth are full of Thy glory!" (*The Raccolta, No. 2*).

An indulgence of 300 days for saying the ejaculation: "My God and my All!" (*The Raccolta, No. 5*).

An indulgence of 500 days for saying the ejaculation: "O God, be merciful to me, the sinner" (*The Raccolta, No. 14*).

An indulgence of 300 days; a plenary indulgence under the usual conditions, if this invocation is devoutly recited every day for a month: "My Jesus, mercy!" (*The Raccolta, No. 70*).

An indulgence of 300 days; a plenary indulgence once a month under the usual conditions, for the daily repetition of: "O Sacrament most holy, O Sacrament divine! All praise and all thanksgiving be every moment Thine!" (*The Raccolta, No. 136*).

249

An indulgence of 300 days; a plenary indulgence once a month on the usual conditions, if this invocation is devoutly repeated daily: "O Mary, conceived without sin, pray for us who have recourse to thee!" (*The Raccolta, No. 357*).

439. How does the Church by means of indulgences remit the temporal punishment due to sin?

The Church by means of indulgences remits the temporal punishment due to sin by applying to us from her spiritual treasury part of the infinite satisfaction of Jesus Christ and of the superabundant satisfaction of the Blessed Virgin Mary and of the saints.

(a) In granting indulgences the Church exercises the power of the keys given to her by Christ.

(b) When the Church, by means of an indulgence, remits the temporal punishment due to sin, this action is ratified in heaven.

SCRIPTURE:

"But not like the offense is the gift. For if by the offense of the one the many died, much more has the grace of God, and the gift in the grace of the one man Jesus Christ, abounded unto the many. Nor is the gift as it was in the case of one man's sin, for the judgment was from one man unto condemnation, but grace is from many offenses unto justification. For if by reason of the one man's offense death reigned through the one man, much more will they who receive the abundance of the grace and of the gift of justice reign in life through the one Jesus Christ. Therefore as from the offense of the one man the result was unto condemnation to all men, so from the justice of the one the result is unto justification of life to all men. For just as by the disobedience of the one man the many were constituted sinners, so also by the obedience of the one the many will be constituted just. Now the Law intervened that the offense might abound. But where the offense has abounded, grace has abounded yet more; so that as sin has reigned unto death, so also grace may reign by justice unto life everlasting through Jesus Christ our Lord" (*Romans 5:15-21*).

"For there is one God, and one Mediator between God and men, himself man, Christ Jesus, who gave himself a ransom for all, bearing witness in his own time" (*I Timothy 2:5-6*).

"But if anyone sins, we have an advocate with the Father, Jesus Christ the just; and he is a propitiation for our sins, not for ours only but also for those of the whole world" (*I John 2:1-2*).

See Scripture, question 435, Matthew 16:19-20.

440. What is the superabundant satisfaction of the Blessed Virgin Mary and of the saints?

The superabundant satisfaction of the Blessed Virgin Mary and of the saints is that which they gained during their lifetime but did not need, and which the Church applies to their fellow members of the communion of saints.

441. What must we do to gain an indulgence for ourselves?

To gain an indulgence for ourselves we must be in the state of grace, have at least a general intention of gaining the indulgence, and perform the works required by the Church.

250

(a) Only baptized persons are capable of gaining indulgences.

(b) The state of grace is required for gaining an indulgence at least at the moment when the prescribed work is finished. Even a person in mortal sin, therefore, can begin to gain an indulgence, unless the prescribed work demands the state of grace, for example, Holy Communion.

(c) Since a general intention is sufficient to gain indulgences, it is well to express from time to time, especially in our morning prayer, the desire to gain all the indulgences attached to the prayers we shall say and to the good works we shall perform.

(d) To gain an indulgence the work required by the Church must be performed fully and according to the prescribed time, place, and manner.

442. Can we gain indulgences for others?

We cannot gain indulgences for other living persons, but we can gain them for the souls in purgatory, since the Church makes most indulgences applicable to them.

SCRIPTURE:

"Then they all blessed the just judgment of the Lord, who had discovered the things that were hidden. And so betaking themselves to prayers they besought him that the sin which had been committed might be forgotten. But the most valiant Judas exhorted the people to keep themselves from sin, forasmuch as they saw before their eyes what had happened because of the sins of those that were slain.

"And making a gathering, he sent twelve thousand drachms of silver to Jerusalem for sacrifice to be offered for the sins of the dead, thinking well and religiously concerning the resurrection.

"(For if he had not hoped that they that were slain should rise again, it would have seemed superfluous and vain to pray for the dead.)

"And because he considered that they who had fallen asleep with godliness had great grace laid up for them.

"It is therefore a holy and wholesome thought to pray for the dead, that they may be loosed from sins" (*II Machabees 12:41-46*).

IMPORTANT TRUTHS ABOUT TEMPORAL PUNISHMENT AND INDULGENCES

In the early days of the Church it sometimes happened that a person was condemned to endure a severe penance; but if he went to a Christian friend who happened to be suffering for the faith in prison, and this friend interceded for the penitent with the bishop, offering his own sufferings for the benefit of the penitent, the bishop would accept them and grant absolution to the penitent, This was the first kind of indulgence granted by the Church. It differed in many details from the type of indulgence with which we are familiar today; but the principal feature of an indulgence was present—namely, the offering of the satisfactions of one member of the Church for another through the ministry of the Church. Down through the centuries the Church has continued to use this power of transferring the satisfactory value of the works of some of her members to others, to obtain the remission of temporal punishment owed to God, thus putting into practice the right conferred on the rulers of the Church by Christ Himself, who said to the apostles and their successors, the bishops: "Whatever you shall loose on earth, shall be loosed also in heaven" (*Matthew, 18, 18*).

The enemies of the Catholic Church ridicule the idea of indulgences, and claim that they induce people to sin more freely. They charge also that indulgences have often been sold for money. To this we reply that indulgences rather induce people to give up sin, because one must be free from mortal sin before he can gain an indulgence. Moreover, although there have been abuses in the past in the matter of indulgences, that is no objection to the proper use of them. Any sacred thing can be abused by wicked persons, but it does not on that account cease to be sacred and beneficial.

Anyone who studies the Catholic doctrine of indulgences must admit that it is most reasonable. It simply means that God in His mercy will accept the satisfactory works of some members of the Church for the benefit of others. Even in human affairs this is a common practice. If one member of a family contracts a debt, and his brothers and sisters give him money to pay it, the creditor accepts the money and regards the debt as paid. God does the same when He accepts the satisfactions of His Divine Son and of the Saints in payment for the debt of temporal punishment due to other members of the Church.

The satisfactory value of the good works performed by members of the Church who have no need of it themselves goes into the spiritual treasury of the Church, and it is then distributed by those who exercise jurisdiction in the Church, the Pope and the bishops. The Pope is not restricted as to the amount of indulgences he can grant, though even he must have a reason for granting an indulgence, since he is only the dispenser, not the owner of the Church's treasury. Nowadays a bishop can grant an indulgence of 100 days, an archbishop 200 days, a cardinal 300 days.

Plenary indulgences are numerous, and the conditions are very easy. One can even gain several plenary indulgences in a single day, by performing various works, each of which has a plenary indulgence attached to it; and even though each may demand confession and Communion, a person need receive these sacraments only once for all the indulgences he can gain in one day. Moreover, the Church allows us to gain many indulgences for the souls in purgatory. There is one indulgence especially which manifests the love of our Church for the faithful departed. It is the indulgence which can be gained on All Souls' Day, November 2nd; and it can be gained from noon of November 1st, until midnight of November 2nd. During this time a person who has been to confession and Communion can gain a plenary indulgence for the poor souls every time he visits a church or public oratory and recites six times the Our Father, the Hail Mary and the Glory be to the Father. This is a special exception to the ordinary law of the Church according to which a plenary indulgence for the same work can be gained only once a day.

When one of the conditions for gaining an indulgence is a prayer for the intention of the Pope, it suffices to say once the Our Father, the Hail Mary and the Glory be to the Father, or some other equivalent prayer. But for a plenary indulgence that can be gained repeatedly on the same day by visiting a church and praying for the Holy Father, one must recite for each indulgence six times the Our Father, Hail Mary and Glory be to the Father.

RESOLUTION: Resolve that on every All Souls' Day you will gain several indulgences for the souls in purgatory, at least one for each deceased member of your immediate family.

STUDY HELPS

A. TRUE OR FALSE. (*Check each of the statements below as either true or false. The correct answers can be found in the previous portions of this lesson*).

TRUE   FALSE

(1) An indulgence of seven years means that a person will have seven years less to suffer in purgatory.   ....

(2) A person must be in the state of grace to gain a partial indulgence, at least when the prescribed work is finished. ....

(3) A plenary indulgence for a certain work can ordinarily be gained only once a day. ....

(4) A person can gain a plenary indulgence every time he makes the way of the cross, even several times the same day. ....

(5) We can transfer indulgences to other living persons if they are in the state of grace. ....

(6) A plenary indulgence takes away the eternal punishment for mortal sin. ....

(7) The Church uses the power of the keys in granting an indulgence. ....

(8) Any bishop can grant a plenary indulgence. ....

(9) An unbaptized person preparing for Baptism can gain indulgences by saying indulgenced prayers. ....

(10) The Holy Communion which may be required for an indulgence can be received within eight days after the day to which the indulgence is assigned. ....

B. PROBLEMS AND EXERCISES. (*Answer the questions orally or write them as your teacher may direct*):

(1) Illustrate the first type of indulgence granted by the Church in the early days of her history.

(2) What essential feature of indulgence is found in present day indulgences and in the type of indulgence found in the early Christian Church?

(3) Thomasine, a buyer in one of the big department stores, comes to the rescue of her brother Reginald who is heavily in debt. She pays his bills and thereby calls off his creditors. Explain why this example is a good illustration of the doctrine of indulgences.

(4) What is remarkable about the indulgence that may be gained for the Poor Souls around the beginning of November? Over what period of time may this indulgence be gained on that annual occurrence? How often may it be gained? How many Paters, Aves and Glorias must be said each time?

(5) Dorinda, a Jewess, Lucretia, a Catholic, and Jemimah, a Protestant all work in the same office. They are lunching together in a cafeteria opposite a Catholic church. On All Soul's Day they notice crowds of people entering and leaving the church, some of them reentering again immediately. Dorinda asks Lucretia what is going on. Lucretia explains that indulgences are being gained for the Poor Souls in Purgatory. Jemimah remarks: "Indulgences! Aren't they permissions to commit sin!" Dorinda says: "No; indulgences are acts that forgive sins, isn't that right, Lucretia?" What answer is Lucretia to make?

(6) Eamon and Constantine are arguing about the meaning of an indulgence of seven years. Eamon, mathematically inclined, figures out

that the indulgence amounts to 2557 days, and claims that one's purgatory is shortened by that amount of time. Constantine says that is not
the idea, but regretfully admits that he has forgotten what the real
explanation is. What is the correct explanation?

(7) After Holy Communion, Natalia recites the crucifix prayer,
"Behold, O kind and most sweet Jesus, etc." for the purpose of gaining a
plenary indulgence. She is sorry for all her mortal sins, and for most of
her venial sins. Does she gain the plenary indulgence? If not, does she
gain any indulgence?

(8) Theodore is trying to gain a plenary indulgence. In praying for
the Holy Father's intention, Theodore recites the "Confiteor" and the
"Apostles' Creed." Does he fulfill that condition? Zaccheus, his brother,
recites the Acts of Faith, Hope, and Charity. Does he satisfy the require-
ment? Florence, their sister, says an Our Father, a Hail Mary, and a
Glory be to the Father. Does she satisfy the demand? Explain.

(9) Myra, anxious to gain a certain plenary indulgence, performed all
the requirements on September the 8th, Our Blessed Lady's birthday;
but she did not go to Communion, the reception of which is required,
for the gaining of the indulgence, until September 15th, the feast of Our
Lady of Sorrows, the feast of her Seven Dolors. Did that delay prevent
Myra from gaining the indulgence?

(10) Althea, her sister, performed all the requirements on September
8th, but her Holy Communion was not received until September 24th, the
Feast of Our Lady of Mercy. Did she fulfill the conditions for the plenary
indulgence? Explain your answer.

(11) Leonore, on All Souls' day, makes seven visits to the parish
church to gain plenary indulgences for her father and mother, her big
brother Gregory and his wife Amabel, her little brother Edgar, herself,
and the only deceased member of the family, her baby sister Nora who
died two weeks after she was baptized. What is your comment about
Leonore's understanding of these indulgences and their application?

(12) Norbert served Mass for a visiting cardinal in the parish church
one morning, and afterward the cardinal said to him: "I am going to
grant you as large an indulgence as I can, because you served Mass so
devoutly." How many days' indulgence did the cardinal grant Norbert?

(13) Fr. Gregory asked the children of the Sunday school if they had
ever heard of the Heroic Act. Apparently nobody had ever heard of it,
so Fr. Gregory explained that a person makes the Heroic Act when he
gives the souls in purgatory all the indulgences he gains, and all the
satisfactory value of his good works, including whatever may be applied
to him after his death. Why is this act called heroic? Why do you think
it is very pleasing to God?

(14) Every morning Seraphinus makes an offering of all the indulgences
that he may gain in the course of the day for the poor souls in purgatory.
Every day he frequently recites, at least mentally, such prayers as:
"My Jesus, mercy" . . . "My God and my all" . . . "Jesus, Mary and
Joseph." What do you think of this custom of Seraphinus? Would it
be commendable for all Catholics to adopt it?

Extreme Unction and Holy Orders

443. What is Extreme Unction?

Extreme Unction is the sacrament which, through the anointing with blessed oil by the priest, and through his prayer, gives health and strength to the soul and sometimes to the body when we are in danger of death from sickness, accident, or old age.

(a) In administering Extreme Unction the priest anoints the eyes, the ears, the nostrils, the lips, the hands, and, if convenient, the feet of the sick person. When the priest judges that there is not sufficient time for multiple anointings, he can administer this sacrament by a single anointing on the forehead.

(b) While anointing the different senses the priest says the prayer: "Through this holy anointing, and His most tender mercy, may the Lord forgive you whatever sins you may have committed by sight" (by hearing, etc.).

SCRIPTURE:

"And going forth, they preached that men should repent, and they cast out many devils, and anointed with oil many sick people, and healed them" (*Mark 6:12-13*).

"Is any one among you sick? Let him bring in the presbyters of the Church, and let them pray over him, anointing him with oil in the name of the Lord. And the prayer of faith will save the sick man, and the Lord will raise him up, and if he be in sins, they shall be forgiven him" (*James 5:14-15*).

444. Who should receive Extreme Unction?

All Catholics who have reached the use of reason and are in danger of death from sickness, accident, or old age should receive Extreme Unction.

(a) A person does not actually have to be dying in order to receive Extreme Unction.

(b) Ordinarily, those who are in danger of death should be advised of their condition. It is false mercy to keep them ignorant of the fact that they may soon face God, their just Judge.

(c) Those who are in danger of death should welcome the sacrament of Extreme Unction. It cannot harm them, and it often helps them physically.

445. What are the effects of the sacrament of Extreme Unction?

The effects of the sacrament of Extreme Unction are:

first, an increase of sanctifying grace;

second, comfort in sickness and strength against temptation;

255a

Extreme Unction

This picture shows a sick person to whom an Apostle is administering the sacrament of Extreme Unction. Above, an angel holds a banner with the words that St. James wrote to the early Christians, "Is any one among you sick? Let him bring in the presbyters of the Church, and let them pray over him, anointing him with oil in the name of the Lord.... The Lord will raise him up, and if he be in sins, they shall be forgiven him." (St. James 5:14-15) Another angel points to heaven with his hand and holds a crown in the other.

255c

The Death of a Just Man
and the Death of a Sinner

This picture shows the death of a just man and the death of a sinner. On top is the just man on his bed of agony, resigned and receiving the last consolations of religion. His guardian angel watches over him and encourages him. His relatives are praying for him. Jesus Christ and the Holy Virgin watch him from heaven and extend their arms towards him. The demon, full of rage and shame, flees to hell.

At the bottom, the dying sinner refuses the priest with contempt. His guardian angel covers his face and departs in sorrow. Before leaving, the priest shows him the crucifix one more time. His relatives are full of dismay and dread. Jesus Christ appears to him and shows him the Cross on which He died to save him and before which He will judge him. The demons surround his bed and wait for the moment when he will breathe his last breath so that they can take possession of his soul.

third, preparation for entrance into heaven by the remission of our venial sins and the cleansing of our souls from the remains of sin;

fourth, health of body when it is good for the soul.

(a) The remains of sin cleansed by Extreme Unction are the spiritual weakness and indifference caused by original or actual sin.

(b) Extreme Unction does not always restore or improve the health of the body. Nor does Extreme Unction effect miraculous cures. But just as God produces spiritual effects through the sacraments, so He often produces the bodily effects of better health through Extreme Unction.

SCRIPTURE: *See Scripture, question 443, James 5:14-15.*

446. When does Extreme Unction take away mortal sin?

Extreme Unction takes away mortal sin when the sick person is unconscious or otherwise unaware that he is not properly disposed, but has made an act of imperfect contrition.

447. How should we prepare ourselves to receive Extreme Unction?

We should prepare ourselves to receive Extreme Unction by a good confession, by acts of faith, hope, charity, and, especially, by resignation to the will of God.

SCRIPTURE:

"My son, in thy sickness, neglect not thyself: but pray to the Lord and he shall heal thee. Turn away from sin and order thy hands aright: and cleanse thy heart from all offense" (*Ecclesiasticus 38:9-10*).

Also, read Luke 22:41-42; and John 21:15-17.

448. Who can administer Extreme Unction?

Only a priest can administer Extreme Unction.

449. When is it advisable to call the priest to visit the sick?

It is advisable to call the priest to visit the sick in any serious illness, even though there be no apparent danger of death, as it is the duty of the priest to visit the sick and to administer to them the sacraments they need.

(a) The following preparations should be made in the home when the priest visits the sick to administer Holy Communion or the last sacraments:

first, in the room of the sick person there should be a small table covered with a clean linen cloth. On the table there should be a crucifix, two blessed candles lighted, holy water, and a spoon;

second, if the priest is bearing the Holy Eucharist, he should be met at the door with a lighted candle. The candle-bearer should genuflect and precede the priest to the sickroom, where all present should kneel. After the priest has sprinkled the room with holy water, if the sick person's confession is to be heard, all should leave the room and return and kneel when the confession is finished.

SCRIPTURE: *See Scripture, question 443, James 5:14-15.*

450. In case of sudden or unexpected death, should a priest be called?

In case of sudden or unexpected death a priest should be called always, because absolution and Extreme Unction can be given conditionally for some time after apparent death.

(a) We are not certain of the moment when the soul leaves the body; the soul may remain united to the body for some time after apparent death. The sacraments of Penance and Extreme Unction can be administered conditionally for several hours after signs of life have ceased, because of the possibility that the soul may still be united with the body.

451. What is Holy Orders?

Holy Orders is the sacrament through which men receive the power and grace to perform the sacred duties of bishops, priests, and other ministers of the Church.

(a) The distinction between clergy and laity is of divine origin, for

first, Christ chose the twelve apostles from among His disciples; and in a special way deputed and consecrated them for the exercise of spiritual ministrations; and

second, the apostles, who could not mistake the will of Christ, administered the sacrament of Holy Orders by consecrating bishops and by ordaining priests and deacons.

(b) A bishop is a priest who has received the fullness of Holy Orders, which gives him the power of administering the sacrament of Holy Orders, and makes him the ordinary minister of the sacrament of Confirmation.

(c) The other orders of ministers of the Church below those of priest are the major orders of deacon and subdeacon, and the four minor orders of acolyte, exorcist, lector or reader, and porter.

(d) Before a man receives Holy Orders he is constituted a member of the clerical state through the ceremony of tonsure in which hair is cut from his head in the form of a cross while he recites a verse from the Psalms to signify that he has dedicated himself to the service of God.

(e) A cardinal is a priest or bishop belonging to the group that has been especially selected to advise and assist the Pope in the government of the Church. Cardinals have the right of electing a new Pope after the death of the reigning Pontiff. Formerly even laymen were elevated to the cardinalate.

(f) An abbot is a priest who exercises over a religious community of men jurisdiction which is similar in some respects to that exercised by a bishop over his diocese.

(g) A vicar general is a priest appointed by a bishop to help him in the government of his diocese, and for this purpose he shares the bishop's power of jurisdiction.

SCRIPTURE:
"And having taken bread, he gave thanks and broke, and gave it to them, saying, 'This is my body, which is being given for you; do this in remembrance of me.' In like manner he took also the cup after the supper, saying, 'This cup is the new covenant in my blood, which shall be shed for you' " (*Luke 22:19-20*).

257

"And the plan met the approval of the whole multitude, and they chose Stephen, a man full of faith and of the Holy Spirit, and Philip and Prochorus and Nicanor and Timon and Parmenas and Nicholas, a proselyte from Antioch. These they set before the apostles, and after they had prayed they laid their hands upon them" (*Acts 6:5-6*).

"Take heed to yourselves and to the whole flock in which the Holy Spirit has placed you as bishops, to rule the Church of God, which he has purchased with his own blood" (*Acts 20:28*).

"I commit to thee this charge, my son Timothy, that according to the prophecies once made concerning thee, thou mayest fight the good fight by means of them, having faith and a good conscience" (*I Timothy 1:18-19*).

"This saying is true: If anyone is eager for the office of bishops, he desires a good work. A bishop then, must be blameless, married but once, reserved, prudent, of good conduct, hospitable, a teacher, not a drinker or a brawler, but moderate, not quarrelsome, not avaricious. He should rule well his own household, keeping his children under control and perfectly respectful. For if a man cannot rule his own household, how is he to take care of the church of God? He must not be a new convert, lest he be puffed up with pride and incur the condemnation passed on the devil. Besides this he must have a good reputation with those who are outside, that he may not fall into disgrace and into a snare of the devil.

"Deacons also must be honorable, not double-tongued, not given to much wine, not greedy for base gain, but holding the mystery of faith in a pure conscience. And let them first be tried, and if found without reproach let them be allowed to serve. In like manner let the women be honorable, not slanderers, but reserved, faithful in all things. Deacons should be men who have been married but once, ruling well their children and their own households. And those who have fulfilled well this office will acquire a good position and great confidence in the faith that is in Christ Jesus" (*I Timothy 3:1-13*).

"Do not neglect the grace that is in thee, granted to thee by reason of prophecy with the laying on of hands of the presbyters. Meditate on these things; give thyself entirely to them, that thy progress may be manifest to all. Take heed to thyself and to thy teaching, be earnest in them. For in so doing thou wilt save both thyself and those who hear thee" (*I Timothy 4:14-16*).

"Let the presbyters who rule well be held worthy of double honor, especially those who labor in the word and in teaching" (*I Timothy 5:17*).

"Do not lay hands hastily upon anyone, and do not be a partner in other men's sins" (*I Timothy 5:22*).

"For this reason I admonished thee to stir up the grace of God which is in thee by the laying on of my hands" (*II Timothy 1:6*).

"For this reason I left thee in Crete, that thou shouldst set right anything that is defective and shouldst appoint presbyters in every city, as I myself directed thee to do. They must be blameless, married but once, having believing children who are not accused of impurity or disobedience. For a bishop must be blameless as being the steward of God, not proud, or ill-tempered, or a drinker, or a brawler, or greedy for base gain; but hospitable, gentle, reserved, just, holy, continent; holding fast the faithful word which is in accordance with the teaching, that he may be able both to exhort in sound doctrine and to confute opponents" (*Titus 1:5-9*).

"For every high priest taken from among men is appointed for men in the things pertaining to God, that he may offer gifts and sacrifices for sins. He is able to have compassion on the ignorant and erring, because he himself also is beset with weakness, and by reason thereof is obliged to offer for sins, as on

258

behalf of the people, so also for himself. And no man takes the honor to himself; he takes it who is called by God, as Aaron was" (*Hebrews 5:1-4*).

"For every high priest is appointed to offer gifts and sacrifices" (*Hebrews 8:3*).

"Now I exhort the presbyters among you — I, your fellow-presbyter and witness of the sufferings of Christ, the partaker also of the glory that is to be revealed in time to come — tend the flock of God which is among you, governing not under constraint, but willingly, according to God; nor yet for the sake of base gain, but eagerly; nor yet as lording it over your charges, but becoming from the heart a pattern to the flock. And when the Prince of the shepherds appears, you will receive the unfading crown of glory.

"Likewise, you who are younger, be subject to the presbyters. And all of you practice humility towards one another; for,
   'God resists the proud,
     but gives grace to the humble' " (*I Peter 5:1-5*).

452. What are some of the requirements that a man may receive Holy Orders worthily?

That a man may receive Holy Orders worthily it is necessary:

first, that he be in the state of grace and be of excellent character;

second, that he have the prescribed age and learning;

third, that he have the intention of devoting his life to the sacred ministry;

fourth, that he be called to Holy Orders by his bishop.

(a) Some of the preliminary signs of a vocation to the priesthood are:

first, that the boy or young man be capable of living habitually in the state of grace;

second, that he be attracted to the priesthood and manifest this attraction by frequent confession and Communion, by a virtuous life, and by a love of serving Mass.

(b) Those who are called by God to be priests ordinarily receive no special revelation to this effect. God expects all to use the gifts of reason and of grace in determining their state of life.

(c) Without a special dispensation no one may be ordained a priest until he is twenty-four years of age. Ordinarily the prescribed learning consists of four years of high school, four years of college, and four years of theology completed in a seminary.

(d) The sacred ministry of the priesthood can be exercised either as a diocesan priest under a bishop, or as a member of a religious community under a religious superior. Priests of religious orders make the vows of poverty, chastity, and obedience. Diocesan priests bind themselves to chastity for life and make a solemn promise of obedience to their bishop.

SCRIPTURE:
"And the Lord spoke to Moses, saying: This is the law of the Levites: From twenty-five years old and upwards, they shall go in to minister in the tabernacle of the covenant" (*Numbers 8:23-24*).

"For the lips of the priest shall keep knowledge, and they shall seek the law at his mouth: because he is the angel of the Lord of hosts" (*Malachias 2:7*).

259a

Holy Orders

The center of this picture shows St. Peter giving the sacrament of Holy Orders to the first seven deacons. This is the occasion on which the diaconate was instituted. Since the number of the first Christians grew each day, the Apostles were unable to fulfil all their functions alone. Therefore, they had seven deacons elected by the assembly of the faithful. The deacons were to be in charge of distributing alms. Those who were elected were led to the Apostles who, "praying over them, imposed their hands upon them" and thus conferred upon them the diaconate.

The power to carry out the ecclesiastical functions came from the Apostles to us by an uninterrupted succession of bishops which will continue until the end of time.

The episcopacy is not an order; rather, it is the fullness of the priesthood. It confers upon those who receive it the power to administer all the sacraments, in particular Confirmation and Holy Orders.

There are seven different orders in the Church: four minor orders and three major orders.

The four minor orders are those of porter, lector, exorcist, and acolyte.

The function of the porter is to open and to shut the doors of the church. At the top far left, a bishop is conferring the order of porter. He has the candidate touch the keys of the church while pronouncing the words which give him the custody of the keys.

Immediately to the right, a bishop is conferring the order of lector, whose function is to read aloud the Old and New Testaments in the church. He has him touch the Missal while pronouncing the words which give him the power to read the word of God.

In the third scene, a bishop is conferring the order of exorcist, whose function is to drive the demon from the bodies of the possessed. He has the candidate touch the book of exorcism, giving him the power to impose hands upon the possessed.

In the right corner, a bishop is conferring the order of acolyte, whose function is to serve the sacred ministers at the altar. He has the candidate touch a candlestick and candle and then the empty cruets and gives him the power to light the candles of the church and to give the wine and water during the Mass.

In the lower left corner, a bishop is conferring the order of subdeacon, whose functions are to serve the deacon at the altar and to sing the Epistle. He has the candidate touch the paten and the book of the Epistles, giving him the power to read it in the church. The sub-deacon is obliged to keep perpetual chastity and to recite the Divine Office every day.

In the lower right corner, a bishop is conferring the order of deacon, whose functions are to serve the priest at Mass, to sing the Gospel, to preach, and to baptize. The bishop imposes his hands upon the candidate while saying, "Receive the Holy Spirit that you may have the strength to resist the demon and his temptations."

In the center of the lower panel, a bishop is ordaining priests. A priest's function is to say the Holy Mass, to preach, and to administer the sacraments. The bishop imposes his hands upon each candidate, as do all the priests who are present, anoints his hands with Holy Oil, and has him touch a chalice containing some wine, and a paten with a host. At the same time, the bishop says to him, "Receive the power to offer sacrifice to God and to celebrate the Mass for the living and the dead."

"Let women keep silence in the churches, for it is not permitted them to speak, but let them be submissive, as the Law also says" (*I Corinthians 14:34*).

"Let a woman learn in silence with all submission. For I do not allow a woman to teach, or to exercise authority over men; but she is to keep quiet" (*I Timothy 2:11-12*).

See also Scripture, question 451, Hebrews 5:1-4.

453. What are the effects of ordination to the priesthood?

The effects of ordination to the priesthood are:

first, an increase of sanctifying grace;

second, sacramental grace, through which the priest has God's constant help in his sacred ministry;

third, a character, lasting forever, which is a special sharing in the priesthood of Christ and which gives the priest special supernatural powers.

SCRIPTURE:
"The Lord hath sworn, and he will not repent: 'Thou art a priest forever according to the order of Melchisedech' " (*Psalm 109:4*).

"On behalf of Christ, therefore, we are acting as ambassadors, God, as it were, appealing through us" (*II Corinthians 5:20*).

See Scripture, question 451, Luke 22:19-20; Titus 1:5-9; and Hebrews 5:1-4.

454. What are the chief supernatural powers of the priest?

The chief supernatural powers of the priest are: to change bread and wine into the body and blood of Christ in the Holy Sacrifice of the Mass, and to forgive sins in the sacrament of Penance.

SCRIPTURE:
"He therefore said to them again, 'Peace be to you! As the Father has sent me, I also send you.' When he had said this, he breathed upon them, and said to them, 'Receive the Holy Spirit; whose sins you shall forgive, they are forgiven them; and whose sins you shall retain, they are retained' " (*John 20:21-23*).

See Scripture, question 451, Luke 22:19-20.

455. Why should Catholics show reverence and honor to the priest?

Catholics should show reverence and honor to the priest because he is the repesentative of Christ Himself and the dispenser of His mysteries.

(a) In showing reverence and honor to the priest one shows reverence and honor to Christ Himself, for the priest in a very true sense is "another Christ." In this country it is the custom to honor priests by addressing them with the title "Father." The custom of tipping the hat to the priest is praiseworthy. The proper way to address a bishop and an archbishop is "Your Excellency"; a cardinal, "Your Eminence." The Pope is addressed as "Your Holiness."

SCRIPTURE:
"With all thy soul fear the Lord, and reverence his priests" (*Ecclesiasticus 7:31*).

"Pray therefore the Lord of the harvest to send forth laborers into his harvest" (*Matthew 9:38*).

"He who receives you, receives me; and he who receives me, receives him who sent me" (*Matthew 10:40*).

"And Jesus drew near and spoke to them saying, 'All power in heaven and on earth has been given to me. Go, therefore, and make disciples of all nations, baptizing them in the name of the Father, and of the Son, and of the Holy Spirit, teaching them to observe all that I have commanded you; and behold, I am with you all days, even unto the consummation of the world' " (*Matthew 28:18-20*).

"He who hears you, hears me; and he who rejects you, rejects me; and he who rejects me, rejects him who sent me" (*Luke 10:16*).

"You have not chosen me, but I have chosen you, and have appointed you that you should go and bear fruit, and that your fruit should remain" (*John 15:16*).

"Now I exhort you, brethren, through our Lord Jesus Christ, and through the charity of the Spirit, that you help me by your prayers to God for me" (*Romans 15:30*).

"Let a man so account us, as servants of Christ and stewards of the mysteries of God" (*I Corinthians 4:1*).

"On the contrary, let us conduct ourselves in all circumstances as God's ministers, in much patience; in tribulations, in hardships, in distresses; in stripes, in imprisonments, in tumults; in labors, in sleepless nights, in fastings; in innocence, in knowledge, in long-sufferings; in kindness, in the Holy Spirit, in unaffected love; in the word of truth, in the power of God; with the armor of justice on the right hand and on the left; in honor and dishonor, in evil report and good report; as deceivers and yet truthful, as unknown and yet well known, as dying and behold, we live, as chastised but not killed, as sorrowful yet always rejoicing, as poor yet enriching many, as having nothing yet possessing all things" (*II Corinthians 6:4-10*).

"Obey your superiors and be subject to them, for they keep watch as having to render an account of your souls; so that they may do this with joy, and not with grief, for that would not be expedient for you" (*Hebrews 13:17*).

456. Who is the minister of the sacrament of Holy Orders?

The bishop is the minister of the sacrament of Holy Orders.

IMPORTANT TRUTHS ABOUT EXTREME UNCTION AND HOLY ORDERS

There is no occasion in life when a person stands more in need of God's assistance and consolation than when his soul is about to take its flight into eternity. Remorse for the past, fear of what may lie before him, the last efforts of the devil to lead him into sin combine with his bodily weakness and pain to make those last hours on earth a time of dreadful anguish. Considering the tender mercy of Our Saviour, we should expect that He would have established a special means of aiding the souls of His faithful followers in that dread hour. Our holy faith tells us that Christ did this, by instituting the sacrament of Extreme Unction for those who are in danger of death from sickness or accident or even old age. There is no reference in the Gospel to the establishment of such a sacrament by Our Lord, though one may say that it was foreshadowed in the anointing of the sick by the apostles in the course of Christ's ministry (*Mark, 6: 13*). However, St. James speaks plainly of this sacrament, saying: "Is any one among you sick? Let him bring in the presbyters of the Church, and let

261

them pray over him, anointing him with oil in the name of the Lord. And the prayer of faith will save the sick man, and the Lord will raise him up, and if he be in sins, they shall be forgiven him" (*James: 5:14, 15*).

This sacrament is called "Unction" because it is conferred through the anointing or unction of the sick person; it is called "Extreme" or "Last" because it is usually given toward the end of a person's life, and also because it is the last of several unctions that the Christian receives in the course of his life, since he previously received anointings in Baptism and Confirmation, and if he is a priest or a bishop at Ordination.

This sacrament is intended to comfort the soul in the distress that normally accompanies weakened bodily powers; hence, it can be given only to one who is in danger of death from some cause actually afflicting his body. It cannot be given to one in danger of death from some cause that has not yet brought about serious bodily weakness—for example, to a soldier on his way to a dangerous battle or to a criminal about to be executed. From this standpoint Extreme Unction differs from the Holy Eucharist as Viaticum which is intended for everyone in danger of death, whatever may be the cause.

The sacrament of Extreme Unction, worthily received, confers noticeable strength of soul and courage on the sick person, so much so that even non-Catholics are astonished at the beneficial effects of this sacrament on the sick. Sometimes it produces restoration to bodily health; however, this effect can be expected only if the sacrament is given before the person comes so near to death that nothing but a miracle can save him. Therefore, Catholics should be glad to receive Extreme Unction whenever there is any danger of death from sickness or accident or old age; above all, they should rid themselves of the erroneous notion that once a person has received the last sacraments he is sure to die. Moreover, in every Catholic household there should be available all that is necessary for the ceremonies of the last sacraments—particularly, two blessed wax candles, a crucifix, holy water, and some cotton.

The sacrament of Holy Orders is mentioned in the Sacred Scriptures, especially in the Epistles of St. Paul to Timothy, in which the apostle refers to the ceremony by which he communicated the priestly power to Timothy: "I admonish thee to stir up the grace of God which is in thee by the laying on of my hands" (*2 Timothy, 1: 6*). Down through the centuries this ceremony has been used to transmit the powers that Our Lord gave to His apostles, to make men priests and bishops. The ceremony of ordination nowadays is more elaborate than in the early Church, yet the rites of laying-on of hands has always been used. We now know with certainty, by reason of a declaration of Pope Pius XII, that the ceremony by which the power and the grace of the orders of deacon, priest and bishop are conferred, is the imposition of the bishop's hands with the prayers that immediately follow. And so, the priests and bishops of today have received their supernatural powers from an unbroken chain of ordination ceremonies going back to the apostles, who received them from Christ Himself.

It is truly a wonderful privilege to be a priest; and any Catholic boy or young man who thinks that he has the qualifications for this sacred calling and a desire to serve God in this ministry should pray fervently that God may guide him aright in his choice of a state of life, and lead him to the priesthood if it be His holy will. However, no one should enter the priesthood for any human motive—for example to please his parents—but only out of the highest motive, to sanctify his own soul and to work faithfully for the spread of God's kingdom on earth.

RESOLUTION: Resolve to pray every day, particularly to St. Joseph, the patron of a happy death, that you will be granted the grace to receive the last sacraments when the hour of your death draws near.

A. WORD SELECTION. (*Select the word or phrase in the parentheses which most exactly and most completely fills out the sentence.*)

(1) Ordinarily a person receiving Extreme Unction is anointed on (three . . . six . . . seven) parts of the body.

(2) When the priest administers Extreme Unction with a single anointing he generally anoints the sick person's (lips . . . hands . . . forehead).

(3) To receive Extreme Unction a person must be (in probable danger of death . . . very close to death . . . certainly dying).

(4) Extreme Unction takes away mortal sin (when the sick person would be sorry for it if he were conscious . . . when the sick person has made a bad confession . . . when the sick person is unaware that he is not properly disposed but has made an act of imperfect contrition).

(5) There are (two . . . four . . . six) minor orders.

(6) A man becomes a member of the clerical state (by receiving the clerical tonsure . . . by becoming a subdeacon . . . by becoming a priest).

(7) The priest in a diocese who shares the bishop's jurisdiction is called the (dean . . . vicar general . . . chancellor).

(8) Without a special dispensation a man may not be ordained to the priesthood until he is (twenty-one . . . twenty-two . . . twenty-four) years old.

(9) The proper way to address a bishop is (Holy Father . . . Your Excellency . . . Bishop).

(10) The ordinary minister of the sacrament of Holy Orders is (a bishop . . . an archbishop . . . a cardinal).

B. PROBLEMS AND EXERCISES. (*Answer the questions orally or write them as your teacher may direct*):

(1) As a rule, what is the first anointing we receive? The second? The last? In how many sacraments are Holy Oils used?

(2) Oswald, a newspaper reporter and a Catholic, watched the priest administer the last rites to a victim of an automobile smashup. He claims that the priest did not anoint the dead man's eyes, ears, etc., but dipped his thumb in the oil-stock, made a small sign of the cross on the victim's forehead, and then wiped it off with a small piece of cotton he had with him. Explain to the reporter what happened and why.

(3) Agnes says that Father Augustine anointed her grandmother yesterday. There seems to be nothing physically wrong with the venerable lady, now in her 82nd year. She doesn't leave the house, as a rule, but she isn't in bed, she walks around the house, reads the papers and her prayerbook, sews, and does a little of the housework too. Agnes is puzzled by what Father Augustine did. Explain the case to her.

(4) Andrew, in the eighth grade, is seriously ill with a blood-stream poisoning. He wants to receive the Last Sacraments; but his mother is frightened out of her wits by his request, and hesitates to send for the priest. She finally yields to his request, but only on condition that Andrew make his confession and receive Holy Communion. She doesn't want him to say a word about being anointed. What do you think of her attitude?

(5) Five Catholic boys go for 'a swim in a neighborhood pond. One of them, Wilfred, drowns. Matthew and Christian recover his body two hours later, and immediately begin first-aid efforts to revive him. Edmund goes to get a doctor. Should Gerald bother about getting a priest? Why?

(6) In serious accidents, crowds quickly gather, and then stand by idly. Should Catholics in the group concern themselves to find out if the victim is a Catholic? Why? If there is reason to believe that the accident victim is a Catholic, should they bother themselves to go for a priest, even if the person is considered dead? Why?

(7) Vergil, a Catholic, in a fit of despondency takes his own life. Harold, a Catholic neighbor, suggests that someone send for the priest right away; his wife Cora says that there's no use of sending for a priest when a person commits suicide. What is your opinion? Explain.

(8) Can dead people receive any sacrament? Explain your reply.

(9) What is the ceremony of the first tonsure? How many of the sacred orders have been received by the bishop of your diocese? By your pastor? By a subdeacon?

(10) Where are the future priests of your diocese being trained? Where do they receive their high schooling? Their college course? Their special training in theology?

(11) Stanislaus, an altar-boy, was helping the pastor to decorate the altar when two clergymen entered the sacristy. The pastor addressed one of them as "Your Excellency" and the other as "Your Eminence." To what ranks of the clergy did these two belong?

(12) Dolores had the great privilege of seeing her brother Francis ordained to the holy priesthood. Among the ceremonies she witnessed were the following: Francis prostrated himself on the ground while the Litany of the Saints was chanted, the bishop imposed his hands on the head of Francis and then recited some prayers, the bishop anointed the young man's hands with blessed oil, then the bishop placed in his hands a chalice and a paten with bread and wine. During which of these ceremonies did Francis become a priest?

(13) After the ordination Francis said to his sister: "This morning I received two great supernatural powers." Which powers?

(14) During the Holy Year Anna visited Rome with her parents and, with a number of other Americans, had an audience with the Pope. When the Pope passed along the line of kneeling people he spoke to Anna, asking her from what part of the United States she came. What title should Anna have given the Pope when she answered him?

(15) Kenneth was out walking with Cyril, a Protestant friend, when they met the pastor coming out of the church, evidently going on a sick-call. Kenneth tipped his hat; the priest bowed slightly but did not stop to talk. Later, Cyril asked Kenneth why he had shown to the priest this sign of respect. Kenneth replied: "First, because he represents Jesus Christ; second, because he was carrying the Blessed Sacrament to a sick person." Can you give Cyril a further explanation?

264

Matrimony

457. What is the sacrament of matrimony?

Matrimony is the sacrament by which a baptized man and a baptized woman bind themselves for life in a lawful marriage and receive the grace to discharge their duties.

(a) Though unbaptized persons can be truly married, only baptized persons can be united in the sacrament of Matrimony and receive the graces of this sacrament.

(b) God instituted marriage when He made Eve as a helpmate for Adam in the garden of Eden.

(c) We know from the constant tradition of the Church that marriage was made a sacrament by Our Lord sometime during His life on earth.

(d) The outward sign in the sacrament of Matrimony is the external expression by the man and woman of their mutual consent to give themselves to each other as husband and wife.

(e) The sacrament of Matrimony is administered by the contracting parties, each of whom confers the sacrament on the other.

SCRIPTURE:

"And God created man to his own image; to the image of God he created him. Male and female he created them. And God blessed them, saying: Increase and multiply, and fill the earth" (*Genesis 1:27-28*).

"And the Lord God said: It is not good for man to be alone; let us make him a help like unto himself.

"And the Lord God having formed out of the ground all the beasts of the earth, and all the fowls of the air, brought them to Adam to see what he would call them: for whatsoever Adam called any living creature the same is its name.

"And Adam called all the beasts by their names, and all the fowls of the air, and all the cattle of the field: but for Adam there was not found a helper like himself.

"Then the Lord God cast a deep sleep upon Adam: and when he was fast asleep, he took one of his ribs, and filled up flesh for it.

"And the Lord God built the rib which he took from Adam into a woman: and brought her to Adam.

"And Adam said: This now is bone of my bones, and flesh of my flesh; she shall be called woman, because she was taken out of man.

"Wherefore a man shall leave father and mother, and shall cleave to his wife: and they shall be two in one flesh" (*Genesis 2:18-24*).

"It was said, moreover, 'Whoever puts away his wife, let him give her a written notice of dismissal.' But I say to you that everyone who puts away his wife, save on account of immorality, causes her to commit adultery; and he who marries a woman who has been put away commits adultery" (*Matthew 5:31-32*).

"And there came to him some Pharisees, testing him, and saying, 'Is it lawful for a man to put away his wife for any cause?' But he answered and said to them, 'Have you not read that the Creator, from the beginning, made them male and female, and said, "For this cause a man shall leave his father and

mother, and cleave to his wife, and the two shall become one flesh"? Therefore now they are no longer two, but one flesh. What therefore God has joined
together, let no man put asunder.' They said to him, 'Why then did Moses
command to give a written notice of dismissal, and to put her away?' He said
to them, 'Because Moses, by reason of the hardness of your heart, permitted
you to put away your wives; but it was not so from the beginning. And I say to
you, that whoever puts away his wife, except for immorality, and marries another, commits adultery; and he who marries a woman who has been put away
commits adultery' " (Matthew 19:3-9).

"Now concerning the things whereof you wrote to me: It is good for man not
to touch woman. Yet, for fear of fornication, let each man have his own wife,
and let each woman have her own husband. Let the husband render to the
wife her due, and likewise the wife to the husband. The wife has not authority
over her body, but the husband; the husband likewise has not authority over
his body, but the wife. Do not deprive each other, except perhaps by consent,
for a time, that you may give yourselves to prayer; and return together again
lest Satan tempt you because you lack self-control. But this I say by way of
concession, not by way of commandment. For I would that you all were as I
am myself; but each one has his own gift from God, one in this way, and another in that" (I Corinthians 7:1-7).

See also John 2:1-10. Our Lord, by attending the marriage feast at Cana and
working His first miracle for the benefit of the bride and groom, thereby
sanctified the married state.

458. What is the chief duty of husband and wife in the married state?

The chief duty of husband and wife in the married state is
to be faithful to each other, and to provide in every way for
the welfare of the children God may give them.

(a) The duty of being faithful to each other means that the privileges of
husband and wife may be shared by them alone.

(b) Parents by the will of God have the primary right and obligation to
feed, clothe, shelter, and educate their children. This God-given right
may not be unjustly interfered with by any power on earth. Any law
which takes away or lessens this right and obligation is unjust.

SCRIPTURE

"Take heed to keep thyself, my son, from all fornication: and beside thy wife
never endure to know a crime" (Tobias 4:13).

"He that loveth his son frequently chastiseth him: that he may rejoice in his
latter end and not grope after the doors of his neighbors.

"He that instructeth his son shall be praised in him and shall glory in him in
the midst of them of his household.

"He that teacheth his son maketh his enemy jealous: and in the midst of his
friends he shall glory in him.

"His father is dead, and he is as if he were not dead: for he hath left one behind
that is like himself.

"While he lived, he saw and rejoiced in him: and when he died, he was not
sorrowful, neither was he confounded before his enemies.

"For he left behind him a defender of his house against his enemies, and one
that will requite kindness to his friends.

"For the souls of his sons he shall bind up his wounds: and at every cry his
bowels shall be troubled.

"A horse not broken becometh stubborn: and a child left to himself will become
headstrong.

266

"Give thy son his way, and he shall make thee afraid: play with him, and he shall make thee sorrowful.

"Laugh not with him: lest thou have sorrow, and at the last thy teeth be set on edge.

"Give him not liberty in his youth: and wink not at his devices.

"Bow down his neck while he is young, and beat his sides while he is a child: lest he grow stubborn, and regard thee not, and so be a sorrow of heart to thee. "Instruct thy son, and labor about him: lest his lewd behavior be an offense to thee" (*Ecclesiasticus 30:1-13*).

"You have heard that it was said to the ancients, 'Thou shalt not commit adultery'. But I say to you that anyone who so much as looks with lust at a woman has already committed adultery with her in his heart" (*Matthew 5:27-28*).

"Be subject to one another in the fear of Christ. Let wives be subject to their husbands as to the Lord; because a husband is head of the wife, just as Christ is head of the Church, being himself savior of the body. But just as the Church is subject to Christ, so also let wives be to their husbands in all things. "Husbands, love your wives, just as Christ also loved the Church, and delivered himself up for her, that he might sanctify her, cleansing her in the bath of water by means of the word; in order that he might present to himself the Church in all her glory, not having spot or wrinkle or any such thing, but that she might be holy and without blemish. Even thus ought husbands also to love their wives as their own bodies. He who loves his own wife, loves himself. For no one ever hated his own flesh; on the contrary he nourishes and cherishes it, as Christ also does the Church (because we are members of his body, made from his flesh and from his bones).

'For this cause a man shall leave his father and mother,
and cleave to his wife;
and the two shall become one flesh.'

"This is a great mystery—I mean in reference to Christ and to the Church. However, let each one of you also love his wife just as he loves himself; and let the wife respect her husband" (*Ephesians 5:21-33*).

"And you, fathers, do not provoke your children to anger, but rear them in the discipline and admonition of the Lord" (*Ephesians 6:4*).

"Wives, be subject to your husbands, as is becoming in the Lord. Husbands, love your wives and do not be bitter towards them" (*Colossians 3:18-19*).

459. Why does the bond of the sacrament of Matrimony last until the death of husband or wife?

The bond of the sacrament of Matrimony lasts until the death of husband or wife because Christ has said: "What therefore God has joined together, let no man put asunder."

(a) Once a man and woman are completely united in the sacrament of Matrimony, they remain truly husband and wife until the death of either of them. A separation, a divorce, or an attempted marriage with another person does not destroy the marriage bond.

(b) It is for the good of husband and wife, for the bodily and spiritual welfare of their children, and for the good of society that God has decreed that the marriage bond can be broken only by death.

SCRIPTURE:

"Do you not know, brethren (for I speak to those who know law), that the Law has dominion over a man as long as he lives? For the married woman is bound by the Law while her husband is alive; but if her husband die, she is set free

267

from the law of her husband. Therefore while her husband is alive, she will be called an adulteress if she be with another man; but if her husband dies, she is set free from the law of the husband, so that she is not an adulteress if she has been with another man" (*Romans 7:1-3*).

"But I say to the unmarried and to widows, it is good for them if they so remain, even as I. But if they do not have self-control, let them marry, for it is better to marry than to burn. But to those who are married, not I, but the Lord commands that a wife is not to depart from her husband, and if she departs that she is to remain unmarried or be reconciled to her husband. And let not a husband put away his wife.

"To the others I say, not the Lord: If any brother has an unbelieving wife and she consents to live with him, let him not put her away. And if any woman has an unbelieving husband and he consents to live with her, let her not put away her husband. For the unbelieving husband is sanctified by the believing wife, and the unbelieving wife is sanctified by the believing husband; otherwise your children would be unclean, but, as it is, they are holy. But if the unbeliever departs, let him depart. For a brother or sister is not under bondage in such cases, but God has called us to peace" (*I Corinthians 7:8-15*).

"A woman is bound as long as her husband is alive, but if her husband dies, she is free. Let her marry whom she pleases, only let it be in the Lord. But she will be more blessed, in my judgment, if she remains as she is. And I think that I also have the spirit of God" (*I Corinthians 7:39-40*).

460. What is meant by the unity of the sacrament of Matrimony?

By the unity of the sacrament of Matrimony is meant that the husband cannot during the life of his wife have another wife, nor the wife during the life of her husband have another husband.

(a) Because of the unity of the sacrament of Matrimony, any other sexual union during the life of either party is adultery.

(b) Laws which permit remarriage during the life of husband or wife are contrary to God's laws. Even though civil law may permit remarriage, such a marriage is sinful and not really a marriage at all, but rather an adulterous union.

461. Why is every true marriage between a baptized man and a baptized woman a sacrament?

Every true marriage between a baptized man and a baptized woman is a sacrament because Christ Himself raised every marriage of this kind to the dignity of a sacrament.

(a) Marriage by its nature is a contract. Marriage between baptized persons is a sacramental contract, that is, a contract which is also a sacrament.

SCRIPTURE: *See Scripture, question 457, Matthew 19:3-9.*

462. Why has the Catholic Church alone the right to make laws regulating the marriages of baptized persons?

The Catholic Church alone has the right to make laws regulating the marriages of baptized persons because the Church alone has authority over the sacraments and over sacred matters affecting baptized persons.

(a) Although the Catholic Church has the right to make laws regarding the marriages of all baptized persons, the Church does not in all cases bind baptized non-Catholics by these laws. Non-Catholics are bound by the laws when, for example, they marry Catholics.

SCRIPTURE:

"For what have I to do with judging those outside? ... For those outside God will judge" (I Corinthians 5:12-13).

See Scripture, question 137, Matthew 16:18; Matthew 28:18-20; also question 459, I Corinthians 7:8-15.

463. What authority has the State regarding the marriages of baptized persons?

Regarding the marriages of baptized persons, the State has the authority to make laws concerning their effects that are merely civil.

(a) By the civil effects of matrimony are meant the rights and obligations of husband and wife as citizens: for example, the right to a share in the property of the other.

SCRIPTURE:

"Then he said to them, 'Render, therefore, to Caesar the things that are Caesar's, and to God the things that are God's'" (Matthew 22:21).

464. What is necessary to receive the sacrament of Matrimony worthily?

To receive the sacrament of Matrimony worthily it is necessary to be in the state of grace, to know the duties of married life, and to obey the marriage laws of the Church.

(a) Matrimony is a sacrament of the living; therefore one must be in the state of grace in order to receive the grace of this sacrament.

(b) Even though one be not in the state of grace, a true marriage nevertheless is contracted.

(c) He who receives this sacrament in the state of mortal sin commits a mortal sin of sacrilege.

(d) It is customary for those who are to be married to go to confession shortly before the ceremony.

SCRIPTURE:

"For we are the children of saints; and we must not be joined together like heathens that know not God" (Tobias 8:5).

See Scripture, question 457, Genesis 2:18-24; Matthew 19:3-9; also question 458, Ecclesiasticus 30:1-13; Ephesians 5:21-33 and Ephesians 6:4.

465. In whose presence do the laws of the Church require a Catholic to be married?

The laws of the Church require a Catholic to be married in the presence of the parish priest, or the bishop of the diocese, or a priest delegated by either of them, and before two witnesses.

269a

Matrimony

In the center, St. Joseph is espousing the Holy Virgin in the presence of the high priest in the temple of Jerusalem. The flowering lily that St. Joseph is holding in his hand recalls the manner in which he was chosen to be the spouse of the Holy Virgin. When the Blessed Virgin Mary was old enough to be married, the high priest gathered the young men of the house of David who wished to marry her and gave to each one of them a blessed branch, ordering them to carve their names upon them. Then he put all the branches on the altar and prayed to the Lord to manifest His choice. When he took the branches from the altar, Joseph's alone was covered with leaves and a white flower similar to a lily. On the right is a young man who, upset at not having been chosen, breaks the branch that he received from the high priest.

At the top left, the young Tobias and Sara prepare themselves for marriage by fervent prayers. The angel Raphael is driving away a demon who had killed Sara's first seven husbands because of the bad dispositions with which they had entered marriage with her. The resolution that Tobias and Sara made to serve God in marriage obtained for them the protection of the angel.

At the bottom, two Catholics are marrying in the presence of a priest.

Above, on the right, is Adam, with Eve, whom God formed from one of Adam's ribs. God is blessing them, saying, "Be fruitful and multiply." (Genesis 1:28)

(a) The marriage of a Catholic before a minister or a civil official, such as a judge, a justice of the peace, a squire, or any clerk of court, is not really a marriage.

(b) Catholics who live together after such a marriage are living in sin just as much as if they had never gone through such a ceremony.

(c) Catholics who attempt marriage in this fashion commit a mortal sin and incur other punishments of the Church.

466. What are the chief effects of the sacrament of Matrimony?

The chief effects of the sacrament of Matrimony are:

first, an increase of sanctifying grace;

second, the special help of God for husband and wife to love each other faithfully, to bear with each other's faults, and to bring up their children properly.

467. What should Catholics do to prepare for a holy and happy marriage?

To prepare for a holy and happy marriage, Catholics should:

first, pray that God may direct their choice;

second, seek the advice of their parents and confessors;

third, practice the virtues, especially chastity;

fourth, frequently receive the sacraments of Penance and Holy Eucharist.

(a) Sinful and unhappy marriages frequently result from the company-keeping of Catholics with non-Catholics.

(b) Keeping company with those who, because of previous marriage or who for any other reason are not free to marry Catholics, ordinarily is a mortal sin.

(c) Catholics who are eligible and who intend to marry should keep company only with Catholics.

(d) The advice of parents and confessors should be sought, for they, more than anyone else, are interested in the welfare of those who intend to marry.

(e) Close association with those of the other sex causes many temptations. Those who are keeping company must be especially diligent in the practice of the virtues, especially chastity, which will lessen the danger of committing sin.

(f) Those who intend to marry will find in the sacraments of Penance and Holy Eucharist the most fruitful source of grace necessary to prepare themselves for a holy and happy marriage.

SCRIPTURE:

"O how beautiful is the chaste generation with glory, for the memory thereof is immortal: because it is known both with God and with men" (*Wisdom 4:1*).

"Or do you not know that your members are the temple of the Holy Spirit, who is in you, whom you have from God, and that you are not your own? For you have been bought at a great price. Glorify God and bear him in your body' (*I Corinthians 6:19-20*).

468. How can Catholics best obtain God's blessing for their marriage?
Catholics can best obtain God's blessing for their marriage by being married at a Nuptial Mass and by receiving Holy Communion devoutly.

(a) In a Nuptial Mass special blessings are asked for the bride and groom.

(b) When Catholics are not married at a Nuptial Mass they should arrange to receive the nuptial blessing at a later date.

(c) Catholics who for any reason cannot be married at Mass should receive Holy Communion on the morning of the wedding day.

SCRIPTURE:

For we are the children of saints: and we must not be joined together like heathens that know not God.

"So they both arose, and prayed earnestly both together that health might be given them.

"And Tobias said: Lord God of our fathers, may the heavens and the earth, and the sea, and the fountains, and the rivers, and all thy creatures that are in them, bless thee.

"Thou madest Adam of the slime of the earth: and gavest him Eve for a helper.

"And now, Lord, thou knowest, that not for fleshly lust do I take my sister to wife, but only for the love of posterity, in which thy name may be blessed for ever and ever.

"Sara also said: Have mercy on us, O Lord, have mercy on us: and let us grow old both togetuer in health" (*Tobias 8:5-10*).

IMPORTANT TRUTHS ABOUT MATRIMONY

Since marriage is one of the most important institutions in human life, it is most natural that Our Lord should have established a special sacrament for married couples. Our Catholic faith teaches us that Christ did so, making the marriage contract of baptized persons the sacrament of Matrimony. Accordingly, whenever two baptized persons are married, they receive this sacrament at the very moment when they make the marriage contract, whether or not they realize that it is a sacrament.

The end to which marriage is primarily directed is that children be brought into the world and properly reared for happiness in this life and in the next. Hence, when a married couple make use of their right to sexual union but perform the act in such a way that the conception of children is positively frustrated, they are guilty of a grave sin. This sin, known as contraception or birth control, is very common nowadays. It was severely condemned by Pope Pius XI in his Encyclical on Christian Marriage. Other purposes of marriage are the love and assistance that husband and wife mutually give and the opportunity of satisfying reasonably and lawfully the inclination to sexual gratification, which is so strong an impulse in human nature.

Just when Our Lord made Christian marriage a sacrament is not clear from Sacred Scripture; but from a text of St. Paul we can infer that Christ did raise marriage to this dignity. Writing to the Ephesians, St. Paul says that the union between a Christian husband and wife is a sign or symbol of the union between Christ and the Church (*Ephesians, 5, 21-33*). From this principle we argue that since the union between Christ and the Church is a supernatural union which produces grace, the union between husband and wife must also be a supernatural union giving grace to the couple—in other words, a sacrament. This doctrine is not indeed clearly stated by St. Paul, but our inference is fully confirmed by the tradition of the Church, which has always regarded marriage as one of the divine means of grace, especially blessed by Our Saviour, intended

271

to aid Christian husbands and wives to be faithful to God and to each other, and to perform exactly all the duties of their state of life.

Since Christian marriage is a sacrament, the Church possesses jurisdiction over the marriages of all baptized persons. The Church uses this authority especially by laying down marriage impediments—that is, by ruling that certain couples may not marry because of a prohibition arising either from the law of God or from the law of the Church. If a couple, bound by an impediment, attempted marriage without a dispensation from the Church, the marriage would be sinful though valid, supposing that the impediment was an impeding impediment, and both sinful and invalid, supposing that the impediment was a diriment impediment. The Church can give a dispensation from an impediment established by ecclesiastical law, but not from an impediment established by divine law.

The fact that a person has taken a private vow of chastity is an impeding impediment; the bond of an already existing marriage is a diriment impediment by divine law; the blood relationship between first or second cousins is a diriment impediment by ecclesiastical law.

Nowadays the state of marriage is degraded by many persons. They enter marriage hastily, with little thought of its sacred dignity, and with small regard for its obligations. After a few years they tire of each other, obtain a divorce and marry again. Sad to say, even some Catholics have not the proper concept of marriage, and though they may not go so far as to seek divorce, they try to rid themselves of the burdens of the married state, and selfishly refuse to live up to the obligations of this state, as God has established it. That is the reason for unhappiness in some Catholic homes.

It is the teaching of the Catholic Church that the marriage of two baptized persons, once they have used their right of sexual union, can never be dissolved except by the death of one of the parties. This rule holds for the marriage of baptized non-Catholics as well as for that of Catholics. In other types of marriage the bond can sometimes be broken with the consent or authority of the Church. There are three types of such marriages, which can be dissolved in exceptional circumstances: (1) If at the time of the marriage both of the parties were unbaptized, and later one receives Baptism and the other refuses to dwell peacefully and sinlessly with the convert. This is called the Pauline privilege. (2) If at the time of the marriage one was a baptized non-Catholic and the other an unbaptized person; (3) If at the time of the marriage both were baptized persons, but they never had sexual relations as husband and wife. Furthermore, sometimes the Church allows a husband and wife to separate or live apart, without having any right to remarry.

Before the marriage of a Catholic couple the law of the Church calls for the publication of the banns—announcements of the coming marriage—to be made in the parish of each of the parties on three Sundays or feast days. Then, if any one believes that they should not marry because of some impediment or other grave reason he should at once inform the authorities of the Church. Those intending to marry should make arrangements with one of the priests in the parish of the intended bride (where the ceremony should ordinarily take place) at least a month before the date of the marriage.

In a Catholic home where the husband and wife live according to the Christian ideals as proposed by the Catholic Church there is true contentment and happiness, even though material comforts and luxuries may be lacking. They bring up their children religiously, with the realization that God has sent them these little ones to be trained in His love and to become one day citizens of heaven. Such a Catholic home is truly an image of the home of Nazareth, in which dwelt the three holiest persons that ever lived on earth—the Holy Family, Jesus, Mary and Joseph.

RESOLUTION: Pray every day for your parents. If they are alive, ask God to help them to live up to their obligations of the holy state of Matrimony; if they are dead, pray that they may soon be admitted to the kingdom of heaven.

STUDY HELPS

A. COLUMN SELECTION. (*Join correctly the parts of the sentences in Columns I and II, by placing the right key letter in the proper parenthesis.*)

I

(1) A civil divorce or a marriage with another party (. .).

(2) Every marriage between baptized persons (. .).

(3) One who marries in the state of mortal sin (. .).

(4) The marriage of a Catholic before a civil official (. .).

(5) To keep company with one who is not free to marry a Catholic (. .).

(6) The marriage impediment between first cousins (. .).

(7) The marriage impediment of one who has taken a private vow of chastity (. .).

(8) The banns of marriage must be proclaimed (. .).

(9) The marriage of two unbaptized persons (. .).

(10) Those planning marriage should frequently receive (. .).

II

(A) can sometimes be dissolved by the Pauline privilege.

(B) is not a real marriage.

(C) is an impeding impediment.

(D) does not break the bond of marriage.

(E) is a diriment impediment:

(F) is a sacrament.

(G) the sacraments of Penance and the Holy Eucharist.

(H) is ordinarily a mortal sin.

(I) is guilty of sacrilege.

(J) in the parish of each of the parties.

B. PROBLEMS AND EXERCISES. (*Answer the questions orally or write them as your teacher may direct*):

(1) Archibald, a baptized Anglican, and Publia, a baptized Huguenot are married by Moses, a Jewish clerk of the Marriage License Bureau in City Hall. In this instance, has the sacrament of Matrimony been administered in City Hall? State the reason for your answer.

(2) What very happy and very holy family group furnishes the ideal or the pattern of the truly Catholic home?

(3) In the commentary on this lesson, the following are linked together: Christ and the Church, husband and wife, grace. What point is made in the paragraph, quoting St. Paul and the foregoing notions?

(4) Fidelis, Guy, and Malachy are Catholic boys in the sixth grade. They were asked to list five favorite movie actors and five favorite movie actresses. Of their 18 heroes and heroines, ten are persons who have been married, divorced, and remarried, some of them several times, and one of them five times. What conclusion do you draw about the wisdom of picking your ideals, your heroes and heroines from moviedom?

(5) Who were the first married couple? Where were they married? Who witnessed their marriage? Did they receive the sacrament of Matrimony? Supply the reason for your answer to this last question.

(6) Zachary and Ulrica, Catholic husband and wife and parents of two small children, have been quarrelling constantly for the past year. Some of Ulrica's friends are suggesting that she get a divorce and marry her first lover, Artemas, who still loves her; she gets a civil divorce. May she now marry Artemas? Please give the reason for your answer.

(7) When the pastor, Father Cyrus, announces the banns of marriage, he adds a remark to the effect that if anyone knows of any impediment to the marriage he is bound in conscience to report that impediment to the proper authorities before the marriage takes place. What does Father Cyrus mean by 'impediment' in this announcement?

(8) Eustace and Melissa, Catholics, are second cousins. They arrange for their marriage, but through ignorance, fail to mention the fact that they are related. Their wedding takes place at a Nuptial Mass. Have they received the sacrament of Matrimony? Explain your reply.

(9) Roy and Leah, Catholics, run away from home to be married. Late Saturday night they appear at the priest's rectory, to be married 'right away'. They grow very angry at the priest who explains to them that he will not marry them since they are without the necessary documents, etc. Were Roy and Leah justifiably angered?

(10) Rudolph and Bertha, a well-instructed Catholic couple, appear at the rectory to arrange for their marriage. With them they bring recently issued baptismal certificates, a marriage license, and a letter from Rudolph's pastor, stating that he is a member of his parish in good standing, and is free to marry Bertha. The pastor then states that he will announce the forthcoming marriage on the three Sundays prior to Rudolph's marriage. The marriage is six weeks off. Rudolph and Bertha wish to be married at a Nuptial Mass. They make two special appointments with the priest, the first, for an instruction on Catholic married life, and the other, to rehearse for the nuptial ceremony. In a paragraph of from 100 to 200 words tell us what you think of this couple's preparation. Contrast it with that of Roy and Leah, the angered, runaway pair.

(11) Emmanuel, a daily communicant and a member of the Third Order of St. Francis, has been married three times. Can that happen, and Emmanuel still remain a good Catholic? Explain your answer.

(12) Victor and Juliana, weekly communicants, have been keeping company for fourteen months. The parents of both have given their consent to the marriage and their approval of it. During the customary two or three visits each week, Victor and Juliana have been very honorable, very modest, and very respectful toward each other; since Victor gave Juliana the engagement ring both of them have been receiving Holy Communion every Sunday, and have been attending the weekly novena devotion in honor of the Blessed Virgin Mary. Their special intention is that they enter upon a happy and successful married career. In three or four sentences tell us why you think this pair, as man and wife, will receive God's special blessing.

The Sacramentals

469. What are sacramentals?

Sacramentals are holy things or actions of which the Church makes use to obtain for us from God, through her intercession, spiritual and temporal favors.

(a) These holy things and actions are called sacramentals because they resemble the sacraments in some ways.

(b) Only Christ could institute the sacraments; the Church has instituted most of the sacramentals.

(c) The sacraments are signs which contain the sanctifying and sacramental grace they signify; the sacramentals are signs but do not contain the graces they signify.

(d) The sacraments have within themselves the power to give grace to those who receive them with the right dispositions; the sacramentals do not have within themselves this power.

SCRIPTURE:

"And they marched from mount Hor, by the way that leadeth to the Red Sea, to compass the land of Edom. And the people began to be weary of their journey and labor:

"And speaking against God and Moses, they said: Why didst thou bring us out of Egypt, to die in the wilderness? There is no bread, nor have we any waters: our soul now loatheth this very light food.

"Wherefore the Lord sent among the people fiery serpents, which bit them and killed many of them.

"Upon which they came to Moses, and said: We have sinned, because we have spoken against the Lord and thee. Pray that he may take away these serpents from us. And Moses prayed for the people.

And the Lord said to him: Make a brazen serpent, and set it up for a sign. Whosoever being struck shall look on it shall live.

"Moses therefore made a brazen serpent, and set it up for a sign: which when they that were bitten looked upon, they were healed" (*Numbers 21:4-9*).

"And as Moses lifted up the serpent in the desert, even so must the Son of Man be lifted up, that those who believe in him may not perish, but may have life everlasting" (*John 3:14-15*).

See Numbers 19:1-22. In this passage God directed the Israelites to use material objects, i. e., ashes, and water of purification in the worship of the Old Law.

470. How do the sacramentals obtain favors from God?

The sacramentals obtain favors from God through the prayers of the Church offered for those who make use of them, and through the devotion they inspire.

SCRIPTURE: *See Scripture, question 469. Numbers 21:4-9.*

471. What are the chief benefits obtained by the use of the sacramentals?

The chief benefits obtained by the use of the sacramentals are:

first, actual graces;

second, the forgiveness of venial sins;

third, the remission of temporal punishment;

fourth, health of body and material blessings;

fifth, protection from evil spirits.

472. Which are the chief kinds of sacramentals?

The chief kinds of sacramentals are:

first, blessings given by priests and bishops;

second, exorcisms against evil spirits;

third, blessed objects of devotion.

(a) Some of the blessings given by priests and bishops are: the blessings of churches, of the sacred vessels and vestments, of the sick, of houses, of crops, of palms, of ashes, and of holy water.

(b) Christ Himself cast out many evil spirits. He also gave His apostles power and authority over all the devils (*Luke 9:1*) and declared that ". . . in my name they shall cast out devils" (*Mark 16:17*).

SCRIPTURE:

"And they came to the other side of the sea, to the country of the Gerasenes; and as soon as he stepped out of the boat, there met him from the tombs a man with an unclean spirit. This man lived in the tombs and no one could any longer bind him, even with chains; for often he had been bound with fetters and chains, and he had rent the chains asunder and broken the fetters into pieces. And no one was able to control him. And constantly, night and day, he was in the tombs and on the mountains, howling and gashing himself with stones.

"And when he saw Jesus from afar, he ran and worshipped him, and crying out with a loud voice, he said, 'What have I to do with thee, Jesus, Son of the most high God? I adjure thee by God, do not torment me!' For he was saying to him, 'Go out of the man, thou unclean spirit.'

"And he asked him, 'What is thy name?' And he said to him, 'My name is Legion, for we are many.' And he entreated him earnestly not to drive them out of the country.

"Now a great herd of swine was there on the mountainside, feeding. And the spirits kept entreating him, saying, 'Send us into the swine, that we may enter into them.' And Jesus immediately gave them leave. And the unclean spirits came out and entered into the swine; and the herd, in number about two thousand, rushed down with great violence into the sea, and were drowned in the sea" (*Mark 5:1-3*).

473. Which are the blessed objects of devotion most used by Catholics?

The blessed objects of devotion most used by Catholics are: holy water, candles, ashes, palms, crucifixes, medals, rosaries, scapulars, and images of Our Lord, the Blessed Virgin, and the saints.

SCRIPTURE:

"Whosoever of you is wise, let him come, and make that which the Lord hath commanded. . . . The candlestick to bear up the lights, the vessels thereof and the lamps, and the oil for the nourishing of fires: the altar of incense, and the bars, and the oil of unction and the incense of spices: the hanging at the door of the tabernacle" (*Exodus 35:10, 14-15*).

"And they kept eight days with joy, after the manner of the feast of the tabernacles, remembering that not long before they had kept the feast of the tabernacles when they were in the mountains and in dens, like wild beasts. Therefore they now carried boughs and green branches and palms for Him that had given them good success in cleansing his place" (*II Machabees 10:6-7*)

"Little children were brought to him then that he might lay his hands on them and pray; but the disciples rebuked them. But Jesus said to them, 'Let the little children be, and do not hinder them from coming to me, for of such is the kingdom of heaven.' And when he had laid his hands on them, he departed from that place" (*Matthew 19:13-15*).

"And the whole multitude of the people were praying outside at the hour of incense" (*Luke 1:10*).

"Then having summoned the twelve apostles, he gave them power and authority over all the devils, and to cure diseases" (*Luke 9:1*).

"Whatever house you enter, first say, 'Peace to this house!' And if a son of peace be there, your peace will rest upon him" (*Luke 10:5-6*).

"Now the seventy-two returned with joy, saying, 'Lord, even the devils are subject to us in thy name'" (*Luke 10:17*).

"Now he led them out towards Bethany, and he lifted up his hands and blessed them" (*Luke 24:50*).

"Now the next day, the great crowd which had come to the feast, when they heard that Jesus was coming to Jerusalem, took the branches of palms and went forth to meet him" (*John 12:12-13*).

474. How should we make use of the sacramentals?

We should make use of the sacramentals with faith and devotion, and never make them objects of superstition.

(a) Sacramentals become objects of superstition when they are considered good luck charms or when they are thought to produce effects apart from the prayers of the Church and from the devotion they inspire.

SCRIPTURE: *See Scripture, question 469, Numbers 21:4-9.*

IMPORTANT TRUTHS ABOUT THE SACRAMENTALS

The word "sacramental" means something connected with a sacrament. When this word was first used it meant the ceremonies that the Church uses in connection with the administration of the sacraments, such as the anointing with oil in Baptism. Later it acquired the meaning of objects blessed by the Church or blessings or exorcisms against the evil spirits, and this is the meaning it has today. The Church is authorized to institute sacramentals because they are useful means toward bringing men to eternal life. We are creatures largely dependent on the use of our senses. Our Blessed Lord established the sacraments as signs appealing to the senses; in establishing the sacramentals, the Church is imitating Him. Of course, there is a vast difference between the sacraments and the sacramentals, inasmuch as the sacraments are instruments of divine power, able of themselves to give grace; whereas the sacramentals inspire to pious sentiments those who use them properly. By means of these pious sentiments they receive grace; the sacramentals also bring to their users the benefit of the Church's prayers. Every day throughout the world millions of Catholics, both the clergy and the laity, unite in prayer to the Almighty. The benefit of these prayers is given to those who devoutly use the sacramentals.

There are many sacramentals. Especially numerous are the blessings given by the clergy of the Church. There are two kinds of blessings, known respectively as constitutive and invocative blessings. The former render a person or object sacred. Such, for example, is the solemn blessing given to a priest when he is made an abbot; also the blessing of a church or a chalice. An invocative blessing is rather a prayer for a person, which is capable of procuring for him spiritual and temporal favors. It may be pronounced directly over the person, like the blessing of the throat on St. Blaise's Day, or it may be pronounced over a thing with the intention of bringing down God's blessings on those who will use it. Such are the blessings of a house or of a ship, or of an automobile. The Ritual, the book used by priests in giving blessings, contains many beautiful prayers composed by the Church to call down divine benediction on her children in the various phases and activities of life. It is well to note that the Church does not hesitate to confer some of her blessings on non-Catholics as well as on Catholics.

Since the evil spirits sometimes obsess or possess a person, the Church has formulated certain solemn exorcisms to be used on such occasions in order to drive the devils away. The law of the Church commands that no one shall perform the solemn ceremony of exorcism except a priest who has been authorized to do so by the bishop. Moreover, the priest is not allowed to use these exorcisms until he has made a diligent examination of the case to discover if the person is really being tormented by the devil. For sometimes people are afflicted with nervous troubles which bear a resemblance to diabolical possession.

In the use of sacramentals Catholics must avoid two extremes. On the one hand, they must not regard them as intended only for children or uneducated persons. They are for all the members of the Church, and no one should consider himself so wise or so cultured as to be above the use of medals and rosaries and scapulars, and the other inspiring sacramentals of the Church. On the other hand, Catholics must not look on sacramentals as charms to bring good luck. They are intended principally for spiritual benefits, and when they do obtain material favors, it is always in conjunction with benefits of soul. There is no infallible assurance that one who wears a scapular will not be drowned, or that one who has a medal of St. Christopher in his automobile will not have an accident. Above all, it would be utterly foolish and contrary to the doctrine of the Catholic Church to imagine that one may lead a bad life, yet because of wearing a medal or a scapular, be assured of the opportunity of conversion when death strikes. Such an attitude toward the sacramentals would be a form of superstition.

RESOLUTION: Resolve to show the sacramentals of the Church the reverence that is due to them.

STUDY HELPS

A. TRUE OR FALSE. (*Check each of the statements given below as either true or false. The correct answers will be found in the preceding portions of the lesson*).

	TRUE	FALSE
(1) The sacramentals contain the graces they signify.	.....	.....
(2) Christ instituted the sacramentals.	.....	.....
(3) Our Lord gave His apostles power over the devils.	.....	.....
(4) The word "sacramental" originally meant the ceremonies used in connection with the administrations of the sacraments.	.....	.....

	TRUE	FALSE
(5) An invocative blessing renders a person or object sacred.	.....	.....
(6) A priest may not exorcise a possessed person solemnly unless he has received permission from the bishop.	.....	.....
(7) The Church bestows some of her sacramentals on non-Catholics.	.....	.....
(8) The sacramentals are intended principally to give us material blessings.	.....	.....
(9) One who wears a scapular can be certain that he will not be drowned.	.....	.....
(10) The blessing of a chalice is a constitutive blessing.	.....	.....

B. PROBLEMS AND EXERCISES. (*Answer the questions orally or write them as your teacher may direct*):

(1) In the earliest use of the word "sacramental", what meaning did the Church attach to the word?

(2) On the afternoon of her First Holy Communion, Loretta was enrolled in the five scapulars. What benefit will she derive from them?

(3) Edwin has his throat blessed on February 3rd, the feast of St. Blaise. A week later he is absent from school with a very sore throat. Did the blessing fail to work?

(4) Domitilla wants to know will it be all right to bring her cousin Prisca, a Protestant child, to the blessing of children ceremony at St. Cecilia's? Domitilla, of course, is a Catholic. St. Cecilia's is her parish church. Let her know if she may take Prisca to receive the blessing.

(5) Dionysia, a Catholic girl in the senior class at an exclusive secular college, goes to Communion once each season of the year. The only ornaments in her room are a dressed doll, and an autographed photograph of her favorite author. In her handbag are the usual feminine requirements, vanity case, etc., but no rosary or crucifix. She never dips her finger in the holy water font, entering or leaving the church. "That's for the common people," is her comment on the practice. Drop Dionysia a courteous note of 50 to 75 words pointing out her error, and suggesting that she make better use of religious and devotional articles.

(6) Anselm, a basketball player at St. Jerome's, fears he is going to be too late for the contest. He "steps on the gas", goes through a couple of red lights, passes the car ahead, as both are traveling up hill, and finally comes to grief in a serious smash-up, gravely injuring himself, and killing a man, his wife, and two children in the other car. Later, in the hospital, he remarks to his sister Eleanora. "I'm awfully sorry about what happened, but I counted on better luck because I had a swell medal of St. Christopher in the old car!" Did St. Christopher neglect Anselm? What is the reason for your answer?

(7) Simon, and three of his companions, go to the lake for a swim. On arriving at the lake, Simon discovers that he left his scapulars at home. The other boys have theirs, and wear them in the water. Martin, one of the boys, knows that Simon will not go into the water unless he has his scapulars with him. The distance back to Simon's house is several

279

miles. Martin calls to Simon: "C'mon in, 'Si' and don't worry about your scapulars! The water's fine!'" Should "Si" take Martin's advice? Why?

(8) Have scapulars, medals, badges and other articles of devotion any spiritual power in themselves? What gives them spiritual value? Spiritually, is there any difference between a bronze medal of the Immaculate Conception, a silver one, and a gold one? Explain your answer.

(9) On what day of the year are candles solemnly blessed? May they be blessed on other days of the year?

(10) Emma, the oldest lady in the parish, is about to be prepared for death by the pastor. What sacramentals will he ordinarily need in the administration of the last rites? Is it advisable to keep these articles in a box or a drawer in your home in case they are needed at any time?

(11) Leonie, in the seventh grade, has never missed a First Friday Communion. She is convalescing at home from a serious illness. Arrangements have been made with Father Genesius who will take Holy Communion to her. At the foot of her bed, where she can see everything easily, is a table, covered with a clean linen cloth. On it are the following articles: a crucifix, two blessed, lighted candles, a glass of fresh water, a small bottle of holy water, two small statues, one of the Sacred Heart, the other, the Immaculate Conception, two small vases of red roses, freshly cut from Leonie's garden, a spoon, rosary beads, and a clean napkin. Which of these articles are not sacramentals?

(12) Enumerate the fifteen mysteries of the rosary, grouping them in the order in which one follows the other. Name each group of mysteries.

(13) Strange incidents began to happen in the Preston home. There were unusual noises, voices were heard, articles were thrown about the room, without any visible cause. Apparently it is a case of diabolical obsession. To whom should the family have recourse? What can the priest do about the matter?

(14) Denis has not been to the sacraments for many years, and when the priest urges him to receive them, he says: "I will receive the sacraments when I am in danger of death. I know I'll have the opportunity of doing so, because I wear a scapular and carry a rosary." Do you think that the attitude of Denis is praiseworthy? What would you tell him about his assurance of receiving the sacraments in the hour of death?

(15) The chain of Mr. Madigan's rosary frequently breaks, some of the beads are lost, and of the remaining beads some are badly cracked. Mrs. Madigan wants to buy him a new rosary but he prefers his old one for sentimental reasons. Would it be better if he got a new rosary with all the beads intact? In that event, what should he do with the old rosary?

(16) Mary's mother keeps two blessed candles in the house. Recently Mary had a party; she wanted to have lighted candles on the dining-room table, but her devout mother refused her the use of the blessed candles for this purpose. Mary, wondering if the blessing had made the two candles holy, talked to the pastor about her problem. He told her that the candles had received a constitutive blessing. Explain this term to Mary. Was her mother's refusal right?

Prayer

475. What is prayer?

Prayer is the lifting up of our minds and hearts to God.

(a) It is the high privilege of angels and men to speak with God in prayer.
(b) We lift up our minds to God by fixing the attention of our mind on Him; we lift up our hearts to Him by love.

SCRIPTURE:
"Let us lift up our hearts with our hands to the Lord in the heavens" (*Lamentations 3:41*).

"Watch and pray, that you may not enter into temptation" (*Matthew 26:41*).

"And he also told them a parable—that they must always pray and not lose heart" (*Luke 18:1*).

"Jesus said to her, 'Woman, believe me, the hour is coming when neither on this mountain nor in Jerusalem will you worship the Father. You worship what you do not know; we worship what we know, for salvation is from the Jews. But the hour is coming, and is now here, when the true worshippers will worship the Father in spirit and in truth. For the Father also seeks such to worship him. God is spirit, and they who worship him must worship in spirit and in truth' " (*John 4:21-24*).

"Ask, and you shall receive, that your joy may be full" (*John. 16:24*).

"Be prudent therefore and watchful in prayers" (*I Peter 4:7*).

See also John 17:1-26.

476. Why do we pray?

We pray:

first, to adore God, expressing to Him our love and loyalty;

second, to thank Him for His favors;

third, to obtain from Him the pardon of our sins and the remission of their punishment;

fourth, to ask for graces and blessings for ourselves and others.

(a) Prayer is a debt we owe to God; a debt of adoration, because He is our Lord and Master; a debt of thanksgiving, because He is our first and greatest Benefactor; a debt of sorrow, because we have offended Him by our sins.

SCRIPTURE:
"Rejoice always. Pray without ceasing. In all things give thanks; for this is the will of God in Christ Jesus regarding you all" (*I Thessalonians 5:16-18*).

477. How should we pray?

We should pray:

first, with attention;

second, with a conviction of our own helplessness and our dependence upon God;

281

third, with a great desire for the graces we beg of Him;
fourth, with loving trust in His goodness;
fifth, with perseverance.

SCRIPTURE:

"The prayer of the humble and the meek hath always pleased thee" (*Judith 9:16*).

"Again, when you pray, you shall not be like the hypocrites, who love to pray standing in the synagogues and at the street corners, in order that they may be seen by men. Amen I say to you, they have received their reward. But when thou prayest, go into thy room, and closing thy door, pray to thy Father in secret; and thy Father, who sees in secret, will reward thee" (*Matthew 6:5-6*).

"Therefore I say to you, do not be anxious for your life, what you shall eat; nor yet for your body, what you shall put on. Is not the life a greater thing than the food, and the body than the clothing? Look at the birds of the air: they do not sow, or reap, or gather into barns; yet your heavenly Father feeds them. Are not you of much more value than they? But which of you by being anxious about it can add to his stature a single cubit? (*Matthew 6:25-27*).

"Ask, and it shall be given you; seek, and you shall find; knock, and it shall be opened to you. For everyone who asks, receives; and he who seeks, finds; and to him who knocks, it shall be opened. Or what man is there among you, who, if his son asks him for a loaf, will hand him a stone; or if he asks for a fish, will hand him a serpent? Therefore, if you, evil as you are, know how to give good gifts to your children, how much more will your Father in heaven give good things to those who ask him!" (*Matthew 7:7-11*).

"Hypocrites, well did Isaias prophesy of you, saying, 'This people honors me with their lips, but their heart is far from me.' " (*Matthew 15:7-8*).

"And all things whatever you ask for in prayer, believing, you shall receive" (*Matthew 21-22*).

"But he spoke this parable also to some who trusted in themselves as being just and despised others. 'Two men went up to the temple to pray, the one a Pharisee and the other a publican. The Pharisee stood and began to pray thus within himself: "O God, I thank thee that I am not like the rest of men, robbers, dishonest, adulterers, or even like this publican. I fast twice a week; I pay tithes of all that I possess." But the publican, standing afar off, would not so much as lift up his eyes to heaven, but kept striking his breast, saying, "O God, be merciful to me the sinner!" I tell you, this man went back to his home justified rather than the other; for everyone who exalts himself shall be humbled, and he who humbles himself shall be exalted'" (*Luke 18:9-14*).

"And whatever you ask in my name, that I will do" (John 14:13).

"If you abide in me, and if my words abide in you, ask whatever you will and it shall be done to you" (*John 15:7*).

"Amen, amen, I say to you, if you ask the Father anything in my name, he will give it to you. Hitherto you have not asked anything in my name. Ask, and you shall receive, that your joy may be full" (*John 16:23-24*).

"Let us therefore draw near with confidence to the throne of grace, that we may obtain mercy and find grace to help in time of need" (*Hebrews 4:16*).

"For Jesus, in the days of his earthly life, with a loud cry and tears, offered up prayers and supplications to him who was able to save him from death, and was heard because of his reverent submission" (*Hebrews 5:7*).

"But if any of you is wanting in wisdom, let him ask it of God, who gives abundantly to all men, and does not reproach; and it will be given to him. But let him ask with faith, without hesitation. For he who hesitates is like a wave of the sea, driven and carried about by the wind" (*James 1:5-6*).

"For the unceasing prayer of a just man is of great avail" (*James 5:16*).

"And the confidence that we have towards him is this, that if we ask anything according to his will, he hears us. And we know that he hears us whatever we ask; we know that the requests we make of him are granted" (*I John 5:14-15*).

478. For whom should we pray?

We should pray especially for ourselves, for our parents, relatives, friends, and enemies, for sinners, for the souls in purgatory, for the Pope, bishops, and priests of the Church, and for the officials of our country.

SCRIPTURE: "It is therefore a holy and wholesome thought to pray for the dead, that they may be loosed from sins" (*II Machabees 12:46*).

"But I say to you, love your enemies, do good to those who hate you, and pray for those who persecute and calumniate you, so that you may be children of your Father in heaven, who makes his sun to rise on the good and the evil, and sends rain on the just and the unjust" (*Matthew 5:44-45*).

"Watch and pray, that you may not enter into temptation. The spirit indeed is willing, but the flesh is weak" (*Matthew 26:41*).

"Now I exhort you, brethren, through our Lord Jesus Christ, and through the charity of the Spirit, that you help me by your prayers to God for me, that I may be delivered from the unbelievers in Judea ... " (*Romans 15:30-31*).

"I urge therefore, first of all, that supplications, prayers, intercessions and thanksgivings be made for all men; for kings, and for all in high positions, that we may lead a quiet and peaceful life in all piety and worthy behavior. This is good and agreeable in the sight of God our Savior, who wishes all men to be saved and to come to the knowledge of the truth" (*I Timothy 2:1-4*).

"Pray for one another, that you may be saved. For the unceasing prayer of a just man is of great avail" (*James 5:16*).

See Scripture, question 476, Matthew 6:9-13; question 477, Matthew 7:7-11; Matthew 21:22; John 16:23-24; and I John 5:14-15.

479. How do we know that God always hears our prayers if we pray properly?

We know that God always hears our prayers if we pray properly because Our Lord has promised: "If you ask the Father anything in My name, He will give it to you."

(a) God is ever ready to grant our salutary petitions, but He requires us to ask Him by prayer to do so. Prayer, therefore, is the condition God has laid down for us to obtain His graces and blessings. He always answers our prayers in the way that is best for us.

SCRIPTURE:

"And whatever you ask in my name, that I will do, in order that the Father may be glorified in the Son. If you ask me anything in my name, I will do it" (*John 14:13-14*).

"If you abide in me, and if my words abide in you, ask whatever you will and it shall be done to you" (*John 15:7*).

See Scripture, question 477, John 16:23-24.

480. Why do we not always obtain what we pray for?

We do not always obtain what we pray for, either because we have not prayed properly or because God sees that what we are asking would not be for our good.

(a) We do not pray properly when any of the conditions mentioned in question 477 are lacking.

(b) God always knows what is best for us. We do not. He knows that often what seems good for us would harm us bodily or spiritually. No prayer is ever unanswered by God, though it is not always answered according to our petitions.

SCRIPTURE:

"Then shall they call upon me, and I will not hear: they shall rise in the morning and shall not find me. Because they have hated instruction, and received not the fear of the Lord, nor consented to my counsel, but despised all my reproof" (*Proverbs 1:28-30*).

"He that turneth away his ears from hearing the law, his prayers shall be an abomination" (*Proverbs 28:9*).

"You ask and do not receive, because you ask amiss, that you may spend it upon your passions" (*James 4:3*).

See Scripture, question 477, Matthew 6:5-6; Matthew 15:7-8; Matthew 21:22; Luke 18:9-14; James 1:5-6; James 5:16; also, question 479, John 15:7.

481. Are distractions in our prayers always displeasing to God?

Distractions in our prayers are not displeasing to God, unless they are willful.

(a) Many distractions arise from natural causes, such as worry, anxiety, or bodily affliction.

(b) Other distractions are temptations of the devil.

(c) The effort made to overcome distractions makes our prayers even more pleasing to God.

SCRIPTURE: *See Scripture, question 477, Matthew 15:7-8; Hebrews 5:7.*

482. How many kinds of prayer are there?

There are two kinds of prayer: mental prayer and vocal prayer.

483. What is mental prayer?

Mental prayer is that prayer by which we unite our hearts with God while thinking of His holy truths.

SCRIPTURE:

"Let thy thoughts be upon the precepts of God, and meditate continually on his commandments: and he will give thee a heart; and the desire of wisdom shall be given to thee" (*Ecclesiasticus 6:37*).

"For the rest, brethren, whatever things are true, whatever honorable, whatever just, whatever holy, whatever lovable, whatever of good repute, if there be any virtue, if anything worthy of praise, think upon these things" (*Philippians 4:8*).

See Psalm 118 for an example of mental prayer.

484. What is vocal prayer?

Vocal prayer is that prayer which comes from the mind and heart and is spoken by the lips.

(a) Vocal prayer can also be taken to mean all bodily prayer, such as genuflections, the bowing of the head, and the folding of hands.

(b) By vocal prayer man recognizes God's sovereignty over the whole man, body and soul.

(c) The use of the voice or the prayerful attitude of the body also excites greater fervor of soul. For example, those who have difficulty in merely meditating on the Passion often find it easy to make the Stations of the Cross, or to say the Sorrowful Mysteries of the Rosary. For many, a simple genuflection is the most expressive of their acts of faith in the Real Presence of Christ in the Eucharist.

(d) Vocal prayer also makes prayer in common possible. Prayer in common is that of many praying as one, such as the prayer of a family or of a congregation saying the Rosary together.

SCRIPTURE:

"With my voice I called upon the Lord, and he hearkened to me from his holy mountain" (*Psalm 3:5*).

"O Lord, thou wilt open my lips, and my mouth shall declare thy praise" (*Psalms 50:17*).

"For where two or three are gathered together for my sake, there am I in the midst of them" (*Matthew 18:20*).

"At the name of Jesus every knee should bend of those in heaven, on earth and under the earth, and every tongue should confess that the Lord Jesus Christ is in the glory of God the Father" (*Philippians 2:10-11*).

485. May we use our own words in praying to God?

We may use our own words in praying to God, and it is well to do so often.

486. What are the prayers that every Catholic should know by heart?

The prayers that every Catholic should know by heart are: the Our Father, the Hail Mary, the Apostles' Creed, the Confiteor, the Glory be to the Father, and the acts of faith, hope, charity, and contrition.

SCRIPTURE:

"Now in the sixth month the angel Gabriel was sent from God to a town of Galilee called Nazareth, to a virgin betrothed to a man named Joseph, of the house of David, and the virgin's name was Mary. And when the angel had come to her, he said, 'Hail, full of grace, the Lord is with thee. Blessed art thou among women.' When she had heard him she was troubled at his word, and kept pondering what manner of greeting this might be" (*Luke 1:26-29*).

"Now in those days Mary arose and went with haste into the hill country, to a town of Juda. And she entered the house of Zachary and saluted Elizabeth. And it came to pass, when Elizabeth heard the greeting of Mary, that the babe in her womb leapt. And Elizabeth was filled with the Holy Spirit, and cried out with a loud voice, saying, 'Blessed art thou among women and blessed is the fruit of thy womb! And how have I deserved that the mother of my Lord should come to me? For behold, the moment that the sound of thy greeting came to my ears, the babe in my womb leapt for joy. And blessed is she who has believed, because the things promised her by the Lord shall be accomplished'" (*Luke 1:39-45*).

See Scripture, question 476, Matthew 6:9-13.

487. How do we usually begin and end our prayers?

We usually begin and end our prayers with the sign of the cross.

SCRIPTURE:

"And Jesus drew near and spoke to them saying, 'All power in heaven and on earth has been given to me. Go, therefore, and make disciples of all nations, baptizing them in the name of the Father, and of the Son, and of the Holy Spirit'" (*Matthew 28:18-19*).

488. Why do we make the sign of the cross?

We make the sign of the cross to express two important mysteries of the Christian religion, the Blessed Trinity and the Redemption.

SCRIPTURE:

"And the Word was made flesh, and dwelt among us" (*John 1:14*).

"And as Moses lifted up the serpent in the desert, even so must the Son of Man be lifted up, that those who believe in him may not perish, but may have life everlasting. For God so loved the world that he gave his only-begotten Son, that those who believe in him may not perish, but may have life everlasting" (*John 3:14-16*).

"And bearing the cross for himself, he went forth to the place called the Skull, in Hebrew, Golgotha, where they crucified him" (*John 19:17-18*).

"Who himself bore our sins in his body upon the tree, that we, having died to sin, might live to justice; and by his stripes you were healed" (*I Peter 2:24*).

See Scripture, Lesson 3; also question 487, Matthew 28:18-19).

489. How are these mysteries expressed by the sign of the cross?

When we say "In the name," we express the truth that there is only one God; when we say "of the Father, and of the Son, and of the Holy Ghost," we express the truth that there are three distinct Persons in God; and when we make the form of the cross on ourselves, we express the truth that the Son of God, made man, redeemed us by His death on the cross.

IMPORTANT TRUTHS ABOUT PRAYER

Our reason tells us that as creatures we are obliged to pray to God, in order to adore Him, to thank Him, to ask Him for what we need, and to seek His pardon for our sins. Faith teaches us the same truth. The Bible abounds with references to man's obligation to pray. And in order to give us an example, Our Divine Redeemer prayed while He was on earth. Sometimes He spent even entire nights in prayer. Two of the most striking incidents of His passion were acts of prayer—His prayer in the Garden asking that, if possible, the cup of suffering might pass away, followed immediately by His sublime act of resignation to His Father's will, and His prayer on the cross, asking pardon for those who were putting Him to death.

Although prayer is intended not only to ask God for favors but also to praise and to thank Him and to make reparation for sin, we often use the word in the restricted sense of asking benefits, whether spiritual or temporal. This is the prayer of petition. To this prayer Christ has attached unfailing efficacy, provided it is offered with the necessary qualities, for He said: "Amen, amen, I say to you if you ask the Father anything in my name, He will give it to you" (*John, 16:23*). Of course, for the fulfillment of this promise we must pray humbly and perseveringly, and confidingly. Sometimes God does not grant us a favor the first time we ask; He wishes us to continue to implore His mercy. Moreover, we cannot expect Him to grant us a temporal favor, such as health and riches, if he foresees that it would be harmful to our soul, any more than we could expect a mother to give her child a knife, for which he is crying, since she knows he would injure himself. Finally, we must remember that Our Lord spoke of prayer offered for ourselves. We can and should pray for others, and we can often obtain for them precious favors; but infallible efficacy is attached to prayer only when a person prays for himself.

Through prayer we can procure for ourselves immeasurable spiritual blessings —the power to overcome temptations, no matter how violent, the grace to increase in love for God, and above all, perseverance in the state of grace and eternal salvation. St. Alphonsus Liguori, who is called the Doctor of Prayer because he wrote so much about it and practiced it so ardently, did not hesitate to say: "He who prays will be saved, he who does not pray will be lost."

Naturally we pray when we go to Mass or receive the sacraments or perform some other religious duty. But we should not limit our prayers to these occasions. In the morning we should pray for God's guidance during the day; at night we should pray for forgiveness of any faults or sins we may have committed in the course of the day and for protection of soul and body during the night. Strictly speaking, it is not a sin to omit morning and night prayers, provided a person prays at some other time; but it is a sin to neglect prayer entirely. The most appropriate place for prayer is the church, where Our Lord is present in the Blessed Sacrament, but we can pray in any place. In time of temptation our first thought should be to pray for divine assistance; above all, frequently in the course of the day we should raise our mind and heart to God in brief but fervent aspirations. Any Catholic who fills his life with prayer in this manner will be living up to the injunction of Our Lord, who said that we must always pray and not lose heart (*Luke, 18:1*).

Mental prayer, which is also called meditation, constitutes one of the most effective means toward sanctification. Hence, the rules of all religious orders call for frequent periods of meditation—sometimes as much as two hours every day. It can be practiced by the members of the laity also, and from it they can derive great spiritual profit. Many good Catholic lay-persons devote fifteen minutes or a half-hour to meditation daily, choosing particularly as the subject of their contemplation and prayer the life and the teachings of Our Blessed Lord. Meditation is especially beneficial in the morning, when we can look forward to the difficulties of the day in a spirit of faith and humbly ask God for light and grace to do His will in all things.

Vocal prayers are also recommended by the Church, and many of them, such as the rosary and the litanies, are richly indulgenced. However, it would be a mistake to imagine that the more vocal prayers a person recites, the holier he is. It is better to say a few vocal prayers slowly and attentively than to recite a large number hurriedly and with little attention.

Spiritual reading is one of the most practical helps toward praying as we should. By this we mean the reading of books about Our Lord, the Blessed Virgin Mary, the Saints, the practice of virtue, etc. In every Catholic home there should be devotional books on hand for the members of the family; above all, there should be a Bible, and the members of the family, old and young, should be accustomed to read it regularly. It is a beautiful custom when all the members of a family assemble at a set time daily—for example, after the evening meal—to hear a portion of the Bible read by the father or the mother or one of the children. Pope Leo XIII granted an indulgence of 300 days to all Catholics who spend at least fifteen minutes in reading Holy Scripture with the reverence due to the word of God and after the manner of spiritual reading.

The sign of the cross, with which we Catholics begin and end our prayers, is not merely our profession of faith in the Holy Trinity and the Redemption, but is also our petition for the blessing of the three divine Persons on our lives and actions. Hence, we should always make the sign of the cross reverently. It is disedifying to see this holy sign made so carelessly and so rapidly that one can hardly recognize what it is intended to be. The Church grants an indulgence of 100 days to the faithful as often as they make the sign of the cross with the prescribed words, and 300 days whenever they make it with holy water.

There is a special value attached to prayer recited in common by several persons—for example, a family, a sodality, a congregation—because Our Lord promised His special blessing on prayer of this kind when He said: "Where two or three are gathered together for my sake, there am I in the midst of them" (*Matthew, 18:20*).

RESOLUTION: Resolve to be most faithful to your morning and night prayers, and to acquire the habit of frequently saying little prayers in the course of the day, particularly at the beginning of every action.

STUDY HELPS

A. WORD SELECTION. (*Select the word or phrase in the parentheses which most exactly and most completely fills out the sentence.*)

(1) We lift our minds to God by giving Him (love ... attention ... praise.)

(2) A prayer endowed with the proper qualities (always obtains what we ask ... may be entirely rejected by God ... is always answered though not necessarily according to our petition).

(3) On the cross Our Lord prayed (that His enemies might be pardoned ... that the chalice might pass from Him ... that His pains might be lessened).

(4) Distractions are not displeasing to God (when they are not wilful ... when they arise from bodily affliction ... when they are temptations of the devil).

(5) Prayer has (two ... four ... six) ends.

(6) The promise of infallible efficacy for prayer was made by (God the Father ... Jesus Christ ... the Blessed Virgin).

(7) In making the sign of the cross we express two truths—the Holy Trinity and (the Redemption ... the Incarnation ... the Resurrection).

(8) When we make mental prayer we are said to (cogitate ... mediate ... meditate).

(9) St. Paul tells us that every knee should bend at the name of (the Holy Ghost ... Jesus Christ ... the Blessed Virgin).

(10) The book of the Bible which tells us that it is a holy and wholesome thought to pray for the dead is (Genesis ... the First Book of Machabees ... the Second Book of Machabees).

288

B. PROBLEMS AND EXERCISES. (*Answer the questions orally or write them as your teacher may direct*):

(1) Madeline finds a prayerbook whose title in golden letters is "Key of Heaven." Is that an appropriate title for a prayerbook? Why?

(2) From memory, write the words of Our Lord's promise concerning prayer.

(3) Zoe finds it hard to pay attention to her prayers at Holy Mass. Advise her what to do during the time of the Holy Sacrifice that will fasten her attention to what is going on at the holy altar of God.

(4) Collette's oldest sister is a nun in the convent. Collette says that her sister makes meditation twice every day. What is meditation?

(5) Helen is trying to persuade the members of her family to recite the rosary in common every evening. What arguments can you suggest that will help her to obtain her request?

(6) Rocco bets Dunstan that he knows more ejaculatory prayers by heart than he does. Dunstan accepts the wager. Fiorello, the judge who is to decide the winner, suggests that they both write out from memory the ejaculations they know. Each writes out his list and hands it to Fiorello. Neither wins, because each of them wrote out nine ejaculations. Can you write out ten? Try it!

(7) George is riding in a bus. His mother is very sick. George is inspired to pray for her as he rides along to his destination. But he stops after the first Hail Mary, as he is ashamed of having peop e see him move his lips in prayer. He noticed a man looking at him, and he felt embarrassed. Could George have prayed without moving his lips? Why?

(8) Barbara likes to clip or copy attractive prayers out of Catholic magazines and the diocesan paper. These she puts in her prayerbook. Once in a while she composes a prayer of her own, and uses it after her Communions during the act of thanksgiving. Are her practices commendable? Why?

(9) Dympna says she finds it hardest to say her meal prayers every day. Eulalia says the morning prayers are the hardest for her to say. Lucy says that for her the hardest of all her daily prayers are the night prayers. Which do you find the hardest to say? Why?

(10) Charlotte spends many precious minutes every morning beautifying herself before she leaves the house. Every week she misses her morning prayers about five times. Write a paragraph of four or five sentences urging Charlotte to beautify her soul also, even if it be necessary to clip off a minute or two from the making-up process.

(11) Why is the church the most appropriate place in which to pray?

(12) What makes our prayers effective?

(13) Explain what is meant by "humble—confident—persevering prayer."

(14) What great Neapolitan saint of the 18th century is called the Doctor of Prayer? What is his well-known saying about the necessity of prayer for the salvation of our souls?

289

LESSON 38

The Our Father

490. Why is the Our Father the best of all prayers?

The Our Father is the best of all prayers because it is the Lord's Prayer, taught us by Jesus Christ Himself, and because it is a prayer of perfect and unselfish love.

SCRIPTURE: *See Scripture, question 476, Matthew 6:9-13.*

491. Why is the Our Father a prayer of perfect and unselfish love?

The Our Father is a prayer of perfect and unselfish love because in saying it we offer ourselves entirely to God and ask from Him the best things, not only for ourselves but also for our neighbor.

SCRIPTURE:
"Jesus said to them, 'My food is to do the will of him who sent me, to accomplish his work'" *(John 4:34).*

See Scripture, question 189, Matthew 22:35-40.

492. Why do we address God as "Our Father who art in heaven"?

We address God as "Our Father who art in heaven," because we belong to Him, our loving Father, who created us and watches over us, who adopts us through sanctifying grace as His children, and who destines us to live forever with Him in heaven, our true home.

SCRIPTURE:
"And God created man to his own image; to the image of God he created him. Male and female he created them" *(Genesis 1:27).*

"But I say to you, love your enemies, do good to those who hate you, and pray for those who persecute and calumniate you, so that you may be children of your Father in heaven" *(Matthew 5:44-45).*

"In my Father's house there are many mansions. Were it not so, I should have told you, because I go to prepare a place for you" *(John 14:2).*

"In that day you shall ask in my name; and I do not say to you that I will ask the Father for you, for the Father himself loves you because you have loved me, and have believed that I came forth from God" *(John 16:26-27).*

"For whoever are led by the Spirit of God, they are the sons of God. Now you have not received a spirit of bondage so as to be again in fear, but you have received a spirit of adoption as sons, by virtue of which we cry, 'Abba! Father!' The Spirit himself gives testimony to our spirit that we are sons of God. But if we are sons, we are heirs also: heirs indeed of God and joint heirs with Christ, provided, however, we suffer with him that we may also be glorified with him" *(Romans 8:14-17).*

"Behold what manner of love the Father has bestowed upon us, that we should be called children of God; and such we are. This is why the world does not know us, because it did not know him. Beloved, now we are the children of God, and it has not yet appeared what we shall be. We know that, when he appears, we shall be like to him, for we shall see him just as he is. And everyone who has this hope in him makes himself holy, just as he also is holy" (*I John 3:1-3*).

See Scripture, question 477, Matthew 6:25-27.

493. For what do we pray when we say "hallowed be Thy name"?

When we say "hallowed be Thy name," we pray that God may be known and honored by all men.

SCRIPTURE:

"Let us sing a hymn to the Lord: let us sing a new hymn to our God.

"O Adonai, Lord, greatest art thou, and glorious in thy power: and no one can overcome thee. Let all thy creatures serve thee: because thou hast spoken, and they were made: thou didst send forth thy spirit, and they were created. And there is no one that can resist thy voice.

"The mountains shall be moved from the foundations with the waters: the rocks shall melt as wax before thy face. But they that fear thee, shall be great with thee in all things.

"Woe be to the nation that riseth up against my people: for the Lord almighty will take revenge on them. In the day of judgment he will visit them. For he will give fire, and worms into their flesh, that they may burn, and may feel for ever" (*Judith 16:15-21*).

"Praise, ye servants of the Lord, praise ye the name of the Lord.

"Blessed be the name of the Lord both now and forever.

"From the rising of the sun unto its going down, may the name of the Lord be praised" (*Psalm 112:1-3*).

494. For what do we pray when we say "Thy kingdom come"?

When we say "Thy kingdom come," we pray that the kingdom of God's grace may be spread throughout the world, that all men may come to know and to enter the true Church and to live as worthy members of it, and that, finally, we all may be admitted to the kingdom of God's glory.

SCRIPTURE:

"Even so let your light shine before men, in order that they may see your good works and give glory to your Father in heaven" (*Matthew 5:16*).

"You therefore are to be perfect, even as your heavenly Father is perfect" (*Matthew 5:48*).

"For the kingdom of God does not consist in food and drink, but in justice and peace and joy in the Holy Spirit" (*Romans 14:17*).

"Now this I say, brethren, that flesh and blood can obtain no part in the kingdom of God, neither shall corruption have any part in incorruption" (*I Corinthians 15:50*).

"Now the works of the flesh are manifest, which are immorality, uncleanness, licentiousness, idolatry, witchcrafts, enmities, contentions, jealousies, anger, quarrels, factions, parties, envies, murders, drunkenness, carousings, and suchlike. And concerning these I warn you, as I have warned you, that they who do such things will not attain the kingdom of God" (*Galatians 5:19-21*).

495. For what do we pray when we say "Thy will be done on earth as it is in heaven"?

When we say "Thy will be done on earth as it is in heaven," we pray that all men may obey God on earth as willingly as the saints and angels obey Him in heaven.

"Not everyone who says to me, 'Lord, Lord,' shall enter the kingdom of heaven; but he who does the will of my Father in heaven shall enter the kingdom of heaven" (*Matthew 7:21*).

"And he himself withdrew from them about a stone's thrown, and kneeling down, he began to pray, saying, 'Father, if thou art willing, remove this cup from me; yet not my will but thine be done' " (*Luke 22:41-42*).

See Scripture, question 491, John 4:34.

496. For what do we pray when we say "Give us this day our daily bread"?

When we say "Give us this day our daily bread" we pray that God will give us each day all that is necessary to support the material life of our bodies and the spiritual life of our souls.

SCRIPTURE:

"Therefore I say to you, do not be anxious for your life, what you shall eat; nor yet for your body, what you shall put on. Is not the life a greater thing than the food, and the body than the clothing? Look at the birds of the air: they do not sow, or reap, or gather into barns; yet your heavenly Father feeds them. Are not you of much more value than they? But which of you by being anxious about it can add to his stature a single cubit?

"And as for clothing, why are you anxious? Consider how the lilies of the field grow; they neither toil nor spin, yet I say to you that not even Solomon in all his glory was arrayed like one of these. But if God so clothes the grass of the field, which flourishes today but tomorrow is thrown into the oven, how much more you, O you of little faith!' Therefore do not be anxious, saying, 'What shall we eat?' or, 'What shall we drink?' or, 'What are we to put on?' (for after all these things the Gentiles seek); for your Father knows that you need all these things. But seek first the kingdom of God and his justice, and all these things shall be given you besides" (*Matthew 6:25-33*).

"Jesus therefore said to them, 'Amen, amen, I say to you, unless you eat the flesh of the Son of Man, and drink his blood, you shall not have life in you' " (*John 6:54*).

"For my flesh is food indeed, and my blood is drink indeed" (*John 6:56*).

"This is why we too have been praying for you unceasingly, since the day we heard this, and asking that you may be filled with knowledge of his will, in all spiritual wisdom and understanding. May you walk worthily of God and please him in all things, bearing fruit in every good work and growing in the knowledge of God" (*Colossians 1:9-10*).

See Scripture, question 476, Matthew 6:9-13.

497. For what do we pray when we say "and forgive us our trespasses as we forgive those who trespass against us"?

When we say "and forgive us our trespasses as we forgive those who trespass against us," we pray that God will pardon the sins by which we have offended Him, and we tell Him that we pardon our fellow men who have offended us.

SCRIPTURE:

"For if you forgive men their offenses, your heavenly Father will also forgive you your offenses. But if you do not forgive men, neither will your Father forgive you your offenses" (*Matthew 6:14-15*).

"Then his master called him, and said to him, 'Wicked servant! I forgave thee all the debt, because thou didst entreat me. Shouldst not thou also have had pity on thy fellow-servant, even as I had pity on thee?' And his master, being angry, handed him over to the torturers until he should pay all that was due to him. So also my heavenly Father will do to you, if you do not each forgive your brothers from your hearts" (*Matthew 18:32-35*).

"And when you stand up to pray, forgive whatever you have against anyone, that your Father in heaven may also forgive you your offenses. But if you do not forgive, neither will your Father in heaven forgive you your offenses" (*Mark 11:25-26*).

498. For what do we pray when we say "and lead us not into temptation"?

When we say "and lead us not into temptation," we pray that God will always give us the grace to overcome the temptations to sin which come to us from the world, the flesh, and the devil.

SCRIPTURE:
"The imagination and thought of man's heart are prone to evil from his youth" (*Genesis 8:21*).

"Because thou wast acceptable to God, it was necessary that temptation should prove thee" (*Tobias 12:13*).

"Therefore let him who thinks he stands take heed lest he fall. May no temptation take hold of you but such as man is equal to. God is faithful and will not permit you to be tempted beyond your strength, but with the temptation will also give you a way out that you may be able to bear it" (*I Corinthians 10:12-13*).

"Let no man say when he is tempted, that he is tempted by God; for God is no tempter to evil, and he himself tempts no one. But everyone is tempted by being drawn away and enticed by his own passion. Then when passion has conceived, it brings forth sin" (*James 1:13-15*).

"Be sober, be watchful! For your adversary the devil, as a roaring lion, goes about seeking someone to devour. Resist him, steadfast in the faith, knowing that the same suffering befalls your brethren all over the world. But the God of all grace, who has called us unto his eternal glory in Christ Jesus, will himself, after we have suffered a little while, perfect, strengthen and establish us" (*I Peter 5:8-10*).

499. For what do we pray when we say "but deliver us from evil"?

When we say "but deliver us from evil," we pray that God will always protect us from harm, and especially from harm to our souls.

SCRIPTURE: "And call upon me in the day of trouble: I will deliver thee, and thou shalt glorify me" (Psalm 49:15).

"I do not pray that thou take them out of the world, but that thou keep them from evil" (*John 17:15*).

IMPORTANT TRUTHS ABOUT THE OUR FATHER

We could not say a better prayer than that which Jesus Christ Himself taught us. Hence, the "Lord's Prayer", or "Our Father", has always been the form of prayer most frequently employed in the Catholic Church. It is the prayer which Our Lord taught us in His Sermon on the Mount (*Matthew, 6: 9-13*), and was repeated by Him in substantially the same form on another

293

occasion when the disciples asked Him: "Lord, teach us to pray" (*Luke, 11: 1-4*). All the elements of prayer—adoration, thanksgiving, petition, atonement—are found in this brief formula; and because of its perfection, as well as its divine origin, the Catholic Church has always used this prayer in its public worship, and urges its members to recite it often in their private devotions. It is sung or recited in the Canon of the Mass, between the Consecration and the Communion; it is said frequently in the course of the Divine Office which priests and religious recite every day; it is one of the prayers which must be learned as a matter of obligation by all Catholics.

In the opening words of the Lord's Prayer we address as "Father" the three Persons of the Blessed Trinity. We say "Our" and not "My" Father to indicate that all human beings are members of one great family of which God is the Father, and that we should pray for one another, not merely for ourselves.

Most Protestants, in reciting the "Our Father" add the words: "For thine is the kingdom and the power and the glory." This phrase is found in some of the texts of the Scripture dating from early days, and in itself this expression is an excellent prayer praising God. Indeed, it is added to the "Our Father" by many Catholics of the Oriental rites. However, Latin Catholics do not say it because the more ancient and more reliable manuscripts of Scripture do not contain it, and the Church in the Latin rite has never adopted it.

In connection with the Our Father it is appropriate to speak of the next best known prayer in the Catholic Church, the Hail Mary, the favorite prayer of Catholics to the Mother of God. This prayer is divided into three parts: (1) "Hail Mary, full of grace, the Lord is with thee" is the salutation given to Mary by the Archangel at the time of the Annunciation. For this reason the Hail Mary is sometimes called the angelic salutation. (2) "Blessed is the fruit of thy womb" is the phrase spoken by St. Elizabeth to Our Lady at the Visitation. (3) "Holy Mary, Mother of God, pray for us sinners now and at the hour of our death. Amen," is the part added by the Church.

The Catholic Church has always honored the Blessed Virgin Mary. However, the use of the "Hail Mary" developed only gradually in the course of the centuries. At first this prayer contained only the portions given in the New Testament in the words of the Archangel Gabriel and St. Elizabeth. Later, around the fourteenth and fifteenth centuries, the custom arose of adding the words: "Holy Mary, Mother of God, pray for us." The form of this prayer as we have it today was officially approved by the Church in the year 1570.

There are many other vocal prayers to Our Lord, Our Lady and the Saints approved by the Church. These can be found in authorized prayerbooks. Among the best known of these prayers to the Blessed Virgin are the "Hail, Holy Queen," the "Angelus," and the Litany of the Blessed Virgin. There are also other Litanies in use in the Church, especially the Litany of the Holy Name of Jesus, the Litany of the Sacred Heart, the Litany of St. Joseph, the Litany of the Saints, and the Litany of the Dying. Every Catholic should have a prayerbook and use the prayers according to his particular needs and devotion. Catholics should be on their guard against unauthorized prayers, especially those known as "chain-prayers", which people pass from one to another, and which are supposed to confer wonderful favors if recited a certain number of times. Such prayers are superstitious, and often even opposed to the Church's doctrines. A Catholic should destroy any copy of such a prayer that is given to him, and should refuse to pass copies to others.

In regard to the use of vocal prayers, two points are to be noted. *First*, we should recite these prayers carefully, and without too great haste. Some Catholics are very diligent in reciting many vocal prayers, but they mumble them hastily, mispronouncing and cutting off syllables. It would be better if they said fewer prayers, but said them reverently. *Second*, we must remember that prayers said with the lips are of no value unless they come from the heart. Hence, while reciting our vocal prayers we should try to avoid distractions and to be attentive to the great act we are performing.

RESOLUTION: Resolve that whenever you recite your prayers, especially the "Our Father" and the "Hail Mary", you will try to pronounce the words properly and realize that you are speaking to God or to the Mother of God.

STUDY HELPS

A. COLUMN SELECTION. (*Join correctly the parts of the sentences in Columns I and II, by placing the right key letter in the proper parenthesis.*)

I

(1) The Our Father is the best of all prayers (. .).

(2) The first part of the Hail Mary (. .).

(3) We pray that all men may know and enter the true Church when we say (. .).

(4) We pray for grace to overcome temptation when we say (. .).

(5) We pray to be protected from all harm when we say (. .).

(6) Prayers said with the lips are of no value (. .).

(7) The Our Father as recited by Protestants (. .).

(8) If a Catholic finds a chain prayer (. .).

(9) The second part of the Hail Mary (. .).

(10) We call God "Our" Father (. .).

II

(A) unless they come from the heart.

(B) was pronounced by St. Elizabeth.

(C) Deliver us from evil.

(D) Thy kingdom come.

(E) Lead us not into temptation.

(F) because it was taught us by Jesus Christ.

(G) was pronounced by an angel.

(H) to indicate that all human beings are one great family.

(I) is longer than the form recited by Catholics.

(J) he should destroy it.

B. PROBLEMS AND EXERCISES. (*Answer the questions orally or write them as your teacher may direct*):

(1) Every now and then after Holy Communion, Willibrord, instead of reading the Acts of Thanksgiving from his prayerbook, recites slowly and thoughtfully the Our Father from five to ten times. Do you think that he is making a good thanksgiving on such occasions? Why?

(2) Earl, Columba, Rene, and Isaac are having a discussion. Earl claims that the Lord's Prayer is addressed to God the Father; Columba says it is to God the Son; Rene holds that it is directed to God the Holy Ghost, while Isaac maintains that the Our Father is said to the Most Blessed Trinity. Who is right?

(3) Is the United States of America our true home, or is it elsewhere?

(4) Olaf is making a campaign speech in behalf of religious and racial tolerance. Several times during his speech he uses the expression "the Fatherhood of God and the Brotherhood of man." Is there anything in the Lord's prayer that indicates the truth of that expression?

295

(5) How many kingdoms of God are discussed in this lesson? Where are they?

(6) Elgius would like to know if the Hail Mary is a prayer of praise. If so, tell him who are praised in the Hail Mary.

(7) Who were the first creatures to utter the terms of praise now enshrined in the Hail Mary?

(8) Daphne, a Catholic teacher in a public school, once asked in a test "Who is the most truly privileged woman of history?" Some of the pupils in her grade answered "Florence Nightingale," others, "Martha Washington," "Mary, Queen of Scots," "Queen Isabella of Spain" and so on. Some of the children wrote the names of famous women living at the present time. Daphne was delighted to note that the five Catholics in her class, without exception, wrote "The Blessed Virgin Mary." Do you agree with them? Why?

(9) When is it most important that we be in the state of grace? Why? Is there any prayer that you can say repeatedly between now and then that will help you at that moment? What prayer is it?

(10) Jack and Tom get into a discussion about the meaning of the word "hallowed" in the Our Father. Jack contends that it means "shouted" while Tom says that it means "repeated." Can you settle the argument by telling in your own words the true meaning of "hallowed"?

(11) Erasmus, Claud, and Crispin know the Litany of the Blessed Virgin by heart. Can you name four other litanies in general use,—litanies approved by the church? Which are they?

(12) Stephen, a Latin Catholic, Calvin, a Protestant, and Athanasius, a Greek boy all belong to the same football team. Once before an important game, they recited together the Our Father for the team's success. Stephen finished his first; Calvin and Athanasius both added an extra phrase at the end of theirs. What is that phrase? Why don't Latin Catholics use it?

(13) Walter finds a chain prayer in the back of the church. He reads it, and becomes frightened because it threatens that bad luck will fall on the one who refuses to write the prayer out nine times and distribute it to nine others. Advise him what to do.

(14) Eligius asked Fr. Honorius why it is that in the Our Father we ask God not to lead us into temptation. Since God is all-good and wishes us to avoid sin, it seems strange that He should ever lead us into temptation. What answer do you think Fr. Honorius gave to Eligius?

(15) Marvin became angry at Juniper one day, because in a game of basketball Juniper was unnecessarily rough and kicked Marvin several times in the shins. When Marvin came home that afternoon he told his mother about the incident, and exclaimed angrily: "Juniper played a mean trick on me, and I won't forgive him until I have a chance to get even with him." His mother made no answer to this remark, but that night, as Marvin was about to go to bed, she remarked gently: "When you say your night prayers, I don't see how you can honestly say all that is contained in the Our Father." To what words of the Our Father do you think Marvin's mother was referring? How could he have disposed his soul so that he could have said those words honestly and sincerely?

Why I Am a Catholic

I. How does our reason point out the truth of the Catholic religion?

Our reason points out the truth of the Catholic religion by these principles:

first, there is a God;

second, the soul of man is immortal;

third, all men are obliged to practice religion;

fourth, the religion God has revealed through Christ is worthy of belief;

fifth, Christ established a Church which all are obliged to join;

sixth, the only true Church of Christ is the Catholic Church.

II. How can we prove that there is a God?

We can prove that there is a God because this vast universe could not have come into existence, nor be so beautiful and orderly, except by the almighty power and the wisdom of an eternal and intelligent Being.

III. How can we prove that the soul of man is immortal?

We can prove that the soul of man is immortal because man's acts of intelligence are spiritual; therefore, his soul must be a spiritual being, not dependent on matter, and hence not subject to decay or death.

IV. How can we prove that all men are obliged to practice religion?

We can prove that all men are obliged to practice religion because all men are entirely dependent on God and must recognize that dependence by honoring Him and praying to Him.

V. How can we prove that the religion God has revealed through Christ is worthy of belief?

We can prove that the religion God has revealed through Christ is worthy of belief, because:

first, Jesus Christ, announcing Himself as the ambassador and the true Son of God, whose coming was foretold by the prophets, preached doctrines which He said all must believe;

second, Christ worked wonderful miracles, which show that the God of truth approved His teachings.

VI. How can we prove that Christ established a Church which all are obliged to join?

We can prove that Christ established a Church which all are obliged to join, because:

first, He gathered about Him a group of disciples, and called it His Church;

second, He promised that this Church would last until the end of time;

third, He declared that all men must believe and be baptized, that is, join His Church, in order to be saved.

VII. How can we prove that the only true Church of Christ is the Catholic Church?

We can prove that the only true Church of Christ is the Catholic Church, because:

first, only the Catholic Church possesses the marks of the Church established by Christ, that is, unity, holiness, catholicity, and apostolicity;

second, the history of the Catholic Church gives evidence of miraculous stength, permanence, and unchangeableness, thus showing the world that it is under the special protection of God.

VIII. Whence do we chiefly derive our historical knowledge of Jesus Christ, His life and teachings, and of the Church He established?

We derive our historical knowledge of Jesus Christ, His life and teachings, and of the Church He established chiefly from the books of the Bible, which can be proved to be reliable historical records.

IX. What else are the books of the Bible besides being reliable historical records?

Besides being reliable historical records, the books of the Bible are the inspired word of God, that is, written by men with such direct assistance of the Holy Ghost as to make God their true Author.

X. How is the Bible divided?

The Bible is divided into the Old Testament and the New Testament; the Old Testament being the inspired books written before the time of Jesus Christ, and the New Testament the inspired books written after His coming.

XI. Are all the truths revealed for us by God found in the Bible?

Not all the truths revealed for us by God are found in the Bible; some are found only in Divine Tradition.

XII. What is meant by Divine Tradition?

By Divine Tradition is meant the revealed truths taught by Christ and His apostles, which were given to the Church only by word of mouth and not through the Bible, though they were put in writing principally by the Fathers of the Church.

XIII. Why must Divine Tradition be believed as firmly as the Bible?

Divine Tradition must be believed as firmly as the Bible because it also contains the word of God.

XIV. How can we know the true meaning of the doctrines contained in the Bible and in Divine Tradition?

We can know the true meaning of the doctrines contained in the Bible and in Divine Tradition from the Catholic Church, which has been authorized by Jesus Christ to explain His doctrines, and which is preserved from error in its teachings by the special assistance of the Holy Ghost.

XV. How can we best show our gratitude to God for making us members of the only true Church of Jesus Christ?

We can best show our gratitude to God for making us members of the only true Church of Jesus Christ by often thanking God for this great favor, by leading edifying and practical Catholic lives, by trying to lead others to the true faith, and by helping the missions.

XVI. How can we help the missions?

We can help the missions:

first, by praying for the missions, home and foreign, and for missionaries that they may fulfill the command of Christ: "Go, therefore, and make disciples of all nations";

second, by knowing the missions and making them known to others;

third, by making sacrifices for the missions, that is, by helping to support them and by personal service;

fourth, by fostering vocations of self-sacrificing young men and women for every need of the missions.

IMPORTANT TRUTHS ABOUT THE REASONS FOR OUR FAITH

Many non-Catholics believe that Catholic faith is a blind acceptance of the Church's teachings without any attempt to use the powers of reason and logic. On the contrary, unless a person uses his own intelligence to come to the conviction that the truths of the Catholic religion have been revealed by God, he can never make a true act of faith. Even a child, before he can make an act of faith, must have some realization that it is reasonable to do so, at least from the testimony of his parents. And if an intelligent person examines the claims of the Church honestly and thoroughly, he will eventually conclude that the Catholic religion is the one true religion of God, and that all are obliged to believe it. Then, if he sincerely prays to God for light and strength to do what is right, he will surely be led to make a firm act of faith in the truths taught by the Catholic Church.

Bearing this in mind, the question naturally arises: Why are there so many persons outside the Catholic Church? There are many reasons for this. Many of those persons have never had the opportunity of studying the Catholic religion; many are so absorbed in the interests of the present life that they have no care for the welfare of their immortal soul; many have prejudices and false ideas concerning the Catholic Church. It must be admitted that sometimes Catholics themselves are to blame, by their wicked lives, which lead people to the erroneous conclusion that the Catholic religion cannot be true. For it is quite usual to judge the merits of a religion by the conduct of some of those who profess it.

Often the statement is made that Catholics are intolerant. This is partially true and partially false. Catholics are not intolerant toward *persons* belonging to other religions; for the Catholic religion commands that we be charitable toward all men and regard those who differ from us in religious matters as being sincere in their belief. But Catholics are intolerant toward *doctrines* opposed to the teachings of the Catholic Church in the sense that they logically regard such doctrines as false since they are contrary to the teachings of the true Church which is protected from error by the Holy Ghost.

The Catholic Church has been authorized by Christ to teach the truths of divine revelation, found in the Bible and in divine Tradition. The Bible contains 72 books—45 in the Old Testament and 27 in the New Testament. Most of the books of the Old Testament were originally written in Hebrew and most of the books of the New Testament in Greek. The Church can teach and explain authoritatively and infallibly not only the doctrines that are contained in the Bible and in divine Tradition, but also doctrines which have not been revealed but are connected with divine revelation; and Catholics are bound in conscience to accept these teachings of the Church.

There is need of Catholics who understand their religion and perceive how reasonable it is to accept its teachings, and who will bring to their non-Catholic friends, when the opportunity is offered, the arguments for their faith. Often a Catholic lay person can be the means of leading a soul to the knowledge of the truth. But only Catholics who know their religion thoroughly can hope to perform such a deed of charity, for objections and difficulties in great numbers are brought up, and if a non-Catholic sees that the Catholic cannot give a satis factory answer, he will wrongly conclude that the Catholic religion offers a very unsatisfactory solution of the problems of the modern world. Of course, the Catholic himself must lead a good, honest life, if he wishes to persuade his non-Catholic acquaintances that his religion is the only true one.

Catholics themselves should show their appreciation of the great gift of the one true faith by studying it constantly and by daily endeavoring to put it more perfectly into practice in their lives. It is indeed a great privilege to be a Catholic. That privilege is possessed by only one out of every six persons in this world. Truly, a sense of gratitude should impel us all to live up to the duties of our Catholic faith so exactly that each day we shall draw nearer to God and increase our merit in the glorious kingdom of Christ, when we shall pass from the Church militant to the Church triumphant.

RESOLUTION: Resolve every day to thank God for the gift of the Catholic faith.

STUDY HELPS

A. TRUE OR FALSE? (*Check each of the statements given below as either true or false. The correct answers will be found in the preceding portions of the lesson.*)

	TRUE	FALSE
(1) All the truths of revelation are found in the Bible.	.....	.....
(2) Christ promised that His Church would last until the end of time.	.....	.....
(3) The immortality of the soul follows from the fact that it is a spiritual substance.	.....	.....
(4) The account of the life of Christ is found in the Apocalypse.	.....	.....
(5) The books of the Bible have God as their true author.	.....	.....
(6) Divine Tradition has as much value as the Bible.	.....	.....
(7) If we read the Bible attentively and prayerfully we are sure to discover its true meaning.	.....	.....
(8) Catholics are intolerant toward false doctrines.	.....	.....
(9) Catholics are intolerant toward those who profess false doctrines.	.....	.....
(10) The Church has the authority to teach infallibly doctrines not contained in divine revelation but connected with it.	.....	.....

B. PROBLEMS AND EXERCISES. (*Answer the questions orally or write them as your teacher may direct*):

(1) Conon, a devout Catholic young man, is accustomed after meals to say this short prayer: "We return Thee thanks, O Almighty God, for Thy benefits, who livest and reignest, world without end. Amen." Is thankfulness for the gift of faith included in this prayer? Why?

(2) Emiliana, a child in the third grade, has been taught by her pious mother, to share her pennies with the Child Jesus. She does this by putting five of them in her penny back each week during the school year. During the Ember seasons, Emiliana, and her classmates, give the pennies to Sister Rosalia, in charge of the Holy Childhood Association. Is little Emiliana helping the Missions? How?

(3) From early youth, Macarius, a non-Catholic, was taught to look down upon Catholics in general, and to despise priests and religious, in particular. If he sees a priest, or a brother, or a sister, approaching him on the same side of the street, he will cross over to the other side to avoid them. Is Macarius tolerant of Catholics? Comment charitably on the case in from 30 to 50 words. Presume that God is going to use you as the instrument of Macarius' conversion.

(4) A Jewish widow, Basilissa, owns a delicatessen store. Every now and then, Christian boys and girls of the neighborhood, torment her, ridiculing her Jewish religious practices, and committing petty thefts of her wares. Can these children be called intolerant? Within 75 words, what would you say to them, if they would listen to you?

(5) In a rain shelter on the golf course, three golfers while away the time discussing the doctrinal intolerance of the Catholic Church. Gerson, a Protestant, is a professor of mathematics in a Baptist College. Laban,

301

a Jew, teaches chemistry in the local high school. Mel, a Catholic, is a structural engineer. Claver, Mel's colored caddy, is an honor pupil in the High School of St. Protus. He is shocked to hear Mel agree with his golfing companions that it doesn't make much difference what a person believes so long as he lives rightly. About to resume the game, Mel asks Claver for his point of view. He is humbly edified and corrected by Claver's answer, which is aptly illustrated by examples from mathematics, chemistry, and engineering. What is doctrinal intolerance? Try to duplicate Claver's achievement in three short letters to Gerson, Laban, and Mel. Confine your letters to about 250 words each.

(6) Lambert, a friend of yours, has no formal religion; but he holds fast to two reasonable principles, namely, that there is a God, and that his own soul will live on forever. Drop him a short note, adding four more principles that will indicate to him as a reasonable friend, the truth of your own Catholic religion.

(7) In the Solomon Islands, Sister Seraphia is teaching the little natives the truth that there is a God. These youngsters are not so familiar as you are with modern inventions; but they are perhaps more familiar with the powers and the grandeur of nature. Write a brief letter to the missionary nun, telling her how you would go about proving God's existence to these simple native children. Confine your letter to 200 words.

(8) Alicia asked the religion teacher whether human beings would be bound to practice religion if God had not made any revelation. What answer do you think should be given? In that supposition, would men be bound to believe in God's existence, the immortality of the human soul, the Holy Trinity, the eternal happiness of heaven?

Days of Fast and Abstinence

Beginning with Lent, 1952,[1] many of the bishops of the United States, using the provisions of Canon Law as modified through the special faculties granted by the Holy See, published the following regulations on fast and abstinence:

ABSTINENCE: All persons over seven years of age must abstain. This means that they may not take meat or meat gravy or meat soup at all on days of complete abstinence, which are all Fridays, Ash Wednesday, and the vigils of the Assumption and of Christmas. They may take meat, but only at the principal meal, on days of partial abstinence, which are Ember Wednesdays and Saturdays, and the vigils of Pentecost and of All Saints' Day. On Holy Saturday meat may not be taken until noon, when both abstinence and fast cease.

FASTS: All persons over twenty-one and under fifty-nine years of age must fast. This means that on a fast day they may have only one principal, or full, meal and two smaller meals. They may eat meat at this principal meal, except on days of complete abstinence. At the two smaller meals they may not have meat, but they may take sufficient food to

---

[1] Since these regulations were issued, Holy Saturday has been made a day of fast and complete abstinence up to midnight by the general law of the Church. However, some Bishops dispense from the abstinence, either wholly or partially, or from the fast, or from both. The fast and abstinence for the vigil of the Assumption (August 14) have been transferred to the vigil of the Immaculate Conception (December 7). In regard to the observance of fast and abstinence on the day before All Saints, Catholics should follow the instructions of their respective Bishops.

maintain their strength. However, these two smaller meals together should be less than a full meal. Eating between meals is not permitted, but liquids, including milk and fruit juices, may be taken at any time on a fast day. The days of fast are the weekdays of Lent up to Holy Saturday noon, the Ember Days, and the vigils of Pentecost, the Assumption, All Saints and Christmas.

Those not bound to fast may eat meat as often as they wish, except on days of complete abstinence (when it may not be eaten at all), and on days of partial abstinence (when it may be eaten only at the principal meal). When a person's health or ability to work would be seriously affected by fasting or abstaining, the law does not oblige. Where doubt arises concerning fast or abstinence, a parish priest or confessor should be consulted.

In granting these concessions the bishops urged the faithful:

to attend daily Mass during the period of fast and abstinence;
to receive Holy Communion often;
to take part more frequently in exercises of piety;
to give generously to works of religion and charity;
to perform acts of kindness toward the sick, the aged and the poor;
to practice voluntary self-denial;
to pray more fervently, particularly for the intentions of the Holy Father.

GLOSSARY

Abbot (ăb′ŭt). A priest exercising over a religious community of men a jurisdiction somewhat similar to that exercised by a bishop over his diocese.

Abel (ā′bĕl). One of the sons of Adam, killed by his brother Cain.

absolution (ăb-sō-lū′shŭn). The forgiveness of sins imparted by the priest in the sacrament of Penance.

abstinence (ăb′stĭ-nĕns). Refraining from food, particularly from meat.

acolyte (ăk′ō-līt). One who has received the fourth of the minor orders; also, one who serves Mass.

actual grace (ăk′tū-ăl). A supernatural help from God, enabling man to perform a good act.

actual sin. Any willful thought, desire, word, action or omission forbidden by the law of God.

Adam (ăd′-ăm). The first man, the father of the entire human race.

adoration (ăd-ō-rā′shŭn). Honor and praise given to someone, particularly to God.

adult (ă-dŭ′lt). One who has attained maturity: One who has attained the use of reason.

Advent (ăd′vent). The penitential season set aside by the Church as a preparation for Christmas.

advocate (ăd′vō-kāt). One who pleads for another. In this context, Jesus.

agility (a-gĭl′ĭ-ti). One of the qualities of a glorified body, enabling it to move rapidly from place to place.

Agnus Dei (ăg′nŭs dăy′ē). A waxen disk bearing the image of Our ·Lord as a lamb, blessed by the Pope; also a small portion of this disk, covered with cloth or silk.

alb (ălb). A long, white vestment of linen worn by sacred ministers in functions—for example, by the priest at Mass.

All Saints' Day. A holyday of obligation to honor all the saints in heaven, November 1.

All Souls' Day. November 2, a day of special prayer for all the faithful departed.

almighty (ôl′mĭ′tĭ). Possessing all power, an attribute belonging to God alone.

altar (ôl′tĕr). The table on which a sacrifice is offered.

amice (ăm′ĭs). A vestment of white linen, worn by sacred ministers about the neck and shoulders.

angel (ăn′jĕl). A created spirit, without body, having understanding and free will.

Angelus (ăn′jĕl-ŭs). A prayer in remembrance of the Incarnation, recited at morning, noon and evening.

Annunciation. The announcement by the Archangel Gabriel to the Blessed Virgin Mary that she was to be the Mother of God; commemorated on March 25.

annulment (ă-nŭl-ment). A declaration by the Church that a marriage is invalid.

303

anti-Christ. A wicked man who is to appear on earth before the end of the world and oppose Christ and His Church.

apostasy (ă-pōs′tă-sĭ). The rejection of the entire Christian faith by a baptized person.

apostle (ă pŏ′sl). One sent by another, particularly one of the twelve chosen disciples of Christ, whom He sent to preach the Gospel to all men.

apostolicity (ă-pŏs-tŏl-ĭ′sĭ-tĭ). One of the notes of the true Church, consisting of its unbroken connection with the Church founded by Christ on the apostles.

apparition (ăp-ă-rĭsh′ŏn). Something which becomes visible.

archbishop. A bishop enjoying a special dignity; usually the bishop presiding over a principal See, with several suffragan bishops affiliated with him.

ascension (ă-sĕn′shŭn). Our Lord's going up into heaven, by His own power.

aspiration (ăs-pĭ-rā′shŭn). A short prayer, also called an ejaculation.

Assumption (ă-sŭmp′-shŭn). The taking up of our Blessed Lady into heaven, in body and in soul, by the power of God.

atheist (ā′thē-ĭst). One who denies the existence of God.

atone (ā-tōn′). To make satisfaction to God's justice for sin and its punishment.

atonement. The act by which God's justice is satisfied, particularly that which Christ performed by His sufferings and death.

attribute (ă′trĭ-būt). A quality belonging to a person or thing, such as the attributes of the Church.

attrition (ă-trĭsh′ŭn). Imperfect contrition, sorrow for sin based on a motive of faith inferior to love for God, particularly that which is based on the fear of punishment.

authority (ô-thŏr′ĭ-tĭ). The right to rule others.

Balm. A sweet-smelling liquid, derived from a terebinth tree, used to make chrism for Confirmation.

banns. The public announcements in church of a forthcoming marriage.

Baptism. The sacrament which gives our soul the new life of sanctifying grace, through the washing of the body with water in the name of the three Divine Persons.

baptism of blood. Martyrdom endured by an unbaptized person for the faith of Christ.

baptism of desire. An act of love for God made by an unbaptized person with the desire to do all that is necessary for his salvation.

baptize. To confer the sacrament of Baptism.

beatific vision. The privilege of the blessed in heaven, to see God face to face.

beatitude (bē-ăt′ĭ-tūd). Happiness, especially the supreme happiness of heaven.

Beelzebub (bē-ĕl′zē-bŭb). One of the names of the leader of the bad angels.

being. Anything which exists; also, the act of existing.

Benediction of the Blessed Sacrament. The function in which the priest blesses the people with the consecrated Host, enclosed in a vessel called the monstrance.

Bethlehem. A small town near Jerusalem, where Christ was born in a stable.

Bible. The collection of inspired writings of the Old and the New Testaments.

blasphemy (blăs′fē-mĭ). Insulting language against God or against holy things or persons.

Blessed Sacrament. The Holy Eucharist, the sacrament containing Our Lord's body and blood under the appearances of bread and wine.

brilliancy (brĭl′yăn-sĭ). One of the qualities of a glorified body, by which it shines with heavenly light.

Cain (kān). Adam's oldest son, who killed his brother Abel.

calumny (kăl′ŭm-nĭ). The sin of injuring another's good name by falsehood.

Calvary (kăl′văr-ĭ). The hill near Jerusalem on which Christ was crucified.

Canon (kăn-ŭn). The part of the Mass between the Sanctus and the Communion; also a law of the Church.

Canon Law. The body of Church laws found in the Code of Canon Law.

canonize (kăn-ŭn-īz). To make an official declaration that a certain person is in heaven.

Cardinal (kär′dĭ-năl). A priest or bishop belonging to the group which advises the Pope and chooses a new Pope when the Pontiff dies.

cardinal virtues. The chief moral virtues—prudence, justice, fortitude, temperance.

catechism (kăt′ĕ-kĭsm). A book of religious instruction, written in the form of questions and answers.

304

catechumen (kăt-ē-kūm'ĕn). A person preparing for Baptism.

Catholic Action. The cooperation of the laity with their bishops in promoting the spiritual welfare of the Church.

ceremony (sĕr'ē-mŏn-ĭ). A sacred function, particularly one connected with the administration of a sacrament.

chalice (chăl'ĭs). The cup used at Mass to contain the wine which is consecrated into the precious Blood of Christ.

character (kăr'ăk-tēr). A spiritual mark imprinted indelibly on the soul by Baptism, Confirmation and Holy Orders.

charity (chăr'ĭ-tĭ). The greatest of the theological virtues, by which we love God above all things for His own sake, and our neighbor as ourselves for the love of God.

chastity (chăs'tĭ-tĭ). The virtue which disposes us to be pure in soul and in body; one of the vows taken by religious.

chasuble (chăz'ū-b'l). The outer vestment worn by the priest at Mass.

Chrism (krĭz'm). A mixture of olive oil and balm, blessed by the bishop on Holy Thursday, and used for Confirmation and certain other functions.

Christmas (krĭs'mǔs). December 25, the feast of Our Lord's birth.

Church. The congregation of all baptized persons, united in the same faith, the same sacrifice and sacraments, and obedience to the same spiritual authority; also, the building in which divine services are held.

churching. The blessing given to a woman after childbirth.

ciborium (sĭ-bōr'ĭ-ǔm). The vessel in which the Blessed Sacrament is contained when reserved in the tabernacle for Holy Communion.

cincture (sĭnk'tūr). The cord worn by the priest about his waist to bind the alb.

citizen (cĭt'ĭ-zĕn). A person who as a member of a civil society, owes allegiance to his government, and is entitled to protection from it.

citizenship (cĭt'ĭ-zĕn-shĭp). State or quality of being a citizen.

cleric (klĕr'ĭk). One engaged in the ministry of the Church, who has received at least the first tonsure.

commandment (kŏm-mănd'mĕnt). A law.

community (kŏm-mū'nĭ-tĭ). A body of people living together under the same laws.

Communion, Holy. *See* Holy Communion.

Communion of Saints. The union of the faithful on earth, the blessed in heaven and the souls in purgatory with Christ as their Head.

confession. The telling of our sins to an authorized priest in order to obtain their forgiveness.

confessional (kŏn-fĕsh'ǔn-ăl). The grated enclosure in which the sacrament of Penance is ordinarily administered.

confessor (kŏn-fĕs'ēr). A priest who hears confessions; also, a male saint who was not a martyr.

Confirmation. The sacrament by which we are made perfect Christians and soldiers of Jesus Christ.

consecration (kŏn-sĕ-krā'shǔn). A solemn blessing; in particular the change of bread and wine into the body and blood of Christ; also the ceremony by which a priest becomes a bishop.

constitutive blessing. A blessing by which a person or a thing is rendered sacred.

consummation (kŏn-sǔm-mā'shǔn). A completion.

contrition (kŏn-trĭ'shǔn). Sorrow for our sins from a supernatural motive, with a purpose of not sinning again.

cope (kōp). A vestment, like a long cape, worn by the priest at certain functions, particularly at Benediction of the Blessed Sacrament.

corporal (kôr'pōr-ăl). The piece of blessed linen on which the Host and the chalice are placed at Mass.

Corpus Christi. A feast celebrated on the Thursday after Trinity Sunday in honor of the Blessed Sacrament.

covetousness. An excessive desire of worldly possessions, one of the capital sins.

create. To make something out of nothing.

Creator. God, who has made all things out of nothing.

creature. Something made out of nothing by God.

Creed. A list of some of the more important Christian doctrines, drawn up and officially proclaimed by the Church.

cremation (krē-mā'shǔn). The destruction of a corpse by burning.

Cross. The instrument of death to which Christ was nailed; also, its representation.

crucifix (krōō'sĭ-fĭks). A cross bearing the image of Christ.

crucifixion. The nailing of Christ to the cross.

curate (kū'răt). A priest who assists a pastor in the care of his parish.

cursing (kûrs'ing). Language calling down some evil on a person, place or thing.

Deacon (dē-k'n). A man who has received the Holy Order next below the priesthood, and is thereby appointed to assist the priest at Mass and at other sacred functions.

deliberate (dĕ-lĭb'ĕr-ăt). With full knowledge and full consent of the will.

depute (dĕ-pūt'). To give a person authority or power to perform a certain task.

despair (dĕ-spâr'). The refusal to trust that God will give us the necessary help for the salvation of our soul.

detraction (dĕ-trăk'shŭn). The sin of making known the hidden faults of another without a good reason.

devil (dĕv'l). A bad angel; particularly, the leader of the wicked angels, Lucifer.

diocese (dī'ŏ-sēs). A portion of the universal Church, governed by a bishop.

diriment impediment. A circumstance, arising from the law of God or of the Church, that renders a marriage null and void.

disciple (dĭ-sī'p'l). One who is a follower and pupil of another; particularly, one who is a follower of Christ.

dispensation (dĭs-pĕn-sā'shŭn). The act by which a superior frees a person from the obligation of obeying a law.

dispense (dĭs-pĕns'). To give a dispensation.

dispositions (dĭs-pō-zĭ'shŭns). The soul's preparation for the worthy reception of a sacrament.

distraction (dĭs-trăk'shŭn). A thought or imaginary picture, during prayer, on some matter not connected with the prayer.

divine (dĭ-vīn'). Belonging to God or coming from God or directed to God.

Divine Office. The official prayer of the Church, recited daily by priests and religious.

divine tradition. Revealed truths given to the Church by word of mouth only, not through the Bible.

divorce (dĭ-vōrs)'. The breaking of the bond of marriage in such a way that the parties are regarded as free to contract another marriage.

doctrine (dŏk'trĭn). A truth pertaining to faith or to morals.

doxology (dŏk-sŏl'ŏ-jĭ). The prayer "Glory be to the Father, etc."; also applied to the *Gloria* in the Mass.

Easter (ēs'tĕr). The day of Our Lord's resurrection from the dead, or its annual commemoration.

Easter Time. The period during which Catholics are bound to receive Holy Communion; in the United States it lasts from the first Sunday in Lent to Trinity Sunday.

ecclesiastical (ĕ-klē-zĭ-ăs'tĭ-kăl). Related to the Church.

ecumenical council (ĕk-û-mĕn-ĭ-kăl). A council of bishops representing the entire Catholic Church, under the presidency of the Pope or of his special delegates.

ejaculation (ĕ-jăk-û-lā'shŭn). A short prayer, also known as an aspiration.

elevation (ĕl-ĕ-vā'shŭn). A solemn ceremony in the Mass, consisting of the raising aloft by the priest of the consecrated Host and Chalice, immediately after the Consecration.

Ember Days. Three days of fast and abstinence, Wednesday, Friday and Saturday, in each of the four seasons of the year.

encyclical letter (ĕn-sĭ'klĭ-kăl). A letter on some important matter sent by the Pope to the faithful through the bishops.

envy (ĕn'vĭ). One of the capital sins, sorrow at another's good fortune.

Epiphany (ĕ-pĭf'ăn-ĭ). The feast celebrating the visit of the Wise Men to the Infant Jesus, January 6.

episcopal (ĕ-pĭs'kō-păl). Pertaining to a bishop.

Epistle (ĕ-pĭs'l). An inspired letter written by one of the apostles and contained in the New Testament.

eternity (ē-tĕr'nĭ-tĭ). Duration without beginning, end or change, possessed by God alone; also duration without end, such as is possessed by angels and human souls.

Eucharist (ū'kăr-ĭst). The sacrament of Christ's body and blood under the appearances of bread and wine.

Evangelical Counsels. The virtues of poverty, chastity and obedience, practiced in accordance with the counsel of Christ.

Evangelist. One who brings good tidings, a term applied to the four writers of the Gospel in the New Testament.

evil spirits. The fallen angels, or devils.

evolution. The development of a higher form of being from a lower; according to some non-Catholics, human beings were developed in this way from animals.

examination of conscience. The act of recalling our sins in order to confess them properly.

excommunication. A penalty inflicted by the Church for a grave crime, excluding one from certain Catholic rights, such as the reception of the sacraments.

existence (ĕx-ĭs'tĕns). The act of being.

exorcism (ĕks'ŏr-sĭsm). A formula employed by the Church against the attacks of the devil.

exorcist (ĕk'sŏr-sĭst). One who has received the third of the minor orders, giving him the power to pronounce exorcisms.

Extreme Unction. The sacrament for those in danger of death, from sickness or accident or old age, conferred through the anointing with oil and the prayer of the priest.

Faith (fāth). The first of the theological virtues, disposing one to believe all that God has revealed because of the authority of God revealing, who can neither deceive nor be deceived.

faithful. The members of the Catholic Church.

faithful departed. Members of the Church who have passed away and are in purgatory.

fast day. A day on which only one full meal is permitted.

Fathers of the Church. Saintly writers who lived in the early centuries and gave testimony to the Church's belief and tradition.

finite (fī'nĭt). Limited; the opposite of Infinite.

first tonsure (tŏn'shûr). The ceremony by which a man becomes a cleric; consisting in the cutting of his hair by the bishop and in certain words pronounced by the recipient.

form. The words pronounced by the one administering a sacrament.

fortitude. One of the cardinal virtues, disposing one to do what is good in spite of difficulty.

foster father. One who takes the place of a real father in the bringing up of a child.

Freemason. A member of a secret society of that name.

free will. The power to choose, according to our own wish, either to perform an action or not to perform it.

fruitful reception of a sacrament. A reception of the sacrament which at once confers grace on the soul.

Fruits of the Holy Ghost. Good works, bringing sweetness and joy, performed under the inspiration of the Holy Ghost.

function (fŭnk'shŭn). A ceremony or religious service.

General Confession. A confession that includes the sins told in previous confessions, either of one's whole life or of a portion of it.

General Judgment. The judgment that Our Lord will pass on all men at the end of the world.

genuflexion (jĕn-û-flĕk'shŭn). An act of reverence, consisting of the bending of the knee or of both knees to the ground.

Ghost (gōst). Spirit; generally applied to the Third Person of the Blessed Trinity, the Holy Ghost.

Gifts of the Holy Ghost. Habits infused together with sanctifying grace, helping one with the assistance of the Holy Ghost to know and to do the will of God.

God. The Supreme Being, self-existing and infinitely perfect, who created all things.

godchild. One for whom a person has acted as sponsor, or godparent, at Baptism or Confirmation.

godparent. A sponsor, who accepts the responsibility of caring for the spiritual welfare of one baptized or confirmed if the parents die or neglect this duty.

Golgotha (gŏl'gŏ-thà). Mount Calvary, the place near Jerusalem where Christ died.

Good Friday. The day on which Christ died, and also its annual commemoration.

Gospel. The account of the life and teachings of Jesus Christ contained in the New Testament, written by Ss. Matthew, Mark, Luke and John.

grace. A supernatural gift of God, given us through the merits of Christ, for our salvation.

Guardian Angel. The angel appointed by God to watch over us in a special manner.

Habitual Grace. A name for sanctifying grace, since it remains as a habit in the soul.

Hail Mary. The Angelical Salutation, the Church's chief prayer to the Blessed Virgin Mary, so called because its first words are the Archangel Gabriel's greeting to Our Lady.

hallowed (hăl'ōd). Made holy.

heaven. The place and state of everlasting happiness in the next life; our eternal home with God, our Father.

heir (âr). One who has a right to an inheritance from his father.

hell. The place and state of everlasting punishment in the next life.

heresy. The obstinate denial of one or more of the truths of divine revelation by one professing to be a Christian.

High Mass. A Mass in which certain portions are chanted by the celebrant.

holiness. Sanctity, one of the marks of the true Church of Christ.

Holy Communion. The receiving of Jesus Christ in the sacrament of the Holy Eucharist, as spiritual nourishment for the soul.

Holy Eucharist. The sacrament which really contains the body and blood of Jesus Christ under the appearances of bread and wine.

Holy Ghost. The third Person of the Blessed Trinity, who proceeds from the Father and the Son; the Soul of the Catholic Church.

Holy Orders. The sacrament by which men receive the grace and the power to perform the sacred duties of bishops, priests and other ministers of the Church.

Holy Saturday. The Saturday of Holy Week, the vigil of Easter.

holyday of obligation. A feastday on which the Church obliges us to hear Mass and to abstain from servile work.

hope. The second of the theological virtues, disposing us to trust that God, because of His power, mercy and fidelity, will give us eternal happiness and the means to obtain it.

hosts (hōsts). A very large number.

humeral veil (hū'mēr-ăl). The veil which drapes the priest's shoulders, arms, and hands at Benediction and at certain other functions.

humility. The virtue which disposes us to acknowledge our limitations.

Idolatry (ī-dŏl'ă-trī). The sin of worshiping a creature as god.

Immaculate Conception. The unique privilege conferred on the Blessed Virgin, whereby she was preserved from original sin from the first moment of her existence in view of the merits of her Divine Son.

immodesty. A sin against the sixth commandment, which is liable to lead to impurity.

immortal. That which will never die.

impassibility. One of the qualities of a glorified body, whereby it is free from suffering and death.

impediment. See Marriage Impediment.

imperfect contrition. Sorrow for sin out of a supernatural motive inferior to love of God; also called attrition.

imperfection. A slight moral defect or a venial sin.

impurity. The sin of unlawful sexual gratification, forbidden by the sixth commandment of God

incarnation (ĭn-kär-nā'shŭn). The union of the second Person of the Blessed Trinity with a human nature.

inclination (ĭn-klĭn-nā'shun). Leaning toward.

indefectibility (ĭn-dē-fĕk-tĭ-bĭ'lĭ-tĭ). The attribute of the Church whereby it will last, as Christ founded it, until the end of time.

indelible. That which cannot be blotted out.

Index of Forbidden Books. The catalogue prepared by the Holy Office in Rome, listing the books which Catholics are explicitly forbidden to read.

indifferentism. The theory that all religions are good, so that it makes no difference which religion a person practices.

indulgence (ĭn-dŭl'jĕns). The remission of temporal punishment due to sins already forgiven granted by the Church from her spiritual treasury.

indwelling. Abiding within a person or thing, such as the constant presence of the Holy Ghost in the Church

infallibility. The attribute of the Church whereby it is preserved from error in faith or morals by the special assistance of the Holy Ghost.

infidelity. Refusal to accept the Christian faith.

infinite (ĭn'fĭn-ĭt). Without limit or measure; applied strictly to God alone.

infusion (ĭn-fū'zhŭn). A pouring in or upon; applied to one of the methods of baptizing; also to the giving of grace and supernatural habits to the soul by God.

inspiration. Enlightenment from God: particularly that given to the persons who wrote the Bible.

intention. An act of the will purposing to do something, such as to administer a sacrament.

invalid (ĭn-văl'ĭd). Not real or genuine, applied especially to a ceremony intended to be a sacrament, but which because of some defect does not constitute a real sacrament.

invocative blessing. A blessing given by the Church to a person, either directly, or indirectly through the use of some object, such as the blessing of a house.

Israelites(ĭz'-rā-ĕl-īts).The Jewish people.

Jesus. A name meaning "Saviour"— the name of the Son of God as Man.

Joseph, Saint. The husband of the Blessed Virgin Mary and foster father of Jesus Christ.

jubilee indulgence. An indulgence granted every 25 years, and on other special occasions, by the Pope.

judgment. The appearance of the soul before God to be rewarded or punished for its good or evil deeds, which will take place twice—immediately after death (particular judgment) and at the end of the world (general judgment).

jurisdiction (jōō-rĭs-dĭk'shŭn). Authority or power; particularly, the Church's power to teach and to rule the faithful.

justice. One of the cardinal virtues, disposing us to render to every one what is due to him.

Kingdom of Heaven. The place and state of happiness in the life to come; also (especially in the parables of Christ) the Church, which brings men to eternal happiness.

Kingship of Christ. Our Lord's authority, even as Man over the entire universe, which is commemorated by the feast of Christ the King on the last Sunday of October.

Laity (lā'ĭt-ĭ). Those members of the Church who do not belong to the clergy or to the religious state.

Latin Church. That portion of the Catholic Church which uses Latin in its liturgy.

laxity. Carelessness and lack of fervor in the practice of religion.

Lent. The penitential season lasting from Ash Wednesay to Holy Saturday, as a remembrance of Christ's fast in the desert and a preparation for Easter.

liberality. A moral virtue which disposes us to use worldly goods rightly and generously.

liberal works. Occupations of an intellectual, cultural or artistic nature, permitted on Sundays and holydays of obligation.

Limbo. The place or state of rest where under the Old Testament the souls of the just who had died before the time of Christ, awaited the Redemption; also, the state or place where infants who die without Baptism enjoy for all eternity a natural happiness.

litany (lĭt'ă-nĭ). A form of prayer to Our Lord, the Blessed Virgin or the saints, consisting of a series of invocations and petitions.

liturgy (lĭt'ŭr-jĭ). The official ceremonies of the Church; in the Oriental churches, the Sacrifice of Our Lord's body and blood under the appearances of bread and wine.

liturgical. Pertaining to the official ceremonies of the Church.

Low Mass. A Mass celebrated by a priest unassisted by deacon or subdeacon, and without chant.

Low Sunday. The first Sunday after Easter.

Lucifer (lū'sĭ-fĕr). The leader of the rebellious angels, also called Beelzebub.

Magnificat (măg-nĭf'-ĭ-kăt). The prayer of praise uttered by the Blessed Virgin on the occasion of her visit to St. Elizabeth.

manifest (măn'ĭ-fĕst). To show plainly.

maniple. The vestment worn by sacred ministers on the left arm at certain functions, such as the Mass.

marks of the church. Certain clear signs by which all men can recognize the true Church of Christ.

marriage. The permanent union of a man and woman as husband and wife; also, the contract by which they enter this union.

marriage impediment. A circumstance determined by the law of God or of the Church which, if present, renders a marriage unlawful or even null and void.

Martyr (măr'tĕr). A person who allows himself to be put to death in testimony of the Christian faith or some other Christian virtue.

Mass. The unbloody sacrifice of the body and blood of Christ, renewing the sacrifice of Calvary.

Matrimony. The sacrament of Christian marriage.

matter. The things or human actions employed in the making of a sacrament.

mediator (mē'di-ā-tēr). One who reconciles two parties that have been in disagreement; usually applied to Our Lord, who reconciled men with God.

mediatrix. A female mediator; usually applied to the Blessed Virgin because she cooperated with Jesus Christ, the Mediator, in reconciling men with God.

meditation. Mental prayer, not expressed in words.

medium. A person claiming to communicate with the spirits of the dead.

Melchisedech (měl-kĭz'ě-děk). A priest of ancient times who offered sacrifice of bread and wine; hence, Christ is called a priest according to the order of Melchisedech, because He offered a sacrifice of His body and blood under the appearances of bread and wine.

merit. The claim to a reward arising from good deeds; also, a good deed deserving of reward.

Messias (měs-ī'ǎs). The Saviour expected by the Jews.

ministry (mĭn-ĭs-trĭ). The performance of a sacred office by one specially chosen for it.

miracle. An extraordinary effect, surpassing the powers of nature, perceptible to the human senses, having God as its chief author.

missal. The book used by the priest for the celebration of Mass; also, a smaller edition or a translation for the use of the laity.

mixed marriage. The marriage of a Catholic with a non-Catholic.

Monsignor (mŏn-sē'nyôr). A title conferred on a priest by the Pope, usually at the request of the bishop, giving the right to wear purple, like a bishop.

monstrance (mon'strǎns). A large sacred vessel, with a glass-covered opening in the centre, to contain the Blessed Sacrament during Benediction.

moral virtue. A virtue disposing us to lead moral lives by treating persons and things according to the will of God.

mortal sin. A grave offense against God's law, which brings spiritual death to the soul by depriving it of its supernatural life, sanctifying grace.

mortification. Self-denial.

mystery (mĭs'tēr-ĭ). A truth which we cannot fully understand.

Mystical Body (mĭs'tĭ-kǎl). A term for the Church with Christ as its Head, because of its resemblance to the living human body.

Nature. That which constitutes a being, and is its principle of action.

Nazareth. A village in Galilee, the home of the Holy Family.

null and void. Worthless, not genuine.

Nuptial Blessing. (nŭp'shǎl). The special blessing given the bride at the conclusion of the Pater Noster in the Mass for a bridal couple.

Nuptial Mass. The special Mass celebrated for a bridal couple immediately after their marriage.

Oath. The calling on God to witness to the truth of what we say or to the sincerity of a promise.

obedience. The virtue which disposes us to do the will of our superiors.

obsession. The tormenting of a person by the devil.

occasion of sin. A person, place or thing that is liable to lead one into sin.

Offertory. That part of the Mass in which the bread and wine are offered up to God in anticipation of their change into the body and blood of Christ.

Oriental Rites. The liturgical ceremonies carried out among Oriental Christians in a manner somewhat different from that employed in the Latin Church and in some of the languages of the East, such as Armenian, Greek or Syrian.

Our Father. The prayer taught us by our Lord, beginning with the words: "Our Father."

original sin. The privation of sanctifying grace with which we come into the world as a result of Adam's sin.

ostensorium (ŏs-těn-sŏ-rĭ-ŭm). A large sacred vessel with a glass-covered opening in the centre, containing the Blessed Sacrament in the form of a large Host, during Benediction to be seen by the worshippers; also called a monstrance.

Pall (pôl). A linen-covered card, used to cover the chalice at Mass.

Palm Sunday. The Sunday immediately preceding Easter, when the Church commemorates the triumphant entrance of Christ into Jerusalem, just before His Passion, on which occasion the people strewed palms before Him as a mark of reverence.

Paraclete (păr'ǎ-klēt). A designation of the Holy Ghost; The Comforter.

parish priest. A priest in charge of a parish, or portion of a diocese; sometimes called a pastor.

310

Partial indulgence. The remission of a part of the temporal punishment due to one's forgiven sins, effected by the Church through the application of her spiritual treasury.

Particular Judgment. The judgment that each soul undergoes before God immediately after death.

Paschal (păs'kăl). Connected with Easter—for example, the paschal candle, lighted for the first time on the vigil of Easter.

Passion of Christ. The sufferings of Our Blessed Saviour, ending with His death on the cross.

pastor. Literally, a shepherd; applied to a parish priest with reference to his parish, also to a bishop with reference to his diocese and to the Pope with reference to the universal Church.

paten. The golden plate on which the sacred Host is placed at Mass.

patience. A moral virtue which disposes us to bear up under difficulties and trials.

patriotism. A moral virtue which disposes us to honor, love, respect and help our country.

Paul, Saint. One of the apostles, chosen by Our Lord through a vision after His Ascension.

Penance. The virtue disposing us to be sorry for our sins; also, one of the sacraments, whereby sins committed after Baptism are forgiven by the absolution of the priest to sinners who confess them with true contrition.

Pentecost (pĕn'tĕ-kŏst). The seventh Sunday after Easter, commemorating the descent of the Holy Ghost on the apostles.

perfect contrition. The contrition based on love of God which restores a sinner to the state of grace even before he goes to confession.

perjury. The grave sin committed by one who takes an oath to what he believes to be false.

person. An intellectual being, independent and distinct from others.

Peter, Saint. The apostle chosen by Christ to be the chief of the apostles and the first Pope.

Peter's Pence. The annual offering made by the faithful to the Pope, the successor of St. Peter.

piety. One of the gifts of the Holy Ghost; (2) a virtue disposing one to honor his parents; (3) in a general sense, the combination of religious virtues.

plenary indulgence (plē'nă-rĭ). The remission of all the debt of one's temporal punishment, granted by the Church through the application of her spiritual treasury.

Pontifical Mass. A solemn Mass celebrated by a bishop or other high dignitary of the Church.

Pontiff. A bishop; often applied to the Sovereign Pontiff, the Pope.

poor souls. The souls in purgatory.

porter. One who has received the first of the minor orders.

positive laws. Laws added to the natural law, either by God or by human superiors.

possession. The indwelling of the devil in a person's body, with a measure of power over the person's faculties.

prayer. The lifting up of our minds and hearts to God.

Preface. The portion of the Mass immediately preceding the Canon, in which thanks are given to God for His blessings.

presbyter (prĕs'bĭ-tĕr). A priest who is not a bishop.

presumption. A sin against hope, whereby a person trusts that he can be saved by his own efforts without God's help, or by God's help without his own efforts.

priest. A man with the power to offer sacrifice.

privileged altar. An altar to which the Church has attached a privilege, whereby a plenary indulgence is granted to any soul in purgatory for whom Mass is celebrated on that altar.

Promised Land. The land of Canaan, or Palestine, which God promised to the Jewish people when they were led by Moses out of Egypt.

prophet (prŏf'-ĕt). A person chosen by God to announce His message to man, particularly things that are to come.

Providence. God's loving care over us.

prudence. One of the cardinal virtues, disposing us to form right judgments in all circumstances about what we must do or not do.

purgatory. The state in the life to come where souls are punished for a time who have died in venial sin or with a debt of temporal punishment unpaid.

purificator. A linen cloth used by the priest at Mass to wipe the chalice and his mouth and fingers after communion.

purpose of amendment. The firm resolution not to sin again, which is included in true contrition.

311

Rash Judgment. A sin against the eighth commandment, whereby a person without sufficient reason believes something harmful to another's character.

Real Presence. The presence of Jesus Christ, truly, really and substantially in the sacrament of the Holy Eucharist under the appearances of bread and wine.

Redeemer. One who releases a captive by paying the price of his ransom; particularly Our Lord, Jesus Christ, who released us from the captivity of sin by offering His sufferings and death to His heavenly Father, as the price of our ransom.

Redemption. The act of redeeming us, performed by our Blessed Lord.

relic. Something belonging to, or connected with Our Lord or the Saints, such as a portion of their bodies or a garment they wore.

religion. The beliefs, laws and ceremonies by which men honor and serve God; also, the virtue disposing us to honor and serve God properly.

Religious. A member of an Order or Congregation approved by the Church, bound to serve God by the vows of poverty, chastity and obedience.

remorse. Anguish of soul because of sin.

repentance. Contrition for past sin.

Requiem Mass (rē'kwĭ-ĕm). A special Mass celebrated for the repose of the souls of the faithful departed at which black vestments are worn.

resurrection. The restoration of a dead body to its life of physical completeness by its reunion with the soul to which it was formerly joined.

revelation. The direct manifestation of truth by God to man; also, the body of truths thus manifested.

rite. A religious ceremony, or a collection of ceremonies.

Rosary. A prayer to the Blessed Virgin Mary, composed of decades of one Our Father and ten Hail Marys each, arranged in three series—the joyful, the sorrowful and the glorious mysteries—each series being composed of five decades; also, the string of beads on which these prayers are counted.

Sabbath. The seventh day of the week, the Lord's day in the Old Testament.

sacrament. An outward sign instituted by Christ, with the power to give grace.

sacramental grace. A special grace given by each sacrament helping the recipient to carry out the particular purpose of that sacrament.

sacramentals. Holy things or actions of which the Church makes use to obtain for us from God through her intercession spiritual and temporal favors.

Sacred Scripture. The inspired writings of the Old and New Testaments, also called the Bible.

sacrifice. The offering of a victim to God by a priest and its destruction in some way, to acknowledge that God is the Creator and Lord of all things.

sacrilege (săk'rĭ-lĕj). A sin against the first commandment, committed when a person mistreats sacred persons, places or things.

Saint. In a general sense, any one in the state of grace; in a more limited sense, one who is in heaven.

salvation. The attaining of the happiness of heaven.

Samaria (să-mā'rĭ-à). One of the regions of Palestine; also, the chief city of that region.

sanctification. The acquiring of sanctifying grace.

sanctifying grace. The grace that confers on our souls a new life that is a sharing in the life of God himself.

sanctuary. That portion of the church, cut off from the body of the church, in which the altar is situated and the sacred functions performed.

Satan (sā'tăn). One of the names of the leader of the bad angels.

satisfaction. What is given to God to pay for the debt of sin or of its punishment, particularly the sufferings of Christ.

Saviour. One who saves others, particularly Jesus Christ, who saved us from the effects of sin.

scandal. A sin against the virtue of charity, whereby a person furnishes the occasion of sin to another.

scapular. A garment worn by some religious, in front and back over the shoulders; also, a miniature form of this garment, blessed and indulgenced, to be worn by the faithful.

Scripture. The inspired writings of the Old and the New Testament.

Scriptural. Having to do with the Scripture.

scruple. An unreasonable fear of sin, based on false ideas of the moral law or on a false application of that law.

scrupulous. Unreasonably anxious about sin, judging things to be unlawful which are not wrong.

312

see. The place in which a bishop resides and rules his diocese.

self-existing. Not owing existence to any other being, a perfection of God alone.

seminary. An institution in which men are prepared for the priesthood.

servile work (sĕr′vĭl). Work which requires labor of body rather than of mind; the type of work forbidden on Sundays and holydays of obligation.

sin. The transgression of God's law; also, as applied to original sin, the privation of sanctifying grace consequent on Adam's transgression.

slander. A sin against the eighth commandment, whereby a person injures the good name of another by false statements.

sloth (slōth). One of the capital sins, laziness of mind or of body which causes a person to neglect his duties.

soul. The principle of life; in man an immortal spirit, endowed with intelligence and free will.

Solemn Baptism. The administration of the sacrament of Baptism with the various ceremonies prescribed by the Church and with specially consecrated water.

Solemn Mass. A Mass, portions of which are chanted, and in which the celebrating priest is assisted by a deacon and a subdeacon.

spirit. An immortal being having understanding and free will, but no body, such as God or an angel.

Spiritism. The practice of trying to get into communication with the souls of the dead.

Spiritist. A person who claims to communicate with the souls of the dead.

spiritual. Having to do with the spirit or the soul, particularly the soul of man, as in the expression "spiritual welfare."

sponsor. One who assumes responsibilities toward another, such as a godparent in Baptism or Confirmation.

stipend (stī′pĕnd). An offering given on the occasion of a sacred function, particularly that given to a priest by the one for whose intentions the priest offers Mass.

stole. A vestment worn about the neck by a bishop, priest or deacon at sacred functions, either crossed over the breast or hanging down.

subdeacon. A man who has received the first of the major orders.

successor. One who follows another in holding an office.

Sunday. The first day of the week, celebrated as the Lord's day in the New Testament.

superabundant satisfactions. Good works performed with the power to make satisfaction for the temporal punishment due to sin, which are not needed by the person who performs them, and which accordingly go into the treasury of the Church to be dispensed in the form of indulgences.

supernatural. Related to God in those aspects of His divine nature which can be known only from revelation, chiefly the Divine Trinity.

supreme (sū-prēm′). Above all others; the highest.

superstition (sū-pĕr-stĭsh′ŭn). A sin against the first commandment, committed when a person attributes to a creature a power which belongs to God alone.

symbol (sĭm′bŏl). A sign of something; for example, marriage is a symbol of the union between Christ and the Church.

Tabernacle. The compartment, usually placed in the middle of the altar, in which the Blessed Sacrament is kept.

temperance. One of the cardinal virtues, disposing a person to control his desires and to use rightly the things that please his senses.

temple. A sacred building, destined for divine worship.

temporal punishment. The punishment which one is obliged to endure for a time, either in this life or in purgatory, for sins that have been forgiven.

temptation. An urge to commit sin, coming either from our own nature or from the world or from the devil.

theology (thē-ŏl′ō-jĭ). The sacred science about God and divine things.

tithes. A tenth of one's income, the offering which Catholics formerly were obliged to contribute to the Church.

tonsure. The cutting of the hair, constituting the ceremony by which a man enters the clerical state, known specifically as the first tonsure; by the law of the Church the clergy in Catholic countries are afterward supposed to keep a portion of the head shaved.

313

tradition. Doctrines handed down without being put in writing; particularly divine tradition, which was given to the Church by Christ and His apostles only by word of mouth, not through the Bible, though later it was put in writing by the Fathers of the Church.

transubstantiation. The change of the entire substance of bread into the body of Christ and of the entire substance of wine into His blood, while the appearances of bread and wine remain—the change effected by Christ through the ministry of His priest at the sacrifice of the Mass.

trespasses (trĕs'păs-sĕz). Offenses, injuries.

Trinity (trĭ'nĭ-tĭ). Three divine Persons in one God.

Trinity Sunday. The first Sunday after Pentecost, the last day for the fulfilment of the Easter duty in the United States.

Unction (ŭnk'shŭn). An anointing, especially that which is given with holy oil in certain sacraments, such as Extreme Unction.

understanding. The power to think and to judge.

unity. The quality by which a being is one, such as the unity of God; or made one, such as the unity of the Church.

universality. The quality of the Church by which it is destined for all times and for all nations, and actually fulfils this destiny.

Valid (văl'ĭd). Genuine, real; particularly in the case of the administration of a sacrament, when it is truly received by the person to whom it is applied.

veil (vāl). A cloth covering, particularly the humeral veil used by the priest to cover his shoulders, arms and hands when he gives Benediction of the Blessed Sacrament; also, the chalice veil and the tabernacle veil.

venial sin (vēn-ĭ-ăl). A transgression of God's law in some slight matter, or even in a serious matter when the sinner believes it is only slightly wrong or does not give full consent.

veracity. A moral virtue, disposing us to tell the truth.

vestments. Special garments worn by the ministers of the Church in sacred functions.

Viaticum (vī-ăt'ĭ-kŭm). Holy Communion received by a person in danger of death.

vicar (vĭ'kẽr). One who represents another; particularly the Pope, who represents Christ in the government of the Church and is called the Vicar of Jesus Christ.

Vicar General. A priest appointed by a bishop to help him in the government of his diocese, and for this purpose sharing in the bishop's jurisdiction.

victim. The thing which is offered and in some way destroyed in a sacrifice.

vigil. The day immediately preceding a great feast; sometimes a day of fast and abstinence.

virtue. A habit of doing good.

vocal. Pronounced with the organs of speech; particularly applied to prayer recited with the lips and tongue, as distinct from merely mental prayer.

vocation. A special call from God to a higher form of life, especially to the priesthood or to the religious life.

vow. A deliberate promise made to God by which a person binds himself under pain of sin to do something especially pleasing to God.

Way of the Cross. A devotion in remembrance of the passion of Christ portrayed by fourteen representations of incidents connected with it, each surmounted by a wooden cross; to make the devotion one visits each of the crosses, meditating on the passion of Christ.

wedlock. The state of matrimony.

Whitsunday (hwĭt's'n-dā). An old name for Pentecost.

wilful. With full consent of the will.

winding-sheet. The cloth in which a dead body is wrapped; particularly the shroud in which Our Lord's body was wrapped.

witness. One who sees an occurrence and is able to give testimony about it.

works of mercy. Certain specially good deeds, performed from a supernatural motive, for the benefit of our fellowmen, such as visiting the sick.

worship. Testimony of reverence and submission to another, particularly the homage we give to God.

314

A CATECHISM OF THE MASS

By

Rev. David J. Sharrock, C. SS. R.

collaborating with

Rev. Francis J. Connell, C. SS. R.

Introductory Questions

Before you start to study this part of the Catechism, go back to Lesson 27 and review what you learned about the Sacrifice of the Mass. This part of the Catechism is going to take for granted that you know that Lesson perfectly.

1. Where do Catholics receive their power to offer the Mass with the priest?

Catholics receive their power to offer the Mass with the priest from their Baptism. By Baptism, each Catholic is united to Christ, the Priest. Confirmation unites a Catholic even more closely with Christ the Priest. Because of these two Sacraments, a Catholic shares in the very Priesthood of Christ and receives from Him the power to *offer* the Sacrifice of the Mass *with* the priest, or to participate in this offering.

(a) Only the priest who has received the Sacrament of Holy Orders can take the place of Christ at the altar, sacrifice Him in an unbloody manner, and offer Him to God. The priest *makes* the Offering. All other Catholics share or participate in this Offering.

2. To whom did Christ give the Sacrifice of the Mass?

Christ gave the Sacrifice of the Mass to His Church. He knew that men would need a Sacrifice to honor God and to beg God to grant them the graces Christ won for them on the Cross. Just the memory of Christ's Sacrifice would not be enough. So He left His Church the perfect Sacrifice, the Sacrifice of Himself, by which God is infinitely honored, and the graces Christ won for men on Calvary are poured into their souls.

3. But is not the Mass Christ's Sacrifice?

Yes. For we must remember that the Church is the Mystical Body of Christ. Christ is the Head of this Body; every Catholic is a member. The Sacrifice of the Mass, therefore, is Christ's Sacrifice and *our* Sacrifice. This is what we mean when we say that Christ gave the Mass to His Church. He gave us, His members, the opportunity to offer the Sacrifice in union with Him.

(a) We use the term "Mystical Body" to describe the union between Christ and His members. We are united to Christ by Baptism, by the open profession of our Faith, by obedience to the Pope, who takes the place of Christ on earth, and, finally, by sanctifying grace, which gives us a share in the Divine Life of God Himself. This sanctifying grace makes us one with Jesus, because He won this grace for us on the Cross, and as Man has the fullness of this grace in His own Soul.

This union between Christ and His member is so close that we call ourselves one Body, with Christ as the Head of this Body.

But this Body is not a physical Body, nor is it a moral Body, e.g., like a men's club, or a young people's club. It is a Body with a Supernatural Head Who is Christ which we enter by the supernatural means of Baptism, live a Supernatural life by sanctifying grace, and profess a Supernatural Faith. So it is a Body that is different from any other bodies we know. It is above nature, or super-natural. So we call the Body a Supernatural or "Mystical Body." It is the Mystical Body *of Christ*, because Christ is the Head of this Body.

(b) On Calvary, Christ alone offered the Sacrifice of His Life. In the Mass, we, the members of His Mystical Body, offer the Sacrifice of His life in union with Him.

(c) Thus at each Mass, Christ is still the Priest offering His Life for us. But He offers that life for us by means of the priest who takes His place at the altar, and in union with us who are members of His Mystical Body.

(d) The Mass is therefore the Sacrifice of the Mystical Body of Christ, which *is* the Catholic Church.

(e) Since the Mass is the Sacrifice of Christ and His members, both Christ and His members will contribute something to the make-up of the Mass. Christ contributes the essential part which is the Consecration of His Body and Blood and the giving of that Body and Blood to us in Holy Communion. His members, besides offering the Sacrifice with Christ, contribute the prayers and ceremonies which surround the essential part. The main part of the Mass (the Canon) has never changed and never will change. But the prayers and ceremonies have both changed and developed through the centuries, as the members of Christ's Mystical Body have lived here on earth. Thus each prayer and ceremony is an expression of the Life of the Church as she has lived on earth. In order to understand many of the prayers at Mass, we must go back to the time they were written, and see why they were composed, and what they meant to the members of Christ's Mystical Body then. Once we understand these things, it will be easy to see what they are to mean to us who are members of this same Mystical Body living in the 20th Century.

So we shall study the prayers and ceremonies of the Mass and see first, how they are an expression of the Life of the Church through the centuries as she has tried to surround the Mass with prayers and ceremonies her children know and understand. Then we shall be able to apply these prayers to our own lives and see the wonderful religion teaching behind each prayer.

316

4. Is the Mass the same throughout the world?

From what we have just studied, we can answer that the Mass, as far as Christ's part in it is concerned, is the same throughout the world. Christ is offered in Sacrifice and given to His people as Food. And His members' part as co-offerers with Him is the same throughout the world. But the prayers and ceremonies which surround this offering may be different. Since different peoples have different ways of expressing themselves to God, they will have different prayers and ceremonies.

(a) Because the prayers and ceremonies which surround the Sacrifice of the Mass are different, we can truly say that the Sacrifice of Christ belongs to the members who offer it with Him. It is part of their lives, because the prayers and ceremonies flow from their own thoughts and actions, as members of the Mystical Body.

5. Which prayers and ceremonies do we use in our Mass?

We use the prayers and ceremonies of the Roman Missal.

(a) Thus the prayers and ceremonies of our Mass are an expression of the Life of the Church as she has lived in the Western part of the world. If we were to study the Mass of the Eastern Catholics, we would find that its prayers are an expression of the Life of the Church in the Eastern part of the world.

6. Why must every Mass in the Roman Rite be celebrated over an altar which contains the relics of some martyrs?

At one time in the Life of the Church, the priest occasionally celebrated Mass over the tomb of some martyr in the Roman catacombs. Gradually, the martyrs came to be so loved and respected that every church in Rome had a martyr buried beneath its altar. This custom spread outside of Rome, too. But some churches could not obtain the whole body of a martyr, but only small relics of some of the martyrs, which they buried in their altars. Finally, what started as a custom was made into a law, so that today, every Mass of the Roman rite must be celebrated on an altar which contains the relics of some of the martyrs.

7. Why must every altar be covered with altar cloths?

Because the altar is a symbol or sign of Christ Himself, and the altar cloths are the Church's way of honoring this symbol.

8. What do we mean by a "symbol"?

A symbol is a material object which is a sign or a representation of some person, *or* thing, *or* idea.

(a) Thus for example, our American Flag is a sign or a representation of our country. It is also a sign or a representation of freedom. When we see the American Flag, we think first of the United States of America, and then of freedom, which is a part of America. For this reason, we call the Flag a symbol of America and a symbol of freedom.

317

(b) Many material objects which are signs are used to represent Christ. These material things are called "symbols." For example, the most common symbol of Christ today is the Cross. Each time we see the Cross, we think of Christ and the Redemption He gained for us by His death on a Cross. So we call the Cross a symbol or a representation of Christ dying for our salvation.

9. Why must the altar cloths be made only of linen?
Because linen cloth has been a sign of purity among people for over 3000 years. It is only right that the Church clothe the symbol of the pure and holy Christ with the cloth that symbolizes purity.
(a) It is because linen cloth is a sign of purity that the finger towels, purificators, and corporals must all be made of linen. Both the purificator and the corporal sometimes touch the Host, and the finger towel is used by the priest who will hold this most pure Host in his fingers.

10. Why must at least two candles be lighted at every Mass?
Candles must be lighted during the Mass, because they are a symbol of Christ Who is the Light of the world; and in the Mass, we offer up this very Light of the world.

11. Which are the vestments used by the priest at Mass?
They are: the amice, the alb, the cincture, the maniple, the stole, and the chasuble.

12. Why are these vestments used?
These vestments are used to draw and keep the attention of both the priest and the people to the wonderful sacrifice being offered.

13. Give a short history of these priestly vestments.
Many years ago, the priestly vestments were the same kind of clothes which most of the Roman men wore, but because of the great dignity of the Mass, they were, even then, more expensive and precious than ordinary clothes. When styles began to change, the Church decided to keep her priests vested as they had always been to make people realize even more deeply how extraordinary the Sacrifice of the Mass really is.
The alb, held together by the cincture, used to be the tunic— the regular "good clothes" of most Roman men. Joined to the tunic was a shawl which covered the shoulders, neck, and head. This is the modern amice. The maniple was the "dress" handkerchief men used to carry. Instead of carrying it in their pockets, they used to pin it to the sleeves of their tunics.
It is hard to find a history for the stole. But very early it was the symbol of priestly power. Finally, the chasuble was the travelling cloak of a man. As a cloak, it used to cover one almost entirely.

The Ordinary of the Mass

Prayers at the Foot of the Altar

The Church as God's representative on earth prepares to offer to God the perfect Sacrifice. She is holy because He has made her holy and therefore worthy to offer this Sacrifice for the sins of all her children. She then begs God, in the words of the Psalmist, to protect her from sinful men, that she may remain holy.

The Beginning of Mass

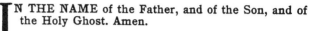

IN THE NAME of the Father, and of the Son, and of the Holy Ghost. Amen.

P. I will go in to the altar of God.

℟. To God, the joy of my youth.

Psalm 42

Give judgment for me, O God, and decide my cause against an unholy people, from unjust and deceitful men deliver me.

℟. For Thou, O God, art my strength, why hast Thou forsaken me? And why do I go about in sadness, while the enemy afflicts me?

P. Send forth Thy light and Thy truth; for they have led me and brought me to Thy holy hill and Thy dwelling place.

℟. And I will go in to the altar of God, to God, the joy of my youth.

P. I shall yet praise Thee upon the harp, O God, my God. Why art thou sad, my soul, and why dost thou trouble me?

℟. Trust in God, for I shall yet praise Him, the salvation of my countenance and my God.

The Meaning of the Opening Prayers

The holy action of the Mass begins with the sign of the Cross to show that the Mass is offered through the power that comes from the Blessed Trinity through the Cross of Christ.

Psalm 42 was originally said on the way to the altar from the sacristy, thus the significance of the verse, "I will go in to the altar of God." Since, however, the distance from sacristy to altar was often very short, it became the custom to start the Psalm only at the altar steps.

God wants each one of us to offer the Holy Sacrifice of the Mass with the Church and the priest. One of the reasons He gave us the Sacrament of Baptism was that we might have the power to offer the Mass with His priest. But He also wants us to be sinless. So right at the very beginning of Mass, even before we walk up to the altar in spirit with the priest, we should stop and see if there are any serious sins on our soul.

1. Why is Psalm 42 said at the beginning of Mass?

Psalm 42 is said at the beginning of Mass to beg God to keep His Church holy and to remind us that we should lead holy lives in order to offer the Mass worthily with the priest.

The Confiteor

The Church is holy because her Head is Christ Himself. Yet her priests who offer the Mass, and her children who offer the Mass with the priest are not perfect. So before the priest ascends the altar, or before the people ascend in spirit with him, the Church has first the priest and then the people humbly confess their sins.

P. Glory be to the Father, and to the Son, and to the Holy Ghost.

℟. As it was in the beginning, is now, and ever shall be, world without end. Amen.

P. I will go in to the altar of God.

℟. To God, the joy of my youth.

P. Our help is in the Name of the Lord.

℟. Who hath made heaven and earth.

Praying the Confiteor

Bowing low, the Celebrant says the Confiteor, and the server answers:

May Almighty God have mercy on you, forgive you your sins, and bring you to life everlasting. P. Amen.

Bowing low, the server says the Confiteor:

I CONFESS to Almighty God, to blessed Mary ever virgin, to blessed Michael the archangel, to blessed John the Baptist, to the holy apostles Peter and Paul, and all the Saints, and to you, Father, that I have sinned exceedingly in thought, word and deed, (*strike breast*

The Meaning of the Confiteor

In the very first book ever written about the Mass, the "Teaching of the Twelve Apostles," we find that the first thing the people did when they came together to offer the Mass with the priest was to confess their sins to God. They did not use the same words that we use today, but the same ideas were there.

When the priest says: "May the Lord forgive us our sins, etc.," he is not absolving the people from their sins. He is simply asking God to pardon him and all the people with him for having offended Him. This history of the Confiteor teaches us how deeply the early Catholics realized that they were offering the Mass with the priest. They were not just onlookers. The Mass was truly *their* Sacrifice. So their hearts and souls had to be as pure and as holy as the soul of the priest himself. For who would dare to offer this most pure Sacrifice with the priest with mortal sin upon his soul?

2. What is the Confiteor?

The Confiteor is the prayer said by the priest and people to beg God to pardon their sins that they may be worthy to offer the Holy Sacrifice.

320

Approach to the Altar

After the Confiteor, and just before going up to the altar, the Church has the priest and people together make one last plea to God to grant them the grace to holily offer this pure Sacrifice. The priest then goes up to the altar and kisses it, saluting the place where the Sacrifice will be offered.

three times) through my fault, through my fault, through my most grievous fault. Therefore I beseech blessed Mary, ever virgin, blessed Michael the archangel, blessed John the Baptist, the holy apostles Peter and Paul, all the Saints, and you, Father, to pray to the Lord our God for me.

P. May Almighty God have mercy on you, forgive you your sins, and bring you to life everlasting. R̳. Amen.

P. May the almighty and merciful Lord grant us pardon, absolution and remission of our sins. R̳. Amen.

P. Thou wilt turn, O God, and bring us life.

R̳. And Thy people shall rejoice in Thee.

P. Show us, O Lord, Thy mercy.

R̳. And grant us Thy salvation.

P. O Lord, hear my prayer.

R̳. And let my cry come unto Thee.

P. The Lord be with you. R̳. And with thy spirit.

P. Let us pray.

TAKE away from us our sins, O Lord, we beseech Thee, that we may enter with pure minds into the Holy of Holies. Through Christ our Lord. Amen.

The Meaning of the Holy of Holies

The Holy of Holies in the prayer of the priest as he ascends the altar refers to the place in the Jewish Temple where God dwelt among His people. Today, the new Holy of Holies is the altar, where God dwells among His people under the appearances of bread and wine. And we have the great privilege of having God dwell with us not just in one place in the world, but in every Catholic church throughout the world!

The Meaning of the Kissing of the Altar

As the priest says "whose relics are here," he kisses the altar. There are several reasons why he does this:

1. Because the altar is the table on which the Holy Sacrifice of the Mass is going to be offered. 2. Because the altar is a symbol of Christ Himself, and 3. Because every altar contains the relics of some Saints and Martyrs. So when the priest kisses the altar, he pays homage to the table of Sacrifice, to Christ Himself, and to the Saints and Martyrs of Christ.

3. What are the sentiments in the prayers at the Approach to the Altar?

The sentiments in these prayers are a plea to God for purity, so that both the priest and the people may be worthy to offer the Sacrifice of His Son.

321

The Introit and the Kyrie

The Introit sets the keynote of the Mass. Every Mass is offered to God alone. But every Mass honors either some special attribute of God Himself, or some part of Christ's life on earth, or the Blessed Virgin, or one of God's Saints. After the Introit, the Church prays the Kyrie, in which she begs Christ to have mercy on her children that they might be more worthy to offer up this most Holy Sacrifice.

WE BESEECH Thee, O Lord, by the merits of Thy saints whose relics lie here and all of the saints: deign in Thy mercy to pardon me all my sins. Amen.

The Introit: See Mass of Day.

The Kyrie

P. Lord, have mercy.	℞. Lord, have mercy.
P. Lord, have mercy.	℞. Christ, have mercy.
P. Christ, have mercy.	℞. Christ, have mercy.
P. Lord, have mercy.	℞. Lord, have mercy.
P. Lord, have mercy.	

He now moves to the center of the altar and recites the Gloria. This is omitted in Lent and Advent and in Masses for the dead.

The Meaning of the Introit and the Kyrie

The Introit helps us at the very beginning of Mass to think about the wonders of God, or of Mary, or of one of the Saints. We beg Christ to give us the grace to imitate Him, or His Mother, or the Saint of the day.

These words, "Kyrie Eleison, Christe Eleison," are the last Greek words left in our Roman Mass. They are short pleas for mercy and salvation. As we are saying them, we realize that the Mass we are about to offer with the priest is the perfect answer to our prayers for mercy and salvation. For the Mass brings to us the mercy and salvation Christ won for us on Calvary.

The Meaning of the Incensing

In Solemn High Mass, the priest incenses the altar right after the Introit. For many hundreds of years before, the Jews used incense to honor God in His Temple. It was fitting that the Church should adopt this custom and incense the altar, which is a symbol of Christ. Then because the priests were the special representatives of God, they too were incensed.

4. What is the Introit of the Mass?

The Introit is the prayer at the beginning of Mass which tells us a particular Mass is going to be in honor of some special attribute of God, or of His life on earth, or of Mary, or of one of the Saints.

5. What is the "Kyrie"?

The "Kyrie" is that part of the Mass in which we tell God how much we need His mercy and salvation, which we hope to obtain through the Mass.

The Gloria

The Church now breaks out in a song of praise. Each one of us has a great deal to thank God for. He created us. He recreated us in grace by sending His Son to die for us. He gives us the Mass to keep us in this life of grace. It should not be difficult for any of us to join fully in this hymn of praise.

GLORY to God in the highest. And on earth peace to men of good will. We praise Thee. We bless Thee. We adore Thee. We glorify Thee.

We give Thee thanks for Thy great glory, O Lord God, heavenly King, God the Father Almighty.

O Lord Jesus Christ, the only-begotten Son.

O Lord God, Lamb of God, Son of the Father.

Who takest away the sins of the world, have mercy on us.

Who takest away the sins of the world, receive our prayer.

Who sittest at the right hand of the Father, have mercy on us.

For Thou alone art holy, Thou alone art the Lord.

Thou alone, O Jesus Christ, art most high. Together with the Holy Ghost, ✝ in the glory of God the Father. Amen.

P. The Lord be with you. R̸. And with thy spirit.

P. Let us pray.

The Meaning of the Gloria

The first words of the "Gloria" are those which the angels sang the night Our Lord was born. The "peace" which they announced to men of good will (men, that is, who had received God's grace) was the peace that Our Lord was to buy for them by His Death on the Cross; the peace of salvation from their sins, and the promise of Heaven forever.

If the coming of Christ gave glory to God and peace to men who were friends of God, how much more does each Mass! For each time the Mass is offered, infinite glory is given to God, and men whom God loves are flooded with the grace that brings peace to their lives and salvation to their souls.

May the Lord be with you.

And may He be with you, also.

NOTE: Each time the priest wants to gain the attention of the people for some very important part of the Mass, he addresses them with these words.

6. What is the Gloria?

The "Gloria" is the Church's hymn of praise to Almighty God which she uses in all her joyful and all her feast-day Masses.

The Collect and the Epistle

The Collect sums up or "collects" all the prayers of the whole Mystical Body, and begs God to grant her and her children all their needs.

The Epistle or Lesson is a Reading of some teaching of the Apostles or the Prophets. It is taken from the Old or New Testament.

The Collect: See Mass of Day.

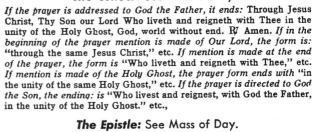

If the prayer is addressed to God the Father, it ends: **Through Jesus Christ, Thy Son our Lord Who liveth and reigneth with Thee in the unity of the Holy Ghost, God, world without end. ℟ Amen.** *If in the beginning of the prayer mention is made of Our Lord, the form is:* "through the same Jesus Christ," *etc. If mention is made at the end of the prayer, the form is* "Who liveth and reigneth with Thee," *etc. If mention is made of the Holy Ghost, the prayer form ends with* "in the unity of the same Holy Ghost," *etc. If the prayer is directed to God the Son, the ending is* "Who livest and reignest, with God the Father, in the unity of the Holy Ghost." *etc.,*

The Epistle: See Mass of Day.

At the end of the Epistle the server says: Thanks be to God.

Gradual, Alleluia or Tract: See Mass of Day.

The priest, bowing down over the altar, says silently the prayer of preparation for the reading of the Holy Gospel:

Munda Cor Meum

CLEANSE my heart and my lips, O Almighty God, Who didst cleanse the lips of the prophet Isaias with a burning coal; in Thy gracious mercy deign so to purify me that I may worthily proclaim Thy holy Gospel. Through Christ our Lord. Amen.

Pray, Lord, Thy blessing. The Lord be in my heart and on my lips, that I may worthily and fittingly proclaim His holy Gospel. Amen.

The Meaning of the Collect, Epistle, Gradual and Tract

As members of Christ's Mystical Body, we should certainly make the prayer of the Church our own prayer. This is a good time to mention our own particular needs as individual members of Christ's Body. It is very important to notice that no Collect is ever ended without some mention of Jesus Christ because it is only through Him and His Death on the Cross that all graces are given.

The reading of the Lesson from Sacred Scripture is a reminder of a service in a Jewish Synagogue. Since the first Catholics were Jews, it is only natural that Jewish customs would appear in the Great Prayer of the Mass.

Even the Gradual or Tract which follows the Lesson is based on the Jewish services. After reading from Sacred Scripture, the Jews would sing some psalms. And our Gradual or Tract is always taken from the psalms.

7. What is the Collect?

The Collect is a prayer for the needs of the Mystical Body which the Church prays for as she is about to offer the Sacrifice by which these graces will be given.

8. What is the Epistle or Lesson?

The Epistle or Lesson is a reading taken from Sacred Scripture, in which God Himself teaches us how to imitate the life of His Son, or the Virgin Mary, or one of His Saints.

324

The Gospel and the Creed

The reading of the Gospel is greater than all the other readings from Sacred Scripture because this is the story of the words and deeds of Our Lord Himself. Because this is such a sacred reading, the book is changed to the left hand side of the altar, the same side from which the sacred words of Consecration are read.

The Gospel: See Mass of Day.

P. The Lord be with you.

℟. And with Thy spirit.

P. The continuation of the holy Gospel according to Saint N. ℟. Glory be to Thee, O Lord.

At the end of the Gospel the server says:

Praise be to Thee, O Christ.

Kissing the words of the Sacred Text, the priest says:

By the words of the Holy Gospel may our sins be blotted out.

The Creed

I BELIEVE in one God, the Father Almighty, Maker of heaven and earth, and of all things visible and invisible. And in one Lord Jesus Christ, the only-begotten Son of God, born of the Father before all ages. God of God, Light of light, true God of true God. Begotten, not made; of one being with the Father; by Whom all things were made. Who for us men, and for our salvation came down from Heaven (*kneel*) and was made flesh, by

The Meaning of the Gospel

Gospel means "good news." Certainly the story of our salvation by Jesus Christ is the greatest news the world has ever heard. It should be our great privilege to try to bring the good news of man's salvation to all of our friends and neighbors. We can do this, especially, by leading the kind of lives Christ urges us to live in each day's Gospel. Before reading the Gospel, the priest announces where it is being taken from in Sacred Scripture for this particular Mass; for the Gospel, too, has a special connection with the feast of the day, and thus changes from day to day. While the priest makes this announcement, he signs himself with the sign of the Cross on his forehead, lips, and breast. This very ancient sign of the Cross fits very well with the Gospel, for by this sign of the Cross, we beg that the Gospel, the Story of our Salvation, be ever in our minds, on our lips, and in our hearts.

9. What is the purpose of the prayers before the Gospel?

Their purpose is to beg God to make a mere man worthy to tell the sacred story of our Salvation by Jesus Christ.

The Creed

On all its more solemn days, like Sundays, feasts of Our Lord and our Lady, and of Doctors of the Church, the Church pauses for a few moments and professes through her priest the one belief of all the members of the Mystical Body of Christ. It should be a great honor for us to join the priest in professing our Faith.

the Holy Ghost of the Virgin Mary: AND WAS MADE MAN (*rise*). He was also crucified for us, suffered under Pontius Pilate and was buried. And on the third day He rose again according to the Scriptures. And ascending into Heaven, He sitteth at the right hand of the Father. And He shall come again in glory to judge the living and the dead; and of His kingdom there shall be no end. And I believe in the Holy Ghost, Lord and Giver of Life, Who proceeds from the Father and the Son. Who together with the Father and the Son is no less adored and glorified; Who spoke by the prophets. And I believe in one holy, catholic and apostolic Church. I confess one Baptism for the remission of sins. And I look for the resurrection of the dead, and the life ✠ of the world to come. Amen.

The Celebrant kisses the altar and says:

P. The Lord be with you. ℟. And with thy spirit.

P. Let us pray.

The Meaning of the Creed in the Mass

As members of Christ's Mystical Body, we profess not only our own Faith, but also the Faith of all those Catholics throughout the world, who, because of persecution, must whisper their Creed behind closed doors. Ever since its earliest days, the Church has always had a creed. In the beginning, however, it was not part of the Mass. But as men came to deny the truth of the Catholic Faith, the Church put her profession of Faith into the Mass itself, so that in her most sacred function, her children might have the chance to profess their Faith again and again. This profession of Faith is known as the Apostles' Creed. When men denied that Jesus is true God, the Church, in the Council of Nicaea, solemnly taught that Jesus is true God and left no doubt in men's minds that she believed in the Divinity of Christ. This teaching of the Council of Nicaea was added to the Apostles' Creed which then became known as the Nicene Creed.

10. What is the Creed?

The Creed is the profession of our Catholic Faith which is included in the more solemn Masses of the Church.

End of the Mass of the Catechumens.

Introduction to the Mass of the Faithful

In ancient times, after the Gospel, the deacon turned toward the people who were not yet baptized (the catechumens) and said: "Go, you are dismissed." Since they were not baptized, the catechumens were not allowed to stay for the sacrifice part of the Mass, and so were not able to offer the Mass with the priest, nor to receive Holy Communion.

THE OFFERTORY—the first principal part of the Mass

The Offertory Verse: See Mass of Day.

The Offering of the Bread

Holding up the host on the paten, the celebrant says:

ACCEPT, O holy Father, Almighty and eternal God, this spotless host, which I, Thy unworthy servant, offer unto Thee, my living and true God, to atone for my numberless sins, offenses and negligences; on behalf of all here present and likewise for all faithful Christians, living and dead, that it may profit me and them as a means of salvation unto life everlasting. Amen.

Making the Sign of the Cross with the paten, he places the host upon the corporal. He pours wine and water into the chalice (blessing the water before it is poured) and recites the prayer:

O God, Who hast established the nature of man in wondrous dignity, and still more admirably restored it, grant that through the mystery of this water and wine we may be made partakers of His Divinity Who has condescended to become partaker of our humanity, Jesus Christ, Thy Son, Our Lord, Who liveth and reigneth with Thee, in the unity of the Holy Ghost, God, world without end. Amen.

The Meaning of the Offertory Verse and Prayers

To teach her children to participate in the Sacrifice, the Church has always urged them to make some offering of material goods as a sign that they wished to offer themselves to God. We should remember that our offering of money stands as a sign of ourselves. By it, we show God that we want to offer ourselves, too, in union with the offering of His Son. While these offerings are being made, a part of a psalm is said in tune with the feast of the day. Also when the priest mingles a few drops of water with the wine, he does this as a symbol that he and all the people offering the Mass with him wish to be united to Christ. In order to understand the prayers at Mass from now until the Consecration, we must remember that each prayer looks forward to the moment of Consecration, when the bread and wine on the altar will become the Body and Blood of Christ. Thus, sometimes even before the Consecration, the Church prays as though this sacred moment had already taken place.

11. What is the Offertory Verse?

The Offertory Verse opens the first principal part of the Mass. During this prayer, on Sundays at least, people make their material offerings and the offering of themselves.

The Offering of the Chalice

The Church, looking forward to the Consecration, sees the chalice of wine already as the Chalice of Christ's Blood—the Chalice of our Salvation. Then the Church has her priest and people look upon their own unworthiness and beg God to accept this wonderful offering from such unworthy hands. And so with the priest we bring humble and sorrowful hearts to this sacrifice.

The Offering of the Wine

The celebrant holds up the chalice of wine, saying:

WE OFFER Thee, O Lord, the chalice of salvation, humbly begging of Thy mercy that it may arise before Thy Divine Majesty with a pleasing fragrance, for our salvation and for that of the whole world. Amen.

Bowing down, he continues:

In a humble spirit and with a contrite heart, may we be accepted by Thee, O Lord, and may our sacrifice so be offered in Thy sight this day as to please Thee, O Lord God.

Raising his eyes to heaven, he blesses the oblation, saying:
Come, Thou Sanctifier, almighty and eternal God, and bless + this sacrifice prepared for the glory of Thy holy Name.

The Meaning of the Offertory Prayers

Each Mass is an offering for the whole of the Mystical Body of Christ. Each Mass also helps thousands of non-Catholics come closer to Christ and to His True Church. For God is so pleased with every Mass that He floods the souls of many non-Catholics with graces that will move them to come into the Catholic Church. Each time, therefore, that we offer the Mass with the priest, we are helping all of the members of Christ's Mystical Body and many, many others outside His Body.

After the offering of the wine, the Church looks forward to what these gifts of bread and wine will become, and begs God to bless these gifts that they might become the Body and Blood of His own Son. As the priest blesses these gifts, he also blesses each one of us who have united ourselves by our personal offerings to the gifts of bread and wine. He begs that we, too, may be made fit to be offered with Christ to His Father.

12. What do the five Offertory prayers teach us?

These five prayers teach us to center our whole life on the Consecration of the Mass, so that our daily lives may be offered as a constant sacrifice to Almighty God.

The Washing of the Hands

Just before the priest enters into the Canon of the Mass, that most sacred part of the Mass in which Christ is really sacrificed, the Church has her priest wash his hands as a symbol to him and to us that our souls should be spotless before we dare to offer the Spotless Victim to God.

The Lavabo

The celebrant goes to the Epistle corner, where he washes his fingers, saying part of Psalm 25:

I WILL wash my hands among the innocent, and will walk 'round Thy altar, O God. To hear the voice of Thy praise and to tell all Thy wondrous deeds.

Lord, I love the beauty of Thy house, and the place where Thy glory dwells.

Destroy not my soul with the impious, O God, nor my life with men of blood. In whose hands there is iniquity, whose right hand is full of bribes.

But as for me, I walk in my innocence, rescue me and be gracious to me. My foot is on the straight way, in assemblies will I bless Thee, O Lord.

The Glory be, etc., is omitted in Masses for the dead and in Passiontide.

Glory be to the Father, and to the Son, and to the Holy Ghost. As it was in the beginning, is now, and ever shall be, world without end. Amen.

The Meaning of the Washing of the Hands

Many years ago, when the people used to hand the priest their offerings, it was necessary for the priest to wash his hands before going on with the Holy Sacrifice. Now, since the priest does not handle the gifts of the people, that is no longer necessary, but the Church has kept this ceremony in the Mass because it is a beautiful symbol. And so during the washing of hands, the priest says some verses from Psalm 25 where the psalmist is telling God how much he wants to keep from sin. The verses of this Psalm express clearly the meaning of the handwashing; by saying these words the priest openly confesses his purpose of celebrating the spotless Sacrifice with the greatest possible purity. What a beautiful way to prepare our souls for the Sacrifice of Christ which will wash our souls in the very Blood of Christ!

13. What is the purpose of the Washing of the Hands?

At one time there was a practical purpose to this ceremony, for the priest had to wash his hands after handling all the offerings of the faithful. Now it is a symbol of our prayer, asking God to wash our souls from all sin before we begin the most sacred part of the Mass.

329

"Receive, O Holy Trinity"

In this prayer, the Church calls upon the Three Persons of the Blessed Trinity (to Whom every Mass is offered) to overlook the unworthiness of the offerers and to accept this Sacrifice. Now as the priest sums up the thoughts of the Offertory we should renew the offering we made of our own lives at the beginning of the Offertory.

Bowing down over the middle of the Altar, the priest continues the prayer of oblation:

Prayer to the Holy Trinity

ACCEPT, Most Holy Trinity, this offering which we are making to Thee in remembrance of the passion, resurrection, and ascension of Jesus Christ, our Lord; and in honor of blessed Mary, ever virgin, blessed John the Baptist, the holy Apostles, Peter and Paul, and of these, and of all the saints; that it may add to their honor and aid our salvation; and may they deign to intercede in heaven for us who honor their memory here on earth. Through the same Christ our Lord. Amen.

The Orate Fratres

He kisses the altar; then, turning to the people and raising his voice, he asks their prayers:

Pray, brethren, that my sacrifice and yours may become acceptable to God the Father almighty.

℟. May the Lord accept the sacrifice from thy hands to the praise and glory of His Name, for our advantage and that of all His holy Church. P. Amen.

The Meaning of the Orate Fratres

The last prayers the Church says before she begins the Sacrifice part of the Mass are prayers which beg God to accept the Sacrifice from the hands of her priest and people, and to bless the gifts of bread and wine which are soon to become the Sacred Body and Blood of His Son. In the prayer "Pray Brethren" we see real proof that it is not just the priest who offers the Mass. The Mass is the priest's Sacrifice, and it is our Sacrifice. It is the Sacrifice of the whole Mystical Body of Christ. And we are members of that Body by Baptism, and so we have the power from Jesus Christ to offer that Mass with the priest.

14. What does the prayer "Accept, Most Holy Trinity" teach us?

This prayer teaches us that every Mass is offered to the Most Blessed Trinity, for God's glory, for the honor of the Saints, and for our salvation.

15. Why is the prayer "Pray Brethren" so important?

This prayer is so important because it teaches us in the words of the Mass itself that we, too, have the power to offer the Mass with the priest.

The Secret Prayer

The Secret Prayer is the last Offertory Prayer; it is recited by the priest silently. In ancient times it used to be called "The Prayer over the Offerings," because it was a prayer which the priest read over the offerings of bread and wine and other gifts which the faithful brought for the Holy Sacrifice. These gifts were a sign that they wished to offer themselves to God.

The Secret Prayer: See Mass of day.

P. World without end. R̶. Amen.

P. The Lord be with you. R̶. And with thy spirit.

P. Lift up your hearts!

R̶. We have them lifted up to the Lord!

P. Let us give thanks to the Lord our God!

R̶. It is fitting and just!

The Preface for Sundays

The following Preface is appointed for Trinity Sunday and all Sundays to which no special one is assigned.

IT IS FITTING indeed and just, right and helpful unto salvation, for us always and everywhere to give thanks to Thee, O holy Lord, Father almighty, eternal God, Who with Thine only-begotten Son and the Holy Ghost art one God, one Lord; not in the unity of a single person, but in the trinity of a single nature. For that which we

The Meaning of the Secret Prayer

This prayer is called the "secret," not because it is now said silently, but because it is the prayer that "sets aside" the gifts of bread and wine which will become the Body and Blood of Christ. The word "secret" is from the Latin word "to set aside." In this Secret Prayer the priest asks God to accept the Sacrifice of Christ that we may be blessed by it; for the time of Consecration is now drawing near when the priest is to offer the Sacrifice of our Lord. "World without end" are the last words of the Secret Prayer. They are sung or recited aloud by the priest in order that we may know that the Secret Prayer of the priest is now ended and in order to invite us to unite our prayers with his by saying "Amen." When we say "Amen" we show that we consent to all the priest said in the Secret Prayer.

16. What is the Secret Prayer?

It is the Prayer that the priest says silently, in which he asks God to accept the Sacrifice that is to be offered in the name of the Church and to bless us with its fruits.

331

The Preface

Now the most solemn part of the Mass begins. The gifts are ready. The offerers are ready. Jesus Christ is about to be sacrificed. The Church begins this act of Sacrifice with what we call the Preface. We might call it the "Invitation to the Sacrifice." Before the priest starts the Preface, he asks each one of us to lift up our hearts and to take them away from worldly things.

believe on Thy revelation concerning Thy glory, that same we believe of Thy Son, that same of the Holy Ghost, without difference or discrimination. So that in confessing the true and everlasting Godhead, we shall adore distinction in Persons, oneness in being, and equality in majesty. This the angels and archangels, the cherubim, too, and the seraphim do praise; day by day they cease not to cry out as with one voice, saying:

The bell now is rung three times.

Sanctus

HOLY, holy, holy, Lord God of hosts. Heaven and earth are filled with Thy glory. Hosanna in the highest.

Benedictus

Blessed is He Who comes in the Name of the Lord. Hosanna in the highest.

The Meaning of the Preface

When the altar boy has assured the priest that we have lifted our hearts and minds to God, the priest begins the Preface. The English words "Let us give thanks to the Lord, our God," do not give the complete meaning of this prayer of the priest. The Preface was once said in Greek, and the Greek meaning goes much deeper than the English words suggest. The Greek words actually mean: "Let us give thanks to God by celebrating the Sacrifice of the Mass." We know, of course, that the Mass is the most perfect way of giving thanks to God. So perfect is it, that to the ancient Catholics, there was no other way of giving thanks to God. The Mass was *THE* Thanksgiving. This is why the Greeks called the Mass the "Eucharist" which is the Greek word for "Thanksgiving." So in the Preface, when the priest invites the people to give thanks to God, he is inviting them to offer the Sacrifice of the Mass with him, the most perfect way of giving thanks to God.

17. What is the Preface?

The Preface is the prayer that begins the Sacrifice part of the Mass. It is the "invitation to Sacrifice" in which the priest invites the people to offer the Sacrifice of Jesus with him as a perfect act of Thanksgiving to God.

332

The Canon of the Mass

The prayers from now until the Our Father are called "the Canon." "Canon" means "Rule"—something that does not change. These prayers are called the "Canon" because they never change. All these prayers are considered part of one single Action. This is how we must try to see the "Canon"— as one Action of sacrificing and offering Jesus Christ.

THE CANON OF THE MASS

Remembrance of the Church

The celebrant bows low over the altar and says:

THEREFORE, most gracious Father, we humbly beg of Thee and entreat Thee through Jesus Christ, Thy Son, our Lord, to deem acceptable and bless

these ✝ gifts,

these ✝ offerings,

these ✝ holy and unspotted oblations

which, in the first place, we offer Thee for Thy holy Catholic Church,

that Thou wouldst deign to give her peace and protection,

to unite and guard her the whole world over,

together with Thy servant, N., our Pope, and N., our Bishop, and all true believers who cherish the Catholic and Apostolic faith.

The Meaning of the Prayer for the Church

Now the Church asks God to accept this Sacrifice from her hands, and because of it to bless the Church, its rulers, and its members. We can see clearly from this prayer that every Mass is offered for the sake of the whole Mystical Body Once we understand that by this Mass we are helping to make holy all the members of Christ's Mystical Body, then will the Mass really mean something to us. Each time there is mention of the gifts of bread and wine that are soon to become the Body and Blood of Christ, the Church has her priest bless these offerings with the Sign of the Cross. All graces, all blessings come to us because Christ died on the Cross. Is it any wonder, then, that the priest reverently makes the Sign of the Cross over these gifts that will soon bring the blessings of the Cross to men today?

18. What is the Canon of the Mass?

The Canon of the Mass is that part of the Mass in which the Action or act of sacrificing and offering Jesus Christ takes place.

19. Why do we pray for the Bishop of our diocese in every Mass?

We pray for the Bishop of our diocese in every Mass, because the Bishop is the head of the Church in the diocese, and it is his duty to see that all the Catholics in his diocese live up to their Catholic Faith.

333

Remembrance of the Faithful

The Church has prayed for the whole Mystical Body. Now she gives the priest and us an opportunity to pray for our own loved ones and friends. But to show Our Lord that we really wish to imitate His great love, we should also pray for those who have hurt us in any way. Once we pray for these people, any feelings of hatred we might have had will disappear.

Remembrance of the Faithful

The celebrant brings to mind those for whom he wishes to pray:

REMEMBER, O Lord, Thy servants and handmaids, N. and N., and all here present, whose faith and devotion are known to Thee, on whose behalf we offer to Thee, or who themselves offer to Thee, this sacrifice of praise, for themselves, families and friends, for the good of their souls, for their hope of salvation and deliverance from all harm, and who offer their homage to Thee, O God, eternal, living and true.

Remembrance of the Saints

In the unity of holy fellowship we observe the memory, first of all, of the glorious and ever virgin Mary, Mother of our Lord and God, Jesus Christ; next that of Thy blessed Apostles and Martyrs, Peter and Paul, Andrew, James, John, Thomas, James, Philip, Bartholomew, Matthew, Simon and Thaddeus; of Linus, Cletus, Clement, Sixtus, Cornelius, Cyprian, Lawrence, Chrysogonus, John

The Meaning of the Remembrance of the Saints

The Church honors the memory of God's Saints with this Sacrifice, and begs these Saints to pray for her and her members. By the sanctifying grace that makes us one with all the members of the Mystical Body, we are also one with all the Saints in Heaven. Because we are one with them, we can apply our Sacrifice to them, not indeed to help them, for they need no help, but to honor them. We must remember that when we honor God's Saints, we are honoring Christ Himself. For on earth Christ lived in these Saints and today He is living in them in Heaven, where they are most intimately united to Christ.

20. What does the prayer for the Remembrance of the Faithful teach us?

This prayer teaches us that in the Sacrament of Baptism, God has given great power to ordinary people of the world. For to every Baptized person, He has given the power to offer the Sacrifice of His Son with His priests.

21. What do the first three prayers of the Canon teach us?

These three prayers teach us once again that the Mass is our Sacrifice, and that we are offering it with the priest for the good of the whole Church, for our own loved ones, and for the honor of the Saints.

Last Prayer of Remembrance

At one time in the Life of the Church, this prayer mentioned every particular intention of all the people present. Later on, because there were too many people present, Pope Gregory changed it to the words we have today. These pray in general for happiness both here on earth and in the next life.

and Paul, Cosmas and Damian, and of all Thy Saints, by whose merits and prayers grant that we may be always fortified by the help of Thy protection. Through the same Christ our Lord. Amen.

The Hanc Igitur

The celebrant spreads his hands over the oblation, and the bell is rung once.

GRACIOUSLY accept, then, we beseech Thee, O Lord, this service of our worship and that of all Thy household. Order our days in Thy peace, save us from everlasting damnation, and cause us to be numbered among Thy chosen ones. Through Christ Our Lord. Amen.

Do Thou, O God, deign to bless ✢ what we offer, and make it approved, ✢ effective, ✢ right, and wholly pleasing in every way, that it may become, for our good, the Body ✢ and Blood ✢ of Thy dearly beloved Son, Jesus Christ, our Lord.

The Meaning of the Last Prayer of Remembrance

Since this prayer used to mention all the intentions of the people present, we can stop for a moment and beg God to hear in a special way the prayers of all the people who are offering this Mass with us today. While the priest prayed for all the people's intentions, he pointed to the offerings on the altar. Gradually, instead of pointing, the priest placed his hands over the offerings. Today we can see a beautiful symbol in this ceremony: In ancient times when a Jewish priest sacrificed an animal, he would first lay his hands on the animal and say: "O God, because of our sins, we deserve death, but we beg You, let this animal take our place." This ceremony was a figure of the Sacrifice of Christ. For God actually *did* lay our sins on Christ and Christ, by His death, took these sins away. At each Mass, we again lay our sins on Christ, and He takes them away as the priest sacrifices Him to His Father.

22. Why does the priest place his hands over the gifts of Bread and Wine?

The priest places his hands over the Bread and Wine as a symbol that he is laying all our sins on Christ, Who will take them away by the Sacrifice the priest is about to make in His Name.

335

Introduction to the Consecration

Finally, all is in readiness for the great moment. We have begged God for purity of mind and heart. We have begged that our gifts of bread and wine be purified. At last, the Church begs God that what is before her priest on the altar may truly become the Body and Blood of Jesus Christ.

Consecration of the Bread

WHO, the day before He suffered, took bread into His holy and venerable hands and having raised His eyes to heaven, unto Thee O God, His almighty Father, giving thanks to Thee, He blessed it ✠, broke it, and gave it to His disciples, saying: Take ye all, and eat of this,

FOR THIS IS MY BODY.

Consecration of the Wine

In like manner, when the supper was done, taking also this goodly chalice into His holy and venerable hands, again giving thanks to Thee, He blessed ✠ it, and gave it to his disciples, saying: Take ye all, and drink of this.

FOR THIS IS THE CHALICE OF MY BLOOD OF THE NEW AND ETERNAL COVENANT: THE MYSTERY OF FAITH, WHICH SHALL BE SHED FOR YOU AND FOR MANY UNTO THE FORGIVENESS OF SINS.

As often as you shall do these things, in memory of Me shall you do them.

The Meaning of the Consecration

In these few words, the Church through her priest sacrifices Jesus Christ in an unbloody way and offers Him to His Heavenly Father. Bread is changed to the Body of Christ. Wine is changed to His Blood. Since Jesus is living now in Heaven, His Body cannot be separated from His Blood, nor His Blood from His Body. So in the Host alone, as in the Chalice alone, the Living Body of Jesus is really and completely present. A double Consecration is necessary because only where there is a separate Consecration of Christ's Body and Blood is Jesus sacrificed again. Since every Mass is the same sacrifice that Christ made on the Cross, every Mass must show forth the death of Christ.

Christ died on the Cross by the real separation of His Body from His Blood. Therefore, every Mass must in some way present again this separation of Christ's Body from His Blood, and the separate Consecration does just this.

23. Who is the Word of God?

The Word of God is the Son of God, the Second Person of the Most Blessed Trinity, Jesus Christ, Our Lord.

24. How does the priest sacrifice Jesus by the words of Consecration?

The priest sacrifices Jesus in an unbloody way by means of the double Consecration. By this double Consecration the bloody Sacrifice which Christ made on the Cross is made present again but in an unbloody way.

Prayers of Offering

In these two prayers, the Church goes back to the theme of the unworthiness of the offerers of this Sacrifice. She reminds herself that God accepted sacrifices from other unworthy creatures, and begs again that He might accept this "Spotless Victim" from the spotted hands of her children. We should learn the lesson of humility from the Mass.

Prayers of Oblation

Mindful, therefore, O Lord, not only of the blessed passion of the same Christ, Thy Son, our Lord, but also of His resurrection from the dead, and finally His glorious ascension into heaven, we, Thy ministers, as also Thy holy people, offer unto Thy Supreme Majesty, of the gifts bestowed upon us, the pure ✝ Victim, the holy ✝ Victim, the all-perfect ✝ Victim; the holy ✝ Bread of life eternal and the Chalice ✝ of unending salvation.

AND this do Thou deign to regard with gracious and kindly attention and hold acceptable, as Thou didst deign to accept the offerings of Abel, Thy just servant, and the sacrifice of Abraham our patriarch, and that which Thy chief priest Melchisedech offered unto Thee, a holy sacrifice and a spotless victim.

Most humbly we implore Thee, Almighty God, bid these offerings to be brought by the hands of Thy holy Angel unto Thy altar above; before the face of Thy Divine Majesty; that those of us who, by sharing in the Sacrifice of this altar, shall receive the most sacred Body and Blood of Thy Son, may be filled with every grace and heavenly blessing. Through the same Christ our Lord. Amen.

The Meaning of the Prayers of Offering

Our Lord said: "Do this in memory of Me," that is, "Offer Me to My Father as a memorial of My passion, resurrection, and ascension." So the Church does just this in her first prayer of offering. At each Mass, the passion and death of Jesus should live again for us. We thank Christ over and over again for what His death on the Cross did for us. Because He died, we live in His grace today and we can rise and live with Him forever in Heaven.

The Mass was Christ's last will and testament to us whom He loved—a priceless treasure to remember Him by! In the second of these two prayers, the Church is already looking forward to that great moment when her children will share in this Sacrifice of Christ by actually eating His Flesh and drinking His Blood.

25. What does the first prayer of offering teach us?

The first prayer of offering teaches us that every Mass is offered to God both as a Sacrifice to Him and as a memorial of Christ's passion, resurrection and ascension.

26. What were the sacrifices of Abel, Abraham, and Melchisedech?

Abel sacrificed a pure lamb; Abraham was willing to sacrifice his only son; Melchisedech sacrificed bread and wine. All these are types or figures of the perfect sacrifice, the Sacrifice of the Lamb of God—Who is the Son of God—under the appearances of bread and wine.

Prayers of Remembrance

Now the Church prays that the Sacrifice she has made may help the souls in Purgatory, and then gives the priest a chance to say a special prayer for himself. As the priest prays that God may grant him a place in Heaven with His Apostles and Martyrs, we should pray for the priest in a special way that God may keep him holy and close to His Heart.

Remembrance of the Dead

REMEMBER also, O Lord, Thy servants and handmaids N. and N., who have gone before us with the sign of faith, and rest in the sleep of peace. To these, O Lord, and to all who rest in Christ, we beseech Thee, to grant, of Thy goodness, a place of comfort, light and peace. Through the same Christ our Lord. Amen.

To us, sinners also, Thy servants, trusting in the greatness of Thy mercy, deign to grant some part and fellowship with Thy holy Apostles and Martyrs: with John, Stephen, Matthias, Barnabas, Ignatius, Alexander, Marcellinus, Peter, Felicitas, Perpetua, Agatha, Lucy, Agnes, Cecilia, Anastasia, and all Thy Saints; into whose company we implore Thee to admit us, not weighing our merits, but freely granting us pardon. Through Christ our Lord.

Through Whom, O Lord, Thou dost always create, sanctify ✛, fill with life, ✛ bless ✛ and bestow upon us all good things.

The Minor Elevation

Through ✛ Him, and with ✛ Him, and in ✛ Him, is to Thee, God the Father ✛ Almighty, in the unity of the Holy Ghost, all honor and glory. World without end. ℟. Amen.

The Meaning of the Final Prayers of the Canon

The Church has shown at last her full membership: The Church Triumphant in Heaven, the Church Militant on earth, the Church Suffering in Purgatory. The Sacrifice which Christ has put into her hands is so infinitely pleasing to God, that it can show honor to every Saint in Heaven, help every member of the Mystical Body on earth, ease the pains of every soul in Purgatory, and still give infinite glory and praise to God. With the short prayer "Through Whom, O Lord," etc., the Canon or the Action of sacrificing and offering Christ is over. Since the Church has just given great glory to God by offering Him His own Son, it is fitting that she end with a prayer that gives glory to God through His Divine Son.

27. What does the first prayer of remembrance teach us?

The first prayer teaches that we are united in Christ not only to the Saints in Heaven and to the members of Christ's Body here on earth, but also to the Souls in Purgatory.

28. What is the purpose of the prayer "Through Him, etc."?

The purpose of this prayer is to end the Canon or Sacrifice part of the Mass with a prayer of praise and honor to God through His Son and through us too, who have been united with His Son.

Preparation for the Sacrificial Banquet

The Church has sacrificed and offered Christ to His Father. Now God gives Christ back to her as food for her children. This is the Banquet part of the Sacrifice of the Mass. To prepare for this Banquet, the Church prays the Our Father, the prayer in which we beg God, Who is Our Father, to give us, His children, the Food of our souls.

The Lord's Prayer

Let us pray: Directed by saving precepts and taught by Thy divine teaching, we dare to say:

OUR FATHER, Who art in heaven, hallowed be Thy Name; Thy kingdom come; Thy will be done on earth as it is in heaven. Give us this day our daily bread; and forgive us our trespasses as wc forgive those who trespass against us. And lead us not into temptation.

℞. But deliver us from evil. P. Amen.

Deliver us, we beseech Thee, O Lord, from all evils, past, present, and to come; and by the intercession of the blessed and glorious Mary, ever virgin, Mother of God, together with Thy blessed Apostles Peter and Paul, and Andrew, and all the Saints.

Grant, of Thy goodness, peace in our days, that, aided by the riches of Thy mercy, we may be always free from sin and safe from all disturbance.

Through the same Jesus Christ, Thy Son, our Lord, Who liveth and reigneth with Thee, in the unity of the Holy Ghost, God.

The Meaning of the Our Father

It is so important for us to receive Our Lord each time we go to Mass and to be well prepared.

In order to prepare us the Church prays the "Our Father," the model of all prayers, taught us by Our Lord Himself. In it we pray for the glory of God, for the fulfilment of His will on earth and for the graces we need in order to fulfill His will. The Our Father teaches us that we should love one another, for we are all children of the one family of which God is the Father.

Because the evil of sin is such a terrible thing in our lives, the priest goes on in the prayer "Deliver us, O Lord" to beg God again to deliver us from evils, whether past, as our past sins, or present, as our temptations, or future, as mortal sins we are in danger of committing. As the priest says this prayer, we should ask ourselves if we are using the grace God is giving us to keep away from persons, places, or things that may lead us into the greatest evil on earth—the evil of mortal sin.

29. Why is the "Our Father" said at Mass?

The *Our Father* is said at Mass, to prepare us who have offered Christ in Sacrifice to His Father to receive Him as our Food from our Heavenly Father.

339

Breaking of the Host

Now the Church prepares the Banquet for her children. At one time, the priest had to break the consecrated Loaves so that all might receive. Now that we have individual Hosts, this is no longer necessary. But the ceremony continues because of what it symbolizes.

P. World without end. R̷. Amen.

P. May the peace ✠ of the Lord be ✠ always with ✠ you.

R̷. And with thy spirit.

May this mingling and consecration of the Body and Blood of our Lord Jesus Christ help us who receive it unto life everlasting. Amen.

The Agnus Dei

LAMB OF GOD, Who takest away the sins of the world, have mercy on us. Lamb of God, Who takest away the sins of the world, have mercy on us. Lamb of God, Who takest away the sins of the world, grant us peace.

O Lord Jesus Christ, Who hast said to Thy Apostles: Peace I leave you, My peace I give you, regard not my sins but the faith of Thy Church, and deign to give her peace and unity according to Thy will. Who livest and reignest, God, world without end. Amen.

O Lord, Jesus Christ, Son of the living God, Who by the will of the Father, with the co-operation of the Holy Ghost, hast by Thy death given life to the world, deliver me by this Thy most sacred Body and Blood from all my sins

The Meaning of the Breaking of the Host and the Agnus Dei

Breaking bread with a person has always meant that one was at peace with that person. Thus we "break bread" to show Our Lord that we wish to be at peace with Him. After the priest breaks the Host into three pieces, he drops a piece into the Chalice of Christ's Blood. This shows the union of the Body and Blood in the risen Lord Whom we are to receive. It also is a symbol of the unity which should exist between all Catholics as members of one Mystical Body.

We are about to receive into our very bodies the Lamb of God, risen and glorious as He is in Heaven. And so at the Agnus Dei, with great humility and sorrow, we should strike our breasts and beg Him Who came to take away the sins of the world to take away our sins that we might receive Him worthily.

30. What does the breaking of the Host and the mingling of the Host and Precious Blood symbolize?

The breaking of the Host symbolizes the peace we wish to have with Christ. The mingling of the Host with the Precious Blood symbolizes the unity which should exist between all the members of Christ's Mystical Body who are fed with the very same Body and Blood of Christ.

31. What is the "Agnus Dei"?

The "Agnus Dei" is a preparatory prayer for Holy Communion. In it we beg Our Lord to take away our sins that we might receive Him worthily.

Prayers Before Holy Communion

In the Breaking of the Host, the Church asked God for peace. Now in the first prayer before Holy Communion, the Church again asks Christ, the Son of God, for the peace and unity that can come only through receiving His Body and Blood. As Our Lord after His Resurrection brought to the Apostles the message of peace and forgiveness of sins, so we now hope to obtain these blessings from the Risen Lord Whom we are about to receive.

and from every evil. Make me always cling to Thy commandments, and never permit me to be separated from Thee. Who with the same God the Father and the Holy Ghost livest and reignest, God, world without end. Amen.

LET NOT the partaking of Thy Body, O Lord Jesus Christ, which I, though unworthy, presume to receive, turn to my judgment and condemnation; but through Thy goodness may it become a safeguard and an effective remedy, both of soul and body. Who livest and reignest with God the Father in the unity of the Holy Ghost, God, world without end. Amen.

The Priest's Communion

I will take the Bread of Heaven, and call upon the Name of the Lord.

The Domine non sum dignus

Lord, I am not worthy that Thou shouldst come under my roof; but only say the word and my soul will be healed. (*Said three times.*)

May the Body of Our Lord Jesus Christ keep my soul unto life everlasting. Amen.

The Meaning of the Prayers before Holy Communion

The peace which the Church prays for is the peace that Christ promised to each of us who believe in Him. "My peace I give to you," He said, "My peace I leave you. Not as the world gives do I give to you . . . For My peace no man shall take from you." It is the peace of knowing that Jesus Christ is living within us, and of knowing that if we keep faithful to Him, no matter what sorrow we have here on earth, He will never leave us and will one day bring us to His Home in Heaven. It is also the peace that exists among the members of the Mystical Body through their love for one another.

The next two Communion prayers used to be private prayers of the priest to prepare himself to receive Holy Communion. After a time, they became part of the Mass itself. They are beautiful prayers for us as well. In them we beg Christ for forgiveness of our sins, fidelity to His commands, and the dispositions we need to receive Him worthily.

32. Why are prayers for peace so fitting at Communion time?

Prayers for peace are fitting at Communion time, because we are about to receive Him Who promised lasting peace to all of us who receive Him.

341

The Communion

At last the moment has come when Christ is about to give Himself as food to the members of His Mystical Body. The Church, realizing how unworthy all her children are, has the priest say the same prayer the Centurion said when Jesus was about to come into his home.

WHAT return shall I make to the Lord for all He hath given me? I will take the Chalice of salvation, and I will call upon the Name of the Lord. Praising will I call upon the Lord, and I shall be saved from my enemies.

May the Blood of Our Lord Jesus Christ keep my soul unto life everlasting. Amen.

The Communion of the Faithful

Behold the Lamb of God, behold Him Who takes away the sins of the world.

Lord, I am not worthy that Thou shouldst come under my roof; but only say the word and my soul will be healed (*said three times*).

May the Body of Our Lord Jesus Christ preserve your soul unto life everlasting. Amen.

What has passed our lips as food, O Lord, may we possess in purity of heart, that what is given to us in time, be our healing for eternity.

May Thy Body, O Lord, which I have eaten, and Thy Blood which I have drunk, cleave unto my very soul, and grant that no trace of sin be found in me, whom these pure and holy mysteries have renewed. Who livest and reignest world without end. Amen.

The Meaning of Holy Communion

While the priest is receiving the Precious Blood, the server says the Confiteor in the name of all the people. We should say it with him and beg God for the last time to purify our souls which are about to receive the pure Body and Blood of His Son. When we receive Our Lord in Holy Communion, we share most completely in the sacrifice of the Mass. For the Mass is both a Sacrifice and a Sacrificial Banquet. We offer Jesus to God as a Sacrifice, and then God offers Him to us as Food. When we receive Jesus as Food, we have not only participated, or taken part in the Sacrifice part of the Mass; we have also participated in the Sacrificial Banquet. This is the most complete and perfect participation. We should ask ourselves if we really consider the eating of Christ's Body as the greatest Banquet we could attend. So often we receive Our Lord just as a matter of habit and never realize that we are receiving into our bodies the Living Body of God Himself.

33. Where does the preparation for Holy Communion begin in the Mass?

The preparation for Holy Communion begins at the *Our Father* in the Mass, which starts the Sacrificial Banquet part of the Mass.

The Thanksgiving Prayers after Holy Communion

The Communion prayer is a prayer that used to be said while the people were receiving Holy Communion. At one time it was a whole psalm which had a relation to receiving Holy Communion and to the feast of the day. In this way, people could think of the wonderful Gift they were about to receive, and at the same time beg the one whose feast was being celebrated to help them receive this Gift worthily.

Communion, Postcommunion: See Mass of day.

P. The Lord be with you. R̅. And with thy spirit.
P. Let us pray.
P. The Lord be with you. R̅. And with thy spirit.
P. Go: you are dismissed. R̅. Thanks be to God — or
P. Let us bless the Lord. R̅. Thanks be to God.

MAY the tribute of my worship be pleasing to Thee, Most Holy Trinity, and grant that the sacrifice which I, all unworthy, have offered in the presence of Thy Majesty, may be acceptable to Thee, and through Thy mercy obtain forgiveness for me and all for whom I have offered it. Through Christ our Lord. Amen.

The Blessing

May Almighty God bless you, the Father, and the Son, ✝ and the Holy Ghost. R̅. Amen.

The Meaning of the Communion and Postcommunion

Today the Communion Prayer is only a verse or two, usually taken from a psalm. For us it makes a short thanksgiving prayer in which we can thank Christ for coming to us, and beg the one whose feast we are celebrating to help us live with Christ for the rest of the day.

"Post" Communion means "after" Communion. In the ancient Church, this was the only prayer said after Holy Communion. This was the official thanksgiving prayer of the Church. In just a few short words, it sums up the special feast of the day, and thanksgiving to God for both the Sacrifice and the Sacrificial Banquet. It also asks God that the fruits of the Sacrifice and of Holy Communion always remain with us. In this prayer, we can once again think of all the intentions we had when we began to offer the Mass with the priest. Even while we are thanking God for His Gifts, we can be begging Him once again to hear all our prayers.

34. What is the Communion prayer?

The Communion prayer is a prayer that used to be said during Holy Communion. Now it is said after Holy Communion and may be used as a thanksgiving prayer.

35. What is the Postcommunion prayer?

The Postcommunion prayer is the prayer in which the Church gives official thanks to God for letting her offer His Son to Him, and for giving His Son to her children as their Food.

The Dismissal and the Last Gospel

The Sacrifice of the Mass is over, so the Church dismisses her children. In all Masses where there is a "Gloria," the priest says: "Go, the Mass is ended." In Masses, where there is no "Gloria," he says: "Let us bless the Lord." Finally, in "Black" Masses, the priest says: "May they rest in peace." All these three phrases mean the same thing: the Mass is ended.

The Last Gospel

P. The Lord be with you. ℟. And with thy spirit.
✞ The beginning of the Holy Gospel according to St. John.
℟. Glory be to Thee, O Lord.

IN THE beginning was the Word, and the Word was with God; and the Word was God. He was in the beginning with God. All things were made through Him, and without Him was made nothing that has been made. In Him was life, and the life was the light of men. And the light shines in the darkness; and the darkness grasped it not. There was a man, one sent from God, whose name was John. This man came as a witness, to bear witness concerning the Light, that all might believe through Him. He was not himself the Light, but was to bear witness to the Light. It was the true Light that enlightens every man who comes into the world. He was in the world, and the world was made by Him, and the world knew Him not. He came unto His own, and His own received Him not. But to as many as received Him He gave the power of becoming sons of God; to those who believe in His Name: who were born, not of blood, nor of the will of the flesh, nor of the will of man, but of God. (*Here genuflect*) And THE WORD WAS MADE FLESH, and dwelt among us. And we saw His glory, the glory as of the Only-begotten of the Father, full of grace and of truth. ℟. Thanks be to God.

The Meaning of the Dismissal and the Last Gospel

The prayer the priest says immediately after the dismissal prayer should be our prayer, too. We, too, have offered the Sacrifice of Christ's Body and Blood to the Most Holy Trinity. We, too, should beg God with the priest to accept this Sacrifice from our unworthy hands. We should beg Him, too, to make our unworthy hands a little less unworthy the next time we offer Him the Sacrifice of His Divine Son.

For many years, the Last Gospel, the last of the dismissal prayers, was not part of the Mass. The priest used to say it as a thanksgiving prayer as he was taking off his vestments. Towards the end of the 16th century, it was made part of the Mass itself. It is truly a beautiful way to end the Mass—to read the story of how the Son of God became man that He might make all of us sons of God. Beautiful—for in each Mass, the Son of God becomes our Sacrifice and our Food, that He may keep us sons of God.

36. How can the prayer "May the tribute, etc." be our prayer, too?

This prayer can be our prayer, too, because we have offered the Sacrifice of the Mass with the priest.

344

Prayers After Low Mass

Hail Mary *(3 times)*

SALVE REGINA

HAIL, Holy Queen, Mother of mercy, hail, our life, our sweetness, and our hope! To thee do we cry, poor banished children of Eve! To thee do we send up our sighs, mourning and weeping in this valley of tears! Turn then, most gracious advocate, thine eyes of mercy towards us; and after this, our exile, show unto us the blessed fruit of thy womb, Jesus! O clement, O loving, O sweet Virgin Mary!

V. Pray for us, O Holy Mother of God.
R. That we may be made worthy of the promises of Christ.

Let us pray

O GOD, our refuge and our strength, look down with favor upon thy people who cry to Thee; and through the intercession of the glorious and immaculate Virgin Mary, Mother of God, of Blessed Joseph, her spouse, of Thy holy apostles Peter and Paul, and all the saints, in thy mercy and kindness hear the prayers which we pour forth to Thee for the conversion of sinners and for the liberty and exaltation of Holy Mother the Church. Through the same Christ Our Lord. Amen.

HOLY Michael, the Archangel, defend us in battle; be our protection against the malice and snares of the devil. May God rebuke him, we humbly pray; and do thou, O Prince of the heavenly host, by the power of God, thrust into hell Satan and the other evil spirits who roam through the world seeking the ruin of souls. Amen.

(10 years indulgence)

Most Sacred Heart of Jesus, have mercy on us. *(3 times)*

(7 years)

345

ALPHABETICAL INDEX

(Arabic numerals refer to Questions, not to pages;
Roman numerals refer to Questions in the Appendix.)

Abbot, 451 (b)
Abel, 358 (b)
Acolyte, 451 (c)
Act of charity necessary,
203 (a)
Act of faith necessary,
201 (b), (c)
Act of hope necessary,
202 (a)
Acts of faith, hope, charity,
contrition, 200, 373, 447,
486
Actual grace, 110, 113, 116
Actual sin, 63-76
Adam and Eve, 51-61, 77,
457 (b)
Adopted sons of God,
315 (a)
Adoration, 200 (d), 476 (a)
Adultery, 256 (b), 460 (a)
Advent, 302
Affinity, 299 (a)
Alb, 362 (f)
All Saints' Day, 172 (a),
283
All Souls' Day, 173 (a)
Altar cloth, 362 (h)
Altar stone, 362 (e)
Ambition, 75 (a)
Amen, 187
Amendment, 384, 388, 406,
407, 426
Amice, 362 (f)
Angels, 11 (b), 13 (b), 36-
46
Angelus, 87 (a)
Anger, 74, 75 (d), 253
Annunciation, 42 (a), 87
Antichrist, 176 (a)
Anxiety, 481 (a)
Apostasy, 205 (a)
Apostles, 162 (a)
Apostles' Creed, 6, 7, 187,
486
Apparent death, 450 (a)
Appearances of bread and
wine, 348 (a)
Archangels, 37 (c)
Ascension, 101, 137 (a)
Ascension Thursday, 283
Ashes, 473
Assumption of the Blessed
Virgin, 87 (e), 178, 283
Athanasian Creed, 6 (b)
Atheists, 1 (a)
Atonement for sin, 420; see
also Satisfaction
Attribute (assign to), 212
Attributes of the Church,
161-165
Attrition, 400 (a)
Authority, 160 (a), 162,
164 (b), 241 (b)

Bad angels, 39, 44-46
Bad Catholics, 157 (d)

Bad example, 253
Baptism, 114 (b), 117 (a),
122 (e), 136 (a), 175 (a),
305, 308 (a), 310, 313-329,
379 (b), 380 (b), 422 (a)
Baptism of blood, 322
Baptism of Christ, 315 (b) ·
Baptism of desire, 323
Baptism of Saint John,
315 (b)
Baptismal character, 314,
317
Beatific Vision, 3 (c), 5 (b),
34 (b), 186 (a)
Beatitudes, 127, 129
Benediction of Blessed Sac-
rament, 378
Bethlehem, 89
Bible, 23 (f), 37 (d), VIII-
XIV
Bishops, 45 (e), 136, 145,
146, 148 (b), 149, 151,
156 (f), 173 (d), 331-334,
336, 451, 456, 472
Bishops can dispense,
289 (c)
Bishops of Rome, 148 (a)
Blasphemy, 75 (d), 233
Blessed Sacrament, 371;
see also Holy Eucharist
Blessed Trinity, 25-33, 82,
105, 488
Blessed Virgin, 62, 81, 86-
89, 178, 285, 439, 440
Blessings, 472
Boasting, 75 (a)
Body of Christ, 136 (b)
Bribes, 261

Cain, 358 (b)
Calumny, 75 (f), 266, 269,
271
Calvary, 93 (a)
Candles, 362 (h), 473
Canon Law, 173 (d), 281 (b)
Canon of Mass, 364 (a)
Capital sins, 74, 75
Cardinals, 148 (c), 451 (e)
Cardinal virtues, 132-134
Catechumens, 357 (a)
Catholic Action, 151
Catholic Church, 5, 6, 136-
169, 190 (b), 462 (a),
VII, XIV; is one, 156 (b);
is necessary, 167 (a)
Catholicity, 158 (a)
Catholic Marriage, 298-303
Catholic Religion, I, V
Catholics, 164 (b), 237 (a),
462 (a), 467 (c)
Causality, 20 (b)
Chalice, 362 (h)

Character of sacraments,
314; of Baptism, 317; of
Confirmation, 337, 339;
of Holy Orders, 453
Charity, 121, 124, 200 (c),
203, 210, 447
Charms, 212, 474 (a)
Chastity, 128, 135, 197,
257, 258, 276, 467 (e)
Chasuble, 361 (f)
Cheating, 261, 266 (d)
Choirs of angels, 37 (d)
Christ, 78-104, 137, 138,
144-148, 330, 343-356,
359, 360, 362, 365, V-
VIII
Christ the Judge, 104 (a),
180 (c)
Christ the King, 78 (d), 103
Christ the Priest, 78 (d)
Christ the Prophet, 78 (d)
Christian burial, 253 (g)
Christian education, 340 (f)
Christian revelation, 23 (d)
Christian sects, 158 (c),
160 (a)-(c)
Christians, 192 (d)
Christmas Day, 89, 283,
370 (b)
Church, 5, 6, 45 (d), 136-
169, 297-302, VI-VIII,
XII, XIV; founded by
Christ, 152 (b); Church
militant, 170 (a); Church
property, 162 (c); Church
suffering, 170 (a); Church
triumphant, 170 (a)
Churches founded by men,
152 (a)
Church, Fathers of, 23 (h),
XII
Cincture, 362 (f)
Circumcision, 283
Circumincession, 107 (a)
Circumstances, 415 (c)
Citizens, 245-248
Civil authority, 243 (a)
Civil effects of marriage,
463
Clergy, 451 (a)
Clerical state, 150 (a), 451
(d)
Code of Canon Law, 281 (b)
College of Cardinals,
148 (c)
Colors of vestments,
362 (g)
Commandments: two great,
189; of God, 54, 55, 195-
278; of Church, 279-302
Communion, see Holy
Communion
Communion in Eastern
Churches, 366 (c)
Communion of Mass, 237
(c), 360 (c)

347

351

IMPRIMATUR FOR CATECHISM TEXT

Paterson, October 31, 1948. *Imprimatur:* ✠ THOMAS A. BOLAND, *Bishop of Paterson.*

IMPRIMATUR FOR ALL OTHER TEXTS

Brooklyn, Aug. 30, 1949. *Imprimi potest:* JOHN M. FRAWLEY, C.SS.R., *Provincial of the Eastern Province.*

New York, Sept. 15, 1949. *Nihil Obstat:* JOHN M. A. FEARNS, S.T.D., *Censor Librorum.*

New York, March 15, 1958. *Nihil Obstat:* JOHN A. GOODWINE, *Censor Librorum.*

Imprimatur: ✠ FRANCIS CARDINAL SPELLMAN, *Archbishop of New York.*

NOTES